The Handbook of Music Therapy

GW00659429

Music therapists work with children and adults of all ages with wide-ranging health-care needs. This handbook traces the history of recent developments in music therapy and the range of current applications, outlining practical requirements for the work and some basic prerequisites for and philosophies of training.

The Handbook of Music Therapy covers material encompassing clinical, practical and theoretical perspectives, and is divided into four main sections, including:

- The recent evolution of music therapy as a paramedical discipline complementing the more traditional areas of child and adult health care
- A clinical section including contributions from music therapy specialists in the fields of autism, adult learning disability, forensic psychiatry, neurology and dementia
- A section on resources necessary to practise as a music therapist including musical illustrations and practical examples
- A focus on issues pertinent to the life of the professional music therapist including job creation, supervision, further training and research.

The Handbook of Music Therapy is illustrated with many case studies and clinical examples throughout, placed within a variety of different theoretical and philosophical perspectives. It will be invaluable to music therapists, other arts therapists and to clinicians such as speech and language therapists, psychotherapists, psychiatrists and social workers.

Leslie Bunt is Visiting Professor of Music Therapy at the University of the West of England where he directs the MusicSpace Trust. He directs the postgraduate Diploma in Music Therapy at the University of Bristol and is the author of *Music Therapy: An Art Beyond Words* (1994).

Sarah Hoskyns is Head of the Music Therapy Department at the Guildhall School of Music and Drama, London. She is a former editor of the *British Journal of Music Therapy* and an Approved Supervisor and Advisory Council member of the Association of Professional Music Therapists.

Contributors: Jonathan Barnes, Richard Bolton, Sandra Brown, Cathy Durham, Helen Odell-Miller, Julian Raphael, Ann Sloboda, Tessa Watson.

The Handbook of Music Therapy

Edited by Leslie Bunt and Sarah Hoskyns

Dear Jo

we'll always have Strasberg and you'll always be in my heart. I couldn't have edited this book without your inspiration.

All my love

Leslie Bunt

Routledge
Taylor & Francis Group

LONDON AND NEW YORK

First published 2002
by Routledge
27 Church Road, Hove, East Sussex BN3 2FA

Simultaneously published in the USA and Canada
by Routledge
270 Madison Avenue, New York NY 10016

Reprinted 2004, 2006 and 2009

Routledge is an imprint of the Taylor & Francis Group, an Informa business

Typeset in Times by Graphicraft Limited, Hong Kong
Printed and bound in Great Britain by TJ International Ltd,
Padstow, Cornwall

This publication has been produced with paper manufactured to strict
environmental standards and with pulp derived from sustainable forests.

Paperback cover image 'A Way In Through Music' by Jonathan Barnes
(inspired by a sculpture by Barbara Hepworth)
Paperback cover design by Louise Page

British Library Cataloguing-in-Publication Data
A catalogue record for this book is available
from the British Library

Library of Congress Cataloging-in-Publication Data
The handbook of music therapy / edited by Leslie Bunt and Sarah
Hoskyns.
       p. cm.
    Includes bibliographical references (p.) and index.
    ISBN 0-415-15707-2 — ISBN 0-415-15708-0 (pbk.)
    1. Music therapy. I. Bunt, Leslie. II. Hoskyns, Sarah, 1959–
ML3920.H266 2002
615.8′5154—dc21   2002025442

ISBN13: 978-0-415-15707-0 (hbk)
ISBN13: 978-0-415-15708-7 (pbk)

In memory of Maggie Pickett, colleague, teacher and friend (1928–2000).

To Benedict Hoskyns who always believed that 'such a *manual* should be written'.

Contents

Illustrations

FIGURES

TABLES

Contributors

Jonathan Barnes is Senior Lecturer in Education at Christ Church University College, Canterbury. He is a past Head Teacher of St. Peter's Methodist Primary School and has held a lifelong passion for the arts in the curriculum. He is a keen practising musician and artist.

Richard Bolton gained an M.Mus. from the University of Sheffield researching jazz improvisation following study at Oxford University and the Guildhall School of Music and Drama. As part of a busy career as a freelance musician and teacher, he teaches improvisation to music therapy trainees at the Guildhall School.

Sandra Brown trained as a music therapist at the Nordoff-Robbins Music Therapy Centre, London and has worked with a wide range of clients. She now works as Senior Therapist at the Centre and as Senior Clinical Tutor on the Centre's Master of Music Therapy degree course. She also maintains a private supervision practice. She is currently training as a Jungian analyst with the Society of Analytical Psychology in London.

Leslie Bunt is visiting Professor of Music Therapy at the University of the West of England. He directs the postgraduate music therapy course at the University of Bristol (also based in Bologna). He has wide clinical experience with children and adults and is currently working with cancer patients and in Guided Imagery and Music. He is the Director of The MusicSpace Trust, a registered charity setting up a network of music therapy centres. He is a Vice-President of the BSMT, a member of the Advisory Council of the APMT and an Approved Supervisor.

Cathy Durham is currently Research Fellow in Music Therapy at the University of the West of England. She teaches on the Bristol and Cardiff training courses. Her areas of clinical experience are in neurology and learning disabilities. She has a special interest in music therapy group work.

Sarah Hoskyns is Head of Music Therapy Department and Director of the postgraduate music therapy course at Guildhall School of Music and Drama.

She has a special interest in working with families and young children and has clinical and research experience with clients in the probation service and in neuro-disability. She is a member of the management board of MusicSpace London. She is a former editor of the *British Journal of Music Therapy*, an Approved Supervisor and an Advisory Council member of APMT. She also acts as APMT representative to the Health Professions Council on training and education.

Helen Odell-Miller is Director of the MA, and postgraduate diploma programme in Music Therapy at Anglia Polytechnic University, Cambridge, UK, and a Senior Music Therapist and researcher in music therapy at Addenbrookes NHS Trust Mental Health Services. Her M.Phil. research studied the outcome of music therapy treatment for elderly mentally ill patients, particularly focusing on those with dementia. She is a founder member of the European Music Therapy Committee, and in the UK she is a past chair of the Association of Professional Music Therapists, and Post Diploma Supervision Panel; and presently Adviser to the Department of Health on Music Therapy.

Julian Raphael is Senior Lecturer in Music at Canterbury Christ Church University College and Programme Director of the Course in Popular Music and Technology. He is an active conductor, composer and arranger of music for *The Maridadi Singers* and directs the College's Salsa Band. He is visiting choral tutor to the UK Dalcroze Society. He has a special interest in rhythmic improvisation and inter-cultural music.

Ann Sloboda is currently Head of Arts Therapies at Three Bridges Regional Secure Unit, West London Mental Healthcare Trust. She is a former Chair of the APMT, a member of the Advisory Council and a recent member of the Arts Therapies Board of the Council for Professions Supplementary to Medicine (CPSM).

Tessa Watson has worked in the area of learning disabilities since qualifying in 1990 and has a special interest in working with clients with profound and multiple learning disabilities. She currently works in a Health and Social Services Community Team for People with Learning Disabilities in London. Tessa also teaches on the Roehampton music therapy course. She maintains a keen interest in professional issues and has worked on the APMT executive committee in various roles.

Acknowledgements

We would like to thank above all the many children and adults who have helped us to understand the processes of music therapy and to thank the staff at the various clinical settings where we have worked. We give our appreciation to our students and colleagues on the music therapy courses at the Guildhall School of Music and Drama, London and the University of Bristol (both British and Italian groups). Special thanks are due to the following people. To our contributors: Sandra Brown, Cathy Durham, Helen Odell-Miller, Julian Raphael (who notated on computer all the musical examples in the text using *Sibeliu*s software), Ann Sloboda, Richard Bolton and Tessa Watson, and to our interviewees: Jean Eisler, Helen Odell-Miller, Elaine Streeter and Tony Wigram. To Jonathan Barnes and Julian Raphael who helped bring the text alive with original pictures and music. To Steve Dunachie for musical ideas for Chapter 12. To the Principal and Research Committee of the Guildhall School of Music and Drama for research funding. To staff of Bristol MusicSpace for advice with Appendix II and the forms in Chapter 13. To staff at MusicSpace West Midlands for information on music therapy provision in schools. To staff of the National Office of The MusicSpace Trust for their support in the final stages of the preparation of the manuscript. To Diana Asbridge and Denize Christophers, Administrators of the APMT and BSMT. To Karin Richards for assistance with transcribing and typing and for helpful advice. To Karen Ryan for administrative support and to Rachel Darnley-Smith for moral support. To Tim Raphael for advice on poetry. To Benedict and Ann Hoskyns for reading part of the manuscript. To Gabrielle Rifkind, consultant supervisor, for new ideas and old wisdom. To the Royal Society of Arts for provision of working space and to the proprietors of cafés in Bristol, Canterbury and London where we have passed many hours in planning and discussion. To Dr Kate Cullen for compiling the index. To our families: Sue Pontin, Laura and Jonathan Bunt; Julian Raphael, Dorothy and Nino Raphael for their continued loving support.

The authors and publisher would like to thank the following for permission to reproduce copyright material:

1 The Association of Professional Music Therapists: Tables 1.1 and 1.2 and Appendix III.

2 Extract from *Captain Corelli's Mandolin* by Louis de Bernières published by Vintage (May 1995). Used by permission of The Random House Group Limited and by Random House Inc. USA (Chapter 10).

3 Two extracts from *A Way of Being Free* by Ben Okri published by the Orion Publishing Group. Used by permission of Phoenix House (Chapter 10 and Endnotes).

4 Extract from 'The Rainstick' from *Opened Ground: Selected Poems 1966–1996* by Seamus Heaney. Copyright © 1988 by Seamus Heaney. Reprinted by permission of Farrar, Straus and Giroux, LLC and Faber & Faber. (Chapter 11).

5 Extract from 'Piano' from *Selected Poems of D.H. Lawrence*. Used by permission of the Estate of D.H. Lawrence.

6 Extract from 'This is not love perhaps' by A.S.J. Tessimond. Used by permission of Whiteknights Press, Department of English, University of Reading.

7 The Editor of *The British Journal of Music Therapy* for reproduction of earlier published research material from Vol. 14, No. 2 (2000) (Chapter 14).

8 The Editor of the *Journal of the Association for Music and Imagery* for permission to use material from Vol. 7 (2000) (Chapter 15).

9 Plate at end of Chapter 15: From a Greek cup: Peleus seizing Thetis – from the Staatliche Museum and with permission from the Bildarchiv Preussischer Kulturebesitz.

10 Plates 1 and 21 from *The Book of Job* by William Blake. © Copyright The British Museum (Endnotes).

Note on confidentiality

All names have been changed and identifying details disguised in order to protect anonymity of patients described in this Handbook. In accordance with the APMT Code of Professional Ethics and Discipline, permission has been sought wherever possible from patients themselves or from carers to use material from music therapy sessions.

Plate 1 Entrance to St George's Asinou, Kakapetria, Cyprus (Jonathan Barnes)

Introduction

Leslie Bunt and Sarah Hoskyns

MUSIC THERAPY ON A THRESHOLD

Music therapy is at an exhilarating stage in its evolution both as a profession and an academic discipline. Gone are the days of it being an *ad hoc* pursuit for the dedicated few. In many parts of the world music therapy is now regarded as a serious clinical profession practised by well-trained and highly motivated practitioners working within a variety of approaches and agreed standards of ethical practice. This commitment to the profession and enthusiasm for the work were demonstrated at a turn-of-the-century conference organised by the British Society for Music Therapy (BSMT) and the Association of Professional Music Therapists (APMT). One of the highlights of this two-day event was a presentation by a group of newly qualified therapists from different training courses. These talented young clinicians outlined their hopes for the future, articulated within a professional approach that celebrated unity and diversity. Similar advances are occurring world-wide.

At the Ninth World Congress of Music Therapy, held in Washington in 1999, the founders of five universally acknowledged music therapy approaches were celebrated: Mary Priestley (Analytical Music Therapy); Clifford Madsen (Behavioural Music Therapy); Rolando Benenzon (Benenzon Music Therapy); Paul Nordoff and Clive Robbins (Creative Music Therapy) and Helen Bonny (Guided Imagery and Music). These approaches were placed in the context of a wide array of presentations from all corners of the globe, representatives of 42 member countries of the World Federation of Music Therapy being present at the congress.

A threshold is an interesting place to be with connotations mainly of entrance but also of exit. It is a place where it is possible to make connections between the past, present and future. A threshold leads from outside to inside; it is a literal and symbolic space between different worlds; it is an image pregnant with anticipation, mystery and not without some superstition. A threshold can also be a doorway or gateway to new understanding and awareness. Overall the image can serve us well in introducing some themes that will be elaborated in further chapters. It can help us pay tribute to the entrances and exits of some important persons in music therapy and the doorways that they opened. It can help us recall some important moments in the development of the profession and the exploration of new pathways through research.

We can start to explore how music, and improvisation in particular, can occupy this space between different worlds: a threshold between the inner and outer, between conscious and unconscious processes, between the individual and the collective, between silence and sound. Even Ruud (1995) has described improvisation as a 'liminal' experience – 'limen' being the Latin for threshold. We can consider training as a 'rite of passage' across a new threshold. Above all we can observe how our patients (interchangeable throughout the book with clients, group members and residents with changes in terminology linked to the context and the therapist's clinical perspective) move across a threshold into a music therapy space. The music therapist meets and attends them at the gate.[1]

The Roman god Janus was the first god of all doorways: public gates through which roads passed and also doors to private homes. What is interesting about him is that he was represented as looking in different directions simultaneously with a double-faced head. He could observe both the entrances and exits of public buildings and the exteriors and interiors of private houses. He was the god of beginnings and endings, of representing transitions between outside and inside, between the world of the country and the city, between primitive life and civilisation. Interestingly for musicians Janus is often depicted holding a key. We know of a key as a device for unlocking and in Roman times the keystone was also the top stone that held an arch together. For musicians there is both the notion of keys on various instruments as points of initial contact and also the means of unlocking a system of a series of related tones. The composer Robert Schumann is attributed as having said:

> Music . . . is the spiritual language of emotion, which is hidden more secretly than the soul . . . just as at the clavier the keys must be touched before they sound; it is only then that the emotion communicates with the slumbering realm of tones.
>
> (Alan 1969 and cited by Cobb 1992: 143)

As Clive Robbins pointed out at the BSMT/APMT conference, his name Clive comes from 'kleis' (Greek) and 'clavis' (Latin) for key (Robbins 2000). It was apt that Clive's work was celebrated at Washington as a major 'door opener' for many music therapists across the world.

---

1 The extended use of the metaphor of a threshold in this introduction has been developed from Leslie Bunt's unpublished keynote address to the BSMT/APMT Annual Conference, February 2000.

There are many ancient triumphal entrances and gateways still to be seen in Rome. As therapists we may find inspiration from them and from images of gateways that lead to different places. Entrances to Egyptian tombs can lead to dark subterranean depths; richly decorated doors can open to hidden treasures within or represent access to other worlds as in Ghiberti's *Gate of Paradise* to the Baptistery in Florence. Let us consider a doorway that is open and inviting and another that is firmly shut. For the first, the entry is potentially celebratory and enlivening – a musical corollary could be Mussorgsky's *Great Gate of Kiev*: for the second, there might be a risk in stepping through; determination or force may be required.

How do we feel, for example, as we witness Tamino being initially refused entrance through the doorways to Sarastro's temple in Mozart's *The Magic Flute*? What do we feel as we contemplate the entrances in the drawings by Jonathan Barnes (see Plates 1 and 2)? A different kind of contemporary artistic version of moving through gateways into different virtual worlds of gardens, houses and seascapes with many transformations *en route* is Peter Gabriel's computer game *Eve* (Gabriel 1996). Within the Maori tradition the gateway to the meeting area known as the 'marae' is an assembly point for visitors. It is a threshold representing the relationship between the hosts and their visitors. Such a potent image emphasises the collective and social aspects of a threshold in addition to any individual journey.

Another pioneer who literally opened many doors for music therapy and music therapists in the UK was Juliette Alvin. The following is typical of her many anecdotes. One day she approached the entrance of a large womens' prison, cello in hand (see Plate 3). She was greeted at what seemed to be a formidable entrance by one of the officers. 'I've come to play my cello to the women' was her clear announcement resulting in nothing or nobody standing in her way. She crossed this threshold, normally locked and inhibiting movement in either direction, with a determination to offer the inmates a new experience that in turn would enable them to move, albeit temporarily, across a further threshold, namely into a musical space.

We shall be celebrating the work of other music therapy 'door-openers' throughout this text. The voices of Jean Eisler, Helen Odell-Miller, Elaine Streeter and Tony Wigram (past students of either Alvin or Nordoff and Robbins and teachers of a new generation of therapists) are heard first in Chapter 3 and then as recurring traces throughout.

Chapter 3 is a bridge between the opening background chapters and the clinical section of the book. This second section includes contributions from colleagues working in the areas of autism, adult learning disability, neurology, forensic psychiatry and dementia. We hope to involve you in these case stories and, through doing so, reveal something of the process of music therapy. Some relevant theory in the field and in other professions with which music therapy is closely associated is identified and explained. We aim to show how this theoretical knowledge informs and underpins practice. The

Plate 2 Entrance to tomb at Muglish, Kazanluk, Cyprus (Jonathan Barnes)

theoretical exploration does not attempt to be comprehensive: the handbook is rooted in practice.

This emphasis on practice is central to the third part of the book describing resources for training. It begins with a chapter by Sarah Hoskyns stressing the fundamental aspects of observation and listening (Chapter 10) with the following two chapters charting some of the personal and musical resources needed for a clinical journey at its various stages (Chapter 12 co-authored with Julian Raphael). In the final section the emerging music therapist crosses a further threshold and steps out into the profession itself. Here issues relating to assessment, supervision and continued personal and musical growth are explored (Chapter 13). Leslie Bunt includes some reflections on research in Chapter 14 followed by his chapter on processes of transformation in Guided Imagery and Music. We round off the handbook with some final thoughts on a range of topical themes.

Plate 3 HM Prison, Holloway, London (Jonathan Barnes)

It will be noticeable that there is a concentration on British music therapy practice and literature. We have planned the book as an overview of music therapy in the UK as the profession moves across a very important threshold, namely the start of a new century. For all of us in this profession a rich challenge is offered to step over and forge new pathways. We hope that the contents will be of use to experienced practitioners and teachers of music therapy and other clinical fields, to those entering the profession and to those interested in inquiring or making further study into the discipline.

> *The music therapist is one of the keepers of the gate*, one of the technicians of the sacred, one who sees the vision and hears the song of the one and the many, the one who dances on the edge of time, *one who can guard the threshold of being, one who waits for sound* . . . [our italics]
>
> (Kenny 1989: Preface)

Part I

Background and context

Chapter 1

Setting the scene

Leslie Bunt and Sarah Hoskyns

INTRODUCTION

The subject of music therapy is creeping gradually into the awareness of the general public. There is growing media interest with articles about music therapy appearing regularly in the press and music therapists being featured on television and radio. Another burgeoning sign of this public recognition is when the character of a music therapist enters a piece of contemporary fiction. In Helen Dunmore's novel *Talking to the Dead* the photographer heroine prepares for a project with children in Romania where she will be joining not just one but two music therapists (Dunmore 1997: 60–61). A further sign is the increasing interest among young people in training for music therapy. The following appeared in a British national newspaper about pupils attending a specialist music school: '70 per cent of Chetham's pupils go on to music college and 30 per cent to university, usually to read music. About a third overall end up earning their living as musicians, as teachers, performers or music therapists' (*The Independent* 11 January 1996).

We often hear comments from teachers at music colleges and university music departments about the growing interest in music therapy as a serious career option for students. The administrator of the British Society for Music Therapy (BSMT), the general body open to all interested in the subject, reports an average of over 2000 enquiries per year. A visit to her office is now included as part of a London taxi driver's training, described colloquially as 'the knowledge' (Christophers 2001). Electronic access to websites has reduced the number of personal enquiries to the BSMT office, as is the case with the professional body, the Association of Professional Music Therapists (APMT). Nevertheless the administrator of the APMT still reports an average of 20 career enquiries per week and these requests are from people of all ages (Asbridge 2001). Regional representatives of the APMT are also local sources of information about music therapy.

We can say confidently that music therapy developed dramatically during the last two decades of the previous century into a mature and respected profession. It has truly come of age. This development was highlighted in the UK in 1997 by the state registration of music therapy as a profession supplementary to medicine. Such a significant step forward is due to the dedication and strength of purpose of many talented practitioners and to the support of clinical allies and forward-thinking managers. This increased recognition has spurred the creation of more music therapy positions in both the public and private sectors. These are important steps forward but vigilance is required to maintain the balance between the numbers of students we train, any development of new courses and the availability and creation of positions. A further sign of maturity is the recognition by practitioners of the importance of regular supervision, matched by a growing number of experienced supervisors. Additionally, a steady output of research is indicating evidence of effective practice in many clinical areas.

It is within this context of an exciting period in the profession's history that we embark on this scene-setting chapter. Within the chapter we will:

- provide a background to the current status and definition of music therapy;
- indicate the range of settings where qualified music therapists work;
- survey some recent, and for the most part, British publications;
- explore some of the qualities needed both to train and practise as a music therapist.

CURRENT MUSIC THERAPY PRACTICE

Definition

In the most recent careers information leaflet published by the APMT music therapy is described as follows:

> Music therapy provides a framework in which a mutual relationship is set up between client and therapist. The growing relationship enables changes to occur, both in the condition of the client and in the form that the therapy takes. . . . By using music creatively in a clinical setting, the therapist seeks to establish an interaction, a shared musical experience leading to the pursuit of therapeutic goals. These goals are determined by the therapist's understanding of the client's pathology and personal needs.
>
> (APMT 2000a)

We quote this definition as it is the one most commonly cited by members of the professional association and one with which members working within many different perspectives seem to be comfortable. A further definition is: 'Music therapy is the use of sounds and music within an evolving relationship between client/patient and therapist to support and develop physical, mental, social, emotional and spiritual well-being' (adapted from Bunt 1994: 8).

Legal background

Since 1976 the APMT has been responsible for monitoring the evolution of the profession. It played a key role in developing professional standards and overseeing a basic level of training. It linked with government departments in the establishment in 1982 of the profession's Career and Grading Structure within the Whitley Council of the Department of Health (see historical summary in Bunt 1994). During 1997 art, music and drama therapies were granted by Act of Parliament the right to become state registered. This involved the creation of an Arts Therapists Board under the Professions Supplementary to Medicine Act 1960, extending the original 1960 Act to include the arts therapists alongside other professionals such as occupational therapists and physiotherapists. In a statement to the House of Lords accompanying the Draft Order of 6 March 1997, Baroness Cumberlege outlined the function of the Arts Therapists Board: 'to promote high standards of professional education and conduct within the umbrella of the Council for Professions Supplementary to Medicine (CPSM).' The main duties of the Board are:

> . . . to prepare and maintain a register; approve training courses leading to state registration and the institutions providing them; determine applications for admission to the register on the basis of qualifications and experience acquired either in the UK or elsewhere; and to set up the investigation and disciplinary committees to produce guidance on conduct and deal with individual cases of misconduct.
>
> (Hansard 6 March 1997: 2026–2029)

Cumberlege's statement continued with the important notice that practitioners who are registered in this way by the Board will be able to call themselves 'state registered arts therapists' and that 'The use of that title by a person who is not registered will be an offence' (ibid.). Clearly these moves have important implications for the provision of a protected professional service to patients and for the stature and respect of the arts therapies professions (for further details of the stages involved in gaining state registration see Barham 1999).[1] Members of the British Medical Association wrote a letter to the CPSM in support of the applications for state registration from both the APMT and the British Association of Art Therapists. They stated:

1 The Health Professions Council took over from the CPSM as the new legislative body for State Registration of Arts Therapists in 2002.

Both organisations appear to fulfil the criteria necessary for state registration. They both have a code of conduct and a central register, set national professional standards for practice and training and can cite substantial research demonstrating the value of their respective therapies. Considering the development they have made over recent years, their relationships with other professionals and their emphasis on their role as members of an inter-disciplinary team, it would seem appropriate for art and music therapists to achieve state registration to protect their status and to bring them in line with colleagues in occupational therapy, speech therapy etc.

(British Medical Association 1991)

Postgraduate training in music therapy

There are currently seven postgraduate training courses in music therapy in the UK (see Appendix 1). The oldest course began in 1968 when Juliette Alvin was invited to introduce music therapy into the Guildhall School of Music and Drama in London. In 1974 Paul Nordoff and Clive Robbins began teaching at Goldie Leigh Hospital in South London. The training course bearing their names is now based at the Nordoff–Robbins Centre in North London. In 1980 a new course was established at Southlands College, Roehampton Institute. A two-year part-time training course was set up at Bristol University in 1991 and the fourth full-time course began at Anglia Polytechnic University, Cambridge in 1994. The most recent courses have been the first course in Wales at the Royal Welsh College of Music and Drama (1997) and in Scotland a new Nordoff-Robbins programme at the University of Edinburgh (2002). Successful students can leave the training courses with a Postgraduate Diploma in Music Therapy. Several courses also offer additional study at Master's level with the other courses moving in that direction. During 2000/2001, all the courses went through a process of review and appraisal in order that they could satisfy requirements for approval by the Arts Therapists Board of the CPSM. State registration is only possible for students who have completed successfully one of the approved courses.

A newly qualified therapist can join the APMT as a provisional member and, after a minimum of 32 hours of supervision with an approved supervisor based on 320 hours of clinical contact time, can then apply for full membership. The APMT also has categories for student and associate membership (retired members or those living abroad).

The range of the work and settings

Music therapists work both with individuals and in small groups. Most therapists are mainly full- or part-time clinical practitioners with a growing number engaged in management, training and research. The majority of therapists work within the statutory agencies of the National Health Service (NHS), Local Education Authorities (LEAs) or Social Services. The Whitley Council's Career and Grading Structure is still used for therapists being employed within the NHS. Employment in schools and decisions about salary structures are often at the discretion of headteachers and school governors. Historically qualified teacher status has been a pertinent issue. Many therapists in schools have tended to obtain a teacher qualification in order to gain longer hours of employment and for their work to be valued financially at the appropriate level. However, increasingly therapists have argued for an equivalent level without necessarily having qualified teacher status. Other therapists are self-employed and some work privately or for charities.

There is a wide range of settings including: pre-school specialist nurseries and centres for children; special schools for children with learning difficulties; mainstream schools; hospitals and centres for adults with learning difficulties, physical disabilities, mental health and neurological problems; nursing homes; centres for children and adults with visual or hearing impairments; hospices and centres for people of all ages living with terminal illness and the prison service. More recent developments include work in designated music therapy or arts therapies community-based centres and local health centres run by groups of general practitioners.

At the end of 2000 there was a total of 490 practising members of the APMT with 402 female members (82 per cent) and 88 male (18 per cent). It is noteworthy that a 1999 survey, reported by Michel (2000), indicated a similar balance of the sexes in the USA. These 490 British members worked across the entire age range (see Tables 1.1 and 1.2). As can be seen in Table 1.1 the numbers working within each subgroup indicate that many therapists work within a variety of areas.

As in earlier APMT surveys work with children and adults with learning difficulties and adults with mental health problems still predominate (for example see Bunt 1994: 10). In Part II of this book we include examples of work across the life span and with people with wide-ranging needs. We cannot give justice to the full range of work and have needed to be selective. Additional case material will be included elsewhere in the book and where we perceive gaps we will direct the reader to the appropriate literature. Here follow summaries of the main areas of work.

Music therapy with children

In 1979 Elaine Streeter completed the first Master's thesis in music therapy in the UK. She explored the connections between rhythmic processes in work with children, particularly those with communication problems, and early patterns in mother–child interaction (Streeter 1979). As we shall see in the clinical chapters these connections became a critical base for much music therapy practice with children. It provided a developmental perspective to the

Table 1.1 Areas of work and ranked numbers of therapists

Area of work	No.
Adult	*210*
Learning difficulties	157
Mental health problems	128
Emotional and behavioural difficulties	119
'Challenging' behaviour	114
Elderly	51
Neurology	37
Forensic psychiatry	25
'Normal' neurotic	23
Stress management	12
Addiction	11
Prison service	1
HIV/AIDS	1
Children	
Pre-school	*138*
Learning difficulties	119
Emotional and behavioural difficulties	99
'Challenging' behaviour	86
Epilepsy	60
Primary	*191*
Learning difficulties	160
Emotional and behavioural difficulties	134
'Challenging' behaviour	120
Epilepsy	74
Secondary	*150*
Learning difficulties	130
Emotional and behavioural difficulties	109
'Challenging' behaviour	98
Epilepsy	64
Adolescent (outside of school system)	51

Source: Association of Professional Music Therapists Survey of Membership, 2000.

work. In 1981 Streeter went on to write a book that provided many practical examples of musical ideas for parents to explore with their children (see Streeter 2001, her latest edition). Parents could easily recognise how musical interaction might aid their child's development of speech and language, physical skills, play, social and emotional maturation. The activities underlined the therapeutic emphasis of working at the child's pace, waiting for the child, care for timing and pacing, use of silence, turn-taking, vocal play and exploration of significant objects (in our case the musical instruments).

The consultant paediatrician with whom Streeter worked, the late Dr Hugh Jolly, would often say that he could gain a fuller picture of each child's level

Table 1.2 Combined areas of interest and ranked numbers of therapists

Area	No.
Adult/child	
Learning difficulties	255
Autism	246
Communication disorders	203
Emotional and behavioural difficulties	201
'Challenging' behaviour	181
Mental health problems	128
Epilepsy	103
Sexual abuse	65
Eating disorders	28
Hospice	23
Student training	
Placements and/or teaching	116
Personal therapy for students	13

Source: Association of Professional Music Therapists Survey of Membership, 2000.

of development, play and potential by observing them in music therapy. Dr Jolly stated in a BBC television documentary that any assessment of a pre-school child was incomplete without a contribution from a music therapist (Wigram 1995: 184). He would often comment that in music therapy a child with communication problems could have influence over an adult and communicate intentions in a way not possible in any other medium. Where else could a child organise an adult in such a way?

Another leading paediatrician, the late Dr Derek Ricks, encouraged Tony Wigram to develop music therapy assessment procedures in his work for Harper House Children's Service, the national assessment centre for children with autism and communication problems based in Hertfordshire (Wigram 1995, 1999a). The late Professor David Baum, Director of the Institute of Child Health in Bristol, Trustee of The MusicSpace Trust and one-time President of the College of Paediatricians considered that:

> By the Institute of Child Health working in conjunction with Music-Space we hope to bring music as a serious therapeutic tool into the medical community. I believe that all people would feel music is good in a broad sense. We would like to be associated with work which shows it is good in a specific sense and is not something 'fringey and out there' but is something which should be prescribable and used as a serious therapeutic tool in serious clinical work.
>
> (Presentation video for The MusicSpace Trust 1991)

The specific approach instigated by Paul Nordoff and Clive Robbins has done a great deal to document and publicise the efficacy of music therapy with children (Nordoff and Robbins 1971, 1977). Many parents and members of the general public have come to know about music therapy through this work. The Nordoff–Robbins approach has been particularly successful in addressing the needs of severely disturbed autistic and psychotic children. It is equally effective with children with major physical disabilities and learning difficulties. More recently the London Centre has developed work with older children with differing problems including eating disorders (Robarts and Sloboda 1994). Sandra Brown, who teaches at the Nordoff–Robbins Centre and is now training as a Jungian analyst, describes the music therapy process of a young autistic child in Chapter 5.

Specialist work with children has also developed in three further areas:

(a) Cathy Ibberson, a clinician with dual training in paediatric nursing and music therapy, is one of a group of therapists who has developed work in children's hospices (Ibberson 1996). The proliferation of music therapy within the hospices has been aided by financial support from Jessie's Fund, a registered charity set up in memory of nine-year old Jessie by her parents who are themselves both professional musicians. The charity also funds short courses and workshops for hospice workers to encourage more use of music in hospices.

(b) Penny Rogers, an experienced therapist, researcher and service manager, has developed research and clinical approaches in music therapy with abused children. She has presented and published widely about this work (for example Rogers 1992, 1993) and has recently been appointed as a clinical specialist in child protection, advising authorities and the courts about the treatment of children suffering abuse.

(c) Joy Hasler organised a successful conference on music therapy with families in June 2000, drawing together the research work of Alison Levinge (1999) and Amelia Oldfield (Oldfield *et al.* 2001) with clinical practitioners around the UK. In Auriel Warwick's review of music therapy in the education system she refers to the results of her collaborative research project with her psychologist colleague, Pierette Muller, into music therapy with autistic children and their families (Warwick 1995). Further discussion of work with children and their mothers is included in Chapter 4 (and see Eleanor Tingle's research involving teachers and other carers in the analysis of 'moments of contact' with children with severe learning disabilities – Tingle 2000).

Some music therapists practise in schools. There has been extensive work convincing LEAs of the value of music therapy for children and young people within the special school system and more recently in mainstream settings, particularly in the area of crisis intervention. In some authorities music therapy has become part of a child's Statement of Special Educational Needs. It can be seen to help a child access the curriculum, for example listening skills, attention, motivation, classroom management with children exhibiting particular behavioural problems. Some of the general aims of music therapy are similar to the aims of the Personal and Social Development in the 5–14 curriculum. The recently developed 'Passport' framework states that 'the personal development of pupils, spiritually, morally, socially and culturally, plays a significant part in their ability to learn and achieve' (Lees and Plant 2000: 26).

Several authorities in the UK employ music therapists as contracted clinicians, as part of the LEA's music service or as freelance sessional therapists. Examples are Oxfordshire and Birmingham, where Auriel Warwick and Angela Fenwick respectively pioneered services in the early 1970s, and more recently Bedfordshire, Cambridgeshire, Leicestershire and Worcestershire. LEAs also contract through charities such as The MusicSpace Trust. The settings where children are seen for therapy vary from dedicated spaces in music therapy centres to shared spaces in pre-school nurseries and rooms of varying quality in schools. The provision of suitable space for therapy is usually improved when there is a clear explanation about the work and close liaison between the visiting music therapist and other staff in these settings (see also Chapters 2 and 13).

Music therapy with adults

Historically music therapy has had a substantial role in the care of adults with learning disabilities.[2] This long tradition began in the large institutions in the 1950s with the late Priscilla Barclay setting up the first music therapy service at St. Lawrence's Hospital in Surrey. This work set the scene for the replication of other departments nationwide. The British government's much criticised 'Care in the Community' policy has caused many changes in the service. As previous hospital residents have been discharged and rehoused in community homes, music therapists have developed a peripatetic and somewhat diffuse service. While in theory these changes are positive steps forward music therapists are keenly aware of the potential danger of isolation; the break-up of close multidisciplinary teams; the dilution of the provision and resources and a dispersal of energy. Residents who have been accustomed to living within the protection of an institution, where a variety of services were on hand, have experienced radical change. Some NHS Trusts have managed this transition well, others not. Nevertheless the process of change has also allowed for the development of alternative community

---

2 We are aware of political and cultural trends in the use of terminology relating to learning disability. We have kept to this term for the most part throughout the text but it could be used interchangeably with 'mental handicap' or the more commonly found 'learning difficulty'.

models of music therapy provision such as the setting-up of local arts therapies resource centres and new charitable trusts.

One significant development in working with adults with learning disabilities has been the furthering of our understanding of the psychological and emotional needs of this group. Several music therapists have been greatly inspired by the research that emerged from London's Tavistock Clinic, for example the work of Jon Stokes (1987) and Valerie Sinason. In her seminal text *Mental Handicap and the Human Condition* Sinason describes how people with learning disabilities can be powerfully affected by what she terms a 'secondary handicap'. She indicates how an individual may make use of the primary damage in a defensive or abusive way (Sinason 1992). Kay Sobey and other music therapists trained at the Roehampton Institute have published case material that links music therapy practice to this notion of 'secondary handicap' (see also Clough 1992; Heal 1989; Ritchie 1991; Sobey 1993; Toolan and Coleman 1995). In Chapter 6, Tessa Watson discusses music therapy within this frame of reference and there are further references to Sinason's work in Chapters 5 and 7.

As can be seen from Table 1.1, adult mental health is the second largest category of employment for music therapists working in the adult field. The pioneering work of, among others, Mary Priestley and her colleagues at the St. Bernard's Wing of Ealing Hospital and Helen Odell-Miller at Fulbourn Hospital, Cambridge has done much to create acceptance and respect for music therapy in NHS mental health teams. The Psychiatric Interest Group of the APMT was formed in the early 1980s and this body of therapists worked hard to debate issues, to disseminate information, promote research and to base music therapy on firm foundations within adult psychiatry.

We include two chapters from psychiatry in this handbook. In Chapter 8 Ann Sloboda and Richard Bolton discuss casework in the field of forensic psychiatry. In Chapter 9 Helen Odell-Miller reviews music therapy work with patients diagnosed with dementia. Further examples of music therapy in psychiatry can be found in compilation texts edited by Aldridge (2000), Bruscia (1991), Wigram *et al.* (1995) and Wigram and De Backer (1999b). A number of journal articles and conference papers also present work in this area (for example Davies 1996; Odell-Miller 1999). For many years Priestley's 1975 classic text on music therapy in psychiatry *Music Therapy in Action* had been difficult to obtain. A great gift to British music therapy has been the publication by Barcelona Publications (under the care of Bruscia) of her *Essays in Analytical Music Therapy*. Four of the chapters come from the earlier book with the remainder resulting from Priestley's other writings in journals and from her teachings in Germany (Priestley 1994). She defines and gives many clinical examples of techniques to probe the conscious and access the unconscious. She introduces some of the basic concepts of Freud and Klein and identifies levels of resistance, various defence mechanisms and manifestations of the Jungian concept of the shadow as encountered in her work.

A growing interest in linking music therapy in psychiatry to theories derived from group psychotherapy and group analysis developed during the late 1980s and 1990s. John Woodcock's article in the revised *British Journal of Music Therapy* in 1987 set the trend (Woodcock 1987). This was followed by stimulating discussion of the effective use of group music therapy linking improvisation with verbal reflection at conferences and then by such writers as Davies and Richards (1998), Stewart (1996), Towse and Flower (1993) and Towse (1997). This seems an important step in theory-building in this field as group work has held such a strong position in mental health treatment in other clinical professions. At the time of writing, Alison Davies and Eleanor Richards were preparing a book on music therapy group work for Jessica Kingsley Publishers. We refer readers interested in group work to this forthcoming text, particularly as there is a major emphasis on individual work in the clinical sections of this text (Davies and Richards 2002).

We conclude this section on the range of clinical practice with passing reference to more recent areas of work with adults. In Chapter 7 Cathy Durham reviews and describes examples of work with adults with neurological illness or injury. Work within this field was the subject of Wendy Magee's doctoral research (summarised in Magee 1999). Although the numbers are still few (see Table 1.1) some therapists in the UK have developed specialist interest in new clinical areas, additionally often setting up conferences and publishing their work. Areas include:

*   anorexia nervosa (Robarts and Sloboda 1994);
*   cancer (Bunt *et al.* 2000);
*   HIV/AIDS (Lee 1996);
*   music therapy students (see Postscript to Part III);
*   offenders (Hoskyns 1995);
*   palliative care (Lee 1995a and see Aldridge 1999);
*   stress management (Holland 1995);
*   respiratory and other physiological problems ameliorated by vibro-acoustic therapy (Skille and Wigram 1995; Wigram and Dileo 1997).

While active work using improvisation is still central to music therapy practice in the UK listening to music and other receptive techniques are gaining ground (see final section of Chapter 12). Helen Bonny's Guided Imagery and Music (GIM) is attracting interest among some music therapists in the UK and some GIM case material is included in Chapter 15.

A SURVEY OF SOME RECENT LITERATURE

As can be noted in the previous section the number of music therapy texts has proliferated since the mid-1990s. Some are compilation texts that have been edited after presentation in previous formats such as music therapy conferences and symposia (for example Wigram *et al.* 1995; Wigram and de Backer 1999a, 1999b); some are collections of case material from different sources or authors (for example Ansdell 1995; Pavlicevic 1999a). The emphasis on the individual and group case study in many of these texts builds on the work of earlier authors. A landmark publication was Bruscia's compilation of 40 case studies from therapists across nine countries (Bruscia 1991).

Several music therapists have contributed chapters on music therapy to other specialist texts. Robarts contributed to a text on autism with a comprehensive literature review and detailed case study of an autistic boy (Robarts 1996). Sloboda has written a chapter on music therapy in relation to psychotic violence (Sloboda 1996), Loth on music therapy in forensic psychotherapy (Loth 1996) and Hughes, Robarts, Rogers and Sloboda have contributed to a book on arts therapies with eating disorders (Dokter 1995). Odell-Miller has written a chapter for a book entitled *Continuing Care for Older People* (Odell-Miller 1997) and Sobey and Woodcock contributed a chapter to *Process in the Arts Therapies*, outlining the specific psychodynamic orientation to the music therapy training at the Roehampton Institute (Sobey and Woodcock 1999). Interest in music therapy practice is not only growing within other clinical fields as demonstrated here but also from within writing on music itself. Bunt contributed an overview of the clinical and therapeutic uses of music in *The Social Psychology of Music* (Bunt in Hargreaves and North 1997). He wrote the entries on music therapy in the latest edition of *The New Grove Dictionary of Music and Musicians* (2001) and *The Oxford Companion to Music* (2002). He recently collaborated with Pavlicevic on a music therapy chapter in a major text on *Emotion and Music* edited by Juslin and Sloboda (2001).

Chapters and articles on music therapy have also recently appeared in texts of a more historical, cultural and philosophical nature. A symposium organised by Horden resulted in the publication of *Music as Medicine: The History of Music Therapy since Antiquity* (Horden 2000). Tyler contributed a chapter to this compilation outlining early recreational approaches of music in hospitals and the gradual emergence of music therapy as a discipline and profession (Tyler 2000). A second symposium with an anthropological perspective was organised by Gouk resulting in the publication of *Music, Healing and Culture: Towards a Comparative Perspective* (Gouk 2000). The music educator Boyce-Tillman has also drawn on historical and anthropological sources in her recent exploration of healing practices and musical traditions within different societies in her book *Constructing Musical Healing: The Wounds that Sing* (Boyce-Tillman 2000). The growing importance given to more philosophical aspects of the work was also apparent at the Fifth European Music Therapy Congress held in Naples in 2001. One of the sub-keynote speakers focused on the aesthetic dimensions of music therapy (Frohne-Hagemann 2001).

The rest of this section on the recent literature is based on a topical issue of debate. As in the other creative arts therapies one of the recurring themes within the profession is how the art – in our case, the music – is construed in relation to the therapist's clinical orientation. In the Introduction to *The Handbook of Art Therapy* we read: 'The theoretical approach of arts therapists is shaped by how "art" and its use in therapy is understood and the orientation of the therapist in coming to this understanding' (Case and Dalley 1992: 2). The recent proliferation of music therapy texts has highlighted an interesting continuum between therapists who underpin their practice with reference to clinical theories from psychology, medicine and, in particular, psychoanalysis and those who are sceptical of theories that are not rooted in or evolve from the music itself. Of course this is not a totally polarised issue and some of the writers we will be highlighting indicate an intention to work in an integrative manner.

In 1995 the art therapist Gilroy and music therapist Lee edited *Art and Music: Therapy and Research*. The text includes descriptions of the research process, clinically worked material and personal narratives (Gilroy and Lee 1995). This shifting continuum between the emphasis on the music and reference to other clinical theories can be seen in the two contributions by music therapists in the section 'The Practice of Research.' Lee's chapter builds from his doctoral work with a focus on a detailed structural analysis of individual improvisations with people living with HIV and AIDS in order to gain further understanding into the music therapy process (Lee 1995b and see Lee 1989, 1990). In the second music therapy chapter Pavlicevic, again building from her doctoral work, discusses music and emotion and outlines her concept of 'dynamic form' in music therapy (see Chapter 4 of this handbook) and some models for understanding the meaning of musical action in therapy. She recommends that music therapists build bridges with practitioners in allied fields, citing literature in the related fields of psychology, psychotherapy, neurology, musical analysis and musical aesthetics (Pavlicevic 1995a). The debate has been set into motion.

Both Lee and Pavlicevic went on write their own books and these texts take the debate further. Lee's *Music at the Edge* is a complete case study of the music therapy experiences of Francis, a musician living with AIDS (Lee 1996). The music is at the centre of this text with examples of Francis' music transcribed and analysed in the text and recordings of some of his own and joint improvisations with Lee available on the accompanying CD. In the keynote address of the musicology section of the Naples congress Ansdell referred to Lee's work as being 'at the forefront of this . . . musicological perspective in music therapy research' (Ansdell 2001: 23). Lee also includes transcribed verbal reflections from both Francis and other listeners on the musical material presented in his book. The juxtaposition of musical and verbal commentary creates many challenges and what Ansdell describes as 'the "gap" between musicologically analysed "musical content" and personal (therapeutic) significance – the attempted link, that is, between the structural and hermeneutic dimensions of the phenomenon' (ibid.: 23).

Like Lee, Pavlicevic trained in the Nordoff–Robbins approach. Her book *Music Therapy in Context: Music, Meaning and Relationship* develops material from her earlier chapter, drawing numerous strands together from a variety of areas including: music theory, music psychology, cross-cultural debates, non-verbal communication particularly early mother–child inter-action and psychodynamic theory. It is also a personal story with references to her clinical work in more than one country, discussions with colleagues, processes in improvisation, life experiences and another ongoing debate, namely between the position of the music and words in music therapy (Pavlicevic 1997). Her text develops theoretical concepts to a more sophisticated level than has previously been attempted in British writing. For example, many music therapists have been enlightened by the theoretical connections between musical process and the observations and theories of Stern and Winnicott but what Pavlicevic achieves here is an effective synthesis and explanation of these different approaches and disciplines. Perhaps this text reflects an evolutionary stage for music therapy, the amassing of clinical mate-rial over the past 30 years now allowing for more concentration on effective discussion of theory.

A central theme of Ansdell's *Music for Life: Aspects of Creative Music Therapy with Adult Clients* is that music therapy 'works in the way music itself works' (Ansdell 1995: 5). Like Lee and Pavlicevic, Ansdell has extended the principles of the Nordoff–Robbins approach to include work with adults (such development builds on, among others, Julienne Cartwright's earlier work in the early 1980s, particularly her work in Scotland). Ansdell's book weaves case studies, for the most part of his own and colleagues' work both in the UK and Germany, with themes that emerge from the studies.

> These short essays concern aspects of the process of Creative Music Therapy such as creating, listening, expressing and meeting in the music: also how the phenomenon of music works in itself within music therapy to quicken people into action, connect them into a group or recall them into integration
>
> (Ansdell 1995: x)

We can note here that a later text by Pavlicevic – *Music Therapy: Intimate Notes* – follows Ansdell's model of weaving the writer's reflective comments between a range of case material, in this case the result of interviews with colleagues working within different specialist areas (Pavlicevic 1999a).

Ansdell's 1995 text is also published with an accompanying CD enabling listeners to understand more of the actual process of Creative Music Ther-apy. In his doctoral and post-doctoral research Ansdell has continued to relate aspects of the 'new musicology' to music therapy (Ansdell 1997, 1999a, 2001).

For example, he is one of a group of researchers who have introduced music therapists to Small's idea of 'musicking'.

> To music is to take part, in any capacity, in a musical performance, whether by performing, by listening, by rehearsing or practising, by providing material for performance . . . The act of musicking establishes in the place where it is happening a set of relationships, and it is in those relationships that the meaning of the act lies.
>
> (Small 1998: 9, 13)

Small sees such relationships as not only existing between the sounds themselves but also metaphorically between the various personal relationships and connections with the outside world. In his Naples keynote speech Ansdell also placed his own work within the context of music's expression of individual and cultural identities. He referred to Ruud's recent writing, in particular *Music Therapy: Improvisation, Communication and Culture* (Ruud 1998). Ruud has also greatly influenced his countryman Stige in his search for 'a better understanding of how the participants create meaning in the communicative processes in the different contexts of music therapy' (Stige 1998: 26 and see his 2001 sub-keynote to the Naples congress when he described an ethnographic approach to clinical research).

The experience of observing a young disabled woman in an individual music therapy session gave the researcher Aldridge 'the impetus to the rest of my professional working life' (Aldridge 1996: 2). In his position as Professor for Clinical Research Methods in the Music Therapy Institute at the University of Witten Herdecke, Germany, Aldridge has been a major influence in the development of music therapy research. In the first of a series of three texts *Music Therapy Research and Practice in Medicine: From Out of the Silence* he brings his research background to a detailed examination of various research methodologies as they relate to music therapy. He calls for a tolerant approach. At the Institute in Herdecke music therapy is viewed as complementary to medical intervention. The work is rooted in both the tradition of the Nordoff–Robbins approach with its emphasis on clinical improvisation, and the anthroposophical writings of Rudolf Steiner. Aldridge places the needs of each patient not only within the perspective of the hospital setting but also within the wider social context. He recommends that any research should be rooted in practice and that it should resonate with the sounds of the music room and the dialogues connecting patient and therapist. Aldridge takes a radical stance in basing his view of health on music. In contrast to relating music therapy to another treatment model such as psychoanalysis he considers that a musical improvisation can be read as a direct expression of the needs of the self.

Some of the chapters in the comprehensive text *The Art and Science of Music Therapy: A Handbook* edited by Wigram *et al.* (1995) continue to explore the continuum. One example of the more music-centred approaches is the detailed description by Howat of a lengthy period of music therapy with an autistic girl, the only chapter to include written-out musical examples (Howat 1995). Towse's chapter stands out for her emphasis on using recorded music when working with the elderly. But her chapter balances her musical approach with her own psychotherapeutic orientation (Towse 1995). John explores more links between psychoanalytic theory and music therapy with his references to Klein, Segal, Winnicott and Bion to support work with psychotic patients (John 1995). In Heal Hughes' chapter a Kleinian approach to mother–infant interaction is compared to work with adults with learning disabilities (Heal Hughes 1995).

To conclude this review, a vigorous restatement of our theme concerning the spectrum of clinical theory and music-based theory was articulated in 1999 in two successive issues of the *British Journal of Music Therapy*. In the first issue, Streeter (1999a) published a challenging paper putting forward the view that finding a balance between musical thinking and psychological awareness is essential for understanding the music therapy relationship. She took one psychological perspective, namely, how basic psychoanalytic concepts could enhance our awareness of musical processes and safeguard therapeutic boundaries. She argued that musical thinking was not robust enough to underpin all aspects of the therapist–client relationship, making a detailed critique of some aspects of the more music-based texts described above. A veritable storm ensued with four therapists replying in the very next issue in the section entitled 'Dialogues' (Aigen 1999; Ansdell 1999b; Brown 1999; Pavlicevic 1999b). All four respondents made their critique of Streeter's assertions. What was surprising about this was the passion that this topic engendered. This theme appears to touch our profession deeply; it is a dichotomy that challenges every music therapist who cares to think more than casually about their work. Because of this constant client–therapist–music triangle we have to work thoroughly to maintain balanced, questioning, tolerant and open attitudes. The subject will not go away, it will not leave us alone. It will continue to surface, need framing and reframing depending on context and the different cultural and political demands. The topic is too powerful a subject to defy any attempt to squash it. It seems highly appropriate that the title of the Tenth World Congress of Music Therapy held in Oxford in July 2002 included the two words: Dialogue and Debate.[3]

---

3 As therapists, trainers and researchers we have both been influenced by varied traditions in psychology (including early mother–infant research and ethology), psychotherapy, musicology and music therapy. We both believe in the importance of integration and of using theory that supports music therapy practice. Our research has also used both quantitative and qualitative approaches when appropriate. We aim to seek a balance between artistic and psychological underpinning to our work.

QUALITIES NEEDED TO TRAIN AND PRACTISE AS A MUSIC THERAPIST

Music therapy training involves developing a wide range of competencies and qualities. The profession requires trainees to be able to integrate their musicality within a sound therapeutic base and an open awareness of individual value and belief systems. The process of selection involves assessors making complex judgements about a person's ability to communicate, to understand human patterns of relating, to be open and self-aware. A potential therapist needs to be flexible and to present a professional attitude. We need to be sure that a trainee is safe (the security of our patients and clients is paramount), reliable and able to reflect. The start of training is only the beginning of a lifelong process of change, reflection and learning.

Music therapy as a career is increasingly appealing to experienced music teachers, other health-care professionals who have continued to maintain a strong commitment to music, younger students of music, specialists in psychology and languages, 'returning' mothers and seasoned professional musicians wishing to complement and broaden their work. In the UK a sustained musical background is a prerequisite before applying to train. This has usually been three years of undergraduate music studies at a university or conservatoire. A comparable level of musicianship needs to be demonstrated if applicants have followed a different entry route. At present there are no approved undergraduate training courses in the UK. As trainers we are often asked, why this emphasis on musical competence? Music therapists often work at a very simple musical level with people who are unpractised musically perhaps using only one or two sounds. In answer we could say that inherent in the musical training process are mirrored some key aspects of the work of a therapist and the therapeutic process itself, for example:

- a keen attention to the smallest detail;
- a highly disciplined approach to work;
- being able to listen very attentively to oneself, for example an instrumentalist's awareness of tuning and pitch discrepancies;
- being able to listen to others, for example in chamber music and small group-playing where there is an absence of a specific director and an intuitive sharing of communications with a subtle blend of leading and following;
- the acute awareness of important musical parameters of timing, phrasing, blending and;
- artistic integration and imaginative risk-taking.

Clearly we are looking for an ability to project any musical utterance in a convincing way and to understand the basis of music as a feeling experience. We are also expecting candidates to share a communication with musical listeners or partners. These are all features of being an effective musician but they are also essential in the process of therapy. The therapist needs to know precisely how and when to 'speak'; to be rooted in feeling experience; to relate sensitively and to be acutely aware of the impact on others. The integration and development of these features are very much the business of training music therapists and we will examine these aspects in Part III in more detail. However, a basic competency in or instinct for each strand in music is a prerequisite, because often our patients will have no words or may feel that words fail them.

In addition to the musical issues there are certain essential personal qualities that are required by all the training courses. These include:

- the ability to empathise with children and adults of all ages with wide-ranging needs;
- tolerance, especially concerning sensitive issues of race and sexuality;
- patience;
- an open and questioning attitude;
- gentleness and strength;
- flexibility and adaptability;
- a sense of humour;
- emotional stability.

Many courses in the UK expect applicants to be a minimum age of 25. The training courses have highly developed and individual ways of assessing these personal qualities. One possibility may be to include an intensive and private interview with a psychotherapist; another may include small group improvisation and discussion with a music therapist; a third method may integrate a personal and musical interview, allowing each area to inform the other.

SUMMARY

In this opening chapter we have tried to set the scene on contemporary music therapy in the UK. We have discussed the current range of work, reviewed some of the most significant recent publications and outlined some of the qualities necessary to train as a therapist. We now need to explore the most common terminology used in music therapy, including brief reference to theory, before moving on to sections dealing in more detail with clinical work and training.

Chapter 2

Practicalities and basic principles of music therapy

Leslie Bunt and Sarah Hoskyns

INTRODUCTION

Chapter 1 charted the recent evolution of music therapy to its current status as a respected profession in its own right. In this chapter some of the practicalities, principles and thinking that underpin music therapy practice are discussed. We begin with a graphic representation of some of the main themes and 'players' present in any music therapy space (see Figure 2.1).

Both patient(s) and therapist will bring to such a music therapy space their unique musical histories, values and life experiences. In every session can be observed a triadic relationship between the individual child or adult, the music and the therapist with the added dynamics of group work. Patients come to therapy with their needs. Therapists respond to these, being vigilant to attend to their own concerns outside in supervision or their own therapy. Hence in Figure 2.1 only needs for the patient(s) are itemised. Other 'players' in this space will be any other people, the instruments, the therapist's theoretical framework and the complex influences of the context and larger cultural,

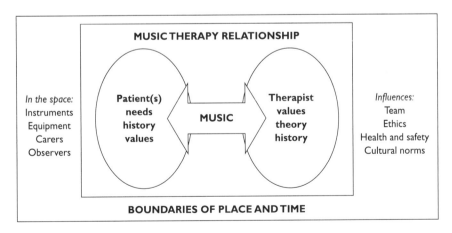

Figure 2.1 The music therapy space.

collective and ethical perspectives. We could also consider the whole frame as a kind of 'gestalt' with a constant fluidity between foreground and background as the various elements within the space shift and change (Zanchi 2001).

CLINICAL EXAMPLE

Case study I

Sergio, a six-year-old boy with dyspraxia[1] and severe difficulties with verbal communication is referred for music therapy. He attends quite willingly but for the first five sessions insists by his gestures and vocalisations that he collects instruments, stores them in available containers and stacks them on top of a low cupboard, where he proceeds to crouch with them for the duration of the sessions. The therapist's expectations of work are to observe the detail and quality of his activity, and to provide any opportunities for musical encounter. He reminds her of a hamster marking his territory (and remembers that in her own childhood she had always wanted one).

On the one hand the therapist follows her music therapy norms and ethical code of practice – the child needs to show freely what are his preoccupations, his capacities and interests for musical play. But the culture of the school says: 'Children should not climb on furniture', and the therapist experiences some tension in justifying the child's actions, especially when he jumps suddenly in session four and hits his head while on top of the cupboard. One of the external influences of the larger team infiltrates the room in the mind of the therapist. She also questions her ability to engage musically with him and feels disempowered. (Thus she experiences her own frustrations but also perhaps the feelings of pain, frustration and incapacity expressed in Sergio's actions.)

Another apparently unacceptable school behaviour (throwing drumsticks at the therapist) is translated into a musical catching game towards the end of the fifth session. The song-game has quite an aggressive quality and is characterised by sharply accented rhythms; Sergio 'fires' the drumsticks like arrows and the therapist catches them in an inverted drum as she sings. The eventual outcome of this process over some weeks is loud, positive and extrovert singing by the child into a stick 'microphone'. Gradually the therapist is gaining some experience of his musical norms, values and potential energy. She has waited for him and understood his needs. Within the boundaries of place and time a musical relationship has begun to be formed and framed.

1 Dyspraxia: the partial loss of ability to plan and execute coordinated movements.

This clinical example is used to illustrate some of the elements in Figure 2.1 and will inform some discussion later in the chapter. We also refer the reader to Ruud's discussion of the Nordoff and Robbins case study of 'Edward' in relation to the interaction between knowledge, values, interests and norms and subsequent action in music therapy (Ruud 1998: 105–108). Parallels can also be drawn with another triangular interaction between the three forces involved in any artistic endeavour and described by Rooley as 'idea, action and fruit' (Rooley 1990: 39).

The rest of this chapter concentrates on:

- the music therapy space;
- the musical instruments;
- boundaries;
- the qualities of the therapeutic relationship;
- some features from psychoanalytic theory;
- the spectrum of therapeutic frameworks;
- the essential 'I's' of music therapy practice: imagination, intuition, improvisation and intellect.

The basic principles discussed in this chapter concentrate on psychological and therapeutic underpinnings of the work, the 'therapeutics'. The central position of music, outlined in the previous chapter, will be clearly reflected in the clinical chapters that form Part II. Reference will be made throughout that section to research that makes biological connections between early musical development and music therapy practice (for example the work of Trevarthen) and to those psychologists who describe human interactions using musical terminology (for example the work of Stern, summarised recently in Pavlicevic 1997).

A PRACTICAL WORKING FRAME FOR MUSIC THERAPY

Each person will use music therapy in a unique way. Many factors contribute to providing a safe and secure space for therapy to take place: the physical conditions; the quality and range of the instruments; the people in the room and above all the evolving relationships between the music and the people within that space. There are many links between external physical features and internal and symbolic aspects of the process. The music therapy frame consequently becomes far more than the sum of its parts. Before we discuss some of the complex links between objective and subjective experience, we need to begin simply by being aware of the physical characteristics of a music therapy room that contribute towards effective work.

The physical space

Ideally all settings should be dedicated music therapy spaces: well lit, warm but airy and with sufficient space to accommodate the participants in the session, a range of instruments and usually a piano or some form of keyboard. Sound-proofing needs careful attention to safeguard both the quality of the acoustic within the setting and any sound disturbance (both ways) that could interfere with the process. Individual and group work obviously present different needs regarding the size of the space. Chairs need to be comfortable but upright enough to encourage alertness. Special or adapted seating is often required for people with physical problems and a physiotherapist or occupational therapist can advise. Disabled access and mobility within the space are prerequisites, as is easy access to a disabled toilet. Storage space is needed for instruments, either in the room or in an adjoining area. Some settings incorporate inbuilt video and audio facilities and/or observation rooms for carers, other professionals and students. In reality this ideal is not often possible and therapists may have to work in rooms used for other purposes besides music therapy. In these cases care and practical common sense are needed to create a self-contained space that guarantees the least distraction. Usually therapists have a minimum list of prerequisites that they regard as essential before any work can commence.

Musical instruments

The provision of high-quality musical instruments is vital. They are the tools of the trade; good care and maintenance of the instruments are prerequisites. All equipment needs to comply with health and safety regulations and to be appropriately insured. In Plate 2.1 we see an empty but inviting music therapy room, purpose-built for clinical work with some tuned and untuned percussion instruments. Plate 2.2 shows a successfully adapted multi-purpose relaxation room with a range of instruments used for music therapy groups. Instruments from Africa, India, the Far East and South America add interest, curiosity, further colour and a range of texture and sound quality to the work. They are suggestible and can evoke a sense of play. Recommendations for a range of instruments for individual and small group work with all ages are included in Appendix II.

The therapist will need to access some kind of harmonic support. Traditionally the piano or a portable keyboard is used and many therapists also use guitar. Stands for the instruments and a good variety of beaters with felt, wood and plastic heads will be needed (sometimes specially adapted beaters will be required). A trolley may be helpful if instruments are to be moved around.

Plate 2.1 A music therapy group room

Plate 2.2 A relaxation room adapted for music therapy

BOUNDARIES

A boundary can be defined as a physical line that delineates an area, as in a field boundary marking out the edge of a territory. Imagine you can walk across this field to the hedge and know that everything this side belongs to you; you have the freedom to walk, gallop, graze or sleep. The other side of the hedge is unavailable for your use. You may feel like jumping over it or breaking it down but you have a sense where the limit is. In some ways the therapist's job is analogous to that of the careful farmer. Good maintenance is the key – keeping the edges in mind and checking on them regularly. A boundary can also delineate a specific action or a pattern of thought. We talk of being out of bounds, off-limits, on the edge or setting our own boundaries. From an early age a child needs to be aware of limits. Parents need to demonstrate consistent handling of not only physical boundaries but also psychological and emotional ones if their child is to feel safe. It is also a natural urge to want to challenge and push through boundaries in our growing attempts at mastery and individuality. In his essay 'On Security' Winnicott reminds us of this lifelong struggle and the ways in which artistic form and creativity are of immeasurable help to us in managing the tension between safety and independence (Winnicott 1965: 30–33). Art can be framed: music has its forms and own kinds of boundaries; for example sound/silence, words/music. We can appreciate these features when working as arts therapists, yet also need to tolerate a certain flexibility of boundaries.

Physical and time-based boundaries

A patient is helped to feel safe and secure if the music therapy session occurs in the same place, at the same time and for the same amount of time each week. The physical layout and features of the room become meaningful and important as therapy develops, contributing to a sense of containment. Often therapists will maintain the instruments and any other objects in the space in the accustomed place for each patient. This all adds to the evolving sense of security and predictability. In group work instruments are presented so that they are easily accessible to all members.

The boundaries of consistent day and time contribute further to the feelings of predictability and expectation: there is a space in the week for the patient to locate thoughts, feelings, actions and music. If sessions start and finish at the same time this engenders a clear sense of beginning and end. The amount of time allocated for each patient depends on the patient's age and nature of the problems. Many music therapists set aside a 'therapeutic hour' (50 minutes for clinical work and 10 minutes to allow time between appointments for departures and arrivals, reflection and note-keeping) for individual adult appointments and 30–45 minutes for children (sometimes less if the child is very young or has a very limited level of concentration).

There is a range from one to two hours for group work. It is important that once an optimum time is established for each context that this is respected. Lack of clarity over timings can lead to insecurity. The approaching end of a session requires careful preparation. Time-based boundary issues often emerge as part of the process requiring periods of reflection and supervision to unravel their potential meaning. Some therapists do not continue with the session if patients wish to stop before the end of the allocated time; others remain in the space even if the patient leaves. There are instances, however, when sensitive adaptability is required, for example when working with terminally ill patients to accommodate for the variable physical and emotional needs of the patients.

The length of any therapeutic contract can be negotiated with verbal patients, for example an initial contract of 12 sessions followed by a review. Much creativity is required when negotiating with non-verbal and highly dependent mentally ill or disabled patients. Here it may be appropriate also to liaise with the primary carers. Careful thought is required in preparing patients for any breaks, in particular for the ending of therapy (see Chapter 13).

An important physical boundary is the non-acceptance of any form of violent behaviour directed either to another patient or to the therapist. Vulnerable patients need to feel safe and that the experience of coming to therapy will not be physically threatening. Destruction or abuse of the environment is also not acceptable, although music therapists recognise the need for patients sometimes to channel very strong negative feelings through instrumental playing. Any additional ground rules can be stated at the outset of the work. Once again this relates to the therapist's value system and clinical orientation.

Professional and ethical boundaries

As professional and student members of the Association of Professional Music Therapists, clinicians practising in the UK must sign an agreement to abide by the Association's *Code of Professional Ethics and Discipline* (see copy in Appendix III). This document outlines significant boundaries important for the protection of patients and therapists themselves.

Of central importance is the requirement to act at all times 'in the best interests of the patient', maintaining a strictly professional relationship and respecting the confidentiality of the patient. Working within institutional settings can present challenges to providing a safe and secure place for the work. Other staff members have to understand that effective therapeutic work can only take place in an undisturbed space. Intrusions push against the safety curtain surrounding patient and therapist and the evolving establishment of trust. They can be felt as invasions of the space. There are practical ways of protecting the space, for example by using a sign to indicate that a private session is in progress. In teamwork there are other complex issues to work through in relation to what material is totally private to the sessions and the ongoing relationships and what can be shared in reports, team meetings and case discussions. Treatment teams need to communicate but to have a high level of regard for the privacy and dignity of patients. If this works effectively the professional boundaries surrounding the members of the team act as another level of security for the patient or client. Music therapists, like all professionals, have to abide by British laws in relation to child protection (the APMT publishes separate guidelines about this attached to the code of ethics). Most clinical work settings will also have agreed procedures for how any disclosures of abuse are handled and reported by individual therapists.

Confidentiality is also a major issue in recording sessions on audio or video for supervision or teaching purposes, presenting work publicly and in written format. Patient consent is essential here and, if granted, it is customary to use just first names, the patient's initial or a pseudonym (as is done for the case material in this book). Seeking informed consent is a delicate issue, particularly when working with non-verbal patients or those highly dependent on others through severe mental illness or disability when the therapist may need to explore creative alternatives or seek assent from the next of kin or the primary care staff (see Chapter 13).

Further ethical issues involve respecting the dignity and autonomy of the patient irrespective of age, gender, sexual orientation, race, legal status and mental state. A book on ethics in relation to music therapy practice has been edited recently by Cheryl Dileo (2000).

Other developmental aspects of boundaries

An aspect of early mother–infant interaction is the baby's strong dependence on the mother and in her meeting of her baby's all-encompassing needs as well as she can, Winnicott's description of 'good enough mothering' is apposite (Winnicott 1965: 145). Ideally a position of trust is soon established (see Erikson 1965 for a discussion of the first polarity of trust versus mistrust). Often a stage like this can be observed in the early sessions of music therapy when a patient seems to be merged in the music with no apparent sense of self or boundaries. Following this early stage in infancy, mother and baby need to separate from each other if the baby is to develop as an individual with an emerging sense of self (and here music therapists have had recourse to other thinkers within the object-relations school such as Melanie Klein). In his 'Spectrum of Consciousness' Ken Wilber describes this process of primary differentiation as the 'skin-boundary' and as 'one of the most fundamentally accepted self/not-self boundaries' (Wilber 1993: 6). The baby comes to terms with all inside as 'me' and all outside as 'not me'. Musical frames and the whole fabric of co-created music within a relationship can be used to help establish these boundaries between 'me' and 'not-me', and self and other.

A further boundary is negotiated as the child begins to draw limits between body and mind (body/ego or soma/psyche). The child begins to assert more autonomy and gain more control over the environment, for example through the development of movement skills and speech. There are also various challenges to overcome including resisting and internalising the adult direction of 'no' (for a concise discussion of these early developmental stages in the context of Erikson's stages of psychosocial development and Freud's classic libido theory, see Brown and Pedder 1991: 37–46). The next boundary appears when the older child begins to separate out parts of the psyche, presenting a particular face to the outside world and hiding away other parts, consciously or unconsciously. We make a further split in our mind, what Wilber refers to as the persona/shadow boundary. Later, once the full adult and functioning ego has been established we appear to find safe ways of loosening the boundaries; of becoming less attached; moving into a place of integration of mind, body and spirit within and beyond our environment. It is as if we have come full circle.

Therapy can help us to put the boundaries in place, to explore what they are, how and why we need them. It can also help to break down unnecessary boundaries, replace them, perhaps eventually help us to dissolve them and, as we move towards the end of our lives, to even live without them. In general terms Western psychological thinking has unravelled many processes in early child and adult development. The connections Wilber makes to Eastern traditions, particularly those linked to the second half of life, may not fit comfortably with a Western approach. Nevertheless they help patients and therapists to explore realms beyond that of the fully integrated ego, particularly the domains of the spiritual and transpersonal (Rowan 1993).

THE QUALITIES OF THE THERAPEUTIC RELATIONSHIP

The Eastern traditions described by Wilber in much of his writing stress a loosening of ego and boundaries. In parallel with some Western monastic traditions there is more focus on individual contemplation, ritual and teaching over and above relationship with others. In his essay 'On Psychological Creativity' James Hillman contrasts such practices with a psychology which 'is created within the vale of living intimacy' (Hillman 1972: 27). The essential ingredient of any therapeutic relationship is seemingly in the meeting of two souls.

To relate implies to refer, to bring into relation to, or to connect. In the contemporary context of therapy is stressed this interpersonal and two-way focus of the patient–therapist relationship. Relationships are the melting-pot for development of 'a sense of self and self in relationship to others' (Pelham and Stacy 1999: 12). The word 'relationship' also implies an evolving dynamic process bringing with it the idea of constant movement, growth and change. Many current theories about personal therapy emphasise the basis in a fluid relationship. Music therapy is founded in this principle as is indicated in the APMT definition quoted in Chapter 1. In his authoritative study *Relationships: A Dialectical Perspective,* the ethologist Robert Hinde analyses and describes central issues in the field of close relationships in adulthood. In outlining some of these features, Hinde emphasises the importance of relationships developing over time:

> Relationships involve (at the behavioural level) a series of interactions between two individuals who know each other, such that each interaction can be influenced by past interactions and by expectations of interactions in the future. Affective and cognitive components are at least as important as the behavioural ones.
>
> (Hinde 1997: 48)

Hinde is describing personal relationships but the professional therapeutic relationship helps patients by exploring the fabric of communication and dialogue within the therapy room. As in personal relationships, the dialogue between patients and therapist matures and grows gradually as trust and mutual understanding are gained. Hinde talks about people who 'know each other'. In therapy there is a need to balance what is known with a sense of not knowing.

> The analyst can learn to follow with one eye those aspects of a patient about which he knows he does not know, while keeping the other eye on whatever he feels he does know. There is a creative tension between this knowing and not knowing.
>
> (Casement 1985: 5)

Music therapists might add 'keeping both ears open' in relation to following the musical communications in the music therapy relationship, listening to both the played and unheard music. The following sections explore aspects of the 'relationship' in therapy and music therapy, how it is built and maintained for effective treatment of patients.

To be with

At a most fundamental level is the need for the therapist just to 'be with' the person who is coming to therapy. Implied in this deceptively simple phrase is one of our hardest tasks. It is difficult to sit alongside and stay with whatever feeling the person is communicating. If the person is in pain, in distress or confused, it is hard to resist the temptation to be active (perhaps to escape from our own intense discomfort) and in our case to play some music or fill the gaps with sound. This is often in direct contrast to the needs of the patient who may be wanting us to attend and wait even if this means staying unobtrusively in silence and to just 'be with' (this little word 'just' again). It could be argued that it is impossible to build up a therapeutic relationship with any child or adult until this fundamental concept of 'being with' is grasped and made apparent in the therapist's approach.

Working alliance

This commonly used term by therapists implies a partnership, a purposeful approach to work and to achieving therapeutic goals. On one level there are practical issues to consider such as keeping appointments and effective time-keeping. In addition, each working alliance will be unique with different patterns and goals. Patients will have varying needs and therapists will need to indicate a sustained willingness to attend to these and continue the work. There are obvious differences in the role limits of both parties and within the process of long-term therapy both therapist and patient(s) work through many different aspects of their alliance. This might involve some significant changes in perception and shifts in power.

Therapeutic attitude and presence

The terms 'therapeutic attitude' (how we think about our work) and 'therapeutic presence' (how we actually are in the room with our patients) are also commonly used. These are difficult concepts to communicate and are more related to the therapist's set of values, beliefs and self-awareness. Patients need to know that their therapists are there for them; they need to feel safe. However, as with all aspects of forming relationships, it is difficult to identify techniques or skills that will help with the growth of a particular attitude. We can observe some therapists working with groups of patients who seem to have a natural therapeutic presence; others seem to struggle in spite of a similar amount of training and range of skills. Therapeutic presence seems to relate to how comfortable and confident therapists feel within and about themselves. It has a lot to do with the quality of attention and listening given to patients who need to feel that their every communication is valued and really heard, features that go beyond any particular clinical orientation. Posture and the therapist's sense of continued alertness are also important. There are some links here with the role of a conductor in a musical ensemble. A music therapist facilitates an unfolding process and exploration of feelings, sounds and words; a sensitive conductor assists the musicians to articulate the composer's intentions. Both roles involve being a kind of sounding or resonating board through which these processes can flow freely.

Musical empathy and resonance

What is meant by empathy? One definition offered by Rogers suggests that it:

> ... involves being sensitive, moment by moment, to the changing felt meanings which flow in this other person, to the fear or rage or tenderness or confusion or whatever that he or she is experiencing. It means temporarily living in the other's life, moving about in it delicately without making judgements.
>
> (Rogers 1980, cited by Egan 1994: 106)

As stated above we have a responsibility to demonstrate that we are listening to our patients with real focused attention. This kind of intense listening to the quality of verbal and non-verbal sounds, to the pace, to the feelings behind any music being played is not an everyday occurrence. The therapist moves across various listening dimensions, listening to the world of the patient and the therapist's own musical and personal responses. Such shifts relate to the different modes of consciousness: the world of the client, the therapist's professional world and the therapist's personal world, as outlined by Bruscia (1995a).

Demonstrating empathy takes us a step further than attentive listening. It links to being open to the other person and to the therapeutic concept of resonance. As musicians we are familiar with this, Rowan quoting the example of a note being struck on one piano in a room and the similar string on another piano in the room resonating in sympathy (Rowan 1993: 55). However, this feeling of identity is not sufficient as we can note in the development of a musical metaphor in the following passage by Casement.

> Empathic identification is not enough, as it can limit a therapist to seeing what is familiar, or is similar to his own experience. Therapists therefore have to develop an openness to, and respect for, feelings and experiences that are quite unlike their own. The greater freedom they have to resonate to the unfamiliar 'keys' or dissonant 'harmonics' of others, the more it will enhance their receptivity to these unconsciously interactive cues that are often central to an understanding of patients.
>
> (Casement 1985: 95)

Inge Nygaard Pedersen develops a total listening attitude in her work with schizophrenic patients. She describes it 'as a state of "being very aware" – as if I am in a state of extreme preparation for resonating with any signal or vibration coming from the patient but, at the same time, not invading the patient' (Pedersen 1999: 31). This is particularly the case when attempting to resonate with those unfamiliar keys of others described by Casement.

Pedersen also discusses states of listening that grow out of this 'being very aware', states that are described as autocentric ways of listening and ones that expand to listening in a slightly altered state of consciousness.

While acknowledging that it is impossible to see or hear the world completely as another person does, we can do all we can to understand the world of our patients from their perspectives. Music therapists are fortunate in having the medium of music as a means of 'sounding out' that we have heard what our patients are trying to communicate to us. We can reflect back sounds and begin to engage in an empathic musical dialogue. We can play a reflective musical phrase in response to a patient's long silence. We can note how the patient's music makes us feel and any subsequent reactions to our musical interventions. Musical empathy is not just imitation or parroting but a subtle dynamic process. We can use both music and words (if appropriate) to reflect back or interpret, for example we can play our response or suggest that 'your music feels like *x or y*'. The varied contribution of patient and therapist (similar or strongly contrasted) can be held together in a delicate or robust web of flexible musical improvisation. There is the possibility that simultaneously the partners can both be themselves and be aware of each other, given the careful listening and responsive framework provided by the music therapist.

SOME FEATURES DRAWN FROM PSYCHOANALYTIC THEORY

Music therapy in the late twentieth century was strongly influenced by psychoanalytic thought. Many music therapists have undertaken supervision with psychotherapists, had personal therapy or analysis and a number have themselves trained as child or adult psychotherapists. Formative discussion by writers such as Priestley (1975, 1994) Odell-Miller (1995), Heal Hughes (1995), John (1995) and Towse (1995) has explored the relationship between psychoanalytic psychotherapy and music therapy practice and highlighted areas of similarity and difference between the disciplines. Heal Hughes and Odell-Miller developed the term 'psychoanalytically informed music therapy' in their writings in the 1990s and some therapists have found this a useful description of practice. The following sections highlight concepts that we consider are being used widely by clinicians to inform their work.

The constructs of holding and containment

The importance of various practical boundaries that help to provide a safe and supportive frame in which the therapeutic process can be protected and begin to be nurtured has been discussed in an earlier section. In describing musical empathy it was suggested that the therapist might 'hold together' disparate communications within a musical structure or web and that this might be helpful to the patient. So what are the holding and containing properties of music and of the therapist?

Therapists constantly refer to holding and containing a patient's feelings. What do we mean by these terms? We can begin by imagining some different kinds of holding: the baby held in a mother's arms, the comfort of a friend's embrace or the intimate holding between lovers. How can we hold a patient effectively in music therapy? What is the most appropriate model? Many therapists use features of the mother's holding as a metaphor for the work. Winnicott (1974) described this early holding as full of contact, nonverbal, highly intuitive and intimate. It is a supportive kind of holding without any judgement, words or interpretation. It is non-invasive and finely balanced; the mother wants both to protect the child and yet encourage individuality. It is of note that the image of the mother or parent holding the baby is commonly associated with a musical 'holding'. The unselfconscious parent will naturally shape vocal melodies to soothe a fretful baby, or sing a lullaby to welcome sleep. The pattern and phrase shape, the tone of voice and the repetition all contribute: the musical form thus 'echoes' the arms of the parent. Initially both aspects go together but gradually music can be used to stand for the embrace. Perhaps at a later developmental stage the child can sing a familiar song alone to hold some particular feelings. Josephine Klein explores in detail the different qualities of holding offered by the therapist (Klein 1995: 72–93). She emphasises the importance of holding as recognising, accepting and understanding feelings of the patient (ideas linked to 'being with' described earlier) and goes on to highlight the idea of pattern in the therapist's use of words:

> Words enable us to make patterns and to hold on to patterns. It is the patterns that give events their meaning and significance . . . Patterns of words enable us to reflect, to communicate and elaborate meaning.
>
> (Klein 1995: 86)

Pattern is also a building block of music; tiny patterns are the starting point of non-verbal contact that may be elaborated and extended in richly varied ways. Words can be added to interpret, spoken or sung by therapist or patient.

In Case study I of this chapter, the therapist needed to recognise and accept how badly Sergio felt when presented with the possibility of playing music. For him the only choice was to put things away and withdraw. The soft guitar music of the first few sessions acknowledged this and the simple musical pattern with chord sequence and voice was perhaps consoling for Sergio. However, a few weeks on, a stronger improvised song could also 'hold' the new energy and aggression of his stick throwing. The holding was achieved by the therapist understanding the need to wait, and by providing gentle and then energetic music to match the moment.

Allied to the concept of holding is containment. What is the purpose of containment in therapy? A patient needs to feel held and supported and also to be aware that the therapist is not only consistent but also able to contain, stay with and manage whatever is communicated, however difficult the expression. Can the therapist contain all the wanted and unwanted parts, all the bits that hurt or need exploring or discarding?

What do we mean by a container? It can be used to hold things; items both wanted and unwanted. Containers can be retained and stored with the contents used at a later date, put out of sight or even discarded. In music therapy there are many opportunities for both the therapist and the music to act as containers. The patient is able to project all kinds of communications not only towards the therapist but also to articulate them musically through the instruments. A myriad of feelings, including difficult and painful ones, can be aired and explored. In this way the instruments – in many instances they even look like physical containers, as in the case of the inverted drum catching sticks for Sergio – can act as containers. When the therapist improvises with the patient, the therapist can begin to get a sense of these feelings, to work with them and to contain them further in organic musical frames. Joint attention can be given to this co-created musical activity. Some meaning may begin to evolve from what in the first instance may sound confused and chaotic. If, for example, the patient presents some very fragmented and confused sounds then the therapist's response may weave some connections between the fragments and help the patient gain insight and understanding.

The constructs of transference and counter-transference

Therapists make different choices about what they notice and attend to in interactions with patients. Clarkson, in giving an overview of a range of psychotherapeutic approaches, argues that a number of different modalities of relationship are present in every therapeutic meeting:

> Like the keys on a piano, some of them may be played more frequently or more loudly than others, depending on the nature of the music. But they are always potentially there in every therapeutic encounter whether or not the pianist uses them, whether or not the composer acknowledges their existence in the written score.
>
> (Clarkson 1994: 28)

Attending to 'transference' might be one of these modalities. The music therapist can choose to note its existence, to feel and recognise its effects and to try to understand what it may mean for the patient, or to work in other ways.

What is commonly understood by the mental construction of transference? Gray observes that there are elements of this phenomenon of 'transference' in all relationships in that we bring expectations and assumptions to new encounters, transferring them from past experience of relating (Gray 1994: 21). When a patient comes to therapy there will invariably be a complex range of feelings directed towards the therapist, some positive and some negative. Feelings or attitudes felt towards earlier significant people in the patient's past life (usually parental or other authority figures) will be transferred in an unconscious way into present relationships and onto the therapist. The therapist may become aware of receiving projections of both a positive (for example loving feelings) and negative kind (for example feelings of attack); or at different times aspects of both.

> The therapist in the opening clinical example receives a striking experience of Sergio's powerlessness within the transference in his packing up and guarding over the instruments. He is perhaps too frightened to engage in any contact with her and school reports show that his halting speech makes verbal contact with others fragmented and frustrating. His mother is very protective and perhaps Sergio expects the therapist to take over? Observing and accepting some of this sustains the therapeutic work – the approach helps the therapist to acknowledge his behaviour and wait till he is ready to make new responses.

Therapists also develop strong feelings towards their patients. These are construed as counter-transferences, defined succinctly by Priestley as 'all of the unconscious reactions that a therapist has towards a patient, and especially to the patient's transference' (Priestley 1994: 74). Originally these feelings were thought to be obstacles, unresolved conflicts in the therapist's past being transferred on to the patient (Brown and Pedder 1991 and see Priestley 1994: 81–85 for a discussion of this classic form of counter-transference). More recently it has been felt that honest and reflective exploration of our counter-transference issues can be a resource in gaining insight into a patient's therapeutic process, a sensitive 'tuning-in' of the therapist's unconscious to the worlds of the patient. Sometimes the feelings are body-based with a particular somatic resonance. By working empathically the therapist can identify with what the patient is feeling/has felt or be able to locate feelings with which the patient is struggling or unable to recognise. Priestley calls this the e-counter-transference (after Racker's 'concordant identification' – see Racker 1968, and Priestley 1994: 87–92). She draws on the musical 'image of a plucked string instrument (the patient) whose music resonates on its sympathetic strings (the therapist) . . .' (ibid.: 86).

Alternatively the therapist may start to feel, for example, in the role of the distant mother or father (Priestley labelling Racker's notion of 'complementary identification' the c-counter-transference – see Racker 1968 and Priestley 1994: 85–87). Carpy observes that the therapist's first task is 'to attempt to tolerate these feelings, without acting them out', while acknowledging that this can be incredibly demanding to achieve (Carpy 1989: 288). Gray notes that in using counter-transference the therapist has to be 'scrupulously honest in determining who is feeling what and why and it should not be the basis for making didactic interpretations. Delicacy, self-questioning and insight are vital, greatly aided by experience of supervision and personal therapy' (Gray 1994: 24).

In the clinical example Sergio's therapist has some contrasting reactions in her own counter-transference. She feels protective towards him (the recall of the hamster she wanted) but also personally redundant and useless. She does not know what to play or do and has to sit with this feeling, trying to understand the implications for Sergio. She also feels quite irritated, wanting to tell Sergio to get on with it, recalling perhaps the control of his parent. The aggressiveness of the arrow song combines her feelings with those of Sergio.

It is usual for a psychotherapist to use words to bring the transferences and counter-transferences into the working context of the therapeutic relationship and to use interpretation to illuminate the process. Music therapists have a range of interesting options, one of which might be to use words. But working with music means that these rather abstract constructions can be articulated in the living forms of active and mutual musical creativity. Streeter (1999b) has developed the notion of the 'musical transference relationship' proposing that 'what we offer in free improvisation is free association within music' (ibid.: 88). As music therapists we can also articulate and express in music aspects of our counter-transference, either if appropriate with the patient or in supervision (see Chapter 13) or privately. We can also articulate counter-transference phenomena in other artistic media, moving or drawing aspects of the dynamics. Bruscia's compilation *The Dynamics of Music Psychotherapy* includes a comprehensive review of both transference and counter-transference phenomena in music therapy with illustrated case material (Bruscia 1998).

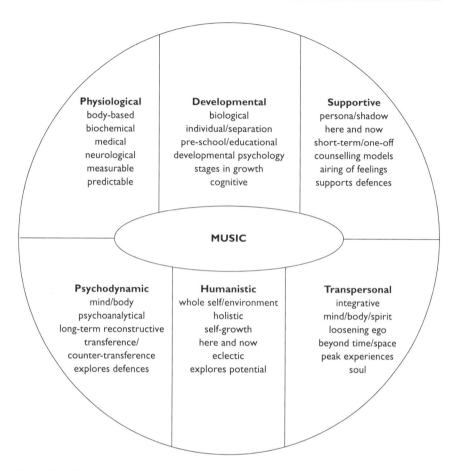

Figure 2.2 The music therapy spectrum.

THE MUSIC THERAPY SPECTRUM

It is clear from the clinical material presented in this book that each therapist brings to the work a particular clinical orientation that can be linked to
personal values and larger philosophical views. At the centre of all the work
is the musical relationship. Hence we place music at the centre of our figure
representing the music therapy spectrum (see Figure 2.2). The spectrum focuses
on six approaches that can underpin music therapy practice. Some of these
selected approaches are directly linked to boundary issues discussed above in
relation to Wilber's 'Spectrum of Consciousness', for example the emphasis
on strengthening the ego boundary at the root of much psychoanalytical practice and conversely the loosening of this in transpersonal therapy. Different

contexts often demand different approaches, for example work with coma or stroke patients in medical settings may emphasise a more physiologically based approach. Obviously this kind of spectrum is not a rigid structure.

A therapist working in a school, for example, might integrate a developmental approach with reflections from a psychoanalytical perspective, not working actively with transference phenomena but using insights from these constructs to inform practice. Pavlicevic has recently described music therapy for the 'whole' child, exploring ' "childhood" and "pathology" from various perspectives without aligning itself with any one at the expense of the another' (Pavlicevic 2001: 14). What we feel is important is to be aware at which level we are working and to position this clearly within our own level of training and experience. The needs of the patients will often dictate the level of work. It may be inappropriate, for example, to work in an active psychodynamic way in short-term open groups on an acute psychiatric ward with very ill and frightened patients. Crisis management with teenagers in mainstream schools may call for short-term intervention at a highly supportive level. Conversely it may be very appropriate to work in a psychoanalytically informed way with an individual contracting for long-term work. We do not want to imply that any one level of work on the spectrum is the more important.

ESSENTIAL 'I's OF MUSIC THERAPY PRACTICE

We now move the discussion to four areas that we consider essential for effective practice. These fields of imagination, intuition, improvisation and intellect are not the sole property of music therapy nor of art itself. In all working situations we feel it is vital to be aware of the enlivening and sustaining nature of these processes.

On imagination

> Imagination is no longer conceived as simplistically opposed to perception and reason; rather, perception and reason are recognized as being always informed by the imagination. With this awareness of the fundamental mediating role of the imagination in human experience has also come an increased appreciation of the power and complexity of the unconscious, as well as new insight into the nature of archetypal pattern and meaning.
>
> (Tarnas 1991: 405)

Imagination occupies a significant space in therapy practice. Though it may be hard to articulate it is one of our most effective tools. William Blake thought that the imagination was the divine principle in man and vitally important to all human existence. In the commentary that accompanies the visionary water-colour painting *The Last Judgement* he states: 'This world of Imagination is the world of Eternity; . . . This World of Imagination is Infinite & Eternal' (Blake's *Notebook for the Year 1810* cited in Keynes 1966: 605). One could argue that a fundamental responsibility of the arts therapist is to provide opportunities for patients to harness their imagination. A depressed patient, for example, can give flight to all manner of imaginative fancy, play with different identities and gain more sense of personal authority and empowerment through active involvement.

Different realities can be created: a very deprived child, for example, can enter a magical realm and feel not only in control but able to influence people and objects. Perhaps nothing else compares to imagination in importance? It is that which inspires and fortifies us: it gets us out and moves us on. Such an idea was movingly encapsulated in the drama therapist Sue Jennings' work with patients undergoing fertility treatment (presented at conferences in the UK in the 1990s). She was passionate about the need for her patients to feel fertile in their minds and hearts, when the apparently fallow ground of their bodies defeated them. Sometimes pregnancy was a reward, but a restored imagination was always achievable. Arts therapies can often make this sort of contribution to a team, evoking all types of imagination including the visual, auditory and tactile. Valuing the imaginative process should be part of our job description.

However, to enable our patients to be in touch with their imagination we have first to be so ourselves. This may not be at all straightforward. It is not a 'given' that we use our imagination, even though there is an implication that those involved with the arts will do so. There is much that stands in the way. It could be that our patients' difficulties affect us dynamically, blocking our ability to think or act clearly. Also just the long days in the caring professions can leave any worker depleted, tired and stuck. We can easily get bored and boring, as in any job. We need to guard against potential 'burnout' (see Chapter 13). However, in arts therapy practice and training, the principle of attending to present feelings within the art form may be one of the best gifts to the imagination. Many professional players who have trained later as music therapists have reported on a reawakening of feeling response, more playful spontaneity, risk and energy in their playing. The reworking of their music in this way has often brought about truer involvement of the personal self. Perhaps we give something back to our parent art forms by such a concentration.

Stephen Sondheim's song about creative process, 'Finishing the Hat' from *Sunday in the Park with George*, emphasises this link between feeling and image. His character George sings of how he maps a sky in his mind. It fills his mental and feeling space and everything else recedes behind his potent vision. All the levels of connection, the word patterns, the weaving of idea, texture and sound are brought together with fine imagination. We each need to find our own sparks and connections. As Winnicott suggests, in his posthumous collection of essays *Home is Where we Start From*, this spirit can be found in unexpected places, as much in doing the cooking as in making art (Winnicott 1986: 51). It is incumbent on all of us to listen carefully to ourselves, to keep in touch with a lively spirit, to refresh our sources of inspiration and to remember our humanity. 'All action is born in the laboratory of the imagination' (Ferrucci 1990: 43).

> . . . imagination activates our psychological and transpersonal resources. First, by inventing possible worlds the mind learns to transcend its own stereotypes. Second, when we use our imagination we are not bound to duties or stopped by obstacles – we are free to play. No longer weighed down by the real world, we can let chance and the unconscious do their part – above all we can laugh. At the same time, inhibitions loosen up and the resources that everyday life perennially restricts can reach full flower. In this way imagination becomes a way to freedom.
>
> (Ferrucci 1990: 46–47)

We need to note however that imagination, like therapy, needs limits and boundaries. Unbridled imagination carries the risk of madness or even death, if not held within a rational frame or perspective. Selection, refinement, form, limits, deadlines – these are thinking processes, which are needed to accompany the imaginative drive. Such a frame of thought gives meaning, focus and safety to the creative process.

On intuition

We are using the words of the historian Theodore Zeldin to make a transition between the worlds of the imagination and intuition. Zeldin observes:

> Imagination has only been truly liberating when it has been constructive . . . It is impossible to feel fully alive unless one takes risks, so those who have refused to take risks . . . have hesitated to live fully.
>
> The direction of thinking has been decided by intuitions, which are sometimes hypotheses and sometimes judgements reached so fast that the reasons for them are not noticed. Women's intuition has been neither magic nor genius but the result of close attention to minute signs and an interest in unspoken emotions: it is as rational, and elusive, as medical diagnosis, using past experience in the face of uncertainty; but it is never easy to learn from experience, because two experiences are seldom exactly alike; an imaginative jump is needed to spot the similarities.
>
> Zeldin (1995: 442)

How can the points that Zeldin makes help us as practising clinicians?

Case study 2

Imagine that a group of severely anxious people have met regularly for six months with their therapist. This week sees the introduction of a student. The therapist has been gently encouraging the group members to take small steps with their feelings and to risk some new encounters. It has been difficult with many obstacles to face: their illnesses, their lack of confidence, diffidence and social isolation. On this day the group has improvised twice with members being somewhat reluctant to articulate any immediate feelings. Perhaps the presence of the student has increased the group's anxiety. The therapist's overall feelings are those of stuckness and lack of direction. The therapist knows what is at stake for each individual and has a reasonable understanding of the needs of the group. But the visiting student provides a new opportunity and challenge for everyone, the therapist included. The therapist feels physically the sense of loss and emptiness within the group – feelings that supervision has revealed regularly and consistently as being part of the dynamic of the group.

The music pauses, the stuck feeling continues and the therapist has an intuitive response that the student could offer something. This is a risk. Some passing gestures and a whispered enquiry bring the idea from the student that she should sing a rather poignant song – an Eastern European folk melody about autumn and the decay of the natural world. The risk pays off because a new connection is made. The group is taken away from the immediate preoccupation of their own painful experiences to a more universal perspective, while still maintaining the link with individual feelings. The group members are very curious about the meaning of the song and talk in an animated way about their reactions. This sense of liveliness has not occurred for many weeks. Out of this intuitive moment has come a shift in the obstacles within the group therapy process. The individual has been linked to the collective. The student is amazed by the potential power of her contribution – a beautifully crafted song presented with an innocent directness, as if telling a story.

In this session an honest risk was involved in inviting the student to sing but the request was also logical in the way it emerged from the natural unfolding of the session. What appeared as spontaneous was embedded in the frame of previous knowledge: of the session; of the group and the therapist's level of expertise, rather in the way that a musician needs the hours of practice before playing can appear natural and spontaneous.

> Intuitive knowledge . . . proceeds from everything we know and everything we are. It converges on the moment from a rich plurality of

directions and sources – hence the feeling of absolute certainty that is traditionally associated with intuitive knowledge.

(Nachmanovitch 1990: 40)

As with the other processes in this section intuition can also link creatively with the rational. 'Intellect has, first, the valuable and necessary function of interpreting, i.e., of translating, verbalizing in acceptable mental terms, the results of intuition' (Assagioli 1965: 223).

On improvisation

Improvisation is at the core of music therapy practice and is the action-product of our musical imagination and intuition, or 'intuition in action' as described by Nachmanovitch (1990: 41). Improvisation forms an interesting link between our discipline and other modes of work in music and the arts. Jazz, Flamenco, Indian and African traditions in music all use improvisation centrally; theatre and dance have long established usage of improvisation in preparation and performance. The *New Grove Dictionary of Music and Musicians* defines improvisation as 'the creation of a musical work, or the final form of a musical work, as it is being performed' discussing its significant existence in 'virtually all musical cultures' of the world (Nettl 2001: 94). An earlier edition of the *Grove Dictionary* in 1954 saw improvisation as 'the art of thinking and performing music simultaneously', an idea that Bailey thought was rather derogatory to the non-improviser playing pre-composed music (cited in Bailey 1992: 66). However, this definition provides a useful link with what music therapists try to do in their work, thinking of musical and clinical requirements while playing 'in the moment'. It also emphasises our theme of connection between the imaginative, spontaneous process and the need for active thought as boundary or shape.

Although the first British texts on music therapy seemed to make some categorical distinctions between playing therapeutic pieces and creative free improvisation, twenty-first-century music therapists would probably have a more fluid idea of their work. Sometimes the music of sessions might start from established repertoire, for example with the song a patient brings to a group, but this can easily become played with and loosened. There might be changes in pace, style and expression, words altered by the patient's current feelings, the group's adaptations, harmony dramatically changed, rhythm adapted to match flagging or rising energy. Likewise, work that begins wordlessly with the exchange of expressive sounds might travel in any direction, perhaps ending with recall of some particular instrumental music or song. There is more the sense of a continuum of improvisation used in clinical practice with free playing at one end working through improvising in various styles, extemporising on themes or pieces back to working loosely with (or even performing) a written piece. Both Darnley-Smith and Simpson describe just such a continuum in their respective work in music therapy with older adults. In this setting the therapist's clinical judgement about the needs of the client dictated the level of pre-composed material, structure and freedom used in the work (Darnley-Smith 2001; Simpson 2000).

Throughout the music therapy profession, there is an emphasis on 'playing' and this being linked to authentic expression of the self. By exploring with colours and textures as the patient, and mixing this with fragments and ideas from musical and personal history, in dialogue with the therapist or other group members, we can be more in contact with ourselves, more alive, more feeling. Interestingly this idea is echoed by a professional classical player, the clarinetist Anthony Pay, who said, in an interview with Bailey, that he thought of improvisation as 'unknown poetry in which I can progress' and contrasted this to playing precisely notated music where he felt he was 'just learning to do better what I already do' (Bailey 1992: 69).

We suspect that cultural influences and late twentieth-century shifts in music practice and education have had their impact here. The Western classical tradition of concert-going (experts play, well-behaved audiences listen) still holds sway but is beginning to be questioned by writers such as Cook (1998) and Small (1998). The edges between traditional and popular forms from diverse cultures begin to be blurred by the improvisatory experiments of celebrated classical and pop artists. Nachmanovitch explores the weight and significance of improvisation in an inspirational way in his book of unusual 'lightness' *Free Play*, quoted at the beginning of this section.[2] Many ideas leap out for consideration, but here are some that emphasise why improvisation is the central force in music therapy. Firstly, the emphasis on the unfolding process rather than the end moment of public performance is a prevailing theme in the book. 'Not only is practice necessary to art, it *is* art' (Nachmanovitch 1990: 68). For the therapist the private work with patients exploring and experimenting with sounds and music has something in common with the musician's world of personal practice. Both are part of 'real music' and by this analogy a necessary process in exploring our real selves.

Secondly, Nachmanovitch argues that improvisation, in its concentration on 'the moment' involves what he calls 'continuous surrender' – giving up control and allowing the surprising to happen. 'Improvisation is acceptance, in a single breath, of both transience and eternity. We know what might happen in the next day or minute, but we cannot know what will happen' (ibid.: 21). Linking with Anthony Pay's 'unknown poetry', this is very much the arena of music therapy, and also the analytic approach described by Casement. 'The therapist's openness to the unknown in the patient leaves more room for the patient to contribute to any subsequent knowing; and what is thus jointly discovered has a freshness which belongs to both (Casement 1985: 26–27).

2 We are grateful to Simon Purcell for introducing us to this thought-provoking book.

A third idea is the 'inside-out' relationship between free play and limits, between spontaneity and security. Nachmanovitch describes all kinds of limits, such as the length of time, the shape and size of our hands, the size of the playing space and suggests that any of these frames or structures can 'ignite spontaneity'. He quotes Stravinsky's reflection that 'The more constraints one imposes, the more one frees one's self of the chains that shackle the spirit' (ibid.: 84), the paradox of structure offering liberation. Therapists might interpret these 'constraints' as strong clear boundaries. Again the notion of bringing an intellectual frame to shape the imaginative, intuitive free musical play comes to the fore.

A final note on intellect

In each of the three sections above – imagination, intuition and improvisation – were included comments that focused on the containing and framing aspects of the intellect. Excessive imagination unregulated by the rational world can lead to chaos and disintegration; we need to translate and make sense of the intuitive moment through the intellect. Improvisations are held in musical pattern and form, the composer Alfred Nieman noting on many occasions during his teaching of music therapy classes that even the freest of improvisations contained within it an inherent logic and formal cohesion.

This rational underpinning or overarching (depending on one's perspective) is a fundamental feature of effective music therapy practice. The 'thinking' of the clinician based on observation, clinical knowledge and experience is what distinguishes music therapy from music-making, education or the pure art. In training and clinical practice, therapists build a body of knowledge about features of illness, human development, theoretical constructs and musical forms and gradually accumulate a framework for shaping differentiated approaches to treatment, based on the needs of different client groups. The therapist needs to interact sensitively with clients, but at the same time to be able to watch the interaction, to note key points and changes and to relate to mental constructs that underpin the work. The intellectual side of the work will also involve reading; relating work to knowledge of the client group; developing aims and strategies; planning for breaks and endings; discussing ideas in clinical teams; exploring appropriate theory and devising research. In this way, the intellect complements and supports the artistic areas characterised in the other three 'I's.

SUMMARY

In this chapter a range of principles in music therapy practice were explored. These ranged from the highly pragmatic – physical aspects of the music space, range of instruments – to the complexities of the different levels and approaches within the work. We return to this subtle synthesis of both the musical and the personal in the relationships within music therapy. Patients with their unique range of musical behaviours and problems come to therapy where they interact with therapists who in turn have to balance their own music and personalities, including their own blind spots, in order to attend a therapeutic process and take part in the journeys with their patients. All this imaginative and intuitive musical free play is contained within the holding forms and conceptual frameworks of music therapy.

The next chapter will introduce four prominent British music therapists, learning something of their musical and personal background and their motivation to train as therapists.

Chapter 3

First meetings with four music therapists

Leslie Bunt and Sarah Hoskyns

INTRODUCTION

The contribution made by practitioners to the development of the music therapy profession has tended to be passed on orally rather than in written documentation. To some extent this has been addressed recently by the series of interviews entitled 'Historical Perspectives' initiated in 1999 by Gary Ansdell and published in the *British Journal of Music Therapy*. This chapter uses interviews with four prominent British music therapists – Jean Eisler, Helen Odell-Miller, Elaine Streeter and Tony Wigram – to explore links between personal history and the motivation to train as a therapist.

Our interviewees, who represent different strands and traditions of practice, have each in their own unique way contributed significantly to the last 30 years of the profession. Jean Eisler is one of a group of therapists who have developed the work of Paul Nordoff and Clive Robbins: their initial emphasis on the importance of the music and the notion of the 'music child' as it extends throughout a person's whole life. Helen Odell-Miller has been passionate about developing specialist work within adult psychiatry, teaching and supervision. Elaine Streeter has made substantial contributions to a reflective understanding of music therapy practice, particularly with links to psychoanalytic perspectives and supervision. Tony Wigram has made a vital contribution to the recognition and professional status of music therapy and has developed procedures for international partnership in practice and research. All our interviewees are experienced trainers and APMT-approved clinical supervisors. They pass on to the next generation of music therapists their expertise, enthusiasm, experience and understanding of clinical practice.

We used the same questions to interview each therapist during summer to autumn 1998. In this chapter we shall focus on their (a) formative musical and personal experiences and (b) motivation to train and training experiences. We shall draw on the interviews throughout the rest of the text, for example when discussing training, supervision and research. In this way the voices of these four colleagues will be woven within our own ideas and reflections. The comments from each colleague are presented in italics with any of our additions being in normal script. Here is a brief description of each therapist's current and past positions:

Jean Eisler is a consultant music therapist at the Nordoff–Robbins Centre in London where students observe her clinical work. Jean is a Governor of the Centre having been connected with the organisation since she joined an early committee in 1972 as minutes secretary. She is currently writing up case studies for teaching purposes and for the archives of the Centre. Jean trained in 1974 with Paul Nordoff and Clive Robbins.

Helen Odell-Miller is Director of Music Therapy Training at Anglia Polytechnic University in Cambridge. She maintains a clinical practice in the field of adult mental health and is an active researcher. Helen has been Chair of the APMT and has for many years liaised on behalf of the profession at governmental levels regarding career and grading structures and state registration. She was involved in the setting-up of the post-training supervision scheme. Helen trained with Juliette Alvin in 1976.

Elaine Streeter is Senior Lecturer in Music Therapy at Anglia Polytechnic University and a tutor at the Guildhall School of Music and Drama. Elaine completed the first Master's degree in music therapy and set up the course based at Southlands College, Roehampton in 1980. She has developed music therapy experiential groups for music therapy students. She was involved with Helen with the setting-up of the post-training supervision scheme and was Chair of the supervision panel for many years. Elaine trained in 1974 with Paul Nordoff and Clive Robbins.

Tony Wigram is Professor of Music Therapy at Aalborg University, Denmark, where he teaches and coordinates the Ph.D. programme. He is Head Music Therapist at Harper House in Hertfordshire, UK, a diagnostic and assessment unit for children with communication disorders. Tony has been Chair of both the BSMT and APMT and President of both the World Federation of Music Therapy and the European Music Therapy Confederation, a group he founded. Tony trained in 1974 with Juliette Alvin.

FORMATIVE MUSICAL AND PERSONAL EXPERIENCES

Jean's story

I had a wealth of music at home throughout my childhood. We all played the piano or string instruments and sang together from a very early age. I was lucky to be at St. Paul's Girls' School when Gustav Holst was Head of Music. When I left school I studied piano and violin in Vienna and then at the Royal College of Music. I had six years of professional string playing including playing second fiddle in the Ebsworth String Quartet. We gave concerts all over the UK and in the National Gallery during the War. I also played in the Jacques String Orchestra, one of the first string orchestras to be founded in this country in the 1930s.

In 1944 I married and in January 1947 left the UK with my Czech husband Paul Eisler and my 6-month old son John. By 1948 I was living in Prague. I had two young children and in 1951 I tried to get into music again and gave my first and only violin recital in Prague. By then my husband was becoming what we nowadays call a dissident and was soon out of work. The political situation was getting quite nasty. I had to earn a meagre living as a translator, which I did for 22 years, mostly humdrum publicity material. But gradually as the political scene slowly eased in the late 1950s and 1960s I translated children's books, books about Czech music and musicians, novels and ultimately two Janáček operas including Osud for the BBC which was performed in concert form in the early 1970s in London. My husband died in 1966 (in a tragic mountain accident). I had been married to a courageous fighter who loved music and believed in people but who was very near to the centre of the political storms that beset Czechoslovakia in the 1950s. In a sense my whole history is made up of my broad musical background and then the intense growth I underwent as a person in those difficult years in Prague. I had a very strong partner who was very loving and 'there' not just for me personally and our family, but for the world and life – a very special person. After he died and once my two boys had completed university and were both in professional jobs in 1972, I returned to the UK.

Helen's story

My earliest musical memories are of having to sing, of literally not being able to stop singing. I don't have early memories of being sung to apart from when I was about 5 or 6 and my father singing to me in quite a jovial way. I remember being very surprised when I was about 9 and went to a new school to discover that lots of people hated singing and tried to get out of singing lessons. I also had a desire to learn the piano and the violin and had a very classical upbringing. My first memories of music I heard at home are of classical music but also of Gilbert and Sullivan operettas and those were my first live musical experiences. I had two older sisters who were learning instruments. I just started to teach myself and make up tunes and even started to write them down when I was quite little. I found some of the formal lessons a bit boring. I suppose the thing I loved most was playing with others.

I came from a very caring and professional family. Most of my ancestors, aunts, uncles and grandparents were either teachers or doctors. My own parents were both doctors. I thought about studying medicine but really I just wanted to pursue literature and music. I suppose rather ironically, although I felt very looked after and very secure in my family, I did go to boarding school but together with my two sisters. How we discussed it was that this was the nearest school that suited us all. When I look back now I think some of my personal desire to express myself through music was to counteract some of the loneliness that I felt when I was at boarding school, especially when I was quite young. I think I only realised that in later years. Other people were very homesick and lonely and a bit directionless at weekends. My weekends were filled up with playing music with other people, singing in choirs, those sorts of thing that happen outside of the ordinary school day. Another feature to do with my personal story is that it never occurred to me not to be looking after others, not to think about making people better or helping them. That was around in my family. After school I went off to study music. *I didn't want to do anything else but to live and breathe music.*

Elaine's story

Elaine expressed strongly that *you cannot disconnect music from people.* In the early part of her interview she explored the relationships with her early music teachers and particularly noted the inspiration of a very warm and influential teacher named Helen Hellier. *I used to go to her house for my piano lessons and it was almost like a second home. She had two pianos in her living room, there was always the possibility of improvisation and she was very kind... I got into a different way of learning and practising and making up my own pieces. The business of being creative and making things – that was my interest rather than performing.*

There was also a connection with Helen's piano teacher. When I went to Guildhall and studied with Buxton Orr he used to go and stay in a cottage in Dorset that was owned by Helen's piano teacher. That was quite a coincidence. She used to belong to the Kensington Music Society and Buxton used to be the chair of that

Society. So I ended up staying in this cottage at one point several years later, probably in my early thirties, and I realised that this was the cottage of my piano teacher's teacher. I can't disconnect the relationships with teachers, the people and the music together.

On deciding to go to music college I started to compose. By the end of the first year I'd left home and was living in a somewhat sophisticated world with very creative people. There were many changes. At the Guildhall you were expected to practise, practise, practise. I wanted to study composition as a first study but I was the only girl who was doing composition so it was a rather difficult thing to try and do. The two teachers there who really influenced me were Edmund Rubbra who was my composition teacher and Buxton Orr. Buxton was a doctor. He and his wife Jean were tremendously sociable. They took me under their wing and held these wonderful parties. Buxton was quite fierce as a teacher. What I can remember was his enormous enthusiasm. He had given up a career in medicine as a physiologist to become a composer. There was a lot on the line for him and I think he brought that into his teaching. He had a deep commitment. His father was in the Glasgow Philharmonic, he had come from a musical background. He'd gone into medicine and escaped into music. He had enormous commitment to music for his own personal reasons and he brought that across. He cared tremendously that we understood. He had a great intensity about music.

I was lucky because I was also with the composer Edmund Rubbra who was an extraordinary man, a very gentle, very quiet man. He was very interested in whatever you brought to him. He – like Buxton – was genuinely interested in notes and how they could live in relation to one another, as all composers are.

Tony's story

I started playing the piano when I was very young, about 4 years old and started to develop playing by ear. I enjoyed playing by ear more than learning to read music. At school Tony enjoyed popularity from being able to play by ear – *television theme tunes and things that other children enjoyed listening to.* Later he was torn between going to a university or conservatoire. *There were a lot of people there (at Bristol university) whom I admired tremendously who were very good musicians. All the musical life of the university was very stimulating. That inspired me tremendously because it was such a rich musical learning experience.* Tony never regretted not going to a conservatoire. His wife went after her degree and commented that *the atmosphere was entirely different from university. It was much more competitive with much less social life and collective music making.*

MOTIVATION TO TRAIN AND TRAINING EXPERIENCES

Jean's story continues

Within four weeks of arriving in the UK I *chanced on Nordoff and Robbins'* 'Therapy in Music for Handicapped Children' *and had met Sybil Beresford-Peirse* (later founder and Director of the N-R Centre). *She'd played me some of their tapes and I'd become totally hooked on the idea of music therapy. Sybil asked me to join a committee she was setting up (someone to take the minutes). The committee was raising money to bring Nordoff and Robbins over from the USA to give their first long-term course in Great Britain, due to start in 1974. In September I joined Sybil for a year as her assistant pianist at the Goldie Leigh Hospital, a residential hospital for handicapped children. I also worked at Harborough School for autistic children. Meanwhile I was earning a little money through piano teaching. In 1974 I was accepted on to the first Nordoff and Robbins course at Goldie Leigh* (as were Elaine and Sybil). *Prior to this, from 1972 to 1973, I was also allowed, as an exception, to join the Guildhall music therapy students in their weekly improvisation group with Alfred Nieman. Otherwise I had had almost no creative improvisation experience in my life and it was an exciting and important preliminary to the course. It was exciting in moving my musical experience away from the printed page. It taught me to begin to listen in a new way and to find the music from within myself. I found it very stimulating. One could now use one's musical ability, skills and awareness for somebody else. There was no performing of this or that. One was 'being' a musician. I loved it.*

There is almost a sense of an epiphany in Jean's awareness of what music therapy meant for her. It was also such a good fit with her personal experiences. *It was the chance to bring together all of my rich musical background along with the quite daunting political experiences of the previous 25 years in Czechoslovakia, a chance to assimilate and use them to understand and help others. Those years taught me many things about myself, about friendships and responsibilities and the cruelties that many people have to face. I knew what it was like to feel alone with a family. In a way we were outcasts and isolated. In the early years this included even speech because I didn't yet speak Czech. I feel so much for a child who cannot speak. I know exactly what it feels like when you sit there dumbly and cannot explain your thoughts and feelings.*

When I first read the N-R book I had never heard of music therapy and in those days in Czechoslovakia handicapped children were kept out of sight. Also we were too absorbed by our own and our friends' troubles.

Jean was very excited with the prospect of training. *I was 57 in 1972. Other professional music jobs were out of the question. I could perhaps have done a little bit of teaching but music therapy was much more exciting. There was no age barrier. It was going to draw on my very strong total life's experiences in a way that perhaps nothing else could have done. It was just made to measure. Instead of coming out of that music shop with easy piano pieces for children I came out with the Nordoff–Robbins music therapy book. It was waiting there for me.*

Paul Nordoff's influence was enormous from a musical point of view *and as part of the training there was also Clive Robbins and his tremendous enthusiasm for the work. He was the person who enlarged on and explained what lay behind the way they were working. Paul brought us his approach to improvisation in his step-by-step way of teaching. Little by little it all gathered momentum and you began to feel you could do it too. Paul's emphasis was on learning to feel and hear sound, learning to listen. Then there was watching and seeing them both work with a child and hearing their case studies. And watching the other students changing and growing in the same way as oneself. It was so new to us all. What was so compelling was the need to learn to rely on one's own inner music and musicality.*

For me there was also the refreshing influence of the musical life of London. *I could go to concerts and hear the latest modern music. For years in Prague even Debussy was declared 'decadent' and you just didn't hear of composers such as Stockhausen and Ligeti. So there was a whole generation of new music and composers that I hadn't heard. Today I find it hard to realise how cut off we were.*

There were also other influences from a general therapeutic point of view. *We had child psychology lectures which were quite daunting for me. There had been no up-to-date literature of that sort available in Prague. Psychotherapy and psychoanalysis had for many years been pretty well taboo. You couldn't have found Freud or Jung in English. So literally I had mountains to read. I now discovered Jung and Winnicott. There I was being enabled and needing to develop and become more aware of a further part of myself if I was to do this work. This was a completely new epoch in my life.*

Helen's story continues

While I was at university I discovered music therapy. *My holidays had been spent being a nursing auxiliary in a hospital in London where my parents worked as doctors. I felt that it was incredible to find something where I could use my musical way of being together with this compulsion to help others. The other side of my personal story was that my father had a major stroke during the time I was at university and that probably not so consciously fed into this desire to help people. He was wheel-chair bound for the rest of his life. Again there was this emphasis on both caring and also on sickness, a sort of disintegration if you like, around me. After university I still wondered if I could go back to the idea of being a doctor. Later on in therapy I looked at it in terms of trying to parallel my parents. If I had been a doctor I'm sure I would have ended up in psychiatry but I just wasn't committed to that type of long academic and scientific study. In a similar way I considered but then ruled out teaching. I remember going to a very deprived comprehensive school in Luton and shadowing a friend of mine there who was already a teacher. I could see it had quite therapeutic benefits in that particular environment but couldn't myself make the music an end in itself. I had a serious look at speech therapy and my parents helped me get some experience sitting in on clinics. But it was just talking, no music. I finally came back to music therapy.*

I was quite young when I decided to be a music therapist. I had been to visit Tony Wigram whom I knew before he was a music therapist because we played in the same orchestras. So I had found out about music therapy and been inspired by talking to him and other people about it. If I was to have entered the profession in Britain now I would be told to probably wait a few years. I would have been seen as rather naïvely wanting to be a music therapist without particularly insightful reasons for doing so. I think at the time I was very enthusiastic, perhaps rather over enthusiastic about it. I spent a lot of my young life being driven around by my father who was off to see a patient the night before they were about to have an operation. I'd go along and sit in the nurse's office or in the car. People chatted to me a lot and took notice. I asked a lot of questions and looked at all their medical books. It just seemed to fit into this idea that I could combine these things. That was a good discovery.

I trained as a music therapist at the Guildhall. As part of my training at the Guildhall I had singing lessons and I had a very inspiring teacher. I listened to a lot of music at that time, went to opera and concerts and played music with other music therapists and other student music therapists. I can remember that listening to new music made a big impression, for example being introduced to Britten's 'Turn of the Screw.'

Once again Alfred Nieman appears as an inspiring teacher. *I hadn't met people like that who were such free spirits. This man was a bit of a rebel in a way, probably musically and maybe in other ways. Here he was, a very wise older man teaching us improvisation. The first thing he said was: 'Here's a piano, you need to forget everything you've learnt and just go and play it.' We spent about six weeks doing this, each person going up in turn and working. It all gathered momentum and I learnt a tremendous amount about form and structure, freedom and creative possibilities in music. I used to look forward to those sessions and to feel that I went into a different musical space. It was my first introduction to much freer improvisation.*

Juliette Alvin inspired me by her drive. She was very to the point and very focused about music. My first response to that was that it was a bit constraining in that she was very definite about her ways of working. If you didn't fit into that model – I think I probably did most of the time – but if you didn't then she was very critical. So she would say things like 'That was just dreadful music' or throw you in the deep end in some clinical situation and then pull whatever you had done to pieces. I'm sure that helped me in some way but at the time I found it quite painful and difficult. Maggie Pickett inspired me as a music therapist in the way that she worked with people with autism. And in her use of piano and song.

I think the major influence was going to a service for people with learning disabilities in Cambridge, to a place that I knew was going to have a post vacant. Tony Wigram was my supervisor and I think he really was a major inspiration. This is interesting as for a while we then worked in different ways. I developed an early interest in working in a psychoanalytically-informed way which he came to perhaps later. Musically he was very inspiring. I think that was where I began to believe in my own improvisation skills at the keyboard. He had such natural skills and I found that I was inspired by the possibilities of what one could do. I'd find that during a session I had composed a song or made a piece of music that had come directly from the work with the clients.

Elaine had a spell teaching various age groups of children after graduating from the Guildhall and before she trained as a music therapist. She enjoyed helping the children to improvise and write pieces. Like Jean she also came across *Therapy in Music for Handicapped Children* by Nordoff and Robbins. She continues:

I remember feeling – this is it, this is what I want to do. I wrote to the publisher because I didn't know anything about music therapy. It turned out that they were just recruiting for the course in Goldie Leigh in '74 so they sent my letter through to Paul and Clive. That was their first course in England. It was all very coincidental. The strange thing was that the audition was held back at the Guildhall and there was Alfred Nieman who had taught me musical history.

It was an extraordinary time both people-wise and music-wise. I recently bumped into Unni Johns who was on the course at a conference in Belgium, the first time I've seen her since the course. We were reminiscing and talking about it. It was an astonishing time but the early '70s were astonishing anyway. Everybody was caught up in an enthusiastic and experimental life-style. It was very dramatic. We had one room in the hospital, like a little storeroom and we were there day in day out being taught by the great masters. There were love affairs that never happened and those that did. It was a passionate time.

I learnt a lot about how to use music and how to teach myself to improvise and ways to practise and to think about music. That was all very good and inspiring. But I rather felt that there was the feeling that if you weren't having the same experience as Paul was having then you were missing it − this marvellous world of the so and so mode. Everybody was going, 'Yes, wow! Isn't it marvellous and wonderful' but if you had a different response, then it wasn't so easy. Looking back, it's difficult to know how much our particular group brought to this guru worship, perhaps Paul would have welcomed more discussion.

There was nothing about your personal experience. There was very little about how you actually felt − in the room with the child and how that affected what you played. It was all about what you played and how the child responded. We edited tapes and heard case studies like Edward and Audrey, marvellous examples, the high points basically. But we were slogging away with these children with very difficult problems and of course they weren't having these kind of high points and there weren't these developments and it wasn't really like that.

I remember Paul's talks on intervals and on music. These have remained with me as an inspiration. He could be quite a scary person but he was a very big influence at that stage. There was no other teacher. He really was a pioneer, in the true sense of the word. I continually draw on his teaching and go back to it, back to the essence of it, with my own students. To listen to the child within and to find a music which can provide a context in which the child can recognise both his or her own responses and those of the therapist. I was extremely lucky to have been taught by Paul and Clive. Their demanding style of teaching was I think driven by Paul's awareness of how little time left he had to train others to take the work further. At the time it felt very intense but it was a time I am deeply grateful to have been part of.

We pick up **Tony's story** while he was still at university. Hearing Juliette Alvin speak was a similar experience to Jean's and Elaine's reading of an inspirational book.

My music professor at Bristol happened to hear of a visit by Juliette Alvin to Bath to give a lecture on music therapy. He called me in to his office and said that this was probably exactly the thing you should do with your particular skills. By this time I was doing a lot of work with the piano playing by ear, jazz and improvisation and doing shows with students. So I went to hear Juliette Alvin and it was the most inspiring thing that I had heard, her talk really attracted different parts of me. It was firstly a fascinating subject, a mixture of music and medicine. Secondly she talked very emotionally about music and I have always been aware of the emotional effects of music. Lots of pieces that I knew, mostly classical, gave me goose bumps and a very big emotional reaction. The idea of being able to use music in therapy work was very interesting. I had very little experience of doing anything at all with people who were ill or sick or disabled so I had to rush off and get some sort of holiday work finding out whether I liked working with people who were disabled or ill. I worked with handicapped children for some time during the holidays.

I went straight from my degree into the post-graduate course at the Guildhall. I didn't take a year off so here was a very naïve and young guy who thought that this was going to be interesting ending up on a course with fourteen girls and me. I went straight into music therapy and have been doing it ever since July 1975. I think I went into training because music therapy was a pioneer profession at this time and the training course had only been going for a few years. The training fitted into my musical background. I could see that I was going to be allowed to do all sorts of crazy musical things in music therapy that I would not have been able to do in music teaching for example.

One of the most significant musical influences was Alfie Nieman (he appears in all four stories) who was teaching improvisation at the Guildhall at this time. He really made you develop an ability to improvise from inside, rather than from some sort of cognitive musical process or learning some sort of technique. He tapped into your potential for expressing yourself in an improvisation and creating amazing sounds that you didn't think you could create. He was always containing it in some way.

The other two people were Juliette Alvin and Maggie Pickett. I actually had placements with both of them and was witness to their different ways of using music with clients. They both had a great intuitive ability to use music communicatively without any inhibitions and that's what impressed me coming from a music degree where you were developing your performance skills but that was more controlled. They were both quite free about how they used music, especially Maggie. I became very impressed with their freedom and their musicality.

Maggie and Juliette were also influential from a theoretical point of view because they were the main people on the course. Juliette was influential because of her interesting mix of analytic viewpoint and orthopedagogical, remedial type of work which she would have used in some educational situations. She taught very author-itatively about the power of music and the influence and effect and development of music as being the foundation of music therapy. Maggie had a tremendously dynamic therapeutic character and you learnt a lot from her by just watching how she interacted with patients. Sometimes you weren't all that comfortable with her style. She had such an uninhibited way of greeting people, right down to walking into the hospital where we were working together and singing 'Good Morning' to the porter on the way in. But she had a very gentle, caring and therapeutic way with the clients. She just wanted them to have as much opportunity as possible to talk about their difficulties and problems and then to find a way of making music that would support their needs. She did it very intuitively. She would perhaps say 'Let's just play something, or let's sing something.' She was very good with patients who became emotional – she was quite an emotional lady herself – so she could give an empathic response to people who became upset, disturbed or distressed during therapy work which is what I learnt as basic tools of your job. From the theoretical point of view what I read about Rogers and his particular approach in therapy probably was the most influential because of his advocacy of equal terms in the relationship and positive regard for your clients.

When we started training at the Guildhall, whilst they would give us models of other people's theoretical approaches, we were in some way responsible for devel-oping our own therapeutic approach. You didn't get stuff rammed down your throat but there are strengths and weaknesses in that and recently we have become more aware of the weaknesses of eclecticism and the need for good strong foundations for therapeutic work. It was useful having applied theory and practice during the training. This is essential for music therapists as they train. It is noticeable with my students now that they are always very interested when they have presenters who show them a theory of work plus clinical examples.

CONCLUDING NOTE

Tony Wigram's reference to presentations that underpin practice with crit-ical reflection provides a convenient bridge to our next section that focuses on a variety of clinical examples, framed within a range of theoretical points of reference. Our four colleagues have all contributed to specific clinical areas: Jean particularly with children, Helen in the area of adult psychiatry (see Chapter 9), Elaine with children and more recently with group therapy for music therapy students and Tony with adults and children with learning diffi-culties and communication problems (for example see Eisler 1990, 1992, 1993,

2001; Odell-Miller 1991, 1995, 1997, 1999; Streeter 1978, 1979, 1999b, 2001; Wigram 1995, Wigram and Dileo 1995, Wigram and De Backer 1999a, 1999b). As mentioned in the introduction to this chapter their voices will also be featured in other sections of the book.

Part II

Clinical chapters

INTRODUCTION

The clinical examples within this section are intended to cover the lifespan, ranging from work with a pre-school child (Chapter 4) to older people with dementia (Chapter 9). Two central areas within the profession, namely music therapy with adults with learning disability and dementia, are reviewed in Chapters 6 and 9, respectively. Children with communication problems and autism are similarly well-established areas of practice: two chapters are included here, one involving work with a child and her mother (Chapter 4) and the other a case study of a school-aged autistic child (Chapter 5). Two further clinical areas that are recently gaining importance are also included: neurology (Chapter 6) and forensic psychiatry (Chapter 8).

The writers of these chapters are all recognised as leading contributors to the particular field in the UK, having previously presented clinical work within their speciality both in verbal and written forms. What they also introduce to this section is the importance of critical reflection. All the work presented in this section is underpinned by reference to supporting theoretical literature and to the author's own particular therapeutic orientation. There is a variety of presentation styles with several chapters also including musical examples as supportive evidence and illustration. Consequently the music therapy work is rooted both within musical frames of reference and related areas of clinical research.

Chapter 4

Suzanna's story: Music therapy with a pre-school child

Leslie Bunt

INTRODUCTION

> It is a paradox, perhaps best captured in music (or tones of voice), that it is sounds and silence that link us to our earliest states of being. Our parents would have spoken words to us as babies, but they were not words to us.
>
> (Phillips 1998: 49)

Young children make spontaneous connections with music as if it has always played a natural part in their development. Here is the very stuff of communication, music reflecting fundamental aspects of what it is to be human. It is noteworthy that researchers are becoming increasingly aware of babies being born with 'an inborn rhythmic coherence of body movements and modulation of effective expressions' (Trevarthen and Malloch 2000: 4). Babies also appear able to make instantaneous connections with the patterned and pulse-based nature of their caregivers' vocal sounds, movements and facial expressions. An interactive 'dance' is quickly established with both partners negotiating highly communicative and emotionally expressive narratives that share such jointly created musical parameters as pulse, tempo, rhythm, accent, stress, loudness, silence, pitch and melody. This is a subtle two-way process with both 'players' mutually influencing the other in order to sustain interaction and modulate emotional expression (see Malloch 1999; Papoušek 1996; Trehub *et al.* 1997; Trevarthen 1999). Musical patterning is at the hub of our emotional development and cognition.

Observation of these early interactive processes can provide a frame for understanding aspects of improvising in music therapy with children. Pavlicevic draws from these early processes in her synthesis of the personal and the musical in the concept of 'dynamic form.' She relates this to Stern's notion of 'vitality affects', namely 'the qualities of shape or contour, intensity, motion, rhythm – "amodal" properties that exist in our minds as dynamic and abstract, not bound to any particular feeling or event, and enabling us to "make sense" of the world' (Bunt and Pavlicevic 2001: 194).

Thus we can make connections, for example, between the speed and contour of a child's hand movement and an adult's response in another modality, for example a vocal sound. Stern uses musical terminology to describe these communicative potentials and, in turn, music therapists can use these links between the personal and musical as a frame when improvising (see Pavlicevic 1990, 1997; Robarts 1996; Stern 1985).

This chapter describes the practical ways in which music therapy assisted a pre-school child on the autistic spectrum who presented with difficulties in communication and the expression of emotions between herself and her caregivers. If we regard musical elements as at the root of our expressive, emotional and communicative life then:

> ... we see that disorders in any of these realms will have musical correspondences. Disturbances in communication may be seen – and experienced directly – through disturbances in the timing, sequencing, amplitude, energy and fluidity of acts and gestures, as well as in disruptions of inter-coordinating acts with another person.
>
> (Pavlicevic 1997: 114)

We shall discover how these disturbances can be observed within the music and how they begin to shift and change over time. Some key features of the child's story will be presented rather than a complete case study. Some psychobiological and developmental underpinnings have already been outlined. Other reflections and concepts that will emerge from this story include:

- changes in the music being mirrored in the child's life outside of the sessions, particularly in the relationships within the child's immediate family;
- the psychoanalytic features of holding and containing within the consistent boundaries of time and space (see Chapters 2 and 11);
- the clinical techniques of reflecting, matching and challenging (see Chapters 11 and 12);
- the creative space, me/not-me, transitional objects and 'good-enough' support (Winnicott 1974 and see Levinge 1999);
- the autistic child's use of hard objects as described by Tustin (1992);
- the teachings from the writings of autistic adults, for example Donna Williams (1996);
- further links to aspects of the child's cognitive, social and emotional development.

An additional reason for selecting the following story is the involvement of other people within the music therapy space (see Chapter 2 for a discussion of the influence of different 'players'). We can read here how the presence of the child's mother became a major feature in the unfolding of the story.

The therapist decided to approach the complex nature of the child's communication difficulties by facilitating as many musical connections as possible between mother and child.

SUZANNA'S STORY

Suzanna was referred to music therapy by her consultant paediatrician when she was 3 years 2 months old. Here are some of the main themes of a period of 22 months of therapy, 64 weekly sessions that ended just after her fifth birthday and move to full-time schooling. She was seen at a community-based dedicated music therapy centre. Her mother was a consistent presence in the sessions and her comments are included here.

Brief background

Suzanna lived with her parents and two older sisters. At the time of her referral there were concerns about her language development and play. Suzanna would point to something she needed and vocalise rather than look. She would take her mother's hand and move her towards an object. There was some situational understanding of words and she had used the odd single word. There was very little sustained play but interest in peek-a-boo-type games was beginning. She interacted well socially with her parents but there was a lack of interest in other children. She had no sense of danger. Her consultant noted a problem in object and context learning, alongside a lack of verbal attention. He considered that Suzanna's problems fell within the diagnostic categories of an autistic spectrum disorder (see Chapter 5 for background on autism).

Music therapy assessment

From the very first session Suzanna demonstrated a lively curiosity in music, developing over the assessment period into a clear preference for a musical rather than a verbal environment. She was most responsive when there was little pressure placed on her or any expectation for her to play. At first she played the instruments in short bursts needing to withdraw from time to time to be close to her mother, to hide behind her or under a chair. Her length of attention to the various sounds increased as the assessment period evolved. She seemed to appreciate both the different qualities and textures of the sounds, sustaining bursts of playing on a variety of tuned and untuned percussion instruments with support from the piano. One or two sounds began to be shared interactively. She would make various high-pitched and seemingly excited vocal sounds as she became more engaged. During the very first session her mother observed what she later described as

Suzanna's angry expression when she found it difficult to hit a suspended cymbal due to a lack of physical control. Her mother described this as a 'bonus' with the angry action being contained in an acceptable activity. This was the first time that she had seen Suzanna express an emotion in such a clear way.

How Suzanna used the different musical activities and parameters

Suzanna quickly indicated her preferred musical activities: drum and cymbal-playing, playing the large tambour and brief excursions around the room to explore the other instruments. At first she would only use one or two instruments. Over the weeks she tolerated the introduction of different ones. Gradually her playing became increasingly refined and sensitive to changes. During the central period of the work she became adept at stopping and starting and would initiate different ways of playing the instruments. She imitated and initiated a range of tempi, levels of loudness and qualities of sounds, exploring quite subtle changes and contrasts. She imitated single and repeated notes and short rhythmic patterns. She clearly demonstrated a sensitivity and flexibility within a musical environment. Towards the end of the sessions there was more sense of a two-way reciprocal interaction in the music.

A description of her music from a typical session (observations taken from video)

This is a description of Session 30 at approximately the halfway stage in her sessions. The session lasts for 30 minutes with approximately the first half being described here.

Preparation – one minute

Suzanna enters the room and immediately pushes a chair towards the drum and cymbal. The instruments are placed in their usual position at the treble end of the piano. She makes a series of high-pitched sounds as she organises the instruments. Her mother encourages her to sit on the chair and I sit at the piano. I gently tap the drum picking up the same tempo of her vocal sounds. I then vocalise in response to some of her high-pitched sounds. She places a large tambour behind the chair, lining up the instruments and chair, as is her custom. She takes a stick with her left hand and points to me for the other stick, which she takes in her right. She points to me to start playing the piano and to her mother to complete the setting-up of the instruments.

*Opening music – meeting and first sustained episode of engagement –
two minutes*

She gives her mother a stick. I play a short, inviting upward phrase in the tempo
of her vocalising (a steady 120 beats per minute). Suzanna taps back in a similar
tempo and with a similar phrase length. Holding the stick with her left hand she
increases the tempo on the drum. I match this. We return to the steady tempo.
This use of a steady pulse to contain and hold her is common to our music, Suzanna
making rhythmic excursions to and from this secure base. She looks towards her
mother who is mouthing sounds to her in the tempo of the drum playing. Suzanna
drops the stick and both her hands continue to flap in what I read as her preferred
steady tempo. We play in this tempo and then explore faster music as she looks
towards her mother and vocalises with her. This feels like the first sustained moment
of contact as she looks towards both her mother and me, moves with flexibility
through different tempi and begins to combine vocalising with her drumming. This
first sustained episode occurs at the peak of her level of excitement during these
opening moments.

Suzanna's song – an episode of mixed levels of engagement – five minutes

I begin her greeting song at the slower tempo of 96 beats per minute. The song
provides a commentary for her drumming and introduces alternations of loud/soft
and fast/slow. She immediately adapts her tempo to suit the phrasing of the song
and her assured manner of playing indicates she knows this music. She anticipates
the changes of speed and loudness. She continues to vocalise with her mother. We
extend the material by improvising together. The music quietens and slows which
she picks up immediately with slower movements and softer playing.

   She suddenly interrupts this calmer engaged period with a single loud hit on the
drum. I reply and stop playing. She laughs at this interruption. This feels like a moment
of real communication, a sharing in the meaning of the gesture she initiated. She
continues to play again and begins to move her feet in the tempo. The song develops with short phrases that increase and decrease both in loudness and tempo. She
hits the side of the drum – we have become accustomed to Suzanna exploring the
instruments in novel ways. She moves her mother's hand in the tempo of the music.
The music slows down. In the quieter passages we see if she wants to change her
vocal sounds to a quieter 'mm' sound but she continues with excited 'da' sounds.
This whole episode is one of a reciprocal exchange and alternation of tempi and
levels of loudness. The material still derives from the song. Sometimes she drums
by herself; at other times she places her hand on top of her mother's hand to control the speed of her mother's drumming.

Cymbal playing – engaged episode – three minutes

I gently touch the cymbal that stops the flow of drumming and causes much laughter. Suzanna hits the cymbal followed by my immediate reply. This episode then becomes characterised by fast alternating individual cymbal crashes and streams of short patterns. The sound of the cymbal not only creates much laughter and high-pitched vocal sounds but also leg and whole body movements. There is also sustained looking at both adults. At times we play the cymbal together in her preferred tempo. Her mother is now sitting back from the instruments. Suzanna plays and laughs and as her excitement increases she looks and vocalises towards her mother. The pattern becomes established: play – look – laugh – my reply. She is very still at the end of each long cymbal sound, as if she is waiting until the vibrations end.

Cymbal – piano exchange – rather scattered episode – three minutes

I pass Suzanna the other stick and she continues playing the cymbal with alternating hands. I return to the piano. The playing is very loud and sustained. She vocalises with streams of 'das'. She includes the drum in her playing. We are now 12 minutes into the session. She gives her mother a stick and begins to include her again in the playing. She then passes this stick to me. I move back to the cymbal. She brings back her idea of the single crash followed by a long pause (usually at least five seconds). I join her in this exchange. There is much laughter again after my reply.

Drum and cymbal-playing supported by piano and with or without vocal sounds provide the musical frame for most of the rest of this session.

Main themes in the therapy

After the establishment of a sense of trust Suzanna's music began to change and develop. Her confidence grew. Her mother began to observe connections between shifts in the way she communicated in the music and her general development outside of the sessions. The following observations within each theme are placed alongside those made by her mother.

Development of trust and confidence

During the first period of sessions after the assessment Suzanna built up sufficient trust in the setting, the music and me in so far as she would enter the room and begin to play immediately. There was soon less need to withdraw and hide. It was important that we respected her need for sameness and familiarity. The instruments were set out each week in the same position. If by any chance they were not she would quickly move them to where they were usually positioned. The session was at the same time and day of the week. The session had a familiarity in the way preferred music and activities were developed. Any new idea was framed within the more familiar structures.

After a period of increased confidence Suzanna would sometimes need to withdraw. These moments felt very ambivalent. It was as if somehow she was aware of how much contact she was making and needed time to assimilate this new pattern. After such a period of consolidation she would then return to her more exuberant self that had become typical of her behaviour.

Her mother often commented on Suzanna's developing trust and confidence. She adds:

> Because of Suzanna's affinity with music she used it as a non-verbal means of contact with us. As her trust in Leslie and the setting grew so did her ability to use this 'way' to accept small changes and eventually to apply it outside this setting. She had not had many 'successes' in her previous encounters with people until she used music as a form of communication. She was then onto a 'winner'.

Indirect communication through the instruments

During the early work Suzanna seemed to have only brief awareness of my music or presence. When playing she would invariably take the lead and I would adapt my playing to support and follow her musical ideas. Any sense of joint communication would develop indirectly through the instruments. She preferred to look at the instruments rather than directly at the two adults in the room. This non-confrontational, indirect communication also helped in assessing Suzanna's limits to sensory and emotional stimulation. How much sound could she tolerate? What kind of sounds, how many and for how long? What were her preferred pitches and timbres? How much musical support was acceptable and what kind? Suzanna would show us what she wanted very clearly and the music was adapted accordingly. Her mother comments:

> Suzanna was terrified by loud, high-pitched noises (e.g. strimmers, vacuum cleaners and certain appliances). In her use of the instruments she discovered she could control the sounds and therefore they were less frightening. This helped ease her fears of the world.

Development of more direct communication and eye contact

We would often play side by side to build up a sense of indirect communication. She began to feel comfortable playing on the same bass xylophone or sitting on her mother's lap while we both played the piano. Gradually, as indirect communication was established through the instruments, Suzanna would begin to give me tentative moments of eye contact. This happened mostly as long as I was at a distance and in my usual place at the piano. She began to tolerate me moving to different instruments as the communications became more two-way and shared. The element of space seemed very important for Suzanna and I was acutely aware of how a sudden change in position or movement could affect her and even create a temporary withdrawal and break in the contact.

As her confidence developed there were little signs that she was beginning to allow me into her musical and internal world. Sometimes it would feel as if she was testing me when she made sudden changes in her music. At other times she would take on some of my musical material directly. By the time of the session described above Suzanna was tolerating a session of 30 minutes, engaging in sustained episodes of direct musical communication without any need to withdraw and avoid contact. Her mother commented that it was important that music therapy provided the opportunity for Suzanna to be in control of the amount of contact. She adds:

> Suzanna used the instruments as a buffer in her contact with Leslie and myself. As her confidence in the situation increased so did her attempts at extended eye contact and direct verbal communication.

Development of vocalisations

During the early work there were some context-based vocal sounds. Her mother reported that there were more vocal sounds at home. One interesting occurrence was the way Suzanna began to open her mouth as if to produce a sound and then not produce one. The use of Nordoff–Robbins reed horns stimulated her to use her voice more confidently. When she was most relaxed there would be a wide range of vowel and consonant-based sounds. She would make these sounds accompanied by a physical gesture, often a hand gesture. These sounds clearly demonstrated her intention to communicate. She would sing to me directly. She would also vocalise in 'chorus' with the adults. We then observed a wide intonation and variety to her sounds: vowel and consonant sounds, for example, 'ah', 'ma', 'da', 'ah-da' and 'mm'. The sounds increased in variety, length, frequency and range throughout the work. Observing the development of her vocal sounds her mother comments:

Suzanna's first verbal sound was 'da'. She used it when she knew you wanted a reply from her but her main use was Makaton and taking me to the item she wanted. As her sessions progressed her range of two-letter sounds increased. Also she realised that any sound was acceptable. There were no wrongs or rights.

Development of turn-taking and reciprocal sharing

During the early sessions Suzanna led most of the joint activity. There were the odd moments of more interactive play. There was also some isolated activity when I felt she did not want to share her music-making or be closely involved in my music. To help in the development of a more reciprocal way of interacting we developed a turn-taking activity. Firstly Suzanna and I would sit on the floor around the large tambour. Suzanna would play and then be invited to pass the stick for me to play my pattern. After a few weeks her mother also took part. Suzanna began to tolerate sharing the activity with two other people and passing the stick to her mother as well.

Music-making also provides opportunities for both synchronous and inter-active play and Suzanna would lead both kinds with growing assurance. Her mother took part in many of these turn-taking interactions and comments:

> For her to allow me to 'play' with her was one of the highlights for me. As she became more comfortable with the order of things to see her enjoyment in sharing and turn-taking was a real turning point for all of us.

Development of planning

From the outset of the sessions Suzanna seemed to have a clear understanding of the situation. She quickly began to make connections and would be clear on what she wanted to play. She connected the appropriate stick for each instrument. The overall shape of the session with a clear beginning, middle and end seemed to help her relax. She was able to plan the order of activities within the overall structure, making each session very much her own.

The patterned-based nature of music seemed to appeal particularly to Suzanna. During the early work she would be quite fascinated by the different ways both sounds and the instruments themselves could be put together and linked in various sequences. She would happily explore up to four different instruments being played in sequence.

Her memory for detail became more apparent as the sessions evolved. She would recall musical aspects of a previous session, reintroducing instruments

or re-exploring a specific musical parameter. She began to tolerate changes
of order. Her mother observed that:

> Suzanna's sense of order of things is very highly developed. She can only func-
> tion when she knows the order of things and when that is in place then she
> can feel free to experiment within those parameters. If she has control in the
> situation as well then she is truly a happy person. Music therapy was an ideal
> place for Suzanna's needs.

Expression of emotions and needs

It was observable from the very beginning that music could provide a
vehicle for Suzanna to express her emotions. By the end of the sessions she
was able to express a range of emotions from excited to calm. Music provided not only an access to her emotions but also a way of Suzanna being
able to express them in a communicative and contained setting. From quite
early on in the therapy Suzanna was able to make her needs felt, either by
gesture, pointing or, as the sessions progressed, by vocalising. She had clear
intentions of what she wanted to do during each session, how, when and
what she wanted to play and hear. She expressed these intentions clearly
and she would always indicate when she had finished and wanted to leave.
It was very easy to understand her intentions in this musical environment.
Her mother witnessed the way Suzanna used the music to express her emotions and communicate her needs and commented:

> She never displayed emotions: happy, sad, angry. She was either OK or clearly
> not OK. The first time I saw Suzanna get angry was her trying to repeat the
> sound from a cymbal that Leslie had just shown her. She was nearly three
> and a half. The first cuddle I ever received was during a session when the
> viola was being played. The sounds of drums would excite her and the piano
> would make her attentive.

Development of imaginary and symbolic play

An important development during the final stages of the work was the use
of cuddly toys. Suzanna was beginning to express an interest for the first
time in cuddly toys and we encouraged her to bring them to the sessions. A
toy fox and a favourite teddy bear were used as intermediary and softer objects.
They would be included in the music, Suzanna playing to them, watching

and listening to their 'responses' as they also would be invited to play. The cuddly toys would dance to the music, start and stop playing, jump up and down to the music, play 'hide and seek' and sometimes fall to the floor. This play also released much spontaneous laughter, a sense of fun and excitement. This was a very positive step forward and her mother reported that such toys were being incorporated into the rest of her play. She was beginning to understand imaginary and symbolic play. About this developing use of imaginary play her mother commented:

> Her using the 'fox' puppet during a session was unintentional in that she never had used it in that way before. She would just carry it around. Seeing the fox hold the drumsticks to 'play' and seeing it jump when she banged on the drum delighted Suzanna. She eventually used the fox to play small games with her sisters. This was the first attempt to play with her sisters.

Development of listening and a closer contact with her mother

The presence of a music therapy student who played the viola provided a further opportunity for Suzanna to listen to music. She would often sit very still while listening to the viola. The listening also enabled Suzanna to have more moments of close contact with her mother. There were some moving moments during the listening times when Suzanna would reach out and give her mother a cuddle, as mentioned by her mother above. Her mother reported that these instances were very rare. The music had been a catalyst for some of the first spontaneous cuddles from Suzanna that she could recall. She adds:

> Suzanna did not like sitting on my lap, a cuddle, holding her hand, or even touching her. My function (in the sessions) was to sit next to her and for her to be able to hide behind me. As her sessions developed she allowed me to take part in turn-taking, in visual contact in seeing my reaction to what was happening and then in her responding to my response. To actually smile and enjoy being part of a group activity was a delightful breakthrough for Suzanna.

Group work at a local pre-school Opportunity Group

During the final stage of her sessions Suzanna also took part in a small group music therapy session at a local Opportunity Group for pre-school children with special needs. She began to transfer some of the skills she had developed in the individual sessions to the social context of a small group with her peers and with a different therapist. Her parents also noted that the achievements and skills developed in music therapy were being slowly transferred to other situations. They made the overall comment:

> We believe a great deal of Suzanna's progress is due to the early application of music therapy with reinforced support from her Opportunity Group. Music therapy was the perfect vehicle for a child with no language and little social awareness. The way it was presented to her accommodated her need of structure with flexibility and control. To see our child find a way to communicate with us, a connection to us, in a way that pleased her was a blessing and a privilege.

Reassessment

After a gap of almost eight months Suzanna attended for a short reassessment session. It was clear that she remembered the setting, the overall structure of one of her typical sessions and me. She explored all the instruments with assurance and a feeling of confidence. She became very excited with the loud sounds. An increase in sustained eye contact was apparent, as was her desire for a direct, sustained and more open communication through the music. She appeared very at ease in the setting and there were more sounds and single words than before. Her exploration of moods ranged from the soft and intimate, including a cuddle with her mother, to the loud and outgoing that involved much laugher and apparent excitement.

Further music therapy for Suzanna

Suzanna's parents wanted 'access to weekly individual music therapy' to be included as an integral part of her Statement of Educational Needs. In preparing reports for this statement her consultant paediatrician wrote:

> Suzanna is under my care with an Autistic Spectrum Disorder. Music therapy has proved crucial in further developing Suzanna's interactions with others. She shows preferential attention to music as opposed to verbal input. I consider that Suzanna will require a high level of musical input as part of her curriculum in school, in order to continue her development. I would also consider that such input would best be in the form of specific music therapy, in the first instance.

This request went to a tribunal before funding was agreed and the new sessions could start. The family later moved to a different part of the country where it was easier for music therapy to be made available. She had access to a further period of music therapy at her new school.

CONCLUDING POINTS

We can note links between Suzanna's story and the underlying premises listed in the introduction and discussed elsewhere in this book. The sounds coming from the music therapy room are described in words although no words can do full justice to the richness of the musical interactions. It is clear that Suzanna became deeply immersed in her musical worlds. We have glimpses of her musical intelligence (Gardner 1985) and how she used music to help herself in understanding the world. The comments from Suzanna's mother made links between the developing patterns in the music therapy process and her world outside of the therapy room. The music clearly helped to deepen the relationship between mother and child. This was demonstrated particularly in the way Suzanna included her mother in the musical play (see Oldfield *et al.* 2001 and Warwick 1995 for further discussion of this steadily growing trend of working with children and members of their families). For Suzanna we can conclude that music therapy provided a rich balance between a valid experience in itself and one that touched many other areas of her general development. It was a source of much pleasure yet at times difficult and discomforting. There was a sense of learning and of beauty, and not only for Suzanna but also for her mother and all involved.

Chapter 5

'Hullo object! I destroyed you!'

Sandra Brown

My introduction to David was indirect. His classroom was across the hallway from the music therapy room in the school for children with autism where I worked as music therapist. In sessions, I would often hear high-pitched squealing from outside and sometimes see a small struggling red-faced boy being held by staff as he kicked and screamed. On speaking with David's teachers, I found them feeling frustrated and impotent: this five-year-old's need for control seemed total and the moment he was asked to take part in an activity he didn't choose, or an interaction with another child thwarted him in some way, he would disrupt the classroom, throwing over the sandpit and water trays, ripping the curtains, screaming continuously in a high-pitched squeal, and hitting and kicking any children or staff around.

Autism is a condition that affects children and adults cognitively, socially and emotionally. Wing (1993) writes of the 'triad of social impairments' of autism, with difficulties emerging in communication, participation in and understanding of interactional social cues, and symbolic and imaginative play. Baron-Cohen also suggests an inherent lack of 'theory of mind' – the ability we have to see things from another's perspective (Baron-Cohen *et al.* 1993). These impairments in social communication of necessity affect the response of others to the child, both in infancy and throughout development, further multiplying social deficits. Furthermore, for the child with a disabling condition such as autism, trying to make life manageable often involves developing behaviour that seems even more dysfunctional, for example becoming obsessional, ritualistic and controlling. Jolliffe, who is autistic, writes:

> Reality to an autistic person is a confusing interacting mass of events, people, places, sounds and sights . . . A large part of my life is spent just trying to work out the pattern behind everything. Set routines, times, particular routes and rituals all help to get order into an unbearably chaotic life.
>
> (Jolliffe *et al.* 1992: 16)

Thus the effect of the original deficit or handicap can be greatly amplified by a child's reaction to and way of coping with their life experiences in relation to that handicap. Sinason refers to this as a 'secondary handicap', writing:

> In children and adults with an organic handicap there is genetic, chromosomal or brain injury. This is real, measurable and incurable. However, the defensive use or abuse the individual makes of the primary damage can sometimes be more powerful than the original handicap itself.
> (Sinason 1992: 112)

This can mean that many autistic children and adults live their lives much below their potential, hampered twice over by primary and secondary handicap. This certainly seemed to be the case for David, where, on top of the confusion and upset he was experiencing in his day-to-day existence, his controlling behaviour was further denying him access to the specialised educational provision that could help him. Following discussion with the school multidisciplinary team, therefore, it was agreed that he should be referred to music therapy, and David and I began working together the following term.

As you will see in the following pages, therapy is a journey where you do not know where you are going until you arrive. New directions can be thought about and planned for but often lead into unexpected country. This journey was devised – and continually revised – by both David and myself and each of us contributed to the direction and manner we travelled. Within David's sessions, much of the clinical work took place within music but some did not. As a music therapist trained originally in the Nordoff–Robbins tradition, it is in general within the improvisational musical relationship that I hope to work to enable the freeing and developing of a child's true potential. Nordoff and Robbins wrote of 'the self-integrative experience' of music, with elements such as pulse, rhythm, tempo, melody, form, and emotionality being 'inherent in the relationship between man and music' (Nordoff and Robbins 1977: 2). Because these elements live deeply in all of us, a child can be motivated by music to move into a musical relationship with another person. If that 'child's being is distorted or damaged (as the result of pathology or emotional disturbance, for example) this will be reflected in every aspect of her or his being – cognitively, psychologically, physically, emotionally, musically' (Brown 1994: 18). By working clinically within the musical relationship, therefore, attending to musical limitations and resistances as well as creative strengths, we can work simultaneously towards healing many other aspects of the child's being.

However, it is important to note that other factors in the therapy room influence and are part of the therapeutic relationship, and each therapeutic process also depends on how the client is able to and wants to work. How this balance is addressed is unique to each therapist, depending on training model, personal awareness and interests, as well as life and clinical experience. As you will see, it was not only his musical being that David brought into the therapeutic relationship, and my knowledge and experience of other clinical models and literature helped to enrich my understanding and usefulness to David throughout our journey.

David and I worked together for two years, with the usual breaks for holidays between each school term. The work of each term, while continuing on from the previous one, seems in retrospect to have had a particular focus or emphasis in relation to the ongoing therapeutic development. I am therefore going to describe the work under termly headings, although of course the relationship between us was more fluid and 'through-composed' than this would imply.

TERM ONE: EXPLORATION

Session one

I go to fetch David from his classroom, and find him squealing, back to the wall, shoes off, standing in the window bay, where staff have resorted to corralling him behind chairs. He has been told he is coming to music therapy and so accompanies me readily to the music therapy room, stopping only to put on his shoes, which he retrieves from the dustbin. In the room, I show him the instruments and explain he will come each week at this time for half an hour. He chooses to play the small glockenspiel and plays each note consecutively from left to right and back again, in a two-note stop/start pattern. I improvise on the piano, picking up the rhythm of this, matching the volume, speed and quality of his playing, singing 'hullo', as David plays on in the left/right pattern.

After a minute or so, I begin to alter the speed, slowing down. David, however, continues in the same manner, showing no awareness of my change. I rejoin his speed and then, a little later, try moving faster. At this point he says 'um', stops playing and reads the letter names of the bars of the glockenspiel, saying 'now let's take where we count our fingers – not a singsong'. He counts the bars on the glockenspiel and begins to take them off one at a time, asking me to instruct him to do this and then to tell him how many bars are left each time. As I do this, I begin to create a song that includes the counting, which has a very clear and predictable structure and is very consonant in sound. David joins me in singing this, with very true pitch, initially a little reluctantly but then with increasing sureness and pleasure.

At the end of each verse, he takes away a bar and then we sing the next verse with the correct number of remaining bars. We sustain this song for about three minutes, despite David several times rather anxiously telling me to stop, then saying 'you don't sing the song yet'. I listen to and acknowledge this but restart each time in order to gauge his response, and he joins in again. However, he eventually stops me completely, saying he has to tell me his 'news'. This involves lengthy and rather repetitive descriptions of yesterday's shopping expedition with his father, and of how the switches work in the room, while switching them on and off. He speaks coherently, but with some incorrect grammatical construction and word usage. I listen, then explain that putting the switches on and off so continuously may be dangerous, and suggest he explores playing the drum and cymbal. After some demurring, he goes to the cymbal and spins it continuously 'like a wheel on the fairground'.

I begin to play the piano and he comes over, hand held out, palm vertical, saying 'that says stop – look, my hand held out'. I stop. He counts the legs on the cymbal. I sing 'three' and he smiles and beats the cymbal. I play again with him, matching his tempo and volume, but when I begin to get louder, he cuts his volume immediately to very quiet, so that I find myself suddenly on my own, and drop mine also. He stops and asks the number of my house. I sing '213', and he is amused and sings it also, playing the cymbal in a rather erratic manner, which I reflect rhythmically but still within a harmonic framework. David then picks up a reed horn from the table and blows it intermittently. I match this and then begin to move towards a more regular pulse. He immediately says 'it's goodbye now'. I ask if we should sing goodbye; at first, he says no, but then agrees, but 'not the piano', and so I vocally improvise a simple goodbye song, which he joins in singing. On the way back to the classroom, he asks if he will come again and I repeat that he will come next week at the same time.

I have illustrated this first session in detail in order to give you some idea of the fluidity and organic development of the process within the session – initiation and response from both of us, each response resulting from a previous contribution, either in continuing the creative flow, or in breaking away from it. From this initial session, several things stand out: firstly, David's predilection for rather obsessional number-counting and cymbal-spinning, both familiar activities with other autistic children, as is his resistance to being involved in a mutual sharing in relationship. His occasional language problems also seem related to his autism, although he is obviously at the 'high-functioning' end of the autistic continuum.

Secondly, his anxiety was clear when I displayed autonomy, for example when I continued playing, or did not count exactly as he asked, and was only relieved when he felt in charge again. He could rarely allow himself to be held in the 'creative now' of the musical experience (Nordoff, cited in Aigen 1996: 10), withdrawing almost immediately from that mutual sharing and living in the music. Thirdly, from a musical perspective, when I got faster, David stopped playing and moved into counting; when I got slower, he didn't register, playing on at the same speed; when I got louder, he immediately cut to a very soft dynamic and then stopped. However, when I created a structured song he was able to join in, singing at pitch and in tempo, with some pleasure. It seemed, therefore, that creative musical gestures from me could be taken up and enjoyed, albeit briefly. However, the moment an unpredictable or unplanned element came in, David would very quickly retreat from it into the security of autistic rituals, and there were also areas where he seemed oblivious to relationship at all.

My thoughts at this point were that David's difficulties did not stem from needing to be over-controlling but from feelings of *lack* of control – that this rigid control covered fear of inner and outer chaos, and from a very tenuous grip on making sense of and managing the world around him, the balance could be easily tipped and then David fell into an inner abyss of uncontrollable frightening fragments. His anxiety when I did not stop playing, with the sense of 'if I give her an inch, she'll take the world', the reassurance and predictability of numbers and counting and the dangers of allowing the needs of the musical relationship to sweep him along, all overpowered the brief flashes of spontaneous play and his real pleasure at engaging in the music. I thought too of Winnicott, who writes of the painful necessity for a child to move from experiencing the world from a position of omnipotence to acknowledging others as 'not-me', separate, autonomous (Winnicott 1990). David's inability to relinquish omnipotence seemed great, and led me to reflect on the added difficulties of achieving this developmental stage for children whose pathology already hinders them in conceptualising another's mind as different from their own, and for whom loss of control can be so terrifying.

My overall therapeutic aims at this point, therefore, could be seen as twofold. Firstly, the building of a relationship of trust, to enable a reduction in David's anxiety concerning loss of control, hopefully thus enabling exploration into the creative possibilities of mutual relationship; and secondly, working for flexibility and adaptability to the 'in the moment' needs of shared music-making, for example in the areas of pulse, tempo and dynamic.

Continuing in term one

As we moved through the first term of work, David often evinced great anxiety after even brief moments of shared experience and mutuality. In general, following where the music led could not be sustained and he would immediately withdraw into the security of counting or telling me repetitively about external happenings in his life. The points of shared musical experience that we did have were again often in song. Although he began to play more extendedly, David's instrumental playing continued to bear little relationship to mine, except where I matched and reflected the quality and tempo of his playing, constantly fitting and attuning myself to him.

I was struck by what a revolutionary idea this had seemed when Nordoff and Robbins first proposed it: rather than ignoring apparently non-communicative behaviours:

we take these manifestations of pathology, and through improvisations
. . . we meet the tempo of whatever the child is doing – the tempo of his
walking, of his headbanging, of his pacing up and down, of his rocking
. . . and we give this back to him in music, so that he has a new experience of what he does habitually.

(Nordoff 1976)

I reflected on how this is not just imitation or reinforcement of autistic
behaviours, but is much more reminiscent of Stern's 'affect attunement', where
'what is being matched is not the other person's behaviour *per se*, but rather
some aspect of the behaviour that reflects the (child's) feeling state' (Stern
1985: 142). This kind of attunement between care-giver and infant plays 'an
important role in the infant's coming to recognise that internal feeling states
are forms of human experience that are shareable with other humans' (Stern
1985: 151). This is clearly a vital starting point for a child such as David
with the social impairments of autism.

In the second session, David had introduced a Monster who stalked the
room, rushing up to eat me and roaring at me, who was kept controlled by
David switching the light off to make it go to sleep. As the term continued,
the description of the Monster's activities became more and more destructive, with David informing me that it 'eats all the flowers and the curtains',
'will eat your piano', 'breaks all the trees up, you hear the big noise'. It felt
very much as though David was increasingly exploring the boundaries of the
room, both as to whether this destructive and 'monstrous' bit of himself could
be brought here, and whether the room – and I – could contain it, while
keeping us both safe. Here, the ability of music to be both structured and
free simultaneously was an essential therapeutic factor on many occasions.
David was able to join me from time to time in brief songs about the Monster.
He had also introduced the 'Teddybears' Picnic' song. A rampaging Monster
was gradually able to be met and contained in this safely known music, with
David/Monster skipping rhythmically round the room as I played and sang,
then hiding and jumping out from behind the piano as 'a big Monster surprise' at the end.

TERM TWO: CONTROL

On returning from the Christmas holidays, David's control issues came more
and more firmly into the room. Musically, he increasingly limited my contribution; as we would be about to start together, David would say 'I don't
know, Sandra – it's not where you sing yet'; instruments were endlessly 'not
quite ready', and had to be adjusted. He would break off to open the top
lid of the piano and peer inside, asking about its workings, moving into

predictable discussions about his 'news'. He also began to move instruments behind the piano and play from there briefly.

My activities became more and more proscribed. From deciding when I should play, he moved to what I should play and then to stopping me from playing at all. I felt increasingly that David was totally unable to relax in case I took over, and that we were centrally dealing with his anxieties about keeping control over his world. Clinically, I wanted to allow him space to explore having this control, to build up his trust that I wouldn't overwhelm him, that I could – and would – keep the room safe in terms of personal and instrumental safety in order to allow him to explore creatively. I felt strongly that until he felt safe enough that his world, including me, wouldn't go out of his control the moment his vigilance wavered, he would not be able to explore what spontaneous interaction and relationship could offer. It felt vital clinically that I should not be drawn into exerting control for the sake of having it, and not feel rendered impotent by David – the very dynamic that he was caught in. Instead, I worked to step sideways into a separate position, where I could maintain free choice to allow David to control the situation or not, depending on the clinical needs of the moment. I did initiate playing, therefore, but stopped when told and accepted David's choice of instruments for me, waiting to see where his chosen route was taking us.

Throughout the term, I had been aware of a growing desire in David to hurt me physically, as he mock-threatened me with beaters, squeezing my fingers 'accidentally'. The Monster by now had materialised into a dangerous Cat that lived behind the piano, and which regularly came out squealing to scratch and eat me – the same squealing that I had heard him do in the classroom. While physically containing David, I sang/spoke rhythmically in a kind of rap about this dangerous fierce Cat, how I could hear it wanted to hurt and eat me and make loud angry noises, and that I was holding him to keep us both safe. The containing and transforming qualities of musical form and pulse were enormously important here, and I mulled over parallels with what Bion describes as 'maternal reverie', where the mother takes in and transforms the baby's chaotic and potentially overwhelming feelings, returning them to the child in a more manageable form (Bion 1962).

TERM THREE: THE DEVELOPING RELATIONSHIP

By the beginning of term three, David was more able to allow me to participate musically, although still under strict control as to what or when to play. He had allowed me a single glockenspiel bar in my hand with one small beater, and I was able to play this, under strict 'start–stop' instruction. I obeyed, closely matching and reflecting what he played in tempo, number of notes and so on. David mainly played the piano and gradually entrusted more and more possibilities to me, risking that I wouldn't take over. From the single glockenspiel bar, sitting at a distance, I was given a cymbal, and a stick; then a drum was added, I was moved closer to the piano and given two sticks. All playing, however, was under strict control of the upraised hand. Nevertheless, as the term progressed I began to test playing or singing without being invited, and this was gradually tolerated for longer periods of time. It became very apparent, now that we could play together more, that David's playing showed no influence or apparent awareness of mine. He would play piano always at the same speed, repeating the same pulse over and over. I would join this speed, but any subsequent alterations I might offer in terms of getting faster or slower he was oblivious to, continuing on and on, not looking at or hearing me in any perceptible manner.

By now, David's anxiety had diminished and he could allow me to play, but no mutually interactive relationship was possible. I constantly strove to help him break through the limitations he and his pathology had imposed on him, working for variation of tempo and dynamic range in relation to my playing. The first indications of change came one session when David for the first time stopped playing a few beats after I did. The second was when his playing became affected by what I did during our playing together – not necessarily relating appropriately to changes I might introduce, but a definite response, for example his pulse becoming erratic when I began to go faster or slower. It felt like a thawing, as when an ice-shelf begins to crack and break up, with change coming but as yet without new definition, and this sense increased as the term went on.

Throughout the term, David continued to be the Cat behind the piano for part of each session. He had also begun to request that I should be the Cat, and increasingly locked me up behind the piano, with chairs to keep me in, while he played boisterously on the piano, shouting commands to me and dropping things over the piano at me mock-threateningly. I was reminded of the corralling of him that I had observed in the classroom. Again here I worked to create a strong containing musical presence, using the back of the piano as a drum, beating out rhythms and singing strongly in a rap-style, drawing him into shared rhythmic interaction, while maintaining boundaries concerning levels of destructiveness and damage.

As David and I sang about this dangerous Cat who could scratch and bite and needed locked up, Tate's paper 'On Ego Development' (Tate 1958) came to mind. In this paper, Tate talks of John, a little boy who brings his destructive self into the sessions in the form of a dangerous lion, who has to be locked in a cage in order to contain him. Rereading this paper proved enormously helpful and reassuring in containing *me* in my feelings of 'unsureness' and not knowing in this section of work and I was struck by the parallels in the present material. More recently, having read Sidoli's paper on the use of lion imagery in the analysis of two adult patients (Sidoli 1998), I became aware of how this use of 'wild cats' to hold aggressive emotions for the child had occurred before in my therapy work, and mused on the connections of this image with Jung's idea of the collective unconscious and archetypal images.[1]

One day, when I was 'locked up' behind the piano, David came to the side, saying 'Oh, in the wind, an egg blowing – inside your cage' – and came in and lay by me. I sang about the egg, and then David called 'Something's hatching – it's cracking open, a baby kitten's coming out'. I reflected this in my singing and he 'miaowed' rather pitifully, and said 'Who will be my mother?', holding on to me. This was repeated in the next session, where again I used singing to hold and contain, rhythmically and melodically. The following session, David came behind the piano beside me, enacting the egg-hatching again. He then told me in urgent tones to hold on to his feet and not let go, and he began to strain and slide on his stomach to move out of the 'cage' through the legs of the stool. He seemed not ready to do this, reversing back in several times, trying again, still insisting I should hold his feet and not let go. I sang about this, acknowledging his actions.

The next week David repeated this, calling 'Hold tight', and 'Pull, pull' as he strained to get out. Suddenly he launched himself away and through, shouting 'I'm gone!' rushing round to play the piano very loudly and triumphantly. I joined in, drumming on the back of the piano and singing, celebrating with him. This was extraordinary to be part of, with a strong sense of David using the sessions purposefully and seriously to do what he needed to do in order to be 'born' and to begin to recognise us as two separate beings. Before this, it seemed David had only two ways of being with me: either totally omnipotently controlling of me, where I wasn't allowed to have a mind or will separate from him, or else wiping me out, as in where we played in parallel, with no acknowledgement of my existence at all. This 'new birth' seemed to reflect developmentally what Winnicott describes as 'the infant's change from being merged with the mother to being separate from her . . . to relating to her as separated and "not-me" ' (Winnicott 1990: 45) – a definite move forward in the task of relinquishing omnipotence.

TERM FOUR: TOGETHER IN MUSICAL EXPERIENCE

What often amazes me is how the process of therapy is maintained and continues to develop during breaks, even of six or seven weeks. In the first session of term four, after the summer holidays, David came in, arranged himself a drumkit, and said 'Hullo song first? Right, start the piano!' and then, for the first time ever, joined me in tempo, with a real feeling for phrase shaping and style. After some minutes, I deliberately slowed down the pulse and, after a few seconds' delay, he hesitated in his playing and looked intently

1 Archetypal images: images containing very powerful emotional content, whose roots are found in the shared unconscious of all human beings (see Jung 1968).

at my hands. He then continued, joining me in the new slow tempo, moving his whole body in response to the music. It was a breath-holding moment and I felt that paradoxically David's growing awareness of me as 'not-me' had enabled the beginning of a true coming together for us. In the rest of the session we improvised, with David listening and responding to pulse and musical changes. He also introduced songs he knew for us to sing and play, with me being allowed to choose songs as well. Throughout this, as well as singing, David created appropriate musical accompaniments with a variety of instruments, and a great deal of enjoyment. This shared instrumental and vocal work was to continue to blossom throughout the term. It was an extraordinary shift and seemed the culmination of the work of the preceding term.

In other ways, this was to be a difficult term for David – his brother had begun school in a lower class, which he found very unsettling and challenging. I felt that both in and out of the sessions he was beginning to try to come to terms with 'the immense shock of the loss of omnipotence' (Winnicott 1974: 83), and that a period of mourning for this had begun. This was apparent in one particular session where, after playing and singing hullo together, he stopped playing and said to me '*you* play'. This was the first time ever that I had been able to play alone and I felt this was an enormous shift for the boy whose fear of loss of control initially meant he had to do all the playing and me none at all. I did continue playing, and David sat, looking and listening, with a sad and rather inward expression, occasionally punctuating my playing with long held notes on the horn. A little later, he wanted to play and sing the Beatles song 'Yellow Submarine' and directed me to the percussion instruments, while he sat at the piano. After a few notes, he stopped and turned to me, saying sadly, 'I can't play the piano – you play it'. We changed places, and then played and sang the song, with David playing the percussion instruments with some panache. This felt deeply significant for him, firstly in the acknowledgement of his limitations, that he couldn't do or control everything, and secondly in the growing sense that allowing the other to be separate and autonomous could potentially be beneficial and enriching.

Throughout the remainder of the term David and I explored and enjoyed ways of being separate and together, playing on instruments simultaneously, separately, swapping over, exploring concepts such as loud/soft, fast/slow, high/low, widening David's musical resources and his cognitive awareness as well as his ability to enter into creative play in a shared and mutual space. Throughout this time, the Cat only appeared minimally and then disappeared altogether, as the work began to be contained totally in the musical relationship. Like Tate's John, who could ultimately lead his Lion safely on a string, David's Cat was becoming more 'tamed', his feared and overwhelming emotions brought to human proportions, able to be contained and managed between us.

TERM FIVE: STRUGGLE

Term four had felt like a consolidation of relationship, of David exploring without anxiety and finding the pleasure of mutuality in relationship in the music. By the end of the term, however, his control issues had begun to come in again: he increasingly repositioned instruments, thereby curtailing playing time, constantly going to the cupboard to get different ones. He also became increasingly directive of my playing again, and now began to introduce 'Yellow Submarine' to avoid and distract away from any spontaneous shared improvisational material we might become involved in. Although his control issues were re-emerging, David's terror of losing control had now gone and we had established a flexible and interactive musical relationship. I felt that he was now ready to tolerate increasing independent action from me, where I might play as I felt appropriate, rather than necessarily as he would like. In this, he would have to begin to acknowledge that what I did I was motivated by choice, not his compulsion – that I was indeed separate and 'not-me'. This would be enormously important work for him, where he could begin to manage the give and take of social relationship, to continue the work in containing his frustration while allowing the other some freedom and needs of their own.

I therefore began to set limits on the constant re-choosing and moving of instruments. David could make a suggestion, which I would implement for the following week, but he had to work with what was set up in the room on the day. He could play as he wished, within the boundaries of safety and damage, but I began to choose what I did, for example which instrument I played, how I played it, which beater, not always going with his desires. Although I introduced this gradually, David found it very frustrating and this was where the music itself was vital to reach in and motivate him to want to join it. On one memorable occasion, we had begun by improvising together very connectedly. David stopped in the middle of this and asked for 'Yellow Submarine'. I continued playing, saying 'let's stay with where we are now', and he seemed very put out, sitting turned away, holding the sticks up under his chin, determined not to play. However, the lilt of the song that developed about 'Here is a boy with two sticks' became too irresistible and he joined in, at first indirectly, still looking the other way while playing, but then with increasing commitment and enjoyment. A little later, he remembered he shouldn't be doing it and deliberately dropped the sticks on the floor, with a flourish, hanging upside down from his chair. I continued with the song and within a minute he was again unable to resist picking up one of the sticks from this position and joining in, playing the chimes from below, still upside down.

TERM SIX: ENDING

Term six came, with a continuation of these therapeutic issues and aims, and with increasing acceptance and compromise being possible between us. We were now covering a large creative area in the sessions – wide and varied mood and emotional exploration, ebullient and calm instrumental playing, many levels of tempo and dynamic; and melody and song, with quiet reflect- ive free singing as well as known structured songs, all within a more mutual relationship.

In his annual school review, David's teacher noted that there had been a great improvement in his behaviour and attitude, and that academically he had made good progress. Although he still could be disruptive in groups, he was now much more able to modify his behaviour. As always in schools and clinics there are children waiting to come for therapy and I felt we were now approaching the point where David could go on developing within the continuing supportive environment of home and school. I therefore told David just before half-term that there would be one more half-term and then we would end music therapy – that when he came back in September, we wouldn't be meeting for music therapy again.

Endings inevitably bring with them all the issues related to death and part- ing – mourning, feelings of loss, of anger, and therapeutic endings can bring a final return of earlier symptoms and difficulties to be addressed in the con- text of ending the relationship. Here David would suffer the death of his creative space with me, of our weekly music-making and relationship. He had not chosen this; I had. This would inevitably touch into these very issues of lack of control and omnipotence that we had been working with from the beginning, and would be a testing time for him. In the final weeks, David would check at the beginning of each session how many were left. Four sessions from the end, he introduced a new theme. The session had begun with him immediately starting singing 'Yellow Submarine'. This felt like an avoidance of a perhaps more emotionally risky improvisational relationship, and so I played on, singing 'No, no, no, time for hullo!' David then began a 'spoken' improvised song, which I supported on piano, in which he banished me to live in various unlikely objects such as toasters, light bulbs and concrete mixers.

At the end of each verse, he would say 'And then what will happen?' I would build and hold the musical tension – there would be a pause – and then David would throw his hands in the air, enact an explosion and shout gleefully 'Dead Sandra!' This would be repeated, with each killing-off notched up – 'Dead Sandra – eleven times!' I felt like Tom in the *Tom and Jerry* cartoon, outwitted, blown up, endlessly resurrected, only to be killed off again. I thought of Winnicott writing of the need of the child to see the object survive their destruction of it in fantasy in order finally to enable the relinquishing of omnipotence (Winnicott 1974). I was also deeply struck by

David's understanding of my 'separate mind', as he tricked me time and again into believing that this time I would be saved, only to deliver the *coup de grâce* with consummate timing. No 'theory of mind' deficit here!

In these final sessions, I pondered on how far David had come. Two years before, his need for omnipotent control was total with the unavoidable failure of maintaining this precipitating terror and rage. His resultant destructive and angry feelings could not be contained and were concretely acted out in the room around him. Now he could bring these feelings into the arena of creative play, both in music and words, and play them, enjoy them, manage them within himself, without the need for destructive enactments. Winnicott writes in terms of growth towards separation of the need for the child's acceptance and recognition of the other's ability to survive their destructiveness:

> The subject says to the object: 'I destroyed you' and the object is there to receive the communication. From now on the subject says 'Hullo object!' 'I destroyed you!' 'I love you.' . . . Here fantasy begins for the individual.
> (Winnicott 1974: 105)

This finding of the separation of fantasy and reality truly enabled David to destroy me over and over again, within the sustaining ongoingness of the creative musical relationship. He was now able to allow me to be a 'not-me', a person other than him; and although he had had to face the frustrations that I was out of his control, autonomous, independent, he was also now at the beginning of another journey, one which leads towards the richness and fulfilment that mutual relationship also brings.

Chapter 6

Music therapy with adults with learning disabilities

Tessa Watson

INTRODUCTION

This chapter considers the ways in which people with learning disabilities can make use of music therapy. An outline is given of British social history of people with learning disabilities and the way their needs have been perceived and met over the past few decades. The reasons why these clients might be referred to a music therapist are discussed, and the process of therapy is outlined. Music therapists have been working with people with learning disabilities since the inception of the profession, and a brief description of this work, and related literature, is given. The author's psychodynamic approach to music therapy is described, and is illustrated by detailed case material of work with a client who has profound and multiple learning disabilities.

LEARNING DISABILITIES – A HISTORY

Two clear definitions of learning disability come from the World Health organisation (WHO) and the Department of Health. The WHO gives a medical definition that is used for diagnosis:

> medical retardation is a condition of arrested or incomplete development of the mind, which is especially characterised by impairment of skills manifested during the developmental period, which contribute to the overall level of intelligence, i.e. cognitive, language, motor and social abilities (1992: 226).

The Department of Health, in its new White Paper 'Valuing People', suggests that:

> The presence of a low intelligence quotient, for example an IQ below 70, is not, of itself, a sufficient reason for deciding whether an individual

should be provided with additional health and social care support. An assessment of social functioning and communication skills should also be taken into account when determining need. Many people with learning disabilities also have physical and/or sensory impairments (DOH 2001: 14).

Historically in the UK, learning disabled people have been cared for either by their families at home, or in institutional care. The numbers of learning disabled children and adults with severe and profound learning disabilities in England was estimated at 160 000 in 1999. Many of these clients live at home. DOH figures show that 7000 of these people are cared for by the NHS and 51 000 live in residential care (DOH 2001). Historically, these clients were often very isolated from their communities, living or working together in institutional buildings and settings. In the past twenty years there has been a great change in government and health services policy about disability in general, including learning disability. Attitudes and language have changed radically. (Sinason 1992 gives an enlightening history of the terminology used to name this client group.) It is now considered that people with learning disabilities can become full members of their local community (Whittaker and McIntosh 2000).

Current thinking places an emphasis on helping clients to live satisfying, full lives in their local community, and to have equal access to community facilities (Mansell and Ericsson 1996). The government launch of the White Paper aims to ensure high standards of service planning and care (Bailey and Cooper 1999). Although services have struggled to change their often unwieldy structures to meet these new ideas, there is now frequently a characteristic of partnership in the work that we undertake with our clients. Rather than the client passively receiving treatment over which they have no influence, clients and professionals are working together.

As a result of these changes in attitude and policy, more independent community living is often possible and desirable. This might mean that clients own a house on a residential street, and have access to their chosen opportunities of everyday life. These opportunities may include making friends with the neighbours, the postman and the local shopkeepers, and using the local facilities including the pub, swimming pool and doctors' surgery. Clients need varying levels of support in order to access their community and to feel happy with their lives, and research and consultation with clients shows that they do not always feel their needs are met in the most appropriate or satisfactory way (Murray et al. 1998).

Community teams were developed in the 1980s, often as a response to clients moving from long-stay hospitals into the community. In 1987 there were 348 such teams in England (DOH 2001). Now these teams are the most usual way that health professionals deliver care to clients living in their area. Many teams are developing to become joint health and social services teams, allowing professionals to work in multidisciplinary partnership with clients to manage change and development for individuals.

If fulfilling community living for people with learning disabilities is to be an actuality, not merely an aim, we must work with the realities and difficulties that this integration brings. The King's Fund notes that learning disabled people need 'special help, support, guidance and sometimes protection to enable them to enjoy the benefits of community life to the full' (1980: 15). This statement is borne out in the referrals that the arts therapists in the author's team receive, where 'special help' is often sought for difficulties with communication, difficulties with self-expression, or problems with relating with others. These referral reasons link with the findings of the *London Learning Disability Strategy Framework* (DOH 2001) where it is suggested that specialist teams should address a variety of areas, including communication, sexuality and relationships, mental health and challenging behaviour.

Sines, considering the maintenance of 'an ordinary life', writes about the importance of exploring feelings and past experiences (which may have been suppressed and introjected), particularly those to do with loss, change and bereavement; 'such feelings are an essential part of life . . . time may be needed for . . . sharing of feelings and emotions' (1988: 45). MacKenzie *et al.* (2000) talk about the importance of recognising and expressing emotion, and the difficulty that clients with learning disabilities can have in this area. Thinking such as this is in stark contrast to previous attitudes to people with learning disabilities, and is refreshing. Much work has been undertaken by clinicians to help clients and staff to work together on the area of emotional issues. Notably, the Tavistock Clinic in London and Harperbury school have worked and written in this area (Nind and Hewett 1994, and The Tavistock and Portman NHS Trust 2001). But Gardner and Smyly find that still they are 'struck by the absence of good quality relationships for some of our clients' (1997: 26). It can be difficult to find ways to work with our clients in the area of emotional relationships; music therapy provides a useful resource.

A LITERATURE REVIEW

British music therapy has a long and interesting history in this clinical area. Literature is available from the start of the profession in the UK in the 1960s, and is fascinating reading. Reviewing the literature, it is clear that music therapists have always been convinced of the efficacy of their work with this client group. Pioneers of the profession documented their work in journals and newsletters; Wing states that even with the most disabled of her clients, 'a thin link of communication has been forged' (1968: 8), and Alvin asserts that 'we know that music is an essentially flexible means of communication which can work at every mental, emotional and social level' (1975: 2) and that 'it [music] can work at a primitive level of understanding and feelings' (ibid.: 150). The clinical work described by these early authors is of a direct-ive style, using well-known pre-composed songs and pieces.

In 1979, Odell documents the developing model of British music therapy, when she writes that she worked 'always from the spontaneous music he [the client] produced, taking up ideas in an improvisatory way, until he eventually made eye contact, and dialogue was possible' (1979: 13). Music therapists continued to develop their work in this field. Clough (1992), Cowan (1989), Gale (1989) and Ritchie (1991) all write in detail about case work, describing the difficulties, approaches and theory behind their work. British music therapy has developed to become, in March 1997, a state reg-istered profession responsible to the Council of Professions Supplementary to Medicine (CPSM 1997). Current characteristics of British music therapy include the use of clinical improvisation. This is described by the Associa-tion of Professional Music Therapists as 'interactive music, spontaneously created by the client and therapist . . . the shared use of sound' (2000a).

A recent proliferation of books published in the area of the arts therapies has produced some useful literature concerning music therapy in the field of learning disabilities. This literature includes Bunt's overall picture of music therapy (1994) and Heal Hughes' readable descriptions of casework (1995). Pavlicevic's recent publications explore the nature of music therapy (1997) and describe case work in detail (1999a). Wigram and De Backer (1999a) provide an international overview. Despite the recent growth in literature, there continues to be a lack of detailed writing about this client area. In the research field, only Hooper and Lindsay (1990), Oldfield and Adams (1990), Toolan and Coleman (1995) and Woodcock and Lawes (1995) have pub-lished their work.

AN OVERVIEW

Music therapists first began work in this area in large mental handicap hospitals, where clients often lived the whole of their adult lives. While work continues in remaining hospitals, it is more usual now for music therapists to be working in the community, perhaps, as in the author's case, as part of a CTPLD (Community Team for People with Learning Disabilities). Working in a team of this sort can allow for close multidisciplinary work and sharing different perspectives and skills within the team. While for the music therapist this teamworking may involve a struggle to speak a langu-age that the team can understand (Pavlicevic 1997: 94), it is clear that the music therapist's integration in the team is productive. In addition to close work with other professionals, liaison with the client's main carers is often desirable, both to share information, and to encourage carers to develop their understanding of the client's difficulties. The London Learning Disability Strategy Group state that this is a strength of community teams (DOH 2001). Liaison with professionals, parents and carers is undertaken with consideration of issues of confidentiality. This might mean discussing with the client how much information can be shared, or talking generally with carers about an area of concern without giving actual details of therapy work.

Clients are seen in music therapy across the range of disability. For example, mildly learning disabled clients might come for therapy to address specific difficulties in their independent community living, and might travel to the session on their own. In contrast, severely learning disabled clients might come for therapy to enable them to start to make emotional connections, and might need to be escorted to sessions by a carer. These examples are given to show the diverse difficulties and situations that clients can experience. In the author's team, group and individual assessment and treatment work can be undertaken in the following areas:

- long-term ongoing therapy with clients to address difficulties relating to communication and emotional issues;
- short-term therapy to support clients through periods of acute emotional distress or to address a specific identified issue;
- therapy with clients whose behaviour challenges staff and services;
- therapy with clients who have a dual diagnosis of learning disabilities and additional mental health problems.

The process of the music therapy referral may vary depending on the resources, situation and clinical orientation of the team. In the author's team, clients are referred by the completion of a referral form to the arts therapies department. The paper referral enables the therapist to gain important information about the client and their needs, and is followed up with an initial appointment. This will usually consist of a home visit, where the therapist meets the client and perhaps a key worker or family member, to give information about music therapy and discuss the referral further. Following the initial appointment, a series of assessment sessions may be offered. Assessment is a useful stage in the process of therapy, allowing both client and therapist to find out if music therapy can be a helpful resource for the client. A set number of sessions will be offered (between 5–8 weekly sessions) and following completion of the sessions, the therapist will meet with the client and carers if appropriate to discuss the process of assessment, particularly in relation to the reasons for referral. Further treatment in a group or individual setting may then be offered. It is important for treatment to be reviewed by the therapist at regular intervals; maybe after each phase of treatment, or at the client's multidisciplinary review meetings.

THEORETICAL FRAMEWORK

Music therapy is a specialised treatment that offers clients a way to address problems in their lives. Toolan and Coleman describe the music therapy structure as 'a time of special attentiveness to meaning; in which anxieties, anger, sadness and thoughts, which may be of overwhelming proportions, can be held and contained by the therapist' (1995: 18). The environment available is one 'within which the patient may explore and deepen his experience of himself and his world' (Steele 1988: 22). The therapist works with the client to address specific identified difficulties by exploring the meaning in the relatedness that is created in the therapy session. Relatedness between the therapist and the client is established through the medium of music; communication is carried in the client's use of the musical instruments, therapeutic relationship and therapy space ('music essentially operates in the realm of analogue and metaphor, providing a transitional area of experience' (Stewart 1996: 22)). The musical medium provides a non-verbal, accessible way for clients to engage in meaningful therapeutic contact.

For clients with a learning disability, words are often a difficult territory, and the musical medium can be used to create an emotional and symbolic landscape where thoughts and feelings can emerge into affective musical articulation and be safely explored and developed.

The author practises psychodynamic music therapy, using the fundamental approach (based on a mother/infant interaction model) taught on the Roehampton postgraduate training course (Heal Hughes 1995; Sobey 1992; Steele 1988, 1991; Stewart 1996; Woodcock 1987). For a detailed explanation of this approach, see Sobey and Woodcock (1999). The author has developed this training further through the influences of personal therapy, supervision and study. Particular psychotherapeutic theorists whose work has informed and enriched the author's use of the psychodynamic music therapy framework include Stern, Klein, Winnicott and Bion. The approach is modulated to provide an appropriate level of therapeutic intervention for individual clients.

In order for the therapist to be a containing and thinking presence, able to receive (in the musical relatedness), all the conscious and unconscious projections, transferences and re-enactments that she will undoubtedly encounter, an ability to think about the process of therapy (in and out of the clinical session) is essential. Levinge speaks of this; 'like the holding of the infant by the mother, I discovered that I not only needed a physical space to carry out the work, but also a space in my mind in which I could think freely' (1993: 220). The psychodynamic music therapy framework provides a specific approach to thinking musically with clients. A central tenet is that 'musical interactions and behaviour are a reflection of what is happening internally for the patient' (Odell-Miller 1995: 86), or that 'in the music-play of

the music therapy relationship, the therapist begins to become ɛ
with the internal landscape of the patient' (Steele 1991).

The musical medium is used to establish relatedness between th
client, and to communicate something of the client's internal expe........
therapist's role is to enable, receive and digest these communications, and to
help the client to find and explore their meaning. She does this in the sessions
through her musical, verbal and thinking processes and interventions. The
therapist will construct and develop a hypothesis about the therapeutic process during and following sessions (in her clinical notes and supervision), and
will continue to develop these hypotheses in subsequent sessions. She works
to enable meaning to emerge and be understood, and patterns of relating to
be recongnised and modulated; thus change and progress may be possible
for the client.

There is a misconception that psychodynamic music therapy work
requires that words be spoken. In fact, much psychodynamic work is undertaken without words. In this music therapy approach, the music and the words
are not separate; the psychodynamic approach does not exist only in the
words, nor the music therapy approach only in the music; rather, they are
one approach. The results of the therapist's thought about the dynamics of
the session can be conveyed in the therapist's music as well as in words.
Pavlicevic describes this in terms of interpretation: 'despite the interpretation being a solitary act that cannot be shared verbally with the client, the
therapist acts musically upon her "private" interpretation and seeks resonance
from the client' (1997: 164). In the author's clinical experience in this area,
words can be useful, and it is important that the therapist has her thoughts
available for use as words when appropriate.

However, the musical embodiment of the therapist's thought is often the
most appropriate intervention. This is particularly germane when working
with learning disabled clients for whom verbal interaction may be inacces-
sible, confusing or threatening. Sinason's statement that 'however crippled
someone's external functional intelligence might be, there still can be intact
a complex emotional structure and capacity' (1992: 74) supports the value
of a means of emotional communication that is not dependent upon verbal
intellect or functional ability. Toolan and Coleman speak of this in specific
relation to music therapy, stating that 'fundamental to the practice of music
therapy is the idea that the emotional world of patients is complex, full of
good and bad experiences and is intact, regardless of the degree of intellectual difficulties or handicap' (1995: 17).

THEORY INTO PRACTICE

Here the practicalities of the clinical session are described. Different
approaches in music therapy may consider different elements of the work in

more detail and the following description represents the psychodynamic approach of the author, who currently works in a community team in London, England. A boundaried approach is used, with sessions taking place on a weekly basis (occasionally twice a week), at the same time and in the same place, and with preparation for breaks in therapy. This consistency of approach encourages the regular contact of the sessions to be relied upon. It also allows for the development of a reliable internal object. The music therapy session is uninterrupted and, where possible, the room is soundproofed. There are a variety of tuned and untuned percussion instruments available for both the client and therapist to use. The length of the session is determined by the needs of the client; in the author's work it is usual that individual sessions are 45 minutes and group sessions 45–60 minutes.

The primary medium of the sessions is that of music, specifically, improvised music, co-created by the therapist and client. Clinical improvisation is a characteristic of British music therapy, and is used widely in work with learning disabled clients. Rogers gives a clear description of the value of improvisation: 'music therapy involves the use of free clinical improvisation through which the therapist examines the relationship between herself and the client, seeking to understand, reflect and interpret (either musically or verbally) therapeutic issues that have particular relevance for the client. Clinical improvisation within the therapeutic environment allows the inner emotional world of the client to be examined and acknowledged' (1993: 206).

The structure of each session may be different, and is determined by the client's use of the therapy space. Beginnings and endings of sessions may be marked with a musical structure, marking the transition in and out of the session in a non-verbal way. The client is then invited to use the instruments with the therapist, in order to create jointly improvised pieces. While some clients may be able to organise the use of the session time spontaneously, others may need the therapist to take the responsibility of organising or structuring the time. The therapist will be sensitive to these differences and will structure the session accordingly. As the joint musical dialogue is created, the client's difficulties (the reasons for referral) can be explored in the context of the dynamic musical relatedness. The therapist's continual examination of the quality of this musical relatedness, and of her response to it, allows the client's communications to be held firmly at the focus of the session. When appropriate, the music within the sessions may be taped and the therapist and client may listen to the tape. It may also be appropriate, as discussed previously, for the client and therapist to talk about the music, or for the therapist to comment on aspects of the session.

After each session the therapist writes comprehensive clinical notes; these will be consulted prior to the next session. The therapist constructs a hypothesis about the work that is modified and developed following each session. Work is reviewed in supervision, in discussion or review meetings with the client, parents/carers or multidisciplinary team.

CLINICAL WORK

The approach described will now be illustrated by the examination of extracts of a clinical case study. The case study is an assessment undertaken with a severely learning disabled woman. The work took place in a resource centre for people with learning disabilities, which is purpose-built and consists of various well-designed and well-equipped clinical spaces. For music therapy sessions, a medium-sized, airy room is used, and is set up with musical instruments, including a metallophone, windchime, cymbal and large drum, and many small percussion instruments. The therapist's cello and guitar are also used. The music therapy service at this resource centre includes the provision of a small, weekly music therapy group for severely learning disabled clients, and the work described is an assessment for this group.

The client was referred to the group in order to develop ways of relating, and for help with self-expression. Having met with the client and key staff in the client's home to discuss the referral, a series of five weekly assessment sessions were offered. Following this assessment, the client was offered a place in the group and she has continued to attend the group on a weekly basis.

This clinical work was studied for a research project. While some details of the research process will be given, extracts are used to explain clinical and theoretical processes, and the research will not be reported in full. The project aimed to explore the hypothesis that 'music therapy interventions can enable severely learning disabled adult clients to experience affective musical contact with the therapist'. Daniel Stern's concept of affect attunement was used to show the presence of affective communication and attunement (Stern 1985). Stern's work with mothers and infants led to the development of this concept in answer to the question 'how can you "get inside of" other people's subjective experience and then let them know that you have arrived there without using words?' (1985: 138). He explored the stages of an intersubjective affective exchange, and considered that there were three different stages to this communication. He developed the idea of different modalities or channels of expression, such as a vocal phrase or an arm movement. The quality or property of affect is communicated by six types of behaviour (absolute intensity, intensity contour, temporal beat, rhythm, duration and shape) that are embodied in the communication between mother and baby.

In order to examine the research hypothesis, clinical music therapy sessions were video-recorded, and documentation was developed in order to analyse the videotape. Three five-minute extracts from the first, second and third weeks of assessment were selected by the therapist and viewed by three music therapists in order to identify the moments of connection and changes in connection berween the client and therapist. This was done through the accurate noting of tape counter numbers and the completion of documentation. The documentation allowed the noting of different elements of connection: musical, facial, gestural and body movement, and a feeling of meaningful connection not directly observable. These identified phases of connection were then notated onto a manuscript (notation including the music of client and therapist, the movement of the client and the therapist's clinical notes), and analysed. This research does not document a whole case study or aim to discuss aims and outcomes of therapy. Rather, this clinical material is considered in a phenomenological way to study what is happening in the contact between therapist and client. A detailed description of segments from each of the three extracts will be given, with comments about the process of the work.

Segment 1

This segment of thirty seconds is taken from the first assessment session. While the therapist has been to the client's house to introduce herself to the client, it is the first time that the therapist and client have met in the clinical setting. There has been a musical greeting at the beginning of the session, and now the therapist and client are embarking on the precarious and exciting task of finding a way of being together in the music therapy situation. In the research, the three viewers have noted this segment as one in which there is connection between the client and therapist. At the point of description (one minute and thirty-two seconds into the extract) the viewers have noted a change in connection, as the client has begun to use her gestures deliberately to influence the musical dialogue.

Figure 6.1 Commentary

The simplicity of the music echoes the tentative strand of contact that is being created. The therapist is working slowly and sensitively, ensuring that she does not overwhelm the client with her musical presence. She is musically reflecting and confirming the quality of relatedness. She has chosen to use firstly her voice, and then the metallophone (an instrument with a gentle ringing sound). Both have a warmth that is welcoming, and not intrusive; they invite rather than demand a response. The client has appeared to hear and take in these musical interventions, and is beginning to respond with a deliberate communication of her own. She lifts her hand and opens it (1:38), and the therapist responds with a musical phrase on the metallophone, reflecting the affective quality of the client's gesture. There is suddenly a different feeling; a stronger connection has been made and is sustained.

The therapist's notes in this session include the following: 'D seemed bewildered at first – a new situation. Making contact at D's pace felt important

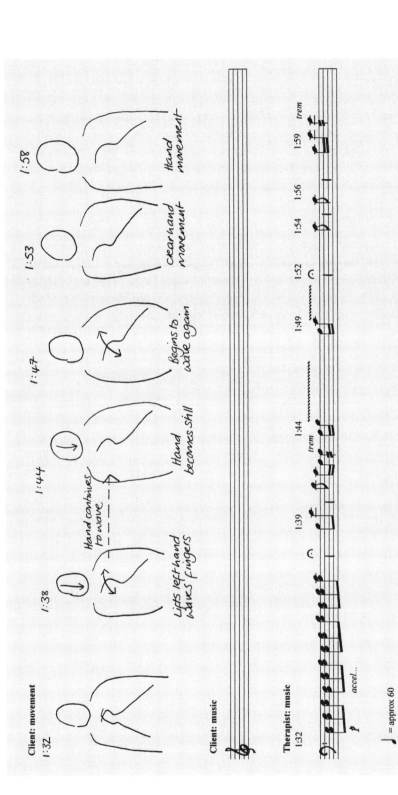

Figure 6.1 Segment 1.

– important not to overwhelm D. Felt *very* important to *wait* for D, *not* to rush in with sound. To create a space where she felt she could make a connection'. In this intitial session the connection feels fragile and uncertain. The therapist, working with the dynamics of the musical relating, is able to process her experience of the contact and develop her therapeutic interventions accordingly. A thinking and musical space is created where a direct connection is possible between the therapist and client.

Manuscript (see Figure 6.1)

The manuscript enables us to see how the relatedness develops. At 1:38 we can see the movement of the client's left hand, and the therapist's clear response to this deliberate gesture (on the metallophone). As the client continues to move her hand, the therapist supports and acknowledges this movement with a repeated note (1:41) and then holds and captures the quality of these movements with a trill, as the client becomes still (1:44) by providing this holding function in her music, she provides a relational and musical environment that the client can easily return to. This is indeed what happens at 1:47 with the client making a number of clear hand movements, and initiating a phrase of strongly imitative responses between client and therapist. In this segment, the manuscript shows how the therapist's music attunes cross-modally to the client's gestures by matching the intensity, timing and movement in physical space of the client's gesture.

Segment 2

This segment of one minute and nineteen seconds is taken from the second assessment session. This segment starts at the very beginning of the session. The therapist is building on the work in the first session, and has chosen to use the chime bars. This both enables the musical quality of the first session to be brought to mind, and allows the therapist to be nearer to the client. She also uses her voice. As the session develops, both client and therapist use their voices.

Figure 6.2 Commentary

Using her understanding of the relating in the previous sessions the therapist has identified a need for a more prominent containing function and uses the

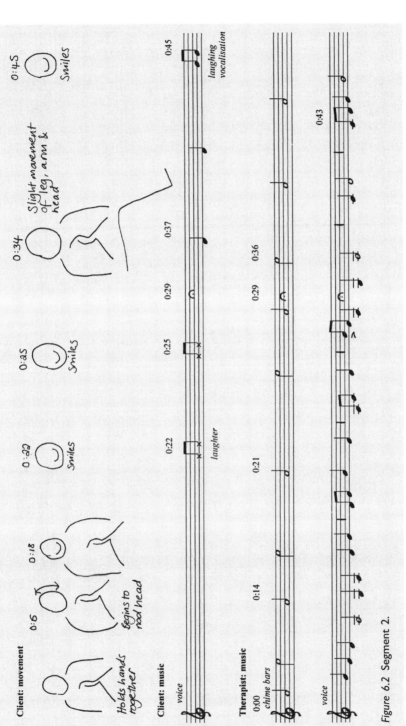

Figure 6.2 Segment 2.

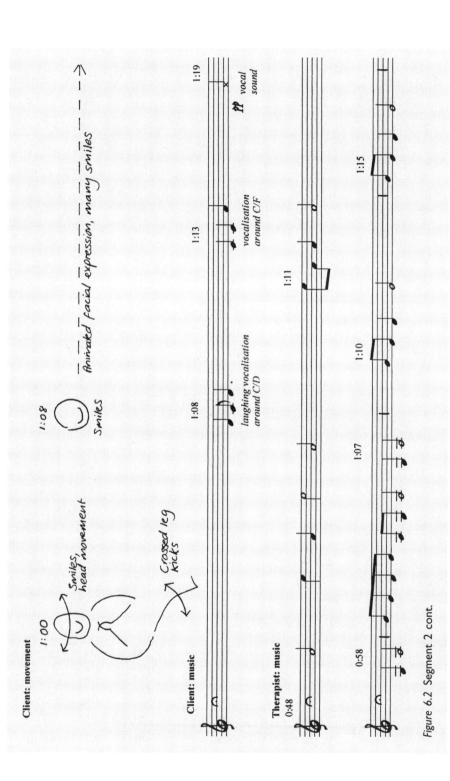

Figure 6.2 Segment 2 cont.

chime bars to provide a musical framework or boundary for the client. She uses only two notes – again matching the minimal nature of the client's movements and sounds. The chime bars act to provide a musical holding or container, within which the therapist and client explore with their voices. The connection begins almost at once, as the client begins to use facial and vocal communications. The therapist uses a vocal line to respond, and excitingly, the client uses her own voice in response. Then follows a vocal dialogue of short musical phrases, which feels strongly connected. As this segment continues, and the contact deepens and intensifies, the client uses musical, facial and gestural modalities, becoming very engaged in the dialogue.

Again the therapist uses her experience and understanding of their relating to develop the process of the session and her notes are useful to explore this: '... finding out will the other respond ... felt fragile, very detailed – tiny sounds, need to respond to these delicate signals'. The contact feels very real, and very fragile and vulnerable. She realises that D's need to have control is important: 'felt D would make the choice whether to become involved; that D would shut off if the contact was not as D wanted it.' She uses the chime bars to provide musical containment, which feels safe, and within this, follows D, responding to vocal, facial and gestural modalities, giving her the control that feels so important. She also notes 'a feeling of delight in this connection', and uses this to inform her musical reponses.

Manuscript (see Figure 6.2)

Again, by following the manuscript, we can see the connections that are described by the therapist. We see from 00:0 to 1:07 the way in which the chime bars provide a continuous regular musical line that acts to contain the musical relatedness. Once the vocal contact is securely established (at 1:13) the chime bar line becomes more flexible, perhaps where it is no longer needed to be a rigid container. We can trace the client's level of engagement on the manuscript, which begins with a movement of the head (1:15), then a smile (0:18), then vocal sounds (from 0:22) and leg movements (0:34 and 1:00). Later in the extract (not shown) the client reaches towards the therapist as they sing together. The vocal dialogue, which the therapist describes as very connected, can be traced between the parts of the therapist and client on the musical staves. There is clearly musical connection that is seen in the rhythmic and harmonic matches beween the parts. The therapist's written notes add to the clinical picture by giving the emotional qualities present in the relating.

Segment 3

This segment of one minute in length is taken from the end of the third assessment. It has felt difficult for the client and therapist to get into contact with each other; it is a hot and muggy day and the client seems to need to rest. She has engaged with the therapist and has used the wind chime, but now has slowly moved to rest her head comfortably on the side of her chair.

Figure 6.3 Commentary

The therapist is using her voice to reflect the different qualities and dynamic feel of the session. She is available to the client for more active involvement but does not demand this. She does not try to generate a different response from the client, but accompanies her mood or 'way of being' in the session. The therapist's notes show how she works with the client's silence: 'therapist's music felt like a match of the quality of D's silence and behaviour'. The therapist responds to the client's use of this part of the session and her own experience of this. She creates a smooth vocal line, which cross-modally matches the client's physical posture (which is relaxed and still), and the calm companionable quality of their relating. The client watches the therapist and is held engaged throughout this part of the session. While the client is not using the musical medium, the therapist is able to 'voice' the characteristics of the connection betwen them, through her clinical improvisation.

Manuscript (see Figure 6.3)

We can see here the importance of documenting the use of modalities other than music, particularly in this field of work where the client may not have the ability to use many instruments. We can see from the line drawing that the client adopts a relaxed and open posture, resting her head on the chair while she watches the therapist (3:12). The therapist's vocal line is quite low in pitch, and is slow, using long sustained notes and many pauses. This echoes the stillness of the client and the increased musical space between them, while maintaining a sense of movement – keeping the engaged quality alive and further musical dialogue possible. The therapist's musical line enables the client to be still and silent (perhaps showing a need for more distance in the relatedness today) while still remaining engaged.

Client: movement
3:12

Rests head on wheelchair

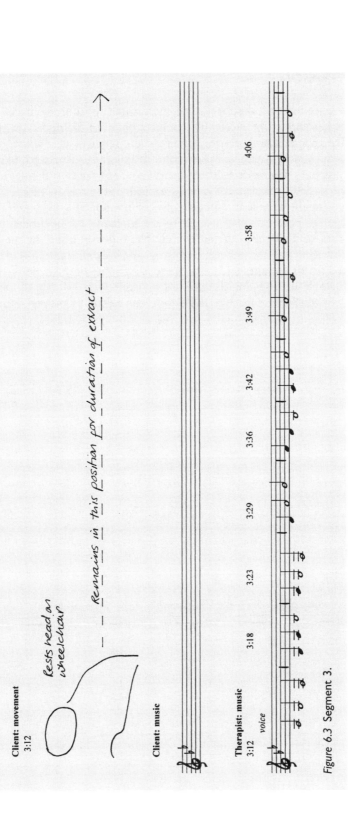

– – – Remains in this position for duration of extract – – – – – – – →

Client: music

Therapist: music
3:12

voice

3:18   3:23   3:29   3:36   3:42   3:49   3:58   4:06

Figure 6.3 Segment 3.

CONCLUSION

The presentation and description of these three short segments of clinical material has shown the incredibly complex detail of the music therapy session. The commentary accompanying each segment has illustrated the author's approach, giving an insight into the therapist's clinical thinking, and displaying, in the manuscript, the practical result of the clinical interventions. The clinical descriptions have given examples of the way in which therapist and client might be able to connect and begin a dialogue in the music therapy situation. Where clients struggle to use language, the possibility of a different kind of dialogue is certainly valuable; more so when the medium of communication has the ability to convey qualities of emotion and feeling. Sinason's words are apposite here: 'there is meaning in the actions and feelings of people with severe disabilties' (Sinason 1992: 77). Music therapy is one way in which these feelings and actions can be communicated and shared.

Chapter 7

Music therapy and neurology

Cathy Durham

INTRODUCTION

Many music therapists will encounter people with some brain damage in the course of their work. This chapter is specifically concerned with people who have led 'normal' lives but who have acquired brain damage later in life due either to trauma, stroke or degenerative neurological conditions such as multiple sclerosis, Parkinson's Disease or Huntington's Disease. However, similar types of disabilities and the emotional distress that accompanies them may be found within the context of different client groups; for example, people brain-damaged at birth within the field of learning disabilities, and those with Alzheimer's Disease in the 'older adult' client group.

This chapter starts with a brief overview of different types of neuro-disability, followed by a discussion of how music affects the brain and then how some music therapy techniques may be used within a neurological context. The three case studies that follow illuminate human dilemmas, which have been worked with in music therapy.

NEURO-DISABILITY

Brain damage usually causes both physical and cognitive disability. With degenerative diseases, the onset may be slow and insidious or rapid. In Huntingdon's Disease (Magee 1995), Parkinson's Disease (Erdonmez 1993) and multiple sclerosis (Magee 1999) the process is irreversible and therefore brings with it perhaps terrifying issues of life and death. With sudden traumatic injury or a stroke, an immediate and sometimes catastrophic change occurs in a person's life. Disabilities may be so extensive and severe that they appear to radically alter pre-morbid personalities. Therefore the patient is not the only casualty; family and friends suffer a loss of the person they once knew. A cerebrovascular accident (CVA or stroke) is caused by bleeding within the brain. Head trauma is caused mainly by road traffic accidents but also from falls, assaults or sporting injuries. Anoxic damage (oxygen starvation of the brain) causes multiple and complex disabilities because the brain damage is often global. Events leading up to the trauma may be distressing in themselves. Anoxia has many causes: violent asphyxiation, heart attacks or drowning. Infections such as meningitis and tumours account for some severe cases of neuro-disability.

When a person has experienced brain injury, they are often referred to a rehabilitation unit once medically stable. The emphasis there is on intensive therapeutic input from a multidisciplinary team over a specific period, generally measured in months rather than years. Much of the work is based on the model of neuroplasticity.[1] Although in some cases extensive recovery is possible for the patient, many people return to the community with complex disabilities and are somehow expected to come to terms with their loss. They may live in nursing homes with minimal therapeutic input. There is an urgent need for any kind of therapy service in the community that will stimulate these individuals and attend to their feelings. There are many people who could be reached by music therapy.

HOW DOES MUSIC AFFECT THE BRAIN?

Our brains are enormously complex and despite recent research we are still at the stage of knowing little about how they work. In fact, some of the research on music and brain function seems contradictory and it is difficult to make generalisations. Certainly people with similar types of traumatic brain injury show unique patterns of response and behaviour, even allowing for personality differences. Some isolated disabilities result in extraordinary and fascinating behaviour as described in the collection of narrative case studies by Oliver Sacks (1985). There is some evidence that some musical skills are anatomically located in specific sites in the brain, for example, timbre discrimination within the right temporal lobe (Samson and Zatorre 1993). However, there is little evidence for a 'musical centre' in the brain (Sloboda 1985: 265). Both Sloboda and Storr (Storr 1997: 37–39) summarise research that identifies the left and right hemispheres in the brain cortex as having different general functions.[2]

A holistic view of brain function in relation to music may be helpful to music therapists. Pribham (1993) and his team at Stanford University have devised holoscapes; a way of representing three-dimensional images of

1 This provides evidence that the brain will respond to injury by reorganisation and adaptation aimed at restoring function. Therefore rehabilitation requires extensive, repetitive, intensive stimulation. New pathways in the brain can be manipulated and restructured.
2 The left hemisphere is specialised for more analytic tasks and the right for more global tasks; or left for abstraction and right for empathy according to Storr (1997). Reverse this for left-handed people.

brain function. Their findings suggest that musical response involves the whole brain.[3] This suggests that music could be a powerful clinical tool to use within neuro-disability.

Musical structure can help us organise and retrieve information. One example is the coordination of body movements to regular rhythmic structure, as in the case of a woman with Parkinson's Disease, who was unable to start walking until the therapist sang a strongly rhythmic song (Erdonmez 1993: 114). A woman I worked with who had anoxic brain damage was unable to walk unless her attention was focused by singing a repetitive song she had memorised. The sequence of manoeuvres required for tying laces was only possible for an autistic boy when put into a song sequence (Nordoff and Robbins 1971: 105). These same techniques could be used with anyone who has difficulties remembering sequences. Reminiscence work with patients with short-term memory problems shows that singing familiar songs helps access long-term memory. Purdie's work with a woman who could sing but not speak demonstrates how music can be used to retrieve language by using different neural pathways (Purdie and Baldwin 1994: 22 and see Simpson 2000). In contrast client and therapist may often explore ways in which music can be made together without the therapist holding any fixed expectations. Thinking about the balance between the need for structure and flexibility is helpful. Precomposed music provides familiarity and set structures that can be altered by the therapist to suit the clinical need. Improvisation incorporating various degrees of structure can be powerful and flexible in an immediate way.

However, there are some common neurological problems that restrict a creative response. A person with *dyspraxia* may have the intention to play an instrument or sing but might be unable to plan and carry out this movement. Sometimes as therapist I have been unable to 'read' the person's intention and remain unaware of what is trying to be done. Heavier breathing is often a sign that someone is trying hard to move. This needs really sensitive understanding. Someone may have problems with *initiating* a movement, or a musical idea. The therapist providing a musical cue with a predictable phrase ending can help someone predict and provide the last note or even begin more continuous music. Others are *disinhibited* and find it difficult to stop playing. The therapist might decide to intervene or distract at this point. *Perseveration* is when a person is stuck in a repetitive sequence of behaviour and may not be aware of this. The therapist may also get musically 'stuck'. I have found that a very clear strong musical challenge is needed if this happens. Some people choose to use their neurological disabilities creatively. One man with *clonus* (tremor) in his left hand used this movement to play rapid triplet beats on a cymbal. In case study two Tom uses his wheelchair as an instrument.

3 This holistic response seems to be regulated by the frontal lobes of the brain. Pribham (1993) suggests that music *in itself* is stored in the brain in some way.

CLINICAL EXAMPLES

The following case study shows how multidisciplinary work can be valuable for someone with such severe disabilities. We will also discover that structure and consistency within a distraction-free environment are essential for someone who is unable to attend selectively to noises in the external environment. These principles are adopted in the practice of sensory stimulation on rehabilitation units.

Case study 1: 'Simeon'

Simeon was a man in his sixties who had a severe stroke. He was admitted to a neurological rehabilitation unit, then referred to music therapy by the team. They were concerned by his agitation and lack of reaction to his immediate environment. Simeon had apparently lost all sight but was likely to respond to sound and touch. He could move his upper body only. He did not speak and did not show any signs of understanding speech. My first impression of him was that he was never still. His left arm constantly wandered seemingly without purpose. His breathing was laboured and he groaned on every out-breath. His eyes were open but unfocused. It seemed as though the only thing that prevented him from pushing himself from his wheelchair onto the floor was a tray fixed in front. Simeon's knees shook[4] and his torso and head rocked. His inner state must have been one of turmoil and confusion.

When I first met Simeon his breathing became a little more shallow and rushed. This gave me some sense that he knew I was there. As I introduced myself his left hand moved from the tray and touched his forehead briefly before returning, something I hadn't seen before.

His relatives described him as a man who had enjoyed a relaxed lifestyle, often drinking in bars until late with friends. He had loved dancing. I reflected, with some irony, that he was still very physically active, in contrast to many of the other patients on the unit who were either paralysed or moved in slow motion. Perhaps together we could find a way that he could relate his body movements to his external environment in a meaningful way, as he used to when dancing. This might also lead to the development of our relationship and possibly help to reduce his inner confusion.

The occupational therapist, Sue, had discovered that Simeon had responded most consistently to sound and touch in sensory tests. She had developed a

---

4 Clonus produces uncontrolled shaking in a particular body part. Sometimes it is possible to stop a leg shaking in this way by leaning gently but firmly on the knee. The foot must be firmly grounded.

Figure 7.1 Synchronising of phrasing with Simeon's breathing.

strong empathic relationship with Simeon. As she could advise on positioning of instruments and how to support Simeon physically, we decided to work
together for his assessment. Eventually we chose to work together throughout the period of therapy, which lasted for seven months.

Faced with difficult decisions about how to use music with Simeon I first
focused on his breathing. Playing minor chords on the guitar, I sang his name
several times, synchronising the phrasing to coincide with his breathing. The
pitch of the first note of each phrase was the same as the pitch he vocalised.
With excitement I noticed that as I sang his breathing slowed a little. After
four phrases his vocalising stopped altogether (see Figure 7.1). Was he
listening? I continued a little and then brought the music to a close. After a
few seconds of tense silence, his vocalising began again and we repeated the
whole process. At the same time, Sue had been stroking his arm. This had
the effect of further calming him. As we continued to work together we
began to synchronise the singing and stroking. Working with a co-therapist
was helpful with such a physically disabled man and I found our shared evalu-
ations after sessions supportive.

Simeon was often fatigued and had difficulty breathing. Coughing left him
exhausted. When this happened I felt the music needed to be rhythmically
solid and consistent, to help him regulate his breathing. Far from just trying

to make communicative contact it began to feel that I was involved in the responsibility of helping him to survive. This belief was reinforced by the observation that Simeon's breathing altered in response to the music. It made me feel almost omnipotent. I decided to increase the sessions to two per week, unconsciously reinforcing this feeling. In the third session Simeon's left hand moved forward and touched the guitar that was balanced on his tray. With a little physical support under his wrist from Sue he was able to move his fingers slightly against the guitar strings.

In the sessions that followed Simeon began to develop his purposeful reaching out to explore other instruments placed at the same point on the tray. He reached out consistently whenever he heard a new sound and seemed particularly motivated by a seed cluster and a beaded calabash. He could grasp them but didn't seem to know what to do next. However, with the guitar Simeon always reached out as soon as the music had started and particularly if the tempo was swung. At times Simeon would spontaneously tap the tray or the side of his wheelchair during strongly rhythmic music I played, influencing the tempo and shaping the music more actively. His left knee jigged more vigorously when the music contained a strong dynamic or pulse, conveying more of his emotional response.

As months passed, Simeon still showed no real indication of understanding language. We had seen him touching his nose spontaneously, but when asked by the speech therapist to do so, he did not. But in relation to the elements of music, Simeon did show more awareness. He was responding to pitch changes in the music by altering his own vocalisations to match my singing more closely. He was responding to rhythmic change in the music by shaking his knee or hand, and was influencing rhythmic change himself. He identified instruments by sound alone and reached out to specific favourites. He also responded to increases in loudness by deeper breathing and more vigorous body movements.

Simeon's responses to formal neuropsychological tests together with brain scans showed he had extensive cognitive damage. Team members said that it was unlikely that he was able to conceptualise what had happened to him, so had minimal insight into his situation. Perhaps this was a blessing? However, I had reasons to suspect that Simeon may have felt a sense of loss and this was addressed in one particular session. He was seized by a burst of racking coughing. As his face grew red I fearfully wondered if he was actually going to survive this episode. Eventually it stopped. Simeon, exhausted, produced huge tears that soundlessly coursed down his cheeks. This felt so right given his circumstances. Sue and I also felt our own tears well up. We left Simeon's

Figure 7.2 Improvised voice and guitar.

tears on his face so he could continue to feel them, eventually drying them off as he was unable to hold a tissue. Then as he continued to weep I sang some improvised music accompanied by the guitar which eventually brought the session to a close (see Figure 7.2).

After this particular session Sue and I were glad we had shared grief with Simeon. His contact with the outside world was so tenuous and crying together was a very normal, human thing to do. It also showed us how hard it was for us to stay with Simeon. Providing much of the musical material myself in Simeon's sessions meant that I relied heavily on what I believed were counter-transference feelings to inform the music. This sometimes weighed heavily on me and I needed to question whether these were Simeon's feelings or my own. It was helpful to explore these doubts in supervision. After this Simeon's agitation lessened for a couple of weeks and his vocalising became more responsive and wide-ranging. We continued to see him twice a week until he was discharged to a nursing home a month later, seeming to be more at peace with himself.

Simeon was one of the few profoundly brain-injured people I have known who actually managed to overtly express such grief. Yet for any non-verbal person who has experienced devastating loss, music continues to be a vital way of reaching and expressing those very deep feelings. In the following story, by contrast, Tom was a verbally articulate man. Here, I used a different way of thinking. This was influenced by the concept of primary and secondary handicap described by Valerie Sinason in relation to the field of learning

disabilities (Sinason 1992: 7, 112). She identifies primary handicap as resulting from organic damage. Secondary handicap, however, is the defensive use
or abuse the individual makes of the primary damage. This can be significantly
more powerful than the primary handicap. With Tom, music therapy offered
some opportunities to combat the primary disability, such as encouraging use
of his left hand to reroute neural pathways, but the main focus of the work
was for him to discover what he felt about his own disabilities and how he
dealt with the reactions of other people.

Case study 2: 'Tom'

When Tom was in his late twenties he had a head-on collision when driving
and sustained damage to the right side and also the frontal lobes of his brain.
Five years later, with Tom living in the family home, his parents sought music
therapy privately. Tom depended on a wheelchair most of the time. His use
of language was fairly unaffected by his accident but speech was slurred and
difficult to understand because of poor physical articulation. Because the right
side of the brain was damaged his left side was weak and he had some perceptual neglect on this side.[5] He had frequent outbursts of temper, likely to
be explained by the frontal lobe damage, since it is this area that is known
to be related to inhibition of responses. This point clearly relates to Tom's
primary handicap.

First meeting

Tom came with his sister who explained that they hoped music therapy would
allow Tom to begin to express some of his 'locked-up' feelings. She said he
needed opportunities to practise his speech in a safe setting with someone
he would get to know. Tom's temper was seriously affecting his life. He would
often get angry and sometimes violent in social situations. Then people would
ask him to leave.

Alone, Tom himself was chatty, friendly and showed quite a developed sense
of humour. He tried a metallophone using a beater with his right hand. He
began with a regular pulse on seemingly random notes and then initiated short,
simple, rhythmic patterns within this. Tom seemed quite comfortable when

---

5 This meant that he simply did not notice objects to his left and was unaware of any stimulus that side.

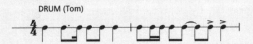

Figure 7.3 Tom's 'rugby' rhythm.

I played quietly with him in the same pulse at the piano but if I shifted the pulse myself even slightly he 'cut off' by putting the beaters down. I soon noted that this musical disconnecting occurred when I made any reference to his future, a subject that must have been painful to him.

Early sessions

Tom agreed to try music therapy on a trial basis for six weeks.

In the first session I set up a 'kit' of percussion instruments grouped together on Tom's right side so he could see and reach them easily. Tom was groggy from anti-epileptic medication. He seemed a little overawed by the situation, and dealt with this by spending ten minutes talking. He told me that he had tried playing the piano at home after his first visit, but that he had been 'unsuccessful' compared to what I could do. I explained that I had been learning the piano for many years, and that one might expect me to have more facility. He agreed, then went on to say that he was 'an expert at doing nothing', laughing in an exaggerated manner. It seemed that if he made a comment that related to his sense of inadequacy, he immediately made light of it by joking. Then he picked up a beater and played loudly a fairly universal rhythm I associated with childhood and he associated with rugby matches (see Figure 7.3). We explored a few minutes of turn-taking just using this rhythm, and Tom tried out each instrument in the room to his right side. Later in the session he fell asleep. I wondered how taxing it was for him to be touching on his feelings in quite a new way.

The following week Tom talked about his accident. He could not remember it, he said, but 'it sounded like a nightmare'. Immediately he started testing boundaries by asking me to 'sit on his knee'. I explained I wouldn't and why, and he immediately began beating the 'rugby' rhythm on a conga drum forcibly. Soon, with some encouragement, he began to use the palm of his weaker left hand to play the same drum. Then he raised his arm very high and stung himself slightly when he brought it down on the drum, taking a risk. Perhaps heartened by this he then asked to play the piano with me. He insisted I played with one finger so that my music wouldn't overwhelm his. As he was leaving Tom went out of his way to say that he had not got annoyed in the sessions so far. By contrast I felt that his feelings of anger had been quite close to the surface. Somehow his contact with the instruments brought up some feelings of inadequacy and fear of failure.

In following sessions strong characteristics emerged in Tom's music. He tested his strength and the durability of the instruments in each session. He said 'I could hit harder, but I don't want to break *your* instruments'. I said I thought *the* instruments were fairly durable; maybe they could stand being hit harder. After this 'permission' he hit drums so hard with a beater in his right hand that I did wonder if the skins would stand up to it; they did. He ended sessions with the loud sustained blast on a reed horn. Later he began to pretend to hit instruments very hard by raising the beater well over his head, bringing it down hard with great control and stopping it centimetres in front of the skin. He laughed if I misread his intent and played something very loud on the piano when he just tapped. I became the one in the session who was allowed to make the 'mistake' of playing dangerously loud. Tom put himself in the position of being the one who contained his feelings. During improvisations when he played on the drum kit and I played the piano, I worked hard at following and mirroring him, providing a sparser texture and a quieter dynamic than his. At first his music was level in volume and speed although after a few improvisations he introduced very slow crescendi.

Over the course of a 15-minute improvisation the volume and speed could slowly creep up, led by Tom. Then he stopped with no warning, saying that I was playing incredibly loud and that my playing was too aggressive. Although much of the time Tom did not seem to be able to own his part of the uncontrolled feeling of the music, during turn-taking exchanges I was aware that some of my piano-playing had an unusually harsh touch. I felt that I was acting out some of the anger that Tom was unable to express. To make this process more conscious I suggested to Tom that he played some of the loudness himself. When he did this, and the instruments still didn't break, Tom laughed a lot and seemed to feel safer. At the end of the session he asked me out of the blue whether I was married. Was this a sign he felt closer?

Exploring expression through loudness

Once the assessment was over Tom agreed to a further six months of therapy, a period where Tom found it very difficult to play music at all. He spent most of the time telling me funny stories about his carers. Once I asked him if he was feeling reluctant to play. He retorted very angrily that I was aggressive, completely wrong, and now I'd be upset for being so wrong. Then he

Figure 7.4 Joint play: Tom and Cathy.

picked up a beater and played the metallophone so quietly I could hardly hear; the notes were random, slow moving and totally different in mood from the predictable rhythms and pulse he generally chose. I joined him using one finger on the piano, and this music continued for some length of time (see Figure 7.4). I felt that Tom was really asking me to listen and making me work very hard not to drown him. This music seemed tentative; a side of Tom that he'd not expressed before in music.

Then as the therapy was extended again, there began a time where he experimented with enormous variety of volume. I had never heard anyone produce such a range of tone colours, note shapes and lengths on a single reed horn. He also began to play on many different surfaces, including parts of his wheelchair. Tom used the carpet, the wall, his leg and his coffee cup as resonating surfaces, and used the ends of beaters, his cigarette lighter, his fingers and his coffee cup on drum surfaces. Using the 'rugby' rhythm, leaving the last two notes for me to play each time, he built up a huge collage of sound. Then he grew tired of this rhythm, and said that he could go on playing this same rhythm for ever, but that would be dull. I commented that by using the same rhythm for weeks he had managed to express it creatively in a very wide variety of ways. He said 'I suppose so' but the tangible evidence of his improved self-esteem was his leaving me in a higher mood than when he arrived. The times when Tom talked rather than played had less of a feeling of avoidance now, being rather a natural resting point from the music.

Facing the trauma of his accident

In one session Tom began describing his week as having been a bit of a 'crash, bang, wallop', demonstrating this on three instruments. He then related this to his life, and said he would have preferred not to have had the 'wallop', which meant his car crash. Immediately he picked up a cimbala[6] and plectrum, and played for about twenty minutes. I supported on the cello. Because of the summer heat one of the cimbala strings began to go out of tune. Tom focused on this note increasingly, so that he was choosing to be 'out of key' with the music. Eventually he almost threw the instrument down and said he had 'played it to death'. He was very quiet then until the end of the session.

The following week he mentioned an ex-girlfriend and an absent family member. He also mentioned walking to the local off-licence. 'It isn't far away but it's a long way *for me*'. It seemed that Tom was beginning to want to talk about things in his life that he had lost. At the same time, he seemed to be seeking my support in the music more. Turn-taking on the 'rugby' rhythm became a focus of exchange; he left much more space for me to play the last two notes, and also he waited for me to play the initial cue several times. He said 'we work well as a team'. Tom also began to try to delay the ends of the sessions, playing after I'd said it was time to finish, and told me several times how much he enjoyed the sessions. He seemed quite emotionally needy at this time.

In one session Tom was very tired, so I played some music for him to listen to. During this he fell asleep. I continued to play for about ten minutes, and found myself playing a lullaby in three-four time as if he were a small child. As I gradually began to enliven the beat, he woke up, and didn't believe me when I said he'd been asleep. He said to me 'I expect you're a mother, aren't you'. This seemed quite a change from his earlier flirtatious self, who tested boundaries by touching my knees with beaters and asking me if I was married.

The following week Tom decided to describe in detail what had happened in the accident, and the consequences. Infuriatingly, this was the only time the privacy of the session was invaded at any point in the therapy. A workman came in, ignoring 'session in progress' signs. This did not put Tom off, and he continued to talk. It helped, I think, that the man had entered the room to Tom's left side where Tom has neglect. Tom then said that anyone else in his circumstances would be '*very pissed off*', but that *he* wasn't. 'I

6 Small harp from Eastern Europe.

generally work very hard at avoiding being pissed off'. This meant that we could talk directly about how he did try to deal with his loss, and the fact that he had a lot of anger stored up that generally surfaced when he was under pressure. He talked about what happened when he lost his temper and how he had been excluded from some places. He said he was afraid of 'losing it' and he was always getting into trouble. Tom then decided to 'have fun' for the rest of the session, and spent most of his time playing the swannee whistle and the flexatone in quite an extreme way, laughing wildly. The music was like *Tom and Jerry* cartoon music.

Three years later

Tom continues to attend music therapy. He has spent much of his time thinking about possible future relationships, but now concentrates more on the good relationships he has now. His sense of humour helps him through the setbacks he continues to face. He tends to sing more in improvisations, an indication of trust and more personal self-expression. He enjoys playing virtuosic flourishes on the piano with his right hand, and I enjoy playing with them.

Within a medical framework, it could be said that Tom displays many traits of someone who has experienced severe brain damage. He is often 'disinhibited' and 'inappropriate', has memory problems and impaired concentration. He has also been described as lacking insight and the ability to fully conceptualise his situation. However, from my experience of my relationship with him I believe that much of Tom's 'inappropriate' anger stems from an extremely painful sense of loss and a keen sensitivity to being patronised. He has found it difficult to articulate what it is that makes him angry, not from misunderstanding the situation but because it is painful to acknowledge where he is.

In Tom's case, he has begun to look positively towards the future. For Frankie, the situation was different because of the disease she had. 'The future' was something that was not broached by either of us. Staying in the 'here and now' of each session was extremely important, as it often is in a palliative care setting.

Case study 3: 'Frankie'

Frankie was referred to music therapy when she left home to live in a nursing home. She was forty and had advanced multiple sclerosis. She was wheelchair-bound, nearly blind with ataxic[7] arm movements. Her son had sought the referral through his GP. He felt that despite being confused, she was very aware of having 'lost' her house. He was afraid she would deteriorate very quickly now, although she had fought the illness for many years. However, she enjoyed singing songs from the sixties, and often would seem happiest when engaged in music in some way. From the way he spoke it was evident that he was struggling with dignity to face the inevitable. His mother had a deteriorating condition and the move to a nursing home was an admission by both of them that she was unlikely to get well again.

When I first met Frankie alone for an assessment session she appeared cheerful, willing to participate in anything. She grabbed instruments firmly that I held out for her to explore and immediately began shaking them rhythmically. Her playing was strangely euphoric. I found myself playing strong Latin rhythms with her when she played any shaking instrument. The music felt almost brash in its vigour and almost out of control. The same thing occurred when she tried the autoharp, playing it using a large plectrum she could grip. She strummed all strings vigorously forcing the autoharp to vibrate so fully I wondered if it would fall apart. This was partly due to the wide sideways ataxic movement produced by her hands. However, by placing the autoharp in front of her at a fixed point across her midline, she could begin to reduce the ataxia and focus her movements down. Frankie seemed cheered by the session and declared 'that was lovely'. She said 'yes' eagerly when I suggested six more sessions before a mutual review. From discussion with other colleagues, clients with multiple sclerosis sometimes show exaggeration of personality in some way, almost larger than life. I thought Frankie had a kind of exaggerated enthusiasm.

In early sessions, Frankie's music was strongly coloured in mood, but with very little variation. Her music was characterised in the following ways:

- the pulse was fixed rhythmically;
- there was no dynamic variation;
- her music would suddenly stop without warning as she tired;
- she seemed only to play 'cheerful' music.

7 Ataxia involves wide shaking movements.

Frankie often responded to an improvisation with comments like 'that was really lovely' but said little else. Her use of language seemed to be as restricted in tone as the moods in the music. I wondered whether the sessions were helping her maintain an almost desperate sense of positive happiness in the face of her illness. Was this a necessary form of denial? I was aware of the feeling I often had of the music being slightly unstable. Therefore, I suggested playing in a more structured way. By alternating short phrases we were generally able to exchange phrases of equal lengths, although soon Frankie still fell into a fixed beating pattern seemingly oblivious to my music. I would often interrupt this pattern in my music to try and contain the sense of 'being out of control'. It felt like trying to stop some kind of runaway vehicle. Frankie usually seemed surprised briefly but then cheerfully resumed the exchange.

In the fourth session, by playing one simple note at a time, the situation changed. Frankie began to explore different ways of playing her note; loud, soft, delayed, resonant or muted. Her language also became more expressive. She said 'gentle' or 'strong' while she played her note, reinforcing her intention. She played one note on a slit drum, said 'I don't like that one, I like this' and swept the wind chimes. I said that the wind chimes sound continued but the slit drum note stopped short. 'Yes', she responded, 'deadened'. The symbolism was obvious. I asked her if it was important that notes 'kept going'. 'Yes', she said emphatically; 'the music must be cheerful'. Notice the connection between 'keeping going' and 'cheerful'.

Frankie was keen on songs by Abba. She often asked to sing one particular song, 'Money, money, money'. She couldn't explain the personal significance; she lacked the words. However, the line 'It's a rich man's world' offered certain possibilities; it was certainly not Frankie's world. Despite forgetting all previous sessions[8] she always asked for the same song. I sometimes suggested other Abba songs. If I said the first word she would remember the rest of the title. During the next five months, Frankie worked on remembering these songs. At first she was able to sing only the last word in a line using the rest of the line as a cue, but later she was able to sing the first verse and chorus of four Abba songs. This was a real achievement, despite increasing memory problems. Our exchanges became more varied in colour and variety. Frankie was gaining ground in terms of her creativity despite a deteriorating condition.

---

8 'Carryover' from one session to the next is significant when clients have serious memory problems.

This was not to last. Frankie had a severe bout of flu and missed six weeks of therapy. She returned with increased ataxia and reduced concentration. She began to fixate on one song, and played no instruments. I felt dismayed; it seemed that our work together had been lost. Was six weeks enough to wipe it all out? Almost in despair I turned to the cello. Frankie sat in silence; I played the melodies of our old songs. And then Frankie began to hum. Was this a new connection between us in the music, or an echo of the old one? For two months we continued in this vein, rarely speaking, but quietly making music. Moods had changed; there was no more euphoria. It was important just to be there alongside. I mourned the loss of the musical connection we once had, maybe bearing just a tiny part of her own losses.

Working with anyone who is dying raises the question of when one actually stops therapy. Sometimes this is determined by external factors or the death itself. In the end, with Frankie, she became quickly very ill and I spent our last session together just playing the songs on the cello before saying goodbye for the last time.

SUMMARY

The music therapist working in a neurological field deals with a range of musical and personal challenges. Because of the wide range of disabilities caused by brain damage (primary handicap), both physical and cognitive, there are very specific limitations imposed on a client's creativity. Structure or simplicity may aid the client to find more freedom of expression and control within these constraints, the use of counter-transference feelings may inform the music when most must be provided by the therapist. In all three case studies, bereavement and loss were the dominant issues. The impact of sudden trauma on any life has far-reaching consequences for that person's future and for those who love them. A degenerative illness produces cumulative loss. Other people's reactions to these changes in circumstance combined with the client's own response often produce a very powerful secondary handicap. In Tom's case, music therapy is enabling him to become aware of his own reaction to his situation, and also how he responds to others. For Frankie, the cheerful mask she presented with each week in the early stages suddenly became less necessary as she approached death.

There are few music therapists who work in this important and interesting area. Specialist knowledge gained from working in a multidisciplinary team can make the understanding of the primary handicap much clearer. Also there are many community clients who could be seen by music therapists who are sensitive to the possible secondary handicap. Regular supervision helps and also the use of adapted instruments, possibly electronic, accessible to those with severe physical disabilities. The most important principles of all are those of flexibility and openness of heart and mind.

FURTHER MUSIC THERAPY READING

Read Usher (1998) and Magee's response (1998) for a discussion of consciousness and a review of the literature. Also read Aldridge (1996, 2000), Bruscia (1991) and Ansdell (1995) for a variety of moving case studies.

Chapter 8

Music therapy in forensic psychiatry: a case study with musical commentary

Ann Sloboda and Richard Bolton

INTRODUCTION (Ann Sloboda and Richard Bolton)

Music therapists are generally required to be able to analyse their music as part of their training. In the workplace their music takes place within a therapeutic relationship. As such, their analysis tends to focus on those aspects of the musical interaction that will inform both their own clinical judgement and that of colleagues who are not trained to interpret musical phenomena. These aspects typically comprise a patient's interaction, communication and self-expression, as indicated by the way a patient plays a musical instrument, or musical parameters such as dynamics and articulation.

In contrast to this broad interpretation of the term 'analysis' (which might in addition be informed by the theory and practice of psychoanalysis), the history of composed music in Western culture has precipitated a parallel and specific tradition of criticism and commentary, the most detailed and revealing of which is termed analysis (see survey by Bent and Pople 2001). Unlike the majority of music therapy publications, which tend to deal with the parameters outlined in the preceding paragraph, the analysis of composed music tends to look at the details of works as they relate to various levels of musical structure – phrase, section, movement or complete work. Whether these analytical methods are valid in the discussion of music outside Western composed art music is open to debate, but it is noticeable that the vast majority of music therapy publications make little or no reference to this analytic tradition. Exceptions include Lee (1989), who, in his detailed study of a therapeutic improvisation, makes use of techniques developed by the German musicologist Heinrich Schenker.

The aim of this chapter is to present the viewpoint of the therapist in two clinical examples alongside a separate discussion of the improvisations written from a purely musicological perspective. By comparing these two discrete approaches to the same material, it is hoped that this chapter may contribute to a greater understanding of the analytic, but often highly intuitive, processes involved in music therapy. The chapter will focus in detail on one case, using musical examples at the beginning and end of treatment to illustrate the process. The case will be discussed therapeutically by the clinician, Ann Sloboda; and, the musical examples will be transcribed, with an accompanying commentary, by Richard Bolton. It is hoped that this will provide a more detailed picture of the musical elements than is often the case, and that conclusions may be drawn from a comparison of the two perspectives.

The chapter is divided into several sections, which reflect its dual author-ship. Following this jointly authored introduction to the chapter, Ann Sloboda surveys the position of music therapy in the world of forensic psychiatry. In the third section, the case material is presented and the musical examples assessed from the viewpoint of the therapist. In the fourth part, the two transcriptions are presented and discussed simply as pieces of music by Richard Bolton. A final section, again written jointly, aims to combine and compare the two perspectives. The purpose of this dual mode of pre-sentation is twofold: to see whether the analytic judgements of the therapist are reflected or contradicted in the musicological analysis; and to demon-strate the existence of empirical musical phenomena that may be used as analytical tools in music therapy.

MUSIC THERAPY IN FORENSIC PSYCHIATRY
(Ann Sloboda)

In recent years there has been a rapid expansion in the field of forensic psychiatry as a speciality within the wider field of general psychiatry. Its practice is regulated as much by law and the criminal justice system as by medicine, and it necessarily deals with three different, but interrelated, areas: society, crime and the offender. A succinct and thorough summary of both political background and therapeutic issues is outlined by Welldon and van Velsen (1996) in *A Practical Guide to Forensic Psychotherapy*. They view the main aims of the forensic therapist as furthering the understanding of the offender patient and providing suitable treatment programmes. Their book is a valuable introduction to psychotherapy with forensic patients and includes chapters on music therapy (Sloboda) and art therapy (Innes). It demonstrates the wide and complex range of professional approaches involved in therapeutic work with this patient group. The parameters of psy-chotherapy, as outlined here, can also be applied to music therapy: to try to understand the psychopathology of the offender and to offer an opportun-ity for the forensic patient to communicate something of their internal world.

My own orientation as a music therapist owes much to these ideas, while recognising that in music therapy the relationship is developed through music-making. Forensic psychotherapy theory emphasises the split between thought and action that affects many patients (Welldon and Van Velsen 1996: 81). In an earlier chapter (Sloboda 1996), I discussed how music, with its capacity to be both concrete and symbolic, could be helpful in addressing this split. The musical activity can be pure, spontaneous, impulsive action, but can also (particularly if a recording is made) become an experience to be reflected upon. This process is illustrated in the case material in this chapter. It is also important to point out that music therapy can offer something to psychiatric patients whose ability to reflect upon their emotional experiences is very limited. In these circumstances music therapy is operating at a pre-verbal level and owes much to the work of attachment theorists, most notably Daniel Stern (1985). These theories are highly relevant to work in forensic psychiatry, as the quality of forensic patients' early attachments is the subject of recent research (de Zulueta 1993).

While it may be argued that, for some patients, the majority of therapeutic work has taken place in the musical relationship, verbal reflection can help to shed some light on this process. Risk assessment is an important component in the rehabilitation of mentally disordered offenders, in that patients are expected to have developed some insight into the fact that they have an enduring mental illness, and some understanding of the relationship between this illness and their offending behaviour. If no such insight or understanding is evident, a patient would often be considered too great a risk to be discharged. This has some bearing on the role of the music therapists as all staff (including the arts therapists) have a responsibility to help the forensic patient communicate verbally, as well as through the art medium, about his or her mental state.

The proliferation of forensic psychiatric units has had an impact on all the arts therapies. In particular, the number of music therapists working in this field has increased rapidly in recent years, compared with general psychiatry, where music therapy services have remained static or have developed very slowly. There are even examples of music therapy posts in general psychiatry 'becoming forensic' as long-stay hospitals close in the move towards community provision, discharging all patients save those requiring secure, locked facilities. At the time of writing these units now appear to be the only ones where people remain as in-patients for a long time and where there is sufficient funding for a multidisciplinary team to do long-term therapeutic and rehabilitative work.

As most acute psychiatric settings have such a rapid turnover of patients, the music therapist is often working in an atmosphere of uncertainty, and is routinely required to run 'open' groups with a continually shifting population. ('Open' is the term used to describe group therapy sessions that offer an open invitation to all patients from a particular ward/unit to attend. These have been found to be appropriate in acute psychiatric settings, as most patients are either too unwell or in hospital for too short a period to commit themselves to regular attendance.)

It was with this background that I moved in 1994 from general psychiatry to a Regional Secure Unit. This was largely motivated by a sense of frustration that, while I could offer patients a musical, and often emotionally powerful, experience, it was difficult to develop this and make a significant contribution to their treatment. This was because their stay in hospital was short and resources for follow-up scarce. At the time I began working in the RSU it was comparatively rare for British music therapists to be working in forensic units. Significant forerunners were Helen Loth and Katie Santos who had presented and published on the topic of music therapy work in secure settings (Santos and Loth 1993; Loth 1996). My initial role was one of sessional specialist, employed one day per week, attending a ward round to pick up referrals, and working, individually at first, with a few patients.

As recounted in a previous chapter (Sloboda 1996) there were striking differences between general and forensic psychiatry, in particular the staff/patient ratios, and the nature of the contact with the multidisciplinary team. In my general psychiatric work, the patients referred for music therapy were unlikely to be undergoing any other type of individual therapy. As such the music therapist functioned as the major therapist, who, in the case of outpatients, held much of the responsibility for providing a supportive link with the mental health services. In contrast, the forensic unit was well staffed by highly skilled professionals of all disciplines offering intensive therapeutic input to the patients. The case that follows is an example of this, with the patient receiving regular mental state examinations from psychiatrists, individual psychotherapy from a psychologist, group art therapy, group occupational therapy, and help with discharge and accommodation plans from a social worker. With so much treatment already being offered, the music therapist's contribution needs to be carefully thought about to complement the rest of the treatment, and to have a specific purpose.

The case in this chapter was one where music therapy, and improvisation in particular, could help to address some of the emotional issues facing the patient. For reasons of confidentiality, biographical details in the case material are kept to a minimum. The focus will be on the process of the therapeutic relationship. One reason for studying this case in particular was that the patient was unusual in his level of musical accomplishment, his music being harmonically more complex than is usual among music therapy patients. This in itself was rare enough in my own 12-year career to warrant further discussion. The issue of the musically accomplished patient in music therapy has been raised at times by both colleagues and students as something of a problem for both patient and therapist. It is often argued that patients skilled in a particular art form may find it difficult to use in a therapeutic context. It can be hard for the patient to put aside technique that has been painstakingly acquired through hours of work, to produce something discordant, messy or uncontrolled. The patient thus faces the significant challenge that music therapists experience in training: that of 'freeing up', putting aside their learned techniques in favour of more exploratory, perhaps even seemingly random paths. A musically skilled patient can also challenge the music therapist. I had become accustomed to helping those with no prior training discover the potential of musical instruments, rather than working with those who might challenge me musically.

Case study: David (Ann Sloboda)

David was a man in his early thirties, with diagnosis of paranoid schizophrenia, with whom I worked individually for eight months. When I met him, he had been in the Regional Secure Unit for several years, admitted on the grounds of diminished responsibility following his conviction for the manslaughter of his girlfriend. He had been acutely psychotic at the time of his index offence, believing that he and his girlfriend were divine beings of one mind, and that she was party to a plan in which she would be killed and they would both be reincarnated. By the time we met, David was making good progress in the unit. He was already using individual verbal psychotherapy and taking part in occupational therapy groups. His psychiatrist and psychotherapist considered him capable of insight with much of his personality intact. While his psychotic symptoms had been successfully controlled by medication, his mental state was still considered fragile at times, and was carefully monitored by the clinical team. David had had some formal training in music, and was skilled in both performance and composition. His main leisure interest was composing modern dance music. He did this alone, using synthesisers, samplers and multi-track recording equipment.

Our first meeting was initiated by David, who approached me asking for piano lessons. I explained that I was not a piano teacher and that music therapy sessions generally involved improvisation. He said that this was new to him but was still interested in having some music therapy sessions. The clinical team then made a formal referral for music therapy. They agreed that the acquisition of skill was not an area of difficulty for David, but that emotional expression was more of a problem. In his case, improvisation, with its emphasis on spontaneity, would be more of a challenge than simply learning to play the piano and could offer an opportunity for self-exploration.

The sessions

His first sessions involved us playing pre-composed classical compositions that he had brought along. In my view, this was his way of exerting the maximum level of control over the musical interaction. The music we played had been selected and practised by him, whereas I had to sight-read, thereby enabling him to test my musical skills while avoiding the possibility of anything un-planned taking place. Music therapy provided a stark contrast to his recent musical experience that had been solitary and highly controlled using elec-tronic instruments. An interactive duet, where the players made no plans but improvised freely on acoustic instruments was a much more immediate and raw experience. David initially felt insecure and at a disadvantage. While I tried to move the focus away from the product and on to the process (that is: exploration, communication and self-expression), David was reluctant to try any instrument on which he did not feel skilled. In the second session he was prepared to improvise but only on his own electric guitar, rather than the instruments in the therapy room.

An extract of our improvisation in that session has been transcribed (see Figure 8.1). David played electric guitar, and I played the piano. We had agreed in advance on the key of the piece, but nothing else. However, the music quickly settled into a sequence of four chords that repeated over and over again for about 20 minutes. Listening to the tape recording of the improvi-sation, the features that were evident were as follows: within the improvi-sation, a repetitive structure with a predictable pattern is established; within this structure, there is nothing unexpected, such as discord, or sudden changes in rhythm or mood. The speed and loudness level vary little through-out the piece. The guitar and piano follow each other very closely; at times they actually play the same notes, without looking at each other. The music has a symbiotic quality; it is difficult to tell the instruments apart, and there is little sense of two different people.

My emotional experience of this piece was one of being drawn in to a sort of musical merging, whereby there seemed to be very little differentiation between patient and therapist. In the light of his case history (in which his delusional material had featured a belief that he and his victim shared the same mind), this particularly concerned me, and was discussed in supervision. The music of the first few sessions seemed to fall into similar repetitive patterns. It was characterised by a hypnotic, trance-like quality, which avoided discord, or changes of loudness or tempo. My role as a participant made it necessary to record the improvisations, in order to listen to the music and attempt to analyse the dynamics of the interaction in retrospect. I began to resist the merging by consciously introducing contrasting elements into the music.

Generally, I encourage verbal reflection on the experience of improvising, and talk about thoughts and feelings that may have arisen while playing. David did not want to do this and difficulties arose when I suggested it. He said

Figure 8.1 Extract 1: Second music therapy session.

that he found my suggestions intrusive and began to be critical of my musical ability. In retrospect, I can see that my attempts to analyse what we were doing signified to him that we were separate people, not 'of one mind', who might have differing views about our experience. Having been initially idealised, I was now denigrated by David. He was reluctant to acknowledge the therapeutic aspects of our sessions, considering them 'just music'; he felt that there was no need to speak, as he talked in his psychotherapy sessions. It was helpful to me that his psychotherapist drew attention to the process of splitting that was going on within the team. David began to miss sessions and said that he would only continue with music therapy if the focus was restricted to musical improvisation. The sessions continued on this basis for several months. Initially any discussion was purely factual, concerning technical aspects of the music. Although I found this constraining, it also struck me that, in view of his initial reluctance to improvise, this was a tremendously important mode of expression for David. Orton highlights the challenging nature of improvisation: '(it) demands total involvement . . . one must be free to initiate ideas, to hear and respond to the contributions of others. An accident or error can be turned around and made musically meaningful' (Orton 1992). As is the case for so many patients whose 'error' has had such tragic consequences, it is not surprising that risk-taking had been experienced as dangerous and something to be suppressed.

Now he was keen to improvise and take risks in a musical context, and probably needed to experience it for a while before being able to hear my thoughts about it. Later David told me that he had felt defensive and threatened at this time. He considered that he was revealing much of himself through his music and that discussing it further was too exposing. I realised that I may have been too quick to offer analyses and interpretations. Gradually, he took more risks, trying out instruments that he hadn't played before. After about six months, he began to discuss the dynamics of the musical relationship, for example who had been taking the leading or supporting role and which of us initiated changes in the music, such as getting louder or faster. He was, in fact, beginning to reflect on the musical experience in the way that I had suggested earlier, but at his own pace. He began to mention things that he found difficult, in particular the issue of ending a piece of music. This was true, as, while I did not wish to impose a musical structure onto him, our improvisations would last for the entire session if I did not bring them to a close. We discussed ways of bringing a piece to a close: fade out, stop suddenly, slow down until reaching a halt, build up to a crescendo and so on. I certainly considered these issues to have relevance beyond the musical sphere, both in relation to his offence and in that he was prepared to think about the relationship between us. The link with his offence and the issue of ending was, of course, that he had ended someone else's life, a linkage maintained in the therapist's mind rather than one which could be frankly discussed with the patient. We experimented with ways he might decide to end a piece and indicate this musically to me. He found this interesting but difficult and realised that all his own compositions did not actually finish, but just faded out.

He finished music therapy after eight months, when he started a full-time college course as part of his rehabilitation (he was still an in-patient at this time, and psychiatric and general clinical input was to continue up to and after his discharge). The second extract (Figure 8.2) is from his final session. I play electric keyboard, while David is playing the piano. It is interesting to recall that he had wanted me to teach him the piano. I resisted this, but had given him a few ideas about how to use it.

In this piece David is much more confident, directing and determining the musical structure rather than simply following me. His playing is now much more exploratory, as he experiments with dissonance, tempo and loudness levels. My role is much less prominent, sometimes elaborating his structure, at other times just playing the occasional note. My function was that of a witness, rather than an equal participant, and the transcription of the music reflects this. The music has some discord, but it is contained within a primarily tonal structure. The piece ends clearly, with a cadence prepared by David, as he plays increasingly slowly and quietly. The music is strikingly different in its intensity to that of the earlier extract. In this piece, David displays an independent voice and identity in the music, greater confidence and range of emotional expression, and a willingness to explore and take risks.

Conclusions

Music therapy was useful in helping him tolerate differences and discord, and in helping him learn to survive a relationship that went through a difficult patch. His typical way of relating to women was that of idealising them, merging with them, and losing his own emotional identity. The music therapy relationship helped him to find a different way of being with a woman, that of being close but individual. I consider any positive changes to be a result of staff working closely together and being able to hold the counter-transference on a team level. I am not attributing these changes to music therapy in isolation, but rather making a case for music therapy within the multidisciplinary team.

Figure 8.2 Extract 2: Final music therapy session after 8 months of work.

Figure 8.2 cont.

MUSICAL COMMENTARY (Richard Bolton)

Introduction

Improvisation can be defined as the spontaneous creation of music in performance. Whether the music belongs to a strictly defined genre (such as jazz or salsa) or avoids preset conditions entirely (as is the case in free improvisation), all improvisations share the feature that responsibility for the creative effect and value of the work lies with the performer. Although the pairing of therapist and patient make for a specialised and unusual type of personnel, the difference between clinical and public improvisation is essentially one of purpose and process rather than content.

The emphasis on improvisation in British music therapy practice can be viewed as one aspect of a widespread revival of musical improvisation in Western culture during the last century. This renaissance of the practice and awareness of improvisation has been closely allied to the development of audio recording technology, which has enabled performers from diverse backgrounds to ingest, disseminate and even notate what had previously been a purely local and aural skill, produced and received solely *in vivo*. The resulting canon of 'masterpiece' recorded improvisations in such fields as jazz and blues have in turn stimulated a considerable quantity of written commentary. Whether as a result of the informal nature of the music itself, or due to the divergent concerns of performers and academics, the vast majority of this writing has taken the form of discography (that is, lists of recordings), pedagogy (that is, 'how-to' manuals) or anecdotal historiography. Although some of this writing is extremely detailed, it seems that musical improvisation has largely failed to stimulate an accompanying canon of in-depth criticism that in any sense parallels the various approaches to music analysis that have characterised the serious discussion of Western composed music.

The past 20 years have nevertheless seen a growing volume of academic literature on the subject (surveyed in Bolton 1998, and including such substantial examples of analytic approaches to improvisation as Berliner 1992); the field is still relatively new, however, and the case for critical, verbal analysis of musical improvisation remains far from proven. Analysis of a music therapy improvisation faces a further philosophical hurdle: that the music has almost certainly not been performed with the intention of producing a clearly defined aesthetic object such as that represented by a commercial recording. Without wishing to judge therapeutic improvisation by the yardstick of published examples by acknowledged experts, some detailed examination of the musical content of music therapy seems warranted by the fact that improvisation forms such a central component of much music therapy practice.

Aside from the fact that every genre of musical creativity is nowadays deemed worthy of close critical scrutiny, it is possible that both music therapists and non-musicians involved in the therapeutic process might find it useful

to consider a detailed account of therapeutic improvisation from an objective standpoint, if only to be able to tell whether such an approach could
usefully support or contradict their original conclusions.

The transcriptions

The two transcribed improvisations (Figures 8.1 and 8.2) represent excerpts
from two separate performances. Both quite short, they have been extracted
by the therapist from two much longer clinical improvisations. The extracts
were chosen as being representative portions of the entire pieces. The first
is performed on piano and electric guitar; the second on piano and electric
keyboard. The patient plays guitar in the first piece and piano in the second
piece; in general, this section of the article will not distinguish between these
respective identities, the aim being to view the pieces simply as two duet
performances. The notated transcriptions can be thought of as a tertiary source.
The primary source, the actual performance, was experienced by only two
people, that is the performers. The secondary source, the recording from which
the transcription was made, has been heard by considerably more. Although
it is not possible to include this recording in this publication, the notated
version serves, in so far as this is possible, as an objective description of the
music upon which to base this discussion. While analytic criticism at any
detailed level would be difficult, if not impossible, without some sort of
transcription of this kind, it should be remembered that it is not universally
accepted that improvisation can be accurately or even usefully rendered in
Western notation (Bailey 1992).

 The transcriptions upon which the following commentary is based are
included so that music readers can cross-check and form their own conclusions. Although some understanding of music theory is assumed, it is
intended that readers unwilling or unable to read music should nevertheless
be able to follow the critical argument. The following sections are termed
'commentary' rather than 'analysis' because their aim is to describe various aspects of the musical events rather than investigate the music from a
specific analytical perspective.

Transcription 1 – commentary

The first piece resembles a pop song in several respects: the chords, textures,
melodies and figurations are all reminiscent of an anodyne, post-1950s' style
of pop music. The music hardly strays from the key of F major – indeed,
the guitar part has no distinct accidentals (although some dissonances are
created by the idiomatic finger-slides, notated by a straight line in the transcription in bars 17 and 18). The piece falls into two halves, the second of
which starts at bar 9. Each half can be subdivided into two phrases, with
only the last phrase extending the characteristic four-bar boundary. The piano

clearly dictates the harmonic movement which varies the following simple chord progression: I (or VI)/ii/V/I. The final phrase extends this formulaic progression simply by lengthening the ii chord to two bars and the V chord to three bars before the final resolution. Typically, the I chord is decorated with an added sixth, the ii and V chord with a flattened seventh. The only point of harmonic variety in the piece is in the approach to the ii chord. The opening tonic sixth (bar 1) is replaced in bar 5 by an F# diminished chord (a standard substitution for the VI chord). The doubling of the harmonic rhythm in bar 9 (I and VI in first inversion) gives a renewed sense of direction and purpose to the start of the second half, whereas the emphatic root position V chord in bar 13 both disguises the predictable repetitiveness of the chord sequence and justifies the extended final cadence.

The piano part largely comprises rolling arpeggios, a typical pop music style of accompaniment. Syncopations such as the ties over the middle of the bar serve to keep the rhythm fluid rather than to provide any starting impetus. The rhythm of the guitar melody is in the main rather four-square. Only in the final phrase (bars 13–20) do the rhythmic values include quavers, a crotchet triplet and quaver syncopations. While the guitar-playing may lack the finesse of expertise, the general style, akin to that of 'West Coast' rock guitar soloing of the mid-1960s, is well caught. It is worth noting how readily incidental dissonances, such as the F#/F natural clashes in bars 5 and 9, or the G against the D7 chord in bar 13, are absorbed by the idiom. Also significant is the way in which the guitarist fashions two large-scale melodic descents. The first, from bar 2 to bar 8, descends through the interval of a major ninth from D to C. Thereafter, the second half of the melodic line climbs quite naturally to the climactic high G in bar 13; from here the line descends, again through the range of a ninth, to the final tonic.

Although the piece clearly displays certain elements of formal design, the rolling piano arpeggios, the predominantly scalic movement of the guitar, the static tonality and the formulaic phrase structure combine to form a sunny, unruffled and unchallenging improvisation.

Transcription 2 – commentary

The second piece is clearly very different in tone. The style of the music veers between two contrasting areas: whereas the first and last sections sound as if they could have been written by a twentieth-century 'classical' composer (for example Samuel Barber or Shostakovich), the two four-bar melodies that constitute the most well-defined section of the improvisation (bars 18ff.) sound much more 'pop', with the characteristic aeolian modal harmony and deliberate 4/4 pacing of 'progressive rock' bands such as Pink Floyd. In some ways, this piece is equally as one-dimensional as the first, as the sustained and sombre mood established at the start continues virtually unchanged for the length of the piece. More specifically, the piano part consists of long bass notes and repeated crotchet chords (generally one harmony per bar) in the right hand. The only exception to this is in bars 17–22, where the piano's right hand plays a single-line melody with predominantly quaver movement. Also, as in the first piece, it is the piano that appears to dictate the structure of the piece (even though it is the patient who is here playing the piano). The keyboard line is at times so quiet that the listener's focus is forced on to the top line of the repeated piano chords. However, this is only one of a number of textural strategies adopted by the keyboardist. At bars 6 and 13, for instance, the keyboard seems to be reinforcing the piano's top line, thereby asserting its melodic role. At other times it seems to be interjecting, or commenting (bars 11, 15, 25 and 26) whereas it clearly 'takes up the baton' of being the main melodic instrument as it is passed from the piano in bar 23.

The piece can be divided into four distinct sections. The first five bars serve as an introduction; after the pause at the end of bar 5, the second section lasts until the piano's right-hand melody begins at the end of bar 17. This third section consists of a four-bar descending chord sequence played twice, the second time featuring the keyboard as the main melodic instrument. The coda, starting at bar 26, is dictated by the pianist both in terms of harmony and tempo, with an *accelerando* in bar 31, followed by the *rallentando* in the climactic bar 34. Apart from the final cadence, several perfect cadences during the piece establish a sense of the overall tonal centre of B (minor at bars 17/18 and 21/22; major at bars 25/26). However, much of the harmonic movement in the first and second parts has a sense of meandering along, as if groping for a stable tonality. This impression is heightened by several pitch clashes between the two performers (that is, A/A sharp in bar 11, D, D sharp in bar 12). The piece thus reaches some very remote tonal areas in comparison to the first example. Furthest away from the prevailing key centre is the second inversion chord of F major in bar 14, which leads to two distinctly bitonal bars as the keyboardist tries to hang on in F major while the pianist steers the piece back to B minor. The clash is absorbed quite easily here, as the A, C and F naturals in the keyboard part can be heard as 'blues' decorations of the pianist's B minor. Some of this harmonic adventurousness may be derived from the physical process of the left hand moving in one direction while the right hand proceeds in contrary motion (bars 12–15 in particular); elsewhere, the inner pedal E in bars 30–33 combines with a series of suspensions and resolutions to create a sophisticated harmonic tension.

Structually, this piece starts (after the introduction) with what seems like a long passage of 'development'; the nearest the piece gets to a recognisable 'theme' is followed only by the climactic coda. Although this sequence of material would be strange in a composition, following as it does no obvious structural template, this type of form is by no means so unusual in free improvisation, where performers might dabble in several areas before finding one that really seems to 'work'. Dance music 'mixes', too, often precede a fully scored (typically, vocal) 'theme' with a lengthy, deconstructed introduction.

Comparison between transcriptions 1 and 2

Looking at the two pieces side by side, the inescapable conclusion is that there is considerably more interaction between the performers in the second improvisation. Although the piano dictates the musical character of both pieces, the single-line playing in the second is much more adventurous and responsive, with a much wider range of approach than the somewhat one-dimensional guitar-playing in the first piece. This enables harmonic dissonance to occur and be resolved without upsetting the musical or structural flow of the improvisation. This is also reflected in the fact that the second piece can accommodate much more tempo fluctuation than the first. The respective histories of both jazz and classical music indicate that the movement away from clear tonal references tends to be accompanied by a similar loosening of adherence to an overt metrical pulse.

DISCUSSION (Ann Sloboda and Richard Bolton)

Improvisation – spontaneous music creation – is viewed in music therapy as an arena where anything can happen; it provides a forum for open discussion and an opportunity to discover something new through a sort of musical 'free association' analogous to that of the verbal psychoanalytic session. This kind of improvisation (sometimes characterised by the term 'associationist', Clarke 1988: 1–26) typically presents a structure that better resembles a narrative than a planned formal design. (Interestingly, patients often liken therapeutic improvisations to film music.) As such it might not easily lend itself to analytic techniques devised to establish the relative structural unity of European compositions written between 1600 and 1900.

While the therapist is primarily interested in the musical interaction as a series of events within a relationship, the musical analysis focuses on the combined effect of these events and seeks to establish their effectiveness as musical performances. As the music therapist did not transcribe improvisations (general clinical practice does not allow the time to do this), so any analysis that took place would be aural. The focus would be less on exactly which notes were played, or even which key, but more on the development of the melodic and rhythmic material, and the place of imitation, repetition and contrasts within the improvisations.

Given the quite discrete foci of the two ways of viewing the music, it is significant that the responses of the therapist are echoed in the musicological description of the two performances. The first piece, described in the musical analysis as 'anodyne', was experienced by the therapist as being pleasant, but saccharine and emotionally one-dimensional. In the case of a patient with a particularly traumatic recent history, such qualities in his improvisation were experienced as exerting subtle control. Certain elements such as tension or aggression were excluded from the music, thus producing the bland quality remarked upon in the musical analysis.

The second and later of the two examples discussed displays aspects of musical structure that could be termed more complex, varied, challenging and, technically, more dissonant. Here, the therapist identified a broadening of the emotional expression in comparison to the first example. This was accompanied by a loosening of control on the part of the patient, allowing unexpected events, such as musical discord, to occur. It also allowed the patient to be more available for a genuine relationship with the therapist involving more exploration, and 'give and take'. These mirrored the changes seen in the way the patient was able to use the music, but also in the way the relationship between patient and therapist had developed. The term 'challenging' in a musicological sense would refer to the challenge the music presented to the listener (or possibly a technical one to the performer), while the same term used in a music therapy context suggests that difficult issues are being addressed rather than avoided or glossed over.

SUMMARY

It proved very useful for the music therapist to have a musical analysis of the session material. It provided concrete evidence that supported her perception of the music, developed intuitively from her own aural and experiential perception of the music. From the analytic point of view, it is clear that the nature of both pieces is dictated by only one of the participants (that is, the patient, even though the therapist clearly influences the direction and structure of the extracts). This one-sided emphasis in collective improvisation is unlikely to yield a genuinely satisfying aesthetic object. Nevertheless, the commentary was able to identify specific aspects of the musical interaction that differentiated the two performances; as such it seems that these aspects could support the therapist's view of the nature of the changes that had taken place in the patient.

Chapter 9

Musical narratives in music therapy treatment for dementia

Helen Odell-Miller[1]

> Stories are instruments of communication by their very form (Shah 1964).
> They cannot be unravelled by ordinary methods alone. It is no use trying
> to count words or correlate metaphors in a story with elevations in blood
> pressure and hope to extract any meaning, but it is possible to under-
> stand them as they are structured as a set of narratives. These narrat-
> ives can be understood as being structured according to the rules of
> construction, as are musical compositions.
>
> (Aldridge 1996: 101)

INTRODUCTION

This chapter aims to give a brief overview of current music therapy practice
in dementia, including some discussion of research questions, and focusing on narrative aspects of the work. In particular, the importance of music
therapy and the continuation of narrative for people with dementia will be
illustrated by case material. The examples from practice will show how
different aspects of narrative can be perceived in both the musical and the
verbal material, arising from clinical improvisations during music therapy
treatment. Research outcomes and evidence will be mentioned briefly but the
focus of the chapter will be case-specific.

COGNITIVE AND NEUROLOGICAL CONSIDERATIONS

The developmental and neurological aspects of understanding music therapy
are important, because it is now well known and well researched that when

1 The material for this chapter was previously presented as a short paper to the Annual Conference
of the Royal College of Psychiatrists in July 2001. We are grateful to Helen Odell-Miller for
agreeing at very short notice for the material to appear here.

brain damage occurs, musical functioning often remains intact, and can be the last faculty to deteriorate (Alajouanine 1948; Basso and Capitani 1985; Gordon and Bogen 1974; Swartz *et al.* 1989; see discussion in Chapter 7). Beatty *et al.* (1988) show findings that indicate that a broad range of complex cognitive abilities may be preserved in patients with dementia of the Alzheimer's type who cannot perform simpler actions. People with probable dementia of the Alzheimer's type have demonstrated preserved skill at painting or piano-playing long after performance of other apparently simpler activities have seriously deteriorated (Crystal *et al.* 1989).

RESEARCH

In terms of an overview of outcome research and literature on music therapy with this population the recent Cochrane updated review (Koger and Brotons 2000) concluded that there has been insufficient conclusive outcome research in music therapy to justify it as a treatment for dementia. There was a dearth of randomised controlled trials (RCTs). However, the report also states '. . . the evidence available suggests that music therapy may be beneficial in treating or managing dementia symptoms . . .'. My particular research in the 1980s, which looked at improvisation in music therapy in a controlled trial with those suffering from dementia, led me to become interested in the ways in which developmental systems become reversed, the more advanced the dementia becomes. Thus improvisation in music therapy, involving spontaneous almost reflexive communicative interactions similar to what Trevarthen (1993) calls 'proto-conversation' in his research with young babies, is essential for those losing their cognitive functions. In summary the research comparing talking therapy with improvisational music therapy in a controlled trial showed the following:

1   Music therapy is associated with higher levels of engagement among participants than in reminiscence therapy, although this difference is not a statistically significant one.
2   Patients who have received music therapy show higher levels of engagement half an hour after they have received music therapy than they show at the same time on a different day, although this difference is not a significant one.
3   Patients show a significantly higher level of engagement during music therapy sessions when involved in this therapy regularly (weekly) than they do when involved intermittently (for further discussion of this research see Odell-Miller 1995).

A recent quite comprehensive overview of the music therapy research and literature in this field (Aldridge 2000) supports the view that music therapy is useful in managing and treating symptoms. This chapter does not attempt to draw any significant conclusions from the case material presented, other than to illustrate how it is possible to use musical evidence for the existence of a person's 'narrative' long after their command of spoken language is damaged. I am using the term narrative in its broadest sense to refer to that fundamental process whereby we understand and make ourselves understood.

MUSICAL NARRATIVE AND IMPROVISATION

Central to narrative expression is language and story telling that form the basis of the therapeutic techniques of psychotherapy generally and drama therapy specifically. In music therapy it is through the use of song and impro-visation that the forgotten and innate narrative structures are encouraged to find expression. Indications for referral to music therapy do not depend on the person having had a musical education. If anything it depends on the person's willingness to engage in a process of musical improvisation that, it is argued, draws on a universal disposition to musicality which is more fun-damental and enduring than spoken language. The rationale for using music as an effective treatment in this way is described elsewhere (Odell-Miller 1995, 1997). I would like to present firstly some general comments on improvisa-tion in music therapy before going on to describe a case presentation in some detail. I will then return to discuss some of the theoretical issues involved.

Here is the way a music therapy group consisting of patients with Alzheimer's Disease might develop. Sessions involve encouraging interaction, awareness and movement using instruments and voice, building improvisations from the sounds and music expressed by group members. At times, this involves developing pre-composed material such as songs, or instrumental material, in improvisations between different members in pairs, threes, small groupings, or as a whole group. For example, if a member begins humming or beating in a particular way, the therapist might listen and subsequently interact mus-ically in order to build on this. The therapist identifies the needs of the patients by observing and getting to know patients as the treatment progresses and the therapeutic relationships develop. Different types of musical interactions are made according to assumptions about what would be helpful. For example, when a patient who had previously shown withdrawn frightened behavi-our begins to beat in a triplet-type rhythm quietly on a metallophone, the therapist might see this as something that could be encouraged musically. This might lead to the patient feeling more able to communicate in other ways. The musical intervention by the therapist is, therefore, made in a way that would help this.

Those with dementia are often confused and express themselves in disconnected regressed speech. Verbal elements, as in ordinary fluent speech and language, are often missing. So music can be an alternative means of expression and communication because a combination of music and sound, often improvised, provides a more accessible mode of communication for this population. This is important because music therapy concentrates on an expressive affect as well as talking and thinking. To reiterate the central point mentioned earlier: when other faculties deteriorate owing to frontal lobe damage of the brain, a natural musical instinct often remains. What the music therapist provides is a musical structure that both encourages and preserves this instinct from the deterioration of these other faculties. Aldridge brings out this point in his discussion of rhythm.

> A feature of her rhythmical playing was that in nearly all the sessions, during the progress of an improvisation, the patient would let control of the rhythmic pattern slip such that it became progressively imprecise, losing both its form and liveliness. The initial impulse of her rhythmic playing, which was clear and precise, gradually deteriorated as she lost concentration and ability to persevere with the task in hand. However, when the therapist offered an overall musical structure during the course of the improvisation, the patient could regain her precision of rhythm. It could well be that to sustain perception an overall rhythmical structure is necessary, and it is this musical gestalt, that is the possibility of providing an overall organising structure of time, which fails in Alzheimer's disease (Aldridge 1996: 198).

Here, the therapist is acting like a musical narrator, offering an overall musical structure when the musical story is not complete. In order to further illustrate points raised above the following case study, which is also discussed in Odell-Miller (1997), will be summarised.

Case study of M

M was 50 years old at the start of music therapy, which took place in a community setting where the multidisciplinary team was functioning well. He was suffering from a particular form of dementia, Simultanagnosia. Areas that integrate the visual field were failing, which meant that M could see one thing, but not many things at once, that is his field of vision was affected. He first presented with a right parietal syndrome, therefore his non-verbal memory was impaired, that is the construction of his visual-spacial memory was affected. He could not distinguish shapes or remember other visual aspects, while his verbal language and cognitive functioning were more intact at first. His life and work had been in the musical field, and particularly in improvisation and composing. His musical memory remained fairly unimpaired although he could not read written music at the time of referral. Thus his ability to improvise was not very much impaired and he was able to return to a musical phrase or section of music used at the beginning of a piece. It is noteworthy that the notion of narrative is taken to mean a story in the least literal sense – a musical story if you like – at that moment in time that reveals different aspects of the person than are revealed in words. For example in M's case there was a shared understanding of mood and also musical keys, demonstrating an implicative form of meaning or narrative about the musical discussion between two people, since these excerpts are all improvised, unplanned and unfolding in that moment in time.

M was first referred by the psychiatrist, who had a clearly defined area of work of music therapy in mind: 'to help him work through some of the emotional implications of his diagnosis'. In later letters, once the therapy had been underway for several months, the psychiatrist wrote that he seemed often depressed, with almost 'too much insight into his condition' but also that: 'Although he has considerable difficulty expressing himself he did explain to me that he found weekly music therapy visits very helpful, and his wife has commented that he seems brighter after these sessions'. This was an ideal use of music therapy. Two other key people involved were the community psychiatric nurse, who visited weekly to help with practical coping strategies and to provide support to M and his wife, and the psychologist's intervention that aimed at 'trying to help the couple understand his neuropsychological strengths and weaknesses'.

An assessment summary as follows illustrates the interrelationship between music and words. After nearly three years of music therapy, he was quite cognitively impaired and sometimes could not identify his wife. Here the idea of musical narrative becomes important. His recognition of me perhaps shows the power of the musical rapport in maintaining some sense of orientation. He developed a rapport with me musically and often said during the first few months: 'I feel this is so good for me – it's just there, music is here – you touch it and you get it'. He also began to improvise on his own between sessions, something that he had no inclination to do when we first met because he was afraid of the piano. His words at this point: 'It comes up to hit me' and his anger towards me at this point seemed linked with his fear of the piano and of losing his skills. It seemed that this fear subsided, the more our work developed, and that through improvising, he recognised a way of expressing himself, in an area he felt relatively expert and confident. By this I mean that long after he could hold a meaningful conversation, he could improvise what seemed to be a meaningful improvisation.

FURTHER THEORETICAL CONSIDERATIONS

The individual case example illustrated is with a professional musician, which raises related issues such as how much his use of music can be seen as intellectually driven rather than expressively or instinctually driven. I mention this because the latter drives are usually the very reason why musical narrative is significant and beneficial for people with Alzheimer's Disease. Aldridge (1996) suggests that the fundamentals of language are musical, and prior to semantic and lexical functions in language development, a view influenced by the findings of Stern (1985), Trevarthen (1993) and see Introduction to Chapter 4. This work in the area of early development with babies and young children supports the notion that it is in this spontaneous area of the music therapy relationship that improvisation seems most powerful in its way of producing and developing interaction and synchronicity where it may have failed as a result of disability or illness.

Music therapists such as Bartram (1991) and Pavlicevic (1995a, b: and, in relation to work in adult psychiatry, see her 1989 paper written with Trevarthen) have been influenced by Stern's use of the term 'vitality affects' to describe mother–infant interactions, as these relate closely to musical terminology such as rhythm, pitch and timbre. Trevarthen's research shows that the apparently irrational incoherent communications of babies are more purposeful than originally thought. Socially constructed meaning is learned as a result of inspiration that comes from early preverbal interactions. Shared meanings even at three to four months old can be observed and concepts that are more implicative in meaning. For example a child beginning to speak is able to understand that the people in the same living space can have shared meanings. Trevarthen uses the analogy of a musical duet to describe the above mechanism, where two performers seek harmony and counterpoint that is synchronised (improvised). They create together a piece of music that becomes a coherent and satisfying narrative of feelings in a time structure that they share in a whole piece. The idea of a narrative 'fit' between mother and baby that functions through such 'proto-speech' focuses on the links between music and the human voice.

A collection of sounds, made up of the elements of pitch, loudness, duration and timbre, leads to the formation of music. Included in this is the importance of rhythmic, melodic and harmonic factors, as the previous example shows, and have been discussed extensively by music therapists (for example Alvin 1975; Bunt 1994; Bruscia 1987; Nordoff and Robbins 1971, 1977). Stages in the vocal development of the child have been researched by, among others, Moog (1976) – see summary in Sloboda (1985). These stages, including spontaneous movement to music and musical babble, are not dependent upon musical training but are part of natural development. They are significant here, in supporting the rationale that when other faculties deteriorate, a natural musical innate instinct often remains as shown in the case example. This can be useful not only in treatment but also in assessment as Aldridge (1996) has shown, comparing convincingly music therapy assessment tasks found in assessment systems for Alzheimer's such as the Mini Mental State, and points to links between musical and non-musical ways of relating.

Emotional responses to music also seem to remain intact in spite of a deterioration of other cognitive faculties (see Juslin and Sloboda 2001 for a comprehensive review of emotion and music). There is also a growing literature on the cultural and social significance of music across the lifespan (for example De Nora 2001).

CONCLUSION

To conclude, music therapy is particularly important for those who find thinking difficult, or communicating using words, but who want to express something. It is of particular benefit for people with forms of dementia, such as Alzheimer's Disease, where severe frustration and depression can result from deterioration in cognitive and verbal functioning. More research is clearly needed in this field but studies up to now show that musical narratives in music therapy with people with dementia allow those without speech to tell their stories in a less specific but metaphoric way. This can relieve some symptoms such as agitation and wandering. Relationships with others can be sustained in a way that is not always possible with words only.

POSTSCRIPT TO CLINICAL CHAPTERS

Leslie Bunt and Sarah Hoskyns

In concluding this major section we return to the voices of our colleagues first heard in Chapter 3 to highlight some key points that have continued to inspire them during their clinical practice.

Jean Eisler has been influenced by the notion of the 'music child' introduced by Nordoff and Robbins.

> There was the core belief in the music child in each person. One needed to learn to really listen to the child's sounds so as to grasp what this meant and how it could be fostered. It was this basic tenet of the 'music person' reflecting the well person.... You work to evoke, meet and develop the 'music person' together. The child can then believe in the relationship and begin to communicate and gain the self-confidence and self-belief needed to face whatever problems they have to cope with.

Helen Odell-Miller stressed the influence of teamwork and learning from other disciplines, music therapists and patients. This helped her in integrating psychoanalytical principles into her work.

> One of the things I helped to develop in the late 1980s was a model not of psychotherapy with music but of music therapy informed by psychoanalytic thinking - the phrase we adopted was 'psychoanalytically informed music therapy'. We took the theory that seemed useful, particularly thinking about transference and countertransference. The music didn't get lost and also one was using a model that worked in reality for people who were often quite disturbed suffering from schizophrenia or manic depression and who wouldn't normally get taken on for traditional analytic psychotherapy. All through the 1980s that was what I was trying to do from

my job in psychiatry in Cambridge. One of the first things I did was to set up the Psychiatric Interest Group and to start with there were only a few people in it: Penny Rogers, John Woodcock, Graham Dickerson and myself. We were people working on our own in large psychiatric institutions.

Elaine Streeter's work at Charing Cross Hospital helped her to develop many different connections between music therapy and other disciplines.

There I was in a Child Development Centre with a team of very interesting people to work with and a good consultant (Dr Hugh Jolly - see Chapter 1). A lot of parents would bring their children and they would want to know how to help them. It's a desperate time at that stage if you've got a child with a difficulty. Nordoff's teaching about improvisation was important because it helped me find ways of making contact directly without words. That was a very important time to not just look at music therapy but at all aspects – psychology, child development, neurology – all these different connections. To come back (to Charing Cross) and to start to integrate that having done a thesis on child development and rhythm was very exciting.

Personal influences, both at home and overseas, contributed a great deal to **Tony Wigram's** career.

In my early years I was influenced and encouraged by Dr Derek Ricks, a consultant paediatrician at Harperbury Hospital (see Chapter 1), an inspiring man and someone keenly interested in music. He had a beautiful way with children and with parents, which inspired me. He would get down on the floor and play with the children the moment they walked in the door.

Travelling has been a very big part of my music therapy life. It started from my first experience of a world congress in Paris in 1983 when I started to meet a large body of other music therapists. I became inspired by different work going on. In 1985 I was awarded a Churchill Fellowship and travelled all over the United States. I wanted to interact with people from different music therapy cultures and countries and get involved with them. That's been something that has virtually taken over my life now. I'm thinking of a lot of different and inspiring people who have affected me whom I've met on the journey including:

- Ken Bruscia who had so much input to us in Denmark in the early 1990s with his lectures. He's written so brilliantly about models of music therapy theory and praxis.
- David Aldridge and Even Ruud in Europe who've really set a standard for music therapy research and theory building.

Over the years I have become a lot more influenced by psychotherapeutic approaches. That was an influence from Aalborg and the analytical model of working there and by the whole area of self-experience and personal therapy. At Aalborg, Inge Nygaard Pedersen from an intuitive therapeutic point of view has been very influential, in her insight into how to work with students, into what their motivations are. Lars Ole Bonde is the quintessential musician with a tremendous knowledge of music and music psychology and musicology but at the same time is very informed about therapeutic praxis as well.

I could make a long list of people I haven't mentioned. Basically you develop in your life by the influence the other people have on you, the way you take on their ideas into yourself, their ways of thinking as you agree with them and find them helpful to you and developing your skills and your process and your personality.

The musical and personal combine in clinical practice and training. This can be clearly observed in the clinical chapters in this section and in the comments made by our colleagues in this postscript to the section. There are many influences that contribute to the effective practice of music therapy. We now need to look more specifically at some of these personal and musical resources in Part III on training.

Part III

Training

INTRODUCTION

Leslie Bunt and Sarah Hoskyns

Music is capable of amazing journeys and meanings.
(Birtwistle 1996 quoted in Andrews 1998)

New trainees enter a course with a range of strengths and weaknesses. Each will have a rich and varied background of musical experiences. Typically students may be music graduates (possibly with professional performance experience) equipped with developed musical skills and sensitivity but with less clinical awareness. Others might have come from a medical or educational background and have much experience in handling patient relationships but less confidence in their use of music. One of our aims as trainers is to build and strengthen the crossovers and basic skills in musical and clinical arenas. A central task of the emergent music therapist is the integration of these areas, the specialist use of a person's music and musical background within a clinical context. As trainers we help to facilitate this integration, this emphasis on underpinning musical know-how with clinical thinking, debate and critical reflection. In practical terms this could mean, for example, that a specific musical resource may be introduced by one of the music teachers on the course and related by the music therapist tutor and supervisor to the clinical setting. Personal development and awareness are vital areas: there is always the need to be flexible, tolerant and to adapt. Nor can we underestimate the development of a student's imagination as part of the training process. A student is helped to integrate these musical, clinical and personal resources throughout the course of their training from a number of sources including:

- clinical improvisation: practising exercises, sharing between students and tutors, role playing, aural and listening practice, instrumental and vocal techniques for both individual and group contexts;
- musical studies, for example: group improvisation workshops, extended vocal and instrumental techniques, styles of improvising (free, jazz, vocal and so on), specific instrumental teaching;

- personal development: personal therapy, experiential music therapy and other group work where the student gains knowledge of the therapeutic process;
- clinical practice: observation on placement of therapists at work, seeing techniques and methods in practice, small group and individual supervision on both observations and each student's own clinical work;
- theoretical studies including: developmental psychology of music, music therapy treatment models, psychological and medical studies.

The journey or pathway is often used as a metaphor for the training process. Students feel much changed by their experiences in training beginning with their attitude to music and how they listen and perform. We notice marked differences between entering and departing from a course and acknowledge the ways in which students struggle to integrate the diverse strands of learning. All the courses expect high commitment and the engagement of the whole self in the training process – the Italians have a nice phrase for this – courses not for 'information' but for 'formation' (*non è un corso di informazione ma di formazione*). This means that to benefit from the experience students will need to be open, brave, reflective and questioning. Students engage with a range of experiences as they work towards evolving their own approach to the work, the development of their music therapy personality. It is a subtle and personal learning process, different for each person, with each student moving through the training in their own unique way.

The courses themselves seem also to adhere to the pattern of a life cycle in microcosm. Students arrive (are born) with all the excitement, curiosity and enthusiasm of new children. They are thirsty for information and the newness is both exhausting and exhilarating. The next developmental phase involves acquiring the skills and tools of the trade and beginning to move out from the safety of the college into the area of clinical placements. We observe much dependence on teachers and supervisors at this stage. Gradually doubts surface and anxiety about competence mounts. Students identify very strongly with the needs of their patients and often begin to challenge the advice and help of staff in sometimes a rather rebellious way. At this stage students may not be able to see alternative interpretations of their work. As the group becomes older protests, storms and disagreements may emerge and it is often hard for the training group to stay united. Striving to be honest has its dangers when a student recognises somebody in the group they originally tolerated now causes intense annoyance. How can such tension be resolved maturely? The ending of the training process gradually comes into focus and, so as to model good therapy practice, careful attention is given to prepare students for how they will feel and cope. Hopefully the course has instilled a curiosity and manner of reflecting critically about the work that will continue to shift and develop as the student moves into the working environment as a trained therapist.

We note that this journey could be described as being within a developmental frame that is be mirrored not only in therapeutic processes but also in the early stages of experiencing supervision as discussed by Hawkins and Shohet (1989) and further in Chapter 13. We begin Part III with a chapter on observation and listening before presenting two resource-based chapters.

Chapter 10

Evolving a capacity for wondering: the development of observation and listening skills

Sarah Hoskyns

INTRODUCTION

This chapter concentrates on the early stages of observational and aural learning in music therapy training, and develops a rationale for its importance. The approaches described are by nature rather general, preparing students to begin their clinical studies in one of a variety of placement settings. As students become more attuned and alert to the overall process of music therapy, their work becomes more patient-specific and thus more specialised observation based on the pathology of particular client groups is needed. This chapter however will be confined to the first stage of work.

Before describing some approaches to teaching, we might start by considering a fictional account of observation and listening.

> . . . never before had she found a piece of music to be so full of surprises. There were sudden flashing tremolos at the beginning of bars, and places where the music hesitated without losing its tempo, or sustained the same speed despite appearing to halve or double it. Best of all, there were places where a note so high in pitch that it could barely be sounded descended at exhilarating pace down through the scale, and fell upon a reverberant bass note that barely had had time to ring before there came a sweet alternation of bass and treble. It made her want to dance or do something foolish.
>
> (de Bernières 1994: 186)

In this passage from *Captain Corelli's Mandolin* the novelist Louis de Bernières is describing one of his characters listening to live music and making observations. The main female character Pelagia watches Captain Corelli playing his beloved mandolin. Initially, Pelagia simply describes what she sees and hears. She makes no emotionally overladen inferences about what the music may actually mean. On one level she makes statements about the music; its hesitation but within a consistent tempo, the high pitch, the speed down the scale to the low bass note. But she is not content with mere musical descriptors. She adds a second level with the adjectives 'flashing', 'exhilarating', 'reverberant' and 'sweet' that obviously have a rich meaning within her own use of language. The music must have had meaning for her in that she found it 'so full of surprises' and she was encouraged to 'dance or do something foolish'. She observes in really careful detail, noting every nuance but also thinks to herself about how it is affecting how she feels and what it makes her want to do.

Soon after this moment the novelist continues:

> . . . she watched wonderingly . . . as the fingers of his left hand crawled like a powerful and menacing spider up and down the diapason. She saw the tendons moving and rippling beneath the skin, and then she saw that a symphony of expressions was passing over his face; at times serene, at times suddenly furious, occasionally smiling, from time to time stern and dictatorial, and then coaxing and gentle. Transfixed by this, she realised suddenly that there was something about music that had never been revealed to her before: it was not merely the production of sweet sound; it was, to those who understood it, an emotional and intellectual odyssey. She watched his face, and forgot to attend any more to the music; she wanted to share the journey.
>
> (de Bernières 1994: 186)

We have now moved on to a deeper level of observation and listening. She 'watched wonderingly' and the language is full of the most beautiful descriptions including her own personal feelings and inferences of mood. She enquires more thoroughly about her own responses. The language is increasingly metaphorical, the 'powerful and menacing spider' gives a different character to the previously innocent left hand of the musician. We infer a sexual undercurrent in the description of the rippling tendons. A tremendous range of emotion is registered by her in this brief musical moment; fury, joy, fear, tenderness. There is a sharing of meaning; the experience is a real encounter between the music, the player and the listener. Pelagia is aware of how deeply she has been affected. She is not just in love with the Captain but is spellbound and transported by her experience of being part of the music. She is drawn into an interaction.

For the music therapist, perhaps the most striking idea is Pelagia's realisation that music is much more than a lovely sound. She discovers the emotional and intellectual process, the possibility of different layers of communication, and consciousness of the idea of journeying (always a helpful metaphor for therapy). Pelagia discovers this by her involvement. Music teaches her something new and profound.

So how might we begin to think about learning to observe and listen in music therapy? There are within these two examples from *Captain Corelli's Mandolin* some interesting lessons on observation and listening. The author gives his heroine ample musical evidence coupled with more vivid language to help the meaning of the scenes come alive for us. In essence he allows his character to use acute and sensitive perceptions, empathy, imagination and an openness to her own feelings. Likewise the trained music therapist uses a delicate balance of all these features in professional practice to gain knowledge of 'the other'. But learning to achieve this balance is complicated and time-consuming. It needs deconstruction, openness and much practice. Overall it is the careful balance of external observation and self-observation and an awareness of the communicative or non-communicative patterns that emerge, which begin to foster the development of a 'therapeutic attitude' referred to in Chapter 2.

Why are observation and listening skills so important to therapists and how do we learn to use and interpret the information gained? In the course of this chapter the intention is to break down the processes of observing and listening, to demystify the role of the experienced practitioner who fluidly combines these complex skills and to think about how we help students get better at these tasks. In order to do this, in the first part of the chapter we can look for some reference points within the traditions and practices of other schools of thought such as psychotherapy, ethology and philosophy and in the description of case work in other professions. A further consideration here is to see how the pursuit of art forms such as literature, music and dance in themselves can teach us something about the process of observation and listening in therapy. In the second part of the chapter we look at a number of different strategies and pathways for developing alertness and responsivity in our perceptual skills and understanding our own reactions. The final section demonstrates an observational exercise undertaken with some filmed clinical work at different stages of training and experience (at the start of training, on completion of training and as an experienced practitioner).

SECTION 1: SOME REFERENCE POINTS FOR OBSERVATION AND LISTENING

The awareness of the need for listening and observation skills is paramount in the early stages in any clinical or therapeutic training. It is the feature that links medicine, psychology and the different therapies; the clinician needs to be able to pay detailed attention to the patient and to be vigilant about what is discovered. Through doing this, we can pinpoint features of the person's physical, communicative and social behaviour and begin to ascertain clues about mood and mental state. Before any treatment can be imagined, we need to 'get to know' the patient; to have collected the fine details of how they are (in relation to self and others); to be able to feel 'in their skin' and gradually to make an assessment of their needs.

As therapists we also need to understand and process our own reactions to what we observe. Trainee doctors learn to 'take a history' and to make a careful examination of the patient, noting any signs or symptoms of illness. These are then related to emerging understanding of normal anatomy and physiology and the study of pathology. Student clinical psychologists might make in-depth observations of patterns of behaviour in their patients and perhaps, for example identify the antecedent events and the consequences of self-injurious behaviour in young people with learning disability. Trainee child psychotherapists make detailed study of early communication and relationships between infants and parents and learn to take a concentrated emotional 'reading' of their encounters with the baby and their family and caregivers. The arts therapies are in an interesting position in that we might see links with a number of more established disciplines and build our practice on some of their methods and procedures. We also have the art form itself to consider; the particular nature of art throws up its own methods and ideas as described later in this section.

Whatever our professional orientation, learning these skills effectively establishes good patterns of clinical practice and is surprisingly tiring and difficult for new trainees. We develop many assumptions about 'reading' people's behaviours and our patterns for doing this need to be re-examined. Initially we need to discover how to be open to possibility; how not to jump to conclusions prematurely but rather to sharpen the clarity and focus of our perceptions.

Mother–infant observations

Some psychoanalytic training courses begin their programmes with close infant observation precisely for this reason – the student focuses solely on the business of being the observer. The task is not to *act* but to wait and pay attention 'to dramas which usually slip away and are forgotten' (Miller *et al.* 1989: 3). It offers a discipline and a method and an intense focus on the inner emotional world of the infant. Time is allowed to take things in and to consider the complexity. The observer also concentrates on the qualities of relating as they are experienced moment by moment, and considers their impact on the observer's own feelings as well as those of the active partners. Music therapy training courses pioneered by the Roehampton Institute, London often use similar or adapted methods to help students orientate themselves towards observation in their work. There are particular benefits to the music therapist in focusing on the preverbal communication of babies and their mothers' responses. Patients may often have little effective speech, through delayed development, learning difficulty, injury or debilitating illness, and looking intensely at the nuances of communication in this nursing partnership focuses the trainee's attention and awareness on non-verbal patterns. Pavlicevic's concept of dynamic form (Pavlicevic 1997: 118) referred to in

Chapters 2 and 4 has been linked to and developed from the musical and affective aspects of mother–baby relationships. The 'music' or 'dance' of early parent–infant contact has often been observed, and many music therapists find this concept persuasive and important in their work, particularly in work with non-verbal clients.

Another important part of close infant observation is the sharing and processing of experience with a teacher and fellow trainee observers. The seminar group can think together about the meaning of things and filter the ebb and flow of events. For example the group can help the observer understand issues such as the impact of the baby's helplessness. The observer is also 'helpless' in a sense, having to sit by and not be able to sort things out. The group might recognise the parallels and see how the baby expresses any difficulties. How are needs met? How does the mother recognise any signals, and how does she feel what the baby feels?

Ethology

Returning to our opening quotation concerning the observation of Captain Corelli playing the mandolin, a nice key or clue is provided by the phrase 'watched wonderingly'. For the character Pelagia this could mean that while she watches, she ponders and thinks, asking herself questions. This process is essential for the professional clinician who acts as a kind of detective (where are the links? what does this signify? is there a pattern to this?). However, Pelagia is also full of amazement at what she observes; there is a sense of wonder, an openness to being taken beyond herself, to seek beneath the surface. Both the artist and the therapist are at home in this area of thought.

By happy accident there is also a nice link in this idea of 'watching and wondering' with the discipline of ethology. This can be defined as the systematic study of animals' behaviour in natural environments, and emerged as a branch of zoology in the 1930s and 1940s. Ethology has refined and specialised the process of observation, initially with birds and animals in natural environments. Bowlby's research on attachment combined his interest in ethology and his training as a psychoanalyst (Bowlby 1969) and other psychologists and clinicians have used the principles of ethology as a rigorous method for understanding the social behaviour of humans (for example Hinde 1979). Tinbergen and Tinbergen (when explaining principles of method in ethology in *Autistic Children: New Hope for Cure*) write about the importance of 'watching and wondering'. Phenomena are perceived as they occur naturally and in all their rich patterning but through doing so systematically, the observer begins to form hunches and test these theories against practice (Tinbergen and Tinbergen 1983: 19–24). Tinbergen and Tinbergen, and latterly, consultant clinical psychologist John Richer have made specialist studies of autistic children and families using ethological principles (for example Richer 1983, 2001). While behaviour lies at the heart of their enquiries, these researchers have also been able to explore the motivation and feelings of their autistic subjects in a way very helpful to therapists interested in the inner world of clients. As teachers and researchers of music therapy, we have both found that borrowing a framework from ethology has often been a very useful way to introduce principles of observation to students, and also to begin to observe for research. The following description of the process of observation seems very pertinent to trainees' experience.

> at first glance, 'behaviour' seems to be an endlessly variable, almost chaotic flow of events (movements, postures and gestures, . . .) a random jumble in which no order can be detected at all . . . The aim of the observer is to refuse to believe that all these events are in fact random; he 'feels in his bones' because he has noticed it unconsciously and intuitively that it is possible to discern some kind of order . . .
>
> (Tinbergen and Tinbergen 1983: 24)

Story-telling

We started with the idea of the novelist describing his characters and perhaps one might say that the job of the therapist does not require the finesse and beauty with language that the novelist pursues by necessity. However, the attention to psychological and perceptual detail is a vital requirement, and the precision and clarity of description is a joy to read and a target to aim for. Maybe our motivation to become therapists comes in part from our interest in clients' stories and how they tell, show or play them to us. This is an attitude clearly shared with the novelist. Ben Okri writes passionately in *A Way of Being Free* of the human importance of story-telling:

> Stories are very patient things. They drift about quietly in your soul. . . . Stories . . . are living things; and their real life begins when they start to live in you. Then they never stop living, or growing, or mutating, or feeding the groundswell of imagination, sensibility and character.
>
> (Okri 1997: 43)

It seems that there is a parallel here with music, and the practice of music therapy. We as music therapists engage in a particular way of sharing musical stories with our patients. We interact with their music and help it unfurl and reveal itself. The process is interactive yet focused on the patient's needs. The patients' stories start to live in us. Of course any individual patient's 'story' may remain in musical form and our responses in the session likewise, but in writing case notes we link with the novelist and try to form the experiences in words. The art of the case study in clinical disciplines is a fascinating way of passing on the history of our work to others and it is done through the revealing of 'story'. Axline's moving case of Dibs, a child she worked with in play therapy, has been in print for many years (Axline 1964); the intriguing stories of Oliver Sacks' neurological patients (Sacks 1985), and the case studies of Freud, such as 'Dora' and 'Little Hans' (Freud 1905) are well known to quite a general public perhaps simply because they are 'tales well told'.

Professor Baum (referred to in Chapter 1) reminded Leslie Bunt to encourage music therapists to 'keep telling your stories' and there are increasing numbers of engaging case stories in the music therapy literature. Recent interesting examples are in Pavlicevic's collection *Intimate Notes* (1999a) where aspects of the therapists' personal histories are set alongside case material and Hibben's *Inside Music Therapy* (1999) where collaborations with families and clients themselves have assisted in telling about the work. In Chapter 9, Odell-Miller examines the idea of music therapy sustaining the narrative skills of Patient M within the course of his treatment. John Sloboda has likened the process of musical improvisation to the 'recounting of a story by a skilled story-teller' (Sloboda 1985: 139–141). The weaving of art forms and the therapy continue to be closely linked.

The music appraiser and analyst

The practice of the arts heightens awareness of our senses and works rigorously on the ordering of information from eye, ear and touch. The development of the eye and 'ways of seeing' for the visual artist is paramount. For musicians, the early years of training will focus our aural acuity in very precise ways. Careful attention to detail for eye and ear among artists and musicians are tools of the trade and promote mastery. But these skills also enhance our understanding of the world around us. Indeed Christopher Small has also argued in his book *Musicking* (Small 1998) that they increase our sense of relatedness and humanity and therefore can profitably be harnessed and integrated for the very rich benefit of the therapeutic discipline. Our artistic imaginative selves have a powerful part to play in understanding our patients: use of imagery, metaphor, pattern, sound and all kinds of non-verbal communication inform us.

The years of work spent by musicians listening to their own sound and that of ensembles can be a great training ground for learning to listen in therapy. It may seem unusual or perhaps too time-consuming to apply a critical or analytic musical ear to the improvisations in music therapy. Certainly it can be a demanding job, but paying attention to this gives interesting rewards as long as we take time to assess the significance within the communication between the partners or group in therapy (Ann Sloboda and Richard Bolton describe these two strands in Chapter 8).

Let us consider an example of how this might work in practice. Fraser Simpson explores the delicacy of his elderly client's vocal changes to the melody line of 'Blue Moon' in his chapter for the book *Music Therapy in Dementia*

Care (Simpson 2000). Simpson identifies and notates the subtle elaborations of both the client and himself as they play with the tune. It is the kind of exercise one might have done for aural notation in 'Advanced Level' Music. But it shows us exactly how Edward builds and lengthens his phrases, plays with 'da, doo and diddly' vocal sounds and eventually how he is motivated to get up from his chair to swing his arms. (Like Pelagia, the music created makes him want to dance.) Simpson, the person and therapist, is very moved by his patient's defiance of his illness – by his real lively spirit. But because of his careful critical analysis of his work as a musician, we see exactly how he comes to that conclusion. Recording, listening, notating, analysing and assessing the meaning: all these are tools of the trained musician and good 'evidence-based practice', a necessary requirement of state registered practitioners in all disciplines in the UK.

The position of the philosopher

The philosopher, according to an account given by Jostein Gaarder in *Sophie's World*, has a special observatory relationship with the world, akin to that of the small child, which perhaps provides a useful reference point here. Gaarder's character argues that 'the world itself becomes a habit in no time at all. It seems as if in the process of growing up we lose the ability to wonder about the world'. This is about having or re-establishing an inno-cent view and thus a genuinely inquiring mind. Little children naturally consider the world astonishing. Adults generally 'accept the world as a matter of course'. Like philosophers, therapists need to avoid habit in their observations and to continue to see the world as '. . . a bit unreasonable – bewildering, even enigmatic' (Gaarder 1991: 16). Perhaps we have to go through a comparable process of reorienting our view of things. A psychotherapist's stance might be to learn to sit with the unbearable anxiety of a child's help-lessness: the philospher's position to stick with the 'huge mystery' and not get too comfortable in the world. However we might think of it, the task seems to be to try to perceive things as they really are, in all their com-plexity and paradox rather than how they seem to be on the surface. We also need to be able to keep the ambiguity of different views in mind. Gaarder's notion is that we need to exist as he describes it 'at the tip of the rabbit's fur' where there is sharpness of focus and clarity, rather than nestled com-fortably at the root, ignoring detail, not wanting to know.

All of this connects to the building of a therapeutic attitude referred to in Chapter 2. It takes time and practice to learn to take things in from differ-ent perspectives. Students regularly begin with a jumble of responses. They may not have a clear distinction between their own feelings and what might be the feelings and reactions of others, and the witnessed events. This is com-plicated. We obviously do have feelings about what we see and hear, and these will yield us important information. But we have to learn to understand and use them. A client's situation can be viewed from many different perspectives. What are the questions to ask? How do we decide what is the truth in any situation? Perhaps the endpoint for therapists is in being able to tolerate ambiguity, to accept complex layers. But first we have to find ways to get at them, to unravel and make sense of the picture. In the next section we look at some methods for building awareness and skill at taking things in (through eyes, ears and feelings) and finding ways to record them.

SECTION 2: SOME STRATEGIES FOR FOCUSING OBSERVATION AND LISTENING IN MUSIC THERAPY TRAINING

Pathways for developing our perceptual awareness can and need to be developed from many angles and there is a whole impact in arts therapy training of the various strands coming together. We sharpen our focus and learn to listen and read situations in more detail. A starting point is to divide up the active relating/playing role and the reflective listening role of the therapist and to concentrate in detail on each. Many courses begin with periods of observational work of various kinds and in order to get students to absorb and feel engaged in this process. It is often hard not to be 'doing' things at the beginning and just starting to try out this reflective stance is in itself useful learning. Chapters 11 and 12 tackle some issues regarding the more active playing and relating side of music therapy. Here we look at the reflective listening one. Three common areas of observational learning in music therapy training are:

1 observation of the general context of music therapy at a placement;
2 observation/listening live music therapy sessions in a music therapy centre or outside placement;
3 study of audio- or videotape of music therapy cases.

Usually this kind of work involves seminar support from a tutor or supervisor who will help and guide the students' perceptions.

General observation of work on clinical placements

Let us consider some general visits to placements first. In the early stages it is easy to get overwhelmed with information and to polarise into one of two positions: either noting everything in great detail and finding it hard to know what is important (pages and pages of notes); or finding it hard to notice anything and writing very little. Decisions need to be made about whether you keep notebook in hand as you go, or whether at fixed points in the day

Table 10.1 Prompts and ideas for general observation on clinical placements

1 *The hospital/centre/school itself*
(a)   The range of illness/handicap/problems dealt with.
(b)   The atmosphere or prevailing mood of the institution as you observe it.
(c)   Interest of staff.
(d)   Integration of staff team.
(e)   Methods of approach to patients by individual staff.
(f)   General interaction of staff and clients within the institution.

2 *Organisation of music therapy*
(a)   Is there one room for work or does the therapist move to the patients/clients?
(b)   Position in room (of patients/clients, staff, equipment etc.).
(c)   What instruments are used?
(d)   Is attendance optional?
(e)   How are clients referred for music therapy and sessions organised?
(f)   How long are the sessions?

3 *Relationships existing*
(a)   Between patients themselves.
(b)   Yourself and therapist (how at ease you are).
(c)   Therapist and staff (how is music therapy viewed?).
(d)   Therapist and clients (what qualities do you observe?).
(e)   Patients and yourself.

Note Do try to notice your own reactions – how at ease you feel with patients, and
the reasons for this (e.g. appearance; extent of handicaps or difficulties; your own
fears; reactions to environment, care of patients etc.).

4 *Within music therapy sessions* (with reference to patients, staff, self)
Try to observe these areas generally and in particular in relation to the music.
(a)   Body position.
(b)   Body contact (use of touch).
(c)   Use of gestures/signs.
(d)   General movement of body and limbs (including repetitive and stereotyped
      patterns).
(e)   Eye contact.
(f)   Facial expression.
(g)   Vocalisation (and/or speech).
(h)   Attention to instruments and people.
(i)   Any instrumental preferences.
(j)   'Social' skills (sharing, waiting, listening, receiving and giving etc.).
(k)   Development or change during session (and is there any observable cause?).
(l)   General behaviour *before* and *after* the music therapy session.
(m)   Specific musical initiatives and responses (in any of these areas: pitch,
      rhythm/duration, timbre, loudness, melody, harmony, form/structure etc.).
(n)   Therapist's style of leadership (high/low structure; directive/non-directive).

These are some issues you might consider in making your preliminary observations
at clinical placements and you may find them useful for reference. The list is not
intended to be compulsory or exhaustive but just a starting point for raising
awareness.

you write up in as much detail as you can remember. The latter is very useful training as you cannot write your notes while you work in sessions, and it helps us stimulate our memory for meaningful events. Mother–baby observations are usually conducted in this way, leaving the listener-observer free to really concentrate.

A frame consisting of prompts or questions to ask yourself can be useful in general visits to placements and indeed some therapists use a kind of prompt sheet as a regular note-writing tool when practising professionally. Table 10.1 shows an example of some prompt questions that might be used to guide observations in early visits. Questions like these jog our memories in various areas that may be significant. They focus our attention on a small part at a time so that we can attend in more detail. Listening is also prompted by these questions and a file with manuscript paper is useful for noting musical ideas and extracts.

At this stage the questions are quite wide-ranging and allow us to notice physical details and also enquire about some of our feeling reactions. Although most of the questions focus on the music therapy session itself there is also attention to the context of the institution. As seen in Chapter 2, norms and values of the therapist and others within the setting have their own impact on practical work with patients, and it is helpful to be aware of this early on. Notes resulting from this kind of observational frame can then be discussed in seminars and trainees can see how others react to their ideas.

How do we begin to observe without making too many inferences?

Early attempts at studying the music therapy process often include a number of personal judgements and preconceptions, as discussed earlier. We need to be aware of when we are stating quite simple easily shared facts or behaviours and when we are having a personal response or hunch (or intuition) about what we experience. Using the concept of being able to 'watch, listen and wonder', our first task might be to take careful note of what we see and hear, but gradually through concentrating in this way we might start to gain a feeling impression of what events could mean. Trainees can explore this idea by concentrating on one area at a time. For example, a class exercise examining an extract of individual music therapy casework on video might be as follows:

Class exercise (a)

Group 1   watches and listens with great attention, taking notes of the easily shared simple practical details, taking care not to make judgements.

Table 10.2 Case notes on music therapy group work with probation clients

WATCHING	WONDERING
Summary of events	Comments and thoughts
Session 9 (for old group)/Session 4 (for new group)	
At the session start-time, no one had arrived. After 7 minutes, client P came in rather hurriedly, quickly followed by D, both clients in the newer group at the centre. D was surprised that there were so few people there and particularly that there was no one from the old group. (7 or 8 clients had been usual in the previous weeks.) I said this session would include some review between the two groups, but that we should do some playing first with whoever came.	It looked as if the more experienced group were vetoing my suggestion that we had a review of the sessions. They don't want to think about working towards leaving? They all said later that they 'had things to finish off' in other workshops.
D said he wanted to play the drum kit so proceeded to assemble it.	Theme of feeling pushed out by the new group still prevails? I feel annoyed/rejected – I'm probably meant to! Hard for the group to discuss the ending?
P could not decide what he wanted to play and looked in the cupboard, but eventually sat down at the piano for a while as D put the drums together. However, he quite quickly got up again and stood by the piano and then paced round the room. Eventually, he spotted the xylophones and glockenspiel and built a structure of xylophones on the closed piano lid and top of the piano. I said that he looked more comfortable standing up to play, and he smiled and waved his arms with the beaters doing a twisting movement.	NB last week's discussion about not having the drum kit, so that people can hear better could not really be pursued as none of old group were around. It feels fragmented to me – undermining what the group builds up. However the new group members have a chance to explore a bit themselves – they can reconstruct the instruments in their own way.

I have not really seen anybody do this before! It was practical – made a stand for the instruments and P seemed a lot happier being able to use some energy/agitation by moving as he played. He was able to stay in contact with the piano (instrument he wants to play) but also shut it off. |
| I collected 3 small hand percussion instruments and suggested that we began playing freely to loosen ourselves up and see what it was like playing together. Music was quite restrained in volume, D played in a hesitant way on the drums but explored the different surfaces of the kit. P had his back to us and his music was quiet but unconnected rhythmically to D or me. he was doing his own thing. | P seems fairly oblivious to the rest of us – but discharging quite a bit of his own tension. |
| E (from the old group) arrived while we were playing and nodded appreciatively and listened until we finished. We went on to discuss his time in the group and I suggested that he possibly had come late because it was uncomfortable to think about leaving. He agreed with this. | It was possible to talk with E about significant achievements he had made, particularly with commitment to the group, and to link his actions and his feelings (i.e. not wanting to come today). This seemed positive and useful for other group members to hear. This surprised me! |

Group 2   wonders about things and is asked to question how it makes them
          feel; to observe themselves and their reactions as they watch; to
          respond to intuitions.

The tutor and class can then discuss the results of these two different perspectives. If a number of trainees do the same Group 1 task, they can compare the different things that are noticed and see which ideas can be shared
and agreed. Trainees can also compare the subjective feeling reactions they
have held in Group 2. There may be overlaps, or striking personal differences. In doing this exercise with a number of training groups in recent years,
one also becomes aware of the wealth of information that can be gleaned.
Trainees are often surprised how much they can discover. Tinbergen suggests the importance of trying to adopt 'a truly enquiring, not prematurely
prejudiced state of mind' but also emphasises how the intuitive hunch
begins to appear if simple careful observation (and listening) is achieved
(Tinbergen and Tinbergen 1983: 19).

   This class exercise can then be applied to a naturalistic setting on placement and the student therapists can observe music therapy from both
perspectives themselves. Table 10.2 gives an example of some case notes constructed in this way. The material is an extract of some semi-open group
work with probation clients to show how one might use this plan to record
clinical work.

   As the training group begin to become more aware of the difference between
simple shared details and their own individual perspective, we can begin to
expand our areas of focus. Another class exercise with a second extract of
filmed case work could be as follows:

Class exercise (b)

Group 1   'Behaviour': this group takes notice of the events, movements, posi-
          tions (much as Group 1 did before).
Group 2   'Interaction': this group pays attention to 'contact between' the
          participants; any gestural, postural, facial connections; vocal or
          verbal; instrumental.
Group 3   'Music': this group listens to and takes note of as much musical
          detail as possible; using manuscript to notate (prompt areas
          suggested in Table 10.1 can be used to guide); and trying to describe
          qualities.

In all groups, the trainees try to avoid making judgements and discuss the
findings together in the class. Overlaps in the categories are noticed (for example, music itself is 'behaviour') but this is inevitable. The class as a whole
then suggest their own perspectives and begin to make inferences about
the significance or meaning of all the information. The point of all of this

is to base our feeling or intuitive reactions on the musical and behavioural evidence. We can use the latter to give weight to our clinical judgement or interpretation.

Class exercise (c) Identifying clinical features

Having amassed a range of information in the previous exercise, the group and tutor can move on to examine the clinical information presented. For example exercise (b) could have shown a four-minute extract of music therapy with an adult with learning disability and challenging behaviour. The group could begin to make an assessment of various areas of general functioning and communication for the patient. This could involve, among other issues, the patient's:

- use of expressive and receptive language;
- willingness to explore instruments;
- use of and reactions to vocalisation;
- tolerance of proximity to another person.

The group might also look at, for example: evidence of cognition; repetitive behaviour; spontaneous communication, communication related to the therapist (dialogue, synchronous music), aggressive gestures and so on. These sorts of features could then help to build on knowledge of the client group and the specific use of music therapy in treatment.

Focus on listening to the music of music therapy

The detailed attention to the aural world of music therapy has always had an important focus in the writings of Nordoff–Robbins-trained therapists, as was seen in Simpson's work above. My teaching at the Guildhall School, London has been influenced by the work of our tutors trained in this approach (Jackie Robarts and Elaine Streeter). We can apply something of the two-stage strategy, described above with mainly *visual* information, to what we hear of music therapy on audiotape. That is, we can transcribe into music notation many of the musical 'events' and describe their form and quality; but then also be aware of our subjective feeling responses to what we hear. A clinical judgement about the material will involve a synthesis of the musical details and our assessment of their meaning.

In training, students study taped material and transcribe parts of their sessions. From the score they can examine the detail of musical interaction or indeed absence of interaction in their work. This work can then be discussed in regular seminars of the training group and students can begin to weigh up the implications of any musical dialogue. Figure 10.1 gives an example of short extracts of case material transcribed from the session

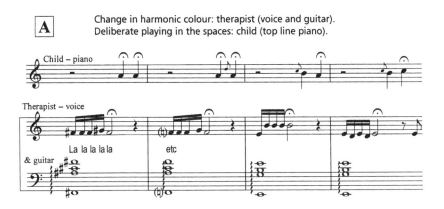

A Change in harmonic colour: therapist (voice and guitar).
Deliberate playing in the spaces: child (top line piano).

B Following the child playing more deliberately, the therapist sings
a longer, more defined melodic phrase with forward movement.

C Child begins a lively triple rhythm and therapist responds with
a dance-like tune.

Figure 10.1 Transcription of short extacts of a music therapy session with Child N.

observed in the final part of this chapter. It indicates the kind of transcription that might be useful for students to undertake.

Elaine Streeter spoke in her interview for this book about the influence of further psychotherapeutic training on her understanding of the importance of listening in music therapy. The combination of the musician's sensitivity to sonorities and forms of sound and the psychotherapist's interest in communication of meaning provide a powerful frame for understanding:

> *You really learn how to listen for everything, to the tone of voice, to the feelings. .. It's about the quality of being with somebody. Listening is probably acknowledged as one of the major skills of the counsellor or psychotherapist. It's listening for meaning, trying to help the person to find significance in a sound or a cry. Sometimes the words used have got nothing to do with what they feel. It's a surface layer. It's about what they might be struggling or daring to say – or very often not being able to put words to. It's not just being able to sit there and listen but being able to be curious and interested by little moments or expressions or tones of voice. I suppose that a lot of our work is about helping people make connections with other sounds that they may have just made so that a sound is not just an isolated incident but can link up with other things that are happening. In music therapy we get interested in the absolute minute details of a sound.*

Rachel Verney examined an interesting process for working receptively and then actively with the intricate musical details of a session at the 2001 BSMT/APMT Conference. She stressed how helpful musical listening can be to inform the work of future sessions and proposed a three-stage model of 'Listening–Thinking–Doing' firstly in the session itself and then in response to an audiotape of the therapy. This process can constantly reflect on and feed into the ongoing work in music therapy (Verney 2001).

The growth of personal awareness

The experiential parts of training courses, music therapy groups, verbal experiential work, therapeutic movement groups and students' personal therapy all assist to heighten general observation skills and self-awareness. These are rather difficult to pinpoint as they are highly personal in nature, but nonetheless affect significantly students' capacity to reflect on the process of music therapy. In my own experience of training groups, students often become much more able to 'read' body language – their own and that of others. They start to see some of their own prejudices in how they think about their work, and more readily can empathise and understand strange and difficult behaviours. They also start to use feelings more actively.

For example, Helen Tyler described the growing understanding gained by students in training of cultural difference through working in movement. The group noticed the difference in meaning of the tiny steps taken by an Eastern student compared to the large relaxed stride of a Westerner (Tyler 1999). Work in mother–infant observation undertaken in various levels of detail on British training courses also helps students identify some of their own emotional responses to infant needs and expression.

The case study as story

As case work develops students collect all their observation, listening and evaluation and begin to shape the story of the work with patients. In this volume, clinical practitioners have filtered, selected and organised periods of work with their patients and explained some of its meaning from different perspectives. In his lively book, *Approaches to Case Study*, Higgins takes the reader through varied uses of the case study and provides helpful advice to the arts therapist on ways to engage the reader. He particularly stresses the importance of giving a real flavour and quality of our therapy (Higgins 1993). Hence, music therapy case stories need to be accompanied by aural illustrations and perhaps we can think musically about how we will unfold the tale?

A simple structure for the information that can be included in case studies is as follows:

(a) name (or pseudonym), age and some description of how the patient presents (this could include musical or other illustration);
(b) diagnosis (if appropriate or known);
(c) background: family history; referral and any other treatment; assessment of needs of patient;
(d) general aims for therapy;
(e) summary of the themes of the work (including examples of music therapy process);
(f) discussion (assessing the meaning of the work);
(g) conclusions and recommendations for the future.

Clearly many case studies do not have this structure and it would be valuable for student therapists to evolve suitable frames of their own, but the above contains some typical details that may be included. (See other suggested references in this chapter and the models used in the clinical chapters of this book.)

SECTION 3: AN ENQUIRY INTO APPROACHES TO OBSERVATION AND LISTENING BY MUSIC THERAPISTS AT DIFFERENT LEVELS OF EXPERIENCE AND TRAINING

This section describes a piece of work where some music therapists at different stages of their training and practice were asked to do the same task as observer-listeners. The study was not controlled but simply a starting point to gather information and to enquire whether music therapists might evolve ways of looking and listening that are qualitatively different at different stages in their training and work. In the process of training we might aim to raise awareness of clinical musical detail and possible meanings as discussed above, but does this really happen?

The task was this. Music therapists at three stages in training and work were each asked to look at the same section of video-filmed case work. The video was shown twice with a few minutes' gap between each playing so that the trainee or qualified therapists could make a few written notes and then watch again. After watching the film for the second time they could make any further notes for a few minutes, and then a short unstructured interview was recorded with the people. The interview began with the following question: '*What do you think is happening here? Please describe and discuss some of your ideas*'. The film lasted four minutes and showed a piece of musical dialogue between a young boy at the piano and the therapist using voice and guitar.

The different stages of training/work of the therapists were:

1 in the first week of training (a group of three new students);
2 in the last week of training (a different group of three students);
3 a clinician of 25 years' experience with children (my co-author).

A summary of the clinical extract on film, as experienced by the therapist, is given below on page 185.

Results of observation and listening

In the three sections shown in Table 10.3 are contained the ideas or constructs that the trainees and therapist developed about the extract in their interview. They observed and listened and some of the issues they discussed are listed in this table.

Clinical extract

Background

The extract shows part of an individual session with N, a young child of six years old, who had quite severely impaired vision and delayed development in his speech and cognition. In his class at school, he also showed patterns of difficult/challenging behaviour and related little to his peers. He experienced much frustration in verbal communication. It was quite hard to understand his limited language and he often stammered. The recent birth of a younger sibling (one year previously) had also put him under a lot of stress emotionally, and he showed many regressed babyish characteristics (falling over, knocking things over, crying and generally needing lots of personal attention). He found it very hard to concentrate especially in class. Originally I worked with N in a group, and decided that he needed more one-to-one time.

The session (see Figure 10.1 for notated musical extracts)

This session took place after about six months of individual work. He was very responsive to musical patterns and easily invested in the work. The sequence shows N sitting down at the piano with his back to me, looking to the side from time to time. I am sitting behind him on the floor playing a guitar and singing (improvising and following his gestures). He is 'doing his own thing' fiddling with the piano keys making little flurries of sound, pushing the keys up and down and experimenting with the pedal. He seems to be aware that I am there, looking over his shoulder from time to time. I have the impression that he becomes increasingly aware that his playing is having an impact on me and what I am doing and starts to play with more emphasis, space and links. We form a quite deliberate dialogue.

I change my playing from little flamenco style 'flutters' to a more dramatic/grandiose 2/2 time and he looks round at me purposefully. I get louder as he looks round again to reinforce our connection. He seems encouraged to get more expansive. He stands up on his chair, begins to bang the frame of the piano. It looks less 'desirable behaviour', but he is part of the music: we are really playing together. As the music becomes louder he stands on the keyboard stretching all round. Sadly I realise the wall-mounted fire is a bit of a threat for safety. I am rather unsure whether to intervene and let it go as long as I can but eventually invite him down. He says 'Hee, hee hee!'. The moment is lost. He's off with something else.

Table 10.3 Results of observation and listening at three stages of experience.

Interview 1: New students in week 1 21.9.98.

1 He seemed very bothered that the therapist was behind him.
2 Even though he has a visual impairment he was turning around a lot.
3 He was very aware of the noises behind him.
4 He knew the therapist was there.
5 I thought he was quite fearless.
6 He was quite inquisitive.
7 Checking to see that the therapist liked what he was doing.
8 Playing with the therapist a little bit.
9 'Ha ha look at what I'm doing'.
10 'I'm not really listening to you'.
11 Such a vivid imagination.
12 Very responsive to what therapist was doing.
13 'Are you still with me?'
14 'I'm going to take control'.
15 'Here's the pace' and therapist matched that.
16 Then it just got really exciting.
17 He takes it one step further (tapping/standing up).
18 He just wanted to keep going.
19 'Is she still with me on this?' Then quickened the pace.
20 I was worried/glad therapist stopped him.

Interview 2: Students in week 36 (last week) 20.7.00.

1 There was a kind of space (physical) and space which allowed the interaction.
2 Started off at random.
3 Seemed to start stopping, when therapist was playing.
4 He'd stop more clearly (while therapist goes 'La la la').
5 A sense of pulse.
6 Became more rhythmic.
7 Tiny phrases between the two.
8 He started to get faster and I think the therapist changed the accompaniment.
9 This flexible pulse became really this kind of frame.
10 Sense of searching with his hand.
11 Music became more structured.
12 Certain stillness in the body like he is listening.
13 Wanting to control.
14 I had the feeling he just wanted the music to grow.
15 Just got too big for the piano.
16 Quite dramatic the way suddenly the music rides?
17 Using just little fingers, then suddenly big sound.
18 Feeling of testing towards the end.
19 'He, he, he, I've got you, you stop what you're doing'.

Interview 3: Experienced therapist (25 years of clinical work) 5.8.00.

1 Use a Stern type idea – here was an adult and child in an engaged moment.
2 Were many elements that were quite contrasting.
3 Overall it had a sort of feel of sustained interaction.

Table 10.3 cont.

4 Matching his first gesture (on the guitar), which seemed to be this little flash of activity on the piano.
5 Keeping a similar intensity and feel to what he gave you.
6 Not just the actual guitar matching but also with your voice.
7 Lovely couple of phrases that some went up (sings) with little Spanish type configurations.
8 It all then felt quite safe, in those early parts (secure in that way of working).
9 It felt that this was like a coming together again (done before?).
10 Within that frame, your input (though changing) seemed to have a very regular pulse to it (even rest points felt pulsed).
11 He may be playing in more random ways but you were keeping it very focused.
12 Sang in a more lyrical way, which seemed to interest him; he turned towards you.
13 Touched a single note with a single finger and you did a loud, more upbeat and more excited type gesture.
14 Experimented with longer phrases led into some mutuality, some reciprocal play.
15 Containing shape or space.
16 Dynamically, at the height of the moment when he was the most with you, it was the time he wrecked it.
17 Quite a lot of concentration for him (2 minutes or so?).
18 Very secure with his little fragments.
19 He didn't get stuck in his patterns/didn't get obsessive.

Discussion

It was interesting to see subtle differences in the three stages of observation indicated here. Group 1 concentrated in some detail on their own thoughts and interpretations. They were very 'case-centred', that is, focused on the patient more than the interaction. Both Group 2 and the experienced therapist paid much more detailed attention to musical events. Group 2 used more phrases like 'I think', 'it seemed', 'I had the feeling'. Group 2 looked more at the overall process and the quality of the relationship. This was even more pronounced with the experienced therapist. The experienced therapist related to theory and was able to balance between an objective overview and the musical fabric. Group 1's observations seemed to contain more assumptions about the meaning of events than the other stages and looked more at single events and not the whole process between the partners. The experienced therapist was also able to bring more clinical knowledge of the client group to the observation as a whole, for example issues about reciprocal play, about the length of the child's concentration and about the lack of obsessive quality in the child's patterns.

To conclude, it seems that this simple enquiry showed that the overall effect of therapy training changes the quality and approach of therapists' observation and listening. Trainees move from a preoccupation with discrete events and a variety of assumptions to a more objective and balanced view of the whole interaction observed. Trainees at the end of their course and an experienced therapist were likely to notice a range of musical details *between* the therapist and patient and to infer suggested meanings from this. Confidence in making inferences and in keeping in mind a complex picture is clearly affected by long experience of the client field. These findings seem to bear out the relevance of Tinbergen's methods and applying careful simple procedures for attending to our work.

SUMMARY

This chapter has attempted to identify some strategies for raising the perceptive skills and sense of enquiry in trainee therapists. More specialisation and refinement of observation will be needed as students develop their clinical work, and it is hoped that colleagues in specialist fields may be stimulated to take these ideas further. This chapter ends with the thoughts of Thomas Moore on the subject of 'observance':

> The basic intention in any caring, physical or psychological, is to alleviate suffering. But in relation to the symptom itself, observance means first of all listening and looking carefully at what is being revealed in the suffering. An intent to heal can get in the way of seeing. By doing less, more is accomplished.

(Moore 1992: 10)

Chapter 11

Beginning the clinical journey

Leslie Bunt and Sarah Hoskyns

INTRODUCTION

There are many practical questions that preoccupy music therapists both in training and practice. There are few formulas or fixed prescriptive answers to these questions but rather we can bring into play a variety of musical/ personal responses and clinical approaches to address them. An experienced therapist makes a number of seemingly instantaneous decisions during a session: for example, whether to play or to attend and listen to the patient without playing; how to engage with the patient's music; how to work with silence; what kind of sounds to play; how to engage with any words in the session. This can all look very baffling to a student, something akin to the 'women's intuition' articulated by Zeldin in Chapter 2. So how are those decisions made?

We aim to explore some of these questions in a straightforward and approachable way, using practical exercises, musical illustrations, quotations and examples from clinical practice. The suggestions in these resource chapters refer in the main to both group and individual practice. We are thinking here about the approach and resourcefulness of the music therapist in general, as applied to various client groups and a range of work. Consequently the exercises are not directed to a particular clinical context but relate more to the therapist's own personal and imaginative development of resources. There are two groups of sections in this chapter that concentrate on beginning the clinical journey: some very basic sound and musical considerations and some fundamental therapeutic issues and personal resources. Although presented in separate sections we are very aware of the integration of both the musical and the personal. We are also aware of overlaps between this and the next chapter, for example empathy is a fundamental quality needed not only at the start of the work but throughout all stages of the therapeutic process.

We anticipate that the ideas in these two chapters can be used flexibly for personal practice or adapted to different kinds of teaching, workshop or training situations. We hope you will pick and choose and play with them. We divide the sections in this chapter accordingly:

The initial musical connection

- Planning and preparing for the first session
- Silence and sound
- Quality of the sound and choice of instrument
- Experience of loudness
- Use of pulse

Fundamental therapeutic and personal issues

- Demonstrating empathy and resonance
- Accompanying, reflecting and matching
- Holding and containing
- Use of words
- Some reflections on interpretation

THE INITIAL MUSICAL CONNECTION

Planning and preparing for the first session

There are a number of issues to consider and decisions to be made before the patient first enters the music therapy room with you. These are rather different plans to ones made for teaching, with which some readers are familiar. They serve the purpose of creating a good working environment and allowing you to think in advance, avoiding practical dilemmas in the midst of new work. Spending time thinking about strategies and allowing time to speak to the team of care staff, therapists or teachers about practical issues can really assist our ability to provide a safe frame for the work, though clearly we cannot control for everything. We have structured this section as questions and answers, using issues commonly raised by students and teachers.

Q: *Should I ask to see the clinical notes before meeting the patient?*

A: This depends on the context and clinical orientation of the therapist. Some therapists study the notes in great detail and take a history before the first meeting; others prefer not to read them until they have met the patient. The very nature of music therapy provides opportunities for a whole picture of a patient to be observed, sometimes with behaviours not observable in other contexts. However, it is very important to assess any potential risks for patient and therapist in beginning work. Here reading of relevant background information and contact with ward staff, teachers and other carers would be very appropriate. For issues of health, safety and general care therapists need to know whether there is:

(a) any physical disability that necessitates special arrangements for positioning or limits particular movements;
(b) any history of epilepsy or other medical condition such as diabetes;
(c) any visual or auditory impairment;
(d) any history of violent or aggressive behaviour or self-injury;
(e) any confidential issues relating to a history of physical or sexual abuse.

Q: *How many instruments should I set out in the therapy room?*

A: For individual work it is useful to provide a range of tuned and untuned percussion (for suggestions see Appendix II). Consideration needs to be given to physical differences and restrictions, for example the thin sticks of beaters may be difficult to hold, and height and accessibility of instruments may need to be adjusted for wheelchair-bound patients or very small children. Remember to provide enough choice but not to overwhelm. If starting a series of sessions other instruments can be gradually offered in subsequent sessions. Make sure you are able to offer quality musical support and that any keyboard or piano is tuned and playable. For group work the same suggestions apply except that a sufficient range of instruments needs to be available for all members of the group to have an instrument. Take care of providing age-appropriate instruments. Be sure also that you can provide the same collection of instruments each week, even if not always used, as patients often evolve a kind of map of the environment in their minds. You need to be aware of the significance of the regularity and familiarity of the 'tools of music therapy' as the work develops.

Q: *Should I use my own musical instrument in the first session?*

A: For pianists this question is not too difficult as the piano can be shared and made accessible to patients. Conversely wind and string instruments, while having enormous potential in therapeutic work, can present challenging problems of ownership and accessibility. Therapists get over these problems in different ways:

(a) placing clear boundaries around their sole use of their own instrument (make sure your own instrument is adequately insured) – it is OK to say 'No';
(b) placing clear boundaries around how the instrument is to be played if offered to patients;
(c) not using their concert instrument in therapy sessions providing alternatives for use by patients, although this opens up dynamic, power and relationship issues (who has the better or best instrument?).

This is a difficult question and we all need to find our individual solutions. As in many issues of this nature it is important to be honest about what is acceptable personally. Aim to be clear and consistent.

Q: *What happens if the patients do not want or are not able to play the instruments?*

A: We need to appreciate this as a communication in itself. Sometimes the fear of becoming involved may be a central theme in our work. However, it is worth considering what is appropriate equipment for patients who are very disabled; for example instruments that can make sounds with a minimum of movement, or computer/electronically generated sounds that can be adapted to the patient's particular physical needs (see Appendix II for further information). We can and do have a role as playing musicians in music therapy and at times it is appropriate to play on our own to our patients. We can listen to music together (music has great potential as a 'co-therapist' in its own right) and we can also be silent together.

Q: *Will I harm the patient if I do anything wrong?*

A: Patients have ways of communicating what they need from their therapists, however confusing or apparently limited their behaviour may be. Approaching any new situation is naturally anxiety-provoking but we need always to listen and observe, taking cues from the patients themselves. We need to trust ourselves to pick up these cues and begin to build a musical relationship from there. Sometimes we can find surprising inner musical and personal resources. The aim is to place ourselves as much as possible in the shoes of the patient, and to shift the point of observation from pre-occupation with self to awareness of others. Sometimes patients are in a very vulnerable state of mind and clearly could be damaged by inexperienced handling. The task of the placement supervisor here would be to choose clients appropriately for student work.

Silence and sound

Catherine, a character in the novel *Grace Notes*, sits by the sea 'lost in her ears' absorbing the quiet play of sea and birds. As a composer, she takes her inspiration from rhythmic cycles of wave and silence. Within her they take on musical pattern and form (MacLaverty 1997: 213). The natural world often inspires artists because of inherent balances or contrasts between space and substance, shadow and light, sounds and quiet and the way they flow and change. When we begin to improvise our focus naturally falls on what sounds we will make because of course that is what music is. Or is it? John Cage's piece *4'33"* famously reminded the musical public that there was more going on than just the sound patterns. In a thoughtful examination of his career in music, Sting describes an interesting paradox:

I'm wondering as musicians whether the most important thing we do is merely to provide a frame for silence. I'm wondering if silence itself is perhaps the mystery at the heart of music. And is silence the most perfect form of music of all? . . . Great music is as often about the space between the notes as it is about the notes themselves.

(Sting 1998: 33)

In this section we would like to think about sounds revealed from or discovered in silence. For the improvising music therapist it can be useful to rebalance our anxieties about what we will play by focusing on space around and between our notes of music.

Exercises

(i) Sit comfortably in your chair. Take a few slow and deep breaths. On the 'in' breath listen to the sounds outside the room. Become aware of them and then let them fade away on the 'out' breath. Repeat this a couple of times. Now on the in breath listen to any sounds in the room. Be aware of them and let them drift gently away. Repeat. Now on the in breath focus on the sounds inside your body. Be aware of them and then let them go. Repeat. Now let the breath return to its normal tempo and depth as you begin to feel more and more still, focused and relaxed.

There are many similar exercises to (i) that help develop internal focus and awareness. They help us develop clarity, clearing our minds and bodies and preparing us to listen acutely to what may take place in the session. The following exercises help to explore the contrast between sound and silence.

(ii) Try and be as still and as quiet as possible. Now make a sound on your out breath. Use the out breaths to make different sounds and the in breaths to take in more energy and prepare for the next sound. Explore the contrast between the two states of sound and silence. This exercise can be done by yourself or in a group. Play and experiment with different sounds perhaps starting with humming then different vowel and consonant-based sounds. Be aware from where the sounds are coming – your stomach, chest, throat, head and so on. What does it feel like to make the sounds? What do the gaps feel like? How synchronised does your breathing become if working with other people?

(iii) Finding the sound. In Michelangelo's theory of sculpture, quoted in *Free Play* (Nachmanovitch 1990), the artist starts with the block of stone but is not cutting the stone into shape and inventing the artwork, but trying to reveal or liberate the form inside the block. It is already hidden there waiting to be found by the sculptor's eye. As musicians, we can think about an unsculpted block of silence. You can use your instruments or voices for this exercise. Let us think about what sounds you will reveal or set free in the quiet space. Concentrate on trying to hear the sounds in the silence – let them find you.

(iv) On your own instrument try exploring slow notes played in the same time frame, sometimes holding the note as long as possible, sometimes with a short duration and rests. Think about bowing, breathing or just waiting in between the notes. Think about the rests. If you are a pianist, you could explore this with or without the sustaining pedal. How is your sound affected by the spaces created?

Clinical example

Peter, a young child with spastic quadriplegia, has no speech and very little natural movement. He presents a calm, quiet personality and it is easy to ignore him in his class at school. In music therapy, the work at first seems like an endless void to the therapist. Peter lies on his back on a mat and watches attentively, but gives few clues for the therapist to catch hold of. After some bursts of over-energetic playing and uncomfortable silences, the therapist gradually relaxes a bit and becomes more comfortable in the space – playing for him gently on a guitar. After a while she notes Peter's eyes widening, his breathing becoming more expansive and recognises a change in atmosphere between them. She plays some sounds on a metal cabasa and then places the instrument on Peter's tummy and waits. He gurgles and then smiles in the pause. After a few seconds the therapist rolls some shapes on his tummy making a little wavy sound with her voice. She stops and Peter seems to wave his eyelids back to her in response.

Summary

Silences are multilayered and allow us to create our own meanings; sometimes welcome moments of rest, useful times to balance out sound, but at other times really anxious and uncomfortable. It was important for the therapist in the above extract to give the space a chance, to take the opportunity to pay attention to Peter. He was much more comfortable with the quiet than she was. Sometimes, music therapists choose not to play at all and to maintain the role of reflective listener. Most commonly this happens in a group where the therapist might step outside the playing in order to observe and to be open to all aspects of the music. Sometimes it is hard to 'keep ears open' when a lot is going on and we are playing too. There are no hard and fast rules except being responsible towards our patients. On the one hand we need to be able to stay with a silence and not intervene; on the other we may need to offer something to a very disabled patient rather than waiting in a long and tense silence.

Noting the use of silence in musical works gives some clues. It can create opening frames that heighten our awareness and get us ready to pay attention to the sound. We can take time to discover how we feel: peaceful, irritated, sad or furious. Sounds are more poised and focused and more specially chosen. We can let them draw to a natural conclusion. A favourite exercise of our teacher Maggie Pickett was to draw an arc with some beautiful antique cymbals, hit them together and then wait with great attention to the very last oscillation of the little cymbals. It was dramatic, completely focused, and allowed her and the class time to reach the natural conclusion. While we did this time was arrested. It was something she also used very effectively with her autistic and mentally ill patients. Claire Flower observes that we need a dynamic and flexible use of music and silence in clinical practice (Flower 2001). If there is too much silence there is 'no alliance': too little and there is 'no space for thinking' or connection between partners. In therapy and in music the creative use of silence allows us to form a quiet reflective space within ourselves.

Quality of the sound and choice of instrument

> Upend the rain stick and what happens next
> Is a music that you never would have known
> To listen for. . . .

> Who cares if all the music that transpires
> Is the fall of grit or dry seeds through a cactus?
> You are like a rich man entering heaven
> Through the ear of a raindrop. Listen now again.
>   From the 'The Rain Stick' by
>   Seamus Heaney (*The Spirit Level*, 1996)

We can be captured in a moment by an evocative or surprising sound. The quality of a friend's voice may be instantly identifiable in their first word on the telephone. We are attracted to particular sounds because they hold meaning or memory for us, or perhaps there is a real recognition of beauty for us in the quality of one specific musical instrument.

Can we think about how we respond to the sound quality and particular characteristics of the favourite instrument we play? Can you remember the first time you heard, saw or touched your instrument? Why do we end up playing what we do? Perhaps it is primarily an enjoyable physical experience, for example cradling a guitar and intimately singing with it, sweeping a bow up and down or gaining pleasure in the finger dexterity required by a Scarlatti sonata. Perhaps we love the look of the instrument or just revel in that particular sound. But at least as important is the linking of outer reality (playing the instrument) and our internal world of feeling and thinking.

Exercises

(i) Within a group, take some time to list and describe favourite sounds. You can include natural sounds or from a wide spectrum of music. (Perhaps this could be prepared for in advance and the group could be encouraged to bring some examples to share). Do the sounds themselves make any special connections for you? Do they have personal associations? Try not to analyse too much – just allow yourself to imagine the sounds and react as honestly as possible.

(ii) Take as much time as you want to explore different tuned and untuned percussion instruments. Try to approach each instrument as if it was the first time you have played it – for this it is useful to explore instruments from other cultures with which you are not familiar. Imagine you are a young child touching the instrument for the first time. Itemise your sensations. How does it feel looking at the instrument, touching and holding the instrument, playing it, listening to the sound? Do you have any associations or memories that connect with the sound? Explore single sounds and as many different ways of playing as possible.

(iii) Play and record a short piece you know well and from memory. After listening back with great attention to the quality of sound, describe your immediate reactions. Let your imaginations wander and list any associations, metaphors, images or feelings.

(iv) Try being as inventive as you can with your own instrument. Listen to some music that exploits contemporary instrumental techniques. Can you bring these techniques into your improvised playing? Make a list of the sounds you discover and your reactions to them.

(v) Try a group improvisation when each person limits their playing to using one favourite sound. Each 'sound gesture' can be repeated as many times as you like during the improvisation but is often more effective the fewer times you play – the old adage 'less is more' comes to mind. Notice if you tend to play your sound after hearing another particular sound. What sounds surround your sound? Are you responding to the sound or the person? Are you aware how many times you played your sound? Try exploring with eyes closed and open. Note any differences.

Clinical examples

(i) Group session

At the start of a one-off session the rainstick is passed around a group of cancer patients and their supporters. This is a way of inviting people to introduce themselves to the group. People are curious about the sound. How is it made? What is inside? Where does it come from? A lot of space and time is taken as each person explores the instrument and makes comments if they wish. There is no rush or pressure to talk or play. There are associations with the sound of rain on roofs, the sea moving backwards and forwards across a pebbled beach, waterfalls, rivers, rain dripping through leaves of trees, breathing. People appreciate the feel and weight of the rainstick. One member of the group uses the metaphor of the ups and downs of life as the rainstick is tilted from one side to the other. The group members talk of feeling increasingly relaxed and of connections with their breathing. They consider how this sound could be used as a focus for meditation. A gradual stillness reduces the initial anxious feelings when the group first encountered the instruments.

(ii) Individual session

Sophie, a seven-year old girl with moderate learning difficulties, has been separated from her natural mother and is in a temporary foster family. She is preoccupied in her music therapy sessions with getting the therapist's violin in and out of its case 'putting it to bed' as she describes it. She compares the violin's shape with a guitar in the room and often asks that they play together, one on guitar one on violin. 'This is you' she observes as the therapist holds the guitar, 'and that's me' pointing to the violin that she has put back in the case. 'They are like a Mummy and a little girl' the therapist suggests, observing the female shape of both. 'Yes' says Sophie, taking the guitar from the therapist, 'I'll sing her to sleep'. Sophie sings the lullaby in a mixture of sweet crooning and rather violent guitar chords (evoking the difficulties of being without her mum?). The therapist is surprised by how easily Sophie uses the instruments like dolls, but can also switch to playing a range of sounds and music to capture her mood.

Summary

Responses to the quality of different sounds are very elemental and often an initial meeting point in individual and group music therapy (as happens with the rainstick in example 1). We are dealing here with notions of choice, personal association and identity. Patients can associate with instruments as objects and playthings (as Sophie does above), connections being made with their quality, feel and sensuous power. Association may of course be tenuous; the person may just like playing, singing and moving, but very often people can feel drawn to the colour, shape and feel of a musical instrument. The meaning of patients' choices is highly subjective and it may take time in therapy to make sense of the significance of the instrument for the patient. Dilemmas or difficulties can be explored and thought about and stories told through the way instruments and sounds suggest things to us.

In conclusion some important issues to note are: allow personal choices and associations with instruments and sounds to develop; allow free access for the person's imagination; encourage playful exploration of sounds and instruments. They may become significant 'intermediary objects' or 'phenomena' for the patient in the way that Winnicott (1974) and Alvin (1977) have discussed. They can be helpful props for story-telling in the best imaginative and therapeutic traditions and give helpful diagnostic data with regard to the patient's needs, difficulties and personality.

Experience of loudness

The scene is a Prom concert in the 2000 season in early September. Bernard Haitink is conducting Beethoven's Ninth (Choral) Symphony. In the final movement, as the orchestra strains to the limits of its wordlessness, the magnificent leonine bass John Tomlinson leaps forward to begin the vocal part of the movement. 'Freude!' is the word, but the sound is extraordinary. Compared with all the vast resources of a full symphony orchestra this seems ironically to be the loudest and most intense moment. How can one bass voice project so loudly? The whole Albert Hall seems to beat and shake to this amazing call to attention.

In polite society being noisy is not very acceptable. One might think of political hecklers shouting, teenagers listening to loud music on a sunny Sunday afternoon with windows open, roadwork machines creating very high decibels and workers wearing earmuffs to protect hearing. The liberation and self-expression of one person's loudness may be a nightmare intrusion to their neighbour. But where an experience of loudness is shared there may be a feeling of power and solidarity, of excitement and exuberance, of energy joyously expelled.

Clearly loud and soft are on a continuum (like sound and silence) and the one exists in balance with the other. In discovering music perhaps one of the attractions might be experimenting with the control of this dimension. In therapy there are important associations with being heard, helping people listen, in the release of feeling energy and being comfortable with quiet.

Exercises: loud and soft

(i) Improvise either by yourself or in a small group aiming to emphasise loud and soft sounds. Explore sudden contrasts of sounds. What is it like to begin softly and then gradually increase loudness? Alternatively how does it feel to begin loudly and become softer? What does it feel like to sustain either very soft or very loud sounds? What about the ending – how does it feel to end very loudly or softly? Try different ways of playing.

(ii) Listen with your eyes closed to colleagues improvising by themselves or in small groups. Be aware of reactions to loud and soft sounds. What are your body-based reactions? How is your breathing affected? Repeat the experience with eyes open and be aware of the links between movement (strength and size of attack, body gestures and so on) and the resulting loudness. How can you describe the sounds? Do you have any associations or images?

(iii) Explore how composers use this element. Take a favourite piece and use the composer's specific use of loudness as a springboard to your own improvisation. Look at a piece such as Bartok's 'Minor Seconds, Major Sevenths' (Mikrokosmos, Volume Six) where the composer explores a gradual increase in loudness linked to a decrease in speed and vice versa. Use this example to explore these connections and what it feels like going against your natural instincts.

(iv) Combine an exploration of loud and soft with high and low pitches. What is it like to play loud and high or loud and low? Compare this with soft and high, soft and low. Make an improvisation exploiting one of these contrasts.

Clinical example

Dan, a very shy and lonely man in his mid-40s, begins to attend a day centre for adults with mental health difficulties and is referred to the music therapy group. He has been feeling depressed for many years and has had periods in hospital and two prison sentences, one for shoplifting and a second for sexual exhibitionism. Socialising is difficult and he is initially very quiet in the group. In the sixth session the impro-visations are all rhythmic and lively and the group becomes very cohesive and encour-aging of each other. Somebody offers Dan a turn on the drum kit and to the great surprise of the group he steps over and sits with feet on the bass drum and high-hat cymbal pedals and begins to join in the next piece. He plays gently and steadily to start with but gradually gains confidence. The group shouts encouragement to him and he begins to grin and gradually builds a tremendous crescendo drum roll, which ends with an explosion on cymbals. Dan leaps to his feet with his arms in the air to the whooping and applause of the group. (Exhibitionism perhaps, but in more acceptable social form?) He bows to everyone and then resumes his seat. In a later review of his sessions, Dan particularly remembers this moment to the therapist. 'It was like having my own little party' he says. 'Everybody listened. They all thought it was good'.

Summary

We all have different sensitivity to loudness but loud and soft are part of the sound palette available to us in music. A real pleasure for the music therapist may be in witnessing patients becoming more flexible in this dimension. 'Dan' in the extract above surprises everybody by showing he has a loud extravagant side to him. He sees himself differently by his 'exper-iment'. Alternatively, a young autistic child might manage to sidestep rigid patterns of beating of drums and cymbal; begin to listen to other sounds in between and discover the pleasure of linking with the therapist's melody, which before has been blotted out. Feeling able to make a loud sound within accept-able limits; being noticed even when your 'song is soft'; experimenting with different levels of intensity: all these can be valuably explored in the music therapy space.

Use of pulse

Pulse moves from rest, to action, to rest unendingly . . . To grasp it intel-lectually is so easy it seems like child's play, but to know it in practice is to understand it *is* child's play.

(Rooley 1990: 117)

The pulse is a musical hinge. In discovering it we may connect and move. A collective pulse is often a strong way for groups to form and feel woven together, as in the clinical example below. But it can also control the time too strongly, and individually we might resist and want to fight it off. In the following exercises, play with its presence and absence, and observe how we compare and contrast our responses with those of others.

Exercises

(i) Take your own pulse and tap it out. If working in a group invite colleagues to do the same. Enjoy the differences and note the range. Play around with different pulses, exploring what it feels like to work with very fast or very slow pulses.

(ii) Work in pairs. Take turns in tuning in to each other's pace of breathing. Make sure you experience both the giving and receiving parts of this exercise. It can be done sitting side by side or with the person receiving the attention lying on the floor. Make sure both parties are comfortable: if person A is lying then do so with legs uncrossed, hands held loosely at the side, any belts or constrictions loosened; person B sitting or kneeling next to A, taking care not to touch A and respecting A's personal space. Person A continues to breathe normally. B observes A's movements and breathing pace and adjusts the breathing accordingly. Take care to keep focused with keen attention on any subtle changes in movement. Synchronise the breathing: as A's diaphragm rises B inhales and as it falls B exhales. After B feels in synchrony with A's breathing B begins to make gentle 'ah' sounds at a comfortable pitch on the out breaths. Continue exploring any shifts in pitch, loudness or duration of the 'ah' sounds as they connect with A's out breath. Come to a gentle resting point and discuss the effects of the process. Swap roles and repeat the exercise. Notice any shifts in states of mind and report your feelings. When feeding back in this and any other exercise make sure each partner has sufficient time both in the reporting and listening mode (another opportunity to practise listening skills).

(iii) Repeat (ii) but this time the 'therapist' weaves a simple wordless melody based on the pulse of the 'patient's' breathing. Pay attention to any small changes in tempo and explore different ways of matching with subtle fluctuations in tempo, phrasing or loudness while trying to keep within the overall pulse of the breathing. Once again swap roles so each can experience this kind of deep listening and matching. Give honest feedback. Do a similar exercise with instruments.

Clinical example: Group work

Let us continue with the story of the cancer patients who have been using the rain-stick (see p. 197). After the initial explorations everybody is invited to choose a differ-ent instrument. Some members of the group are very keen to play an instrument that strikes their fancy and get up to try things out. Others are rather more diffident and sit back in their chairs, the therapist needing to spend more individual time encour-aging and pointing out some of the qualities of the various instruments. Here is the first example of being sensitive to the different 'pulses' of the group. Some people are quick off the mark; others need more time. The therapist is also aware intuitively of an overall pulse of the group at this stage in the session and surmises this to be quite steady – quite a few people appear rather cautious. The exploration of the rain-stick has also created a rather reflective general atmosphere. Eventually everyone has an instrument. Some people begin to scrape, tap and explore. The therapist listens, observes and wonders it there could be an underlying pulse that will unite these fragments of sounds. A steady heartbeat pulse emerges. The members of the group are invited to play anything they like, keeping the pulse as a background and trying to internalise it. There are many smiles as people feel quickly that they are all playing together, playing in a 'groove'. Some people appear to want to explore a faster pulse and some of the foreground changes as different personalities emerge from the texture. The therapist picks these changes up and introduces a gradual shift in speed. The group accepts the invitation and also follows a gradual slowing of the pulse.

The rest of the improvisation is a subtle exploration of slow, medium and fast pulses with more fluidity of direction between members of the group and the ther-apist. In the following discussion there is a general amazement on how cohesive the music felt. Some members had been suspecting a general cacophony of sounds with 13 people playing together. The group is pleased with their first group piece. The pulse acts as a holding principle. It helps to create trust right from the beginning.

Summary

Pulse is linked to fundamental human processes. It is the bedrock of all that helps us to feel held, safe and secure. Without a sense of pulse how can we predict events in time, a necessity for the time-based actions involved, for example, in movement and speech and language development? The cancer patients used playing within the same pulse as a safe container at the start of a session. They could then emerge from this secure position to explore more independent and challenging freer improvisations. Here different pulses could be negotiated as a healthy adult exchange of playing with and within similar pulses or not, depending on how the music evolved. At times in music therapy we meet patients whose particular difficulties prevent them from externalising a sustained pulse. Their sounds appear as disjointed and fragmented. Here any co-created music with the therapist can help any individual or fragmented sounds to be placed in a larger and more evenly pulsed framework. The therapist can work to find connections between the patient's fragments.

These reflections on pulse, particularly our prime responsibilities of working to link with an individual's pulse or finding the common pulse of a group, can form a transition to the next section.

FUNDAMENTAL THERAPEUTIC AND PERSONAL ISSUES

Demonstrating empathy and resonance

> This is not Love perhaps – Love that lays down
> Its life, that many waters cannot quench, nor the floods drown –
> But something written in lighter ink, said in a lower tone
> Something perhaps especially our own:
>
> . . .
>
> A need for inns on roads, islands in seas, halts for discoveries to be
>   shared,
> Maps checked and notes compared;
> A need at times of each for each
> Direct as the need of throat and tongue for speech.
>   (Tessimond 1985: 50)

Human connection, companionship and sensitive relating lie at the heart of the music therapy frame. Empathy in the most general sense may be to know how to act as an 'inn on the road' or an 'island in the sea' for our fellows. As in the old Eskimo saying, we should not jump to conclusions about a person until 'we have walked a mile in their moccasins'. If we use the analogy of music therapy being the giving and receiving of a musical story, then Okri has some useful thoughts about the listener to the story (the therapist position). He observes that the listening process importantly involves 'silence, openness and thought'. While the joy for the teller of the story is 'artistic exploration', the joy for the listener is in 'imaginative identification' (Okri 1997: 48). These ideas seem very in tune with Rogers' definition of empathy involving 'being sensitive, moment by moment, to the changing felt meanings which flow in this other person' quoted in Chapter 2. They also suggest active work done by the listener in thought and imagination. We can demonstrate in the music we play with our patients that we are listening carefully and showing this imaginative identification.

Resonance is a therapeutic concept with a significant musical correlate. Musicians are aware of the resonating capacity of their instruments and the notion of sympathetic resonance when a string or part of an instrument resonates in sympathy with a sound. Different spaces have their own unique resonating frequency. So it is not too big a step for musicians to be able to apply this concept to a broader one of resonating with a patient's music and feelings, including those dissonant and difficult ones.

Exercises

(i) Work in pairs – neither partner is allowed any words – take it in turns to lead. You sit together and try through gesture, and posture and any movements to empathise with and reflect the feelings of your partner. Swap over leadership. Try the exercise again also using vocal sounds.

(ii) This exercise is based on John Steven's 'Triangle' from *Search and Reflect* (Stevens 1985: 77). Work in groups of three and choose similar sorts of instruments (you might have a group of string or woodwind players trying this). Sit in an equilateral triangle, imagining that the other two people are your sound system, and you are playing with the stereo sound you hear. Each person does the same in the triangle. You do not start to play until you hear your 'sound system' playing: try to feel with the sounds and 'play what you hear'. (Breathing, scrapes and any music.) Listen to the different pieces created by different trios. Try with dissimilar instruments.

(iii) If you are a piano player, look at some of Bach's *Two-part Inventions*. Consider each part as a character, showing empathy to the other, and play it through. How do the parts mutually complement? Are they exactly the same, what does the difference in register do?

(iv) In pairs, imagine one of you is the 'backing singer' to the other. The main singer chooses a melody well known to both of you. The backing singer sings an *obligato* melody that simply harmonises with the main vocalist. Swap over and find a new melody. Repeat the exercise but improvising the main melody this time.

(vi) Work in pairs. Play to each other and be open to where and how you experience both playing and receiving the music. Where is the locus of any resonance – feelings, an idea, part of your body?

(vii) Facilitate a group improvisation. Try to be open to how and where you resonate with the sounds. Allow the sounds into your body. Feed back as honestly as you can. What did the sounds make you feel both physically and emotionally? How did they influence your thoughts?

Clinical example: Carla

This wiry and wary eight-year-old, with emotional and behavioural problems, provided a challenge to the therapist's ability to provide a safe space and to truly empathise with her rapidly changing feelings. Carla certainly provoked hard – and the therapist often had the experience of being wrong-footed, feeling cross and frustrated and certainly insensitive to Carla. (Anger and lack of control were experienced as counter-transference by the therapist; these were combined with the therapist's own struggle to hold limits.) Carla's parents had a very volatile relationship, her mother often leaving home and her father changing address. Two schools had found her behaviour unmanageable.

The therapist worked with Carla for nearly two years, until her father moved on again. The mutual 'difficulties with boundaries' remained a feature, though in the second year it seemed as if they represented more creative opportunities for Carla (more in keeping with a lively rebellious spirit that needed nurturing, than the rage, injustice and pain that they seemed to embody to begin with). Carla was small, thin and athletic constantly needing to be 'ahead', always beating the therapist to the music therapy room. In many ways she was very quick-thinking; fascinated by detail and perceptive about how things worked, but there was a desperation and panic in her activity.

The opportunity to empathise came about through the focus on some musical work together, based loosely around the use of songs and themes from 'Mary Poppins'. Carla would often act parts of it, both she and the therapist would sing, and Carla also improvised on a kind of 'drum kit' she put together from mixed percussion. The therapist played violin and guitar and Carla would impulsively want the violin on a regular basis. As Carla sang 'Feed the Birds' and 'Chim Chiminee' the therapist had a really strong sensation that these songs were her feelings, the loss, the battle with adults, the wish for magical musical powers. Empathy was easy then. The violin and 'Mary Poppins' took up much of the first two terms together and gradually Carla allowed herself to diversify and to play more freely on a larger range of instruments.

Summary

Music therapy can work with empathy in interesting ways. The active role of the therapist in making music with the patient allows for a direct expression of 'feeling with' the patient. Feedback can be shared almost instantaneously about the 'changing felt meanings' described by Rogers. For further discussion on musical empathy and resonance see Chapter 2.

Accompanying, reflecting and matching

> How inspiring for the singer when rehearsing to feel that his partner at the piano has given the song as much study as he has, knows the poem, is aware of that awkward corner just approaching, anticipates with him – not responding after – to this inflexion and that.
>
> (Moore 1962: 199)

To accompany with such flexibility can appear as almost second nature in the hands of an artist of Gerald Moore's sensitivities. Orchestral musicians are also used to accompanying soloists and when playing pure orchestral music to moving between a foreground and background position within the movement of any one piece. Players in chamber and jazz groups regularly tread this balance between soloist and accompanist. Singers can be in the solo spotlight or part of a group. In music therapy it is a humbling experience to provide a musical accompaniment to children and adults as they begin to narrate their stories in sounds and music. We can begin to know and study their personal songs and anticipate with them as the musical relationship evolves. We can work to find the kind of accompaniment that is most fitting to each clinical situation. One day this might be a young child with limited attention, the next a group of highly articulate adults with acute anxiety and depression. This property of music to act as an accompaniment yet enabling the players to feel both supported and free to explore is one of the great gifts of music therapy.

Reflecting is a classic technique in supportive counselling. Reflecting not only the words but also the intonation and quality of the feelings can contribute to a development of trust. The patient feels heard. Musically this can also be relevant in the early stages of the work when the therapist reflects back using a similar musical gesture to the patient. A negative aspect of this technique is the potential slide into parroting with the dangers of sounding like an automatic response.

We prefer to concentrate here on the concept of matching. Here reflection is used but there is also more active listening to the feelings behind the musical presentation (in verbal work some counselling colleagues often refer to listening to the music behind the words). The listening attitude works across the different modalities. A child plays a series of soft sounds on a xylophone. The therapist might then match these sounds by playing at the same level of pitch, loudness and duration but use a different timbre, for example the piano. This technique of matching is closely related to Stern's notion of 'vitality affects' (Stern 1985) and Pavlicevic's development of 'dynamic form' (Pavlicevic 1990; see Introduction to Chapter 4).

Exercises

(i) Work in pairs. A plays an instrument and B accompanies, aiming to provide a musical frame for A's music. The aim is for B to concentrate on providing a safe atmosphere to support A's music concentrating on going alongside A at A's pulse and level of loudness. What does it feel like to play alongside A's music? Spend time discussing the experience from both musical and personal perspectives. Swap roles and explore different music and expression of feelings.

(ii) A plays a short phrase to B; B listens to A and reflects back the phrase as accurately as possible using the same instrument and musical parameters of timbre, pitch, duration and loudness. How does A feel to have the sounds reflected back? Swap roles and try out different kinds of musical gestures. As the exercise progresses pay increasing attention to reflecting back the kind of emotional world that is being communicated. Explore this using different instruments, some similar and some not.

(iii) Continue to work in pairs. Again B chooses a different instrument to A but one that can easily match A's sounds – for example wood for wood, metal for metal, pitch for pitch . . . A plays to B and B attempts in the reply to match the overall mood of A's communication. B pays attention to matching the parameters of pitch, loudness, duration and timbre but is not so preoccupied with an exact reflection. Explore ways of matching the feelings being communicated. Again discuss and swap.

(iv) Take everything one stage further with one of the pair trying to facilitate the other's expression. A plays and B helps to encourage A's exploration of the instrument and feelings by putting into practice the accompanying, reflective and matching techniques described above. Discuss the kinds of musical gestures and support that facilitated your communications.

(v) Practise facilitating different group improvisations by listening for any musical common denominators that can help you to make reflective well-matched interventions.

Clinical example

This example illustrates the themes of this section alongside references to the matching of pulse and pitch, pacing and the emergence of a meeting and dialogue in sound.

Louise is sitting head-down in her specially adapted chair. She is 10 years old, pro-foundly disabled and has no speech. The therapist has been working with Louise for six months and has been trying to understand her story by creating accom-panying sounds that connect to her pace, movements, breathing and level of under-standing. He has learnt that everything has to be extremely slow – movements, sounds, gestures – and in effect even slower than what he imagines is slow enough. Today he starts by observing the tempo of her breathing and reflects this by playing one long sound on some beautiful Indian bells, a sound that has previously attracted Louise's attention. The sound begins from and ends in silence. A long gap ensues during which time Louise begins to move her head towards the source of the sound. After another longish pause he plays a second sound, taking great care to attend to her breathing and to how long the sound lasts. Again Louise looks up but this time after a shorter gap. This interaction continues for a while with the one bell sound. There is the beginning of a smile and Louise makes a quiet and sustained vocal sound. The therapist matches the pitch, duration and intensity of this sound. She makes another sound. The therapist replies with a slightly longer vocal phrase and incorporates Louise's name. The vocal sounds within this more sustained dialogue extend in pitch and length as the pace livens. Looking back on video it is clear to see the emerging contact at the child's pace and level of understanding.

Summary

The techniques of accompanying, reflecting and matching are fundamental ways of demonstrating to a patient that the therapist is carefully attending and listening. We can adapt our music to accompany different personal stories as patients sing out their individual songs. The quiet pragmatic skills of the accompanist provide much on which we can draw. It is not a flashy role in music but its essential underpinning of the instrumental or vocal soloist makes a skilful accompanist like gold dust. Great musicianship is needed to subtly time and tone the accompanying part, and the work of the music therapist is very linked to this. We draw on all aspects of our musical and personal resources in creatively reflecting and matching what people bring to us in therapy.

Holding and containing

Softly, in the dusk, a woman is singing to me
Taking me back down the vista of years, till I see
A child sitting under the piano, in the boom of the tingling
    strings
And pressing the small, poised feet of a mother who smiles as
    she sings.

In spite of myself, the insidious mastery of song
Betrays me back, till the heart of me weeps to belong
To the old Sunday evenings at home, with winter outside
And hymns in the cosy parlour, the tinkling piano our guide.
. . .
      From 'Piano' *Selected Poems* (D.H. Lawrence 1950: 30)

Lawrence wrote in a letter to a friend of his attempts to 'get an emotion out in its own course, without altering it' in his writing of poetry (Williams 1950). There are links here to improvised music with the desire for spontaneous expression – the wish to not intellectualise but to express in the moment. In this poem 'Piano', a clear part of the observation is music's power to evoke memory, but it could also give an idea of its 'holding' and 'containing' qualities. In Chapter 2, we noted Winnicott's concept of the mother holding the baby, emotionally and physically being akin to the therapist 'holding' the patient. Here Lawrence captures the mother as musician, the child close by under the instrument and the intimacy of the contact. The child is held in her smiling song, pressing her foot perhaps to continue or control the sound.

The music therapist can use the dual function of holding the patient in mind, as the therapist, and also holding the patient's communications by the way music is framed.

Exercises

(i) Explore the qualities of different containers either in your imagination or as a prepared exercise. Ask members of the group to describe their chosen container. In what way does it hold objects, liquids and so on?

(ii) Listen to the Act II Finale of Mozart's *The Marriage of Figaro*. Listen to the way the many motivations of character are held together in the musical structure. How is this achieved? What musical means does Mozart use to hold the singers' parts together?

(iii) In pairs explore ways of holding and containing a range of different emotions. Person A thinks of a particular emotion, spends a few moments getting into the role and plays out the emotion. B uses all the musical and personal resources discussed so far to try and hold and contain A's music. Spend time discussing and then swap and try out different emotions. As you feel more comfortable you may feel able to play what you are really feeling. Paradoxically we find that it is sometimes easier to reach this place of honest communication after working through a more role-based exercise. Playing as if once removed can often produce very imaginative and spontaneous playing (freedom within the structure).

(iv) Explore ways of trying to contain fragmented and disjointed sounds. Long sustained notes or drones may be very effective here, a kind of cocoon of sound that surrounds. You may like to come back to this exercise after experimenting with the melodic, and rhythmic suggestions in the next chapter.

Clinical example: Lisa

This little girl aged seven, with mild learning difficulties, had a difficult and painful life, living in foster care after her mother had discovered her sexual abuse by several male relatives. Her foster family was caring and supportive but Lisa was deeply affected by the loss of her mother and the trauma of the abuse. Lisa's time at school was landmarked by whirlwind tantrums and crises. She was contained very warmly and strongly by a teacher and a care assistant but it was enormously difficult for her to engage in any one-to-one work, as the intensity was often unbearable. She was very interested in the idea of coming to music therapy and effectively referred herself by her constant requests to come. However, rarely was she able to come at the right time or to stay more than a few minutes in the first few months of work. The therapist fought against the pressure to fill her slot as lots of other children had been referred – but was unsure if Lisa could take anything from her.

Then a song came along.

One afternoon, she had not wanted to come and the therapist sat doodling at the piano, thinking about her and wondering what she was feeling. The tune that emerged was a Beatles song 'A Little Help from my Friends'. Initially the words were not the first thought, but the tune just kept revolving around in the therapist's mind. She became preoccupied with the idea of the two other staff mentioned earlier and trying to help Lisa 'get by' – and how difficult that task felt. The next week the therapist told Lisa on collecting her that she had been thinking of her when she wasn't there and had a song for her. Lisa beamed, jumped up and ran straight to the room. 'Sing me the song, sing it to me, I want to hear it' she enthused. The therapist was stunned, having no idea that it would be so motivating. But perhaps the surprise for Lisa that the therapist had held her in mind, and sung something for her when she was not there had helped her keep a thread of contact. Perhaps the therapist could be trusted, or maybe more likely the song itself was trustier. It was something she could grasp, when she couldn't 'get hold' of people. Something they could focus on and share together, without so much emphasis on relating to a person, which she dreaded. She became fixated on the phrase in the song 'I just need someone to love'. The song was singing of her needs, her difficulties. The idea of it 'held' her when it was almost impossible to do this in person. It also held the relationship together.

Note: for more discussion of these themes see Chapter 2.

Use of words with music – a continuum

> There was speech in their dumbness, language in their very gesture.
>
> Shakespeare, *The Winter's Tale*, V.2.13

> . . . when anyone speaks to me, I listen more to the tonal modulation in his voice than to what he is actually saying, what he is like, what he feels . . . Life is sound, the tonal modulation of the human speech . . . I have been taking down speech melodies since the year 1897 . . . they are of the utmost importance to dramatic music.
>
> (Janáček in Harvey 1999: 49)

To use words or not to use words – this is a subject of continuous debate in music therapy. We propose a pragmatic approach with the use of words relating to context, an obvious example being the appropriate use of words when working, for example with groups of elderly mentally ill patients or of preverbal children. How each therapist responds and uses words relates to theoretical orientation. Within our particular styles of work, we would both encourage students, at the most basic level, to feel comfortable greeting patients and using any everyday conversation as part of creating a relaxed and safe environment. But anomalies do occur, for example if we have already greeted an individual or group member, is this moment the start of the session or when the first musical sound is made? What is the function of the frame of a greeting song if we have already greeted people with words? Is the traditional use of 'Hello' and 'Goodbye' songs in music therapy therefore only relevant with people of certain ages and range of disabilities?

The student music therapist requires training in using words so that they can flow in and out of the music if this is required. For example a pattern that is often used when working in adult psychiatric groups is for an improvised piece of music to lead naturally and continuously into some verbal discussion raising awareness of the group members' feelings about the music and each other before returning to some more music. A beginning student may often feel apprehensive about handling such a delicate process. Learning some simple counselling skills including the use of reflecting and open questions can help the student begin to work more confidently with these transitions. If the therapist wishes to work at a level beyond the supportive (see therapeutic spectrum in Chapter 2) then further training in individual or group psychotherapy, group analysis or other systems is recommended.

Clearly the use of words in a therapeutic encounter moves beyond the everyday and the therapist needs to take care in handling words. At times words are redundant in sessions: how often do we feel lost for words after a particularly moving musical experience? Words can also block or defend against emotional expression. The elemental nature of music can be a significant release for people without access to words. However, the powerful combination of experiencing feeling in music and subsequent identifying meaning in words should be accessible to and valued by music therapists. We recommend respect for this continuum between words and music and an approach based on common sense, appropriate clinical techniques and balanced integration. We would like to think that all students leaving their training feel comfortable handling verbal material if it arises in sessions and for any words to be held within a supportive framework.

Exercises

(i) Improvise some small group pieces. Take turns to facilitate the process and help the members of the group to discuss their experiences of the music and of playing together. Be aware of the balance between words, non-verbal sounds (the very important supportive 'mms' and 'ahs') and the music. Do any themes emerge for the development of further improvisation, the words forming a transition to the next piece of music?

(ii) Practise listening to the sound shapes and inflection of speech around you. How do different people sound? How does sound quality contribute to meaning? It is useful to listen to different languages that you do not understand. Try this on the Tube in London, or travelling abroad. Go for colour and expression.

(iii) In pairs, try to match some words to your partner's improvised music. In contrast offer some music to some free words your partner says. Swap the playing and the speaking and take turns with both.

(iv) Think of the things your patients say as their own sort of music. Examine the intensity, pitch inflections and 'voice print'. Improvise some free singing or accompany a spontaneously invented song in the privacy of your own practice.

(v) Choose a poem that suggests 'music' to you (such as e.e. cummings' 'In Just-spring when the world is mud-luscious' (1960: 1) or Hopkins' 'Binsey Poplars' (1953: 39)) and practise reading it aloud with attention to all the sound qualities (rhythm, timbre, fluidity). Work in pairs and share your poems. Improvise a short piece together on instruments inspired by the poem's sounds. Discuss how the poem and the improvised sounds relate.

(vi) In a small group try singing a nursery rhyme in three different ways, working on contrasting styles and instrumentation. How do your different styles alter the meaning of the words?

Clinical example: Jimmy and the 'Seedmaid'

Jimmy is a fair-haired freckly boy of seven years with a mild learning disability. His home life is quite deprived and he has three street-wise older brothers. He is verbally fluent and lively and explores the instruments as tools in a variety of cowboy and army games. His speech is often stern and 'sergeant majorish' and he barks orders to the therapist. It is hard to sustain any music on instruments Jimmy allows the therapist to play. He is always moving on, like a sound track in fast-forward. The therapist makes a point of trying to hold on to his verbal ideas and to elaborate on how they sound and feel in little songs, but it is always hard to keep up.

One day, Jimmy asks the therapist to climb inside the soft guitar case. She is uncertain as quite a lot of Jimmy's suggestions involve controlling, tying up, things that feel uncomfortable. However, he says 'Please. Go on, you can sing. You're a Seedmaid'. The words he says are important, he has recognised that she keeps trying to put things into music. Also, here is a rich metaphor – the sea, the mermaid, the seed and so on. The 'Seedmaid' sings for some time on her 'rock' in the middle of the room, a lyrical line, wordless to start with and then something about being lonely and beautiful. Jimmy jumps up, having been listening quietly. 'Hallo I'm the Seedmaid-boy, can I have the tail?' Jimmy takes the guitar case and puts his legs in and sits on the 'rock'. He sings in a sweet treble voice, of swimming and fishing and then 'lahs' for several minutes. It is the most sustained musical-verbal exchange they have had in their work together of four months. Words and music are shared between the partners in a simple easy way. The Seedmaid girl and boy are then the 'seed' of several months of future work.

Summary

We mused about pragmatism at the beginning of this section. Being free to do what works and what seems to be comfortable for client and therapist is important. Words and music have always had close allegiance in song, opera, music theatre and musical. These forms are popular and easily accessible and music therapists can make good use of their traditions. Sometimes we might try a kind of recitative (providing a sung commentary to what is happening); or *sprechstimme* (inflected/heightened speech); at other times a clear division between the musical period and the talking period is needed. At another point we may have no words, in another session, no music.

Some reflections on interpretation

Interpretation in psychoanalytic work is one of the ways in which the analyst suggests a link between the present relating moment and a feeling in the patient that is not consciously recognised. The use of interpretation needs awareness, sensitivity and good timing for it to be helpful. Malcolm Pines makes an interesting exploration of the roots of interpretation, including analogies of language interpreters, 'translating from one person's language into another's' (Pines 2000: 138). He also thinks about a musical 'interpretation' (musicians are familiar with 'style and interpretation' classes in their education). Here 'interpretation' means one person's personal view of the music, their 'style' and what understanding they bring. There is much food for thought in this for the music therapist, for example improvising their understanding or interpretation back to the patient.

We are getting closer to developing more rigorous interpretation procedures in music therapy. For example at the recent Naples conference Giacomo Gaggero and Barabara Zanchi presented their early explorations of integrating a musical interpretation of events in music therapy within more psychological and overriding philosophical frames of reference. On the Bologna music therapy course the students are encouraged to 'read' improvisations on a number of planes:

- *the descriptive plane*: direct and spontaneous of what actually happens;
- *the resonance plane*: more intersubjective, including transference and counter-transference dynamics and physical/mental/emotional resonance;
- *the symbolic plane*: picking up any symbols in their musical guise including images and moods and any archetypal, collective, cultural or mythological features;
- *the stylistic plane*: very linked to how the music is used and relating to specific and personal form;
- *the rough interpretation plane*: insights from the therapeutic encounter placed in the context of the personal, family and environmental background (including history of any pathology); insights from the other *planes* linking with the music therapist's intuitions – all moving towards an initial working interpretative hypothesis (Gaggero *et al.* 2001).

CONCLUDING POINTS

We have explored some essential musical and personal resources that will equip us not only for the start of a therapeutic process but also for continuing the work. We have begun to explore central themes that will form part of many therapeutic encounters throughout our training and our working lives as therapists. We now need to turn to some more complex musical resources for the therapist that will assist in helping patients to continue to move through the therapy process.

Chapter 12

Developing the musical journey

Julian Raphael, Leslie Bunt and Sarah Hoskyns

INTRODUCTION

Our focus now moves from simple features of sound and early stages of therapy described in Chapter 11 to a series of practical exercises that concentrate on more complex elements of melody, harmony, rhythm and form. The intention here is to attend to the needs of a range of musicians (singers, guitarists, single-line instrumentalists, first- and second-study pianists) providing shapes and inspiration for practice and useful structures to assist improvisation in music therapy. The exercises are obviously relevant at any stage in the therapeutic process but we give most attention in this chapter to ideas that help to sustain interaction or move the process forward. In the main, the musical ideas in this chapter are framed to enable readers without much experience of improvising with patients to have a try at developing their ideas and skills; but we also hope more experienced music therapists might find something new to do.

While the exercises are presented in a straightforward musical way, you may find it helpful to keep in mind some of the following clinical questions:

- How can these elements be used to accompany a person's music?
- How can these ideas be used to help sustain focused concentration in musical play?
- What helpful musical connections can we make (taking account of the person's personal taste, culture and musical experience)?
- What kind of musical interventions can be used to challenge (when appropriate) any obstacles in the flow of interactive communication? For example a client's loud continuous playing, repeating obsessive patterns, continuous beating, fragmented or disconnected moments?
- How can these exercises be adapted for both individual and group work?
- How can these elements be used to help prepare a client for the ending of therapy?

In this way you can make your own imaginative exploration of how the principles behind the exercises can be applied in the music therapy room.

The main areas and sub-sections of this chapter are:

12.1 Practical music exercises

- Common modes
- Pentatonic sets from other musical cultures
- Varied starting points for improvisation
- Accompaniment patterns
- One-note 'turnarounds'
- Simple 12-bar blues
- Two-chord vamps
- Rhythmic grooves
- Exploration of song and accompaniment style: 'Amazing Grace'

12.2 On listening to music

- Open listening as part of training
- On working with individuals and groups

PRACTICAL MUSIC EXERCISES

See over.

3 Common Modes

The Mixolydian mode; white keys G - G, with the flattened 7th has a soft, major key feel without the functional certainty of the raised leading note.

Do Re Mi Fa So La Tor Do

The Dorian mode; white keys D - D (here transposed to G) has a minor 3rd but a major 6th, which adds a certain brightness to the minor tonality.

Do Re Mor Fa So La Tor Do

The Aeolian mode; white keys A - A (here transposed to G) has both a minor 3rd and minr 6th and can easily summon-up melancholy.

Do Re Mor Fa So Lor Tor Do

Modes can be performed on any instrument, but vocal practice will help tune the ear into the different interval characteristics. Modes work well over a tonic drone, while a rhythmic ostinato accompaniment can provide momentum and facilitate musical phrasing.

Figure 12.1 Common modes.

3 Pentatonic Sets

These are some examples of 5 note scales from other musical cultures.
Working with such combinations of intervals will allow the musician to produce distinct sound worlds of colour and mood. Remember it is often the notes that are left out that give the right flavour and this will need practice. Instruments such as xylophones can be prepared to aid performance in the desired mode.

This set of notes comes from the rag system of Indian classical music. The scale has a bright, spacious character.

This set is built on the tetrachord system of Japanese scales. This is but one combination. Make up more of your own.

The top 5 notes of the harmonic minor scale can be used to create melodies in the Hebrew style, particularly if harmonised like the example below.

Figure 12.2 Pentatonic sets from other musical cultures.

Starting Points

Even a simple clapping rhythm can be made to sound dynamic with a back-beat pulse. This makes a good warm-up before rhythmic improvising. Make up variations or generate call and response ideas.

Here is one of the oldest of West African rhythms, usually known as the 12/8 bell pattern. To play it fluently over a foot pulse is rather difficult until you finds its groove. But keep trying; its rewards are many, as are its applications and, once mastered, never forgotten.

Try playing a simple ostinato on tuned percussion while clicking a back-beat. Swap hands to develop balanced co-ordination.

On single line instruments you could develop ideas using different scales (see Pentatonic Sets). Here is the start of a melody using a whole-tone scale.

Develop your left hand piano skills with a boogie bass line. You could sing or play some simple riffs over it.

Figure 12.3 Varied starting points for improvisation.

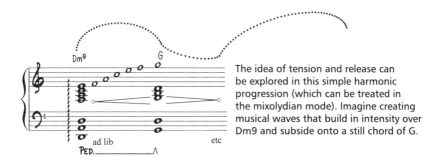

The idea of tension and release can be explored in this simple harmonic progression (which can be treated in the mixolydian mode). Imagine creating musical waves that build in intensity over Dm9 and subside onto a still chord of G.

Explore pan-diatonic progressions that offer variations in colour and light. Here the right and left hands play different primary triads in A major.

The cycle of 5ths is in every sense a classic structure for improvisation. This version alternates root chords with first inversions resulting in smaller steps in the bass. As an exercise try creating a variation for each repetition of the cycle.

Here is cadential sequence in a popular style that avoids the dominant chord, using instead the triad on bVII and chord IV. Much heard in Beatles songs and Country rock.

Accompaniments

These accompaniment patterns using primary chords are designed to develop co-ordination and rhythmic precision. They are suitable for both experienced and non-specialist keyboard players. Work in partnership with a singer, improvising melodies, then lyrics. For further challenge, memorise and transpose into different keys.

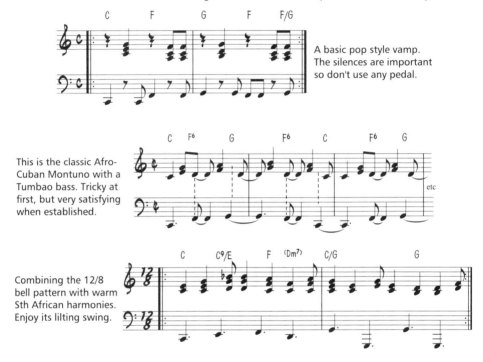

A basic pop style vamp. The silences are important so don't use any pedal.

This is the classic Afro-Cuban Montuno with a Tumbao bass. Tricky at first, but very satisfying when established.

Combining the 12/8 bell pattern with warm Sth African harmonies. Enjoy its lilting swing.

A Samba-like rhythm can generate energy and excitement when well articulated. Try RH pattern 1 over the bass before the more complex agogo-like 2nd version.

A more 'traditional' progression in this bar would be Dm7 -G7.

Figure 12.4 Accompaniment patterns.

One Note Turnarounds

These examples demonstrate just some ways in which a repeated single pitch can be harmonised. The first 2 remain diatonic while the last 2 introduce functional chromaticism.

A gentle sequence that avoids treating the G as a tonic.

This sonorous vamp around a repeating tonic has opened many a popular song:

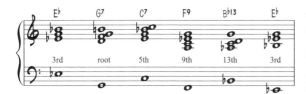

You will find versions of this classic turn-around in Liszt's 'Liebestraume' and in 'Basin Street Blues'.

Notice the relationship of the G to each chord.

Contrary motion chromatic lines rising to a 6/4 are resolved with a typical cadential figure:

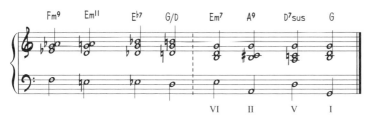

See also "Ein Tone" by Praetorius and Jobim's "Samba de Uma Nota" for some alternative one note harmonisations.

Figure 12.5 One-note turnarounds.

Simple 12 bar Blues in E

This is a good key for the blues if you have diatonic tuned percussion; just remove the F and B tone bars and you have an instant blues pentatonic scale. The voice, however is the best instrument for blues melodies.

Start improvising melodic shapes with just 3 notes from the E minor pentatonic scale,

With a gentle swing

maybe add the 4th note here,

and the 5th note here.

Figure 12.6 Simple 12-bar blues.

12 bar Blues in E with a Walking Bass

Over a walking bass line alternate sustained and 'stab' two-note chords (playing 3rd and 7th). This keeps the texture light and gives a charateristic blues-jazz sound.

Walk like a cat in the low octave.

Try different right hand inversions and syncopated rhythms.

Concentrate on the right feel rather than just note accuracy.

To complete the effect improvise a vocal melody over the top.

Figure 12.7 12-bar blues with walking bass.

Vamps with 2 Chords

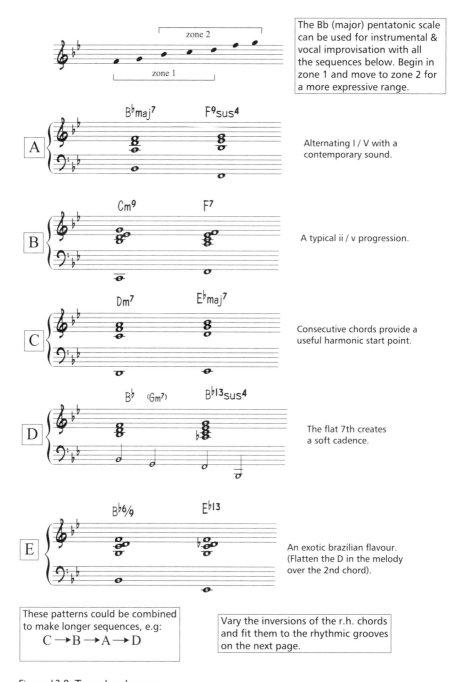

The Bb (major) pentatonic scale can be used for instrumental & vocal improvisation with all the sequences below. Begin in zone 1 and move to zone 2 for a more expressive range.

A — Alternating I / V with a contemporary sound.

B — A typical ii / v progression.

C — Consecutive chords provide a useful harmonic start point.

D — The flat 7th creates a soft cadence.

E — An exotic brazilian flavour. (Flatten the D in the melody over the 2nd chord).

These patterns could be combined to make longer sequences, e.g:

C → B → A → D

Vary the inversions of the r.h. chords and fit them to the rhythmic grooves on the next page.

Figure 12.8 Two-chord vamps.

Rhythmic Grooves

These patterns can work as 1 or 2 bar grooves.
Practise them first away from an instrument to
establish hand independance.

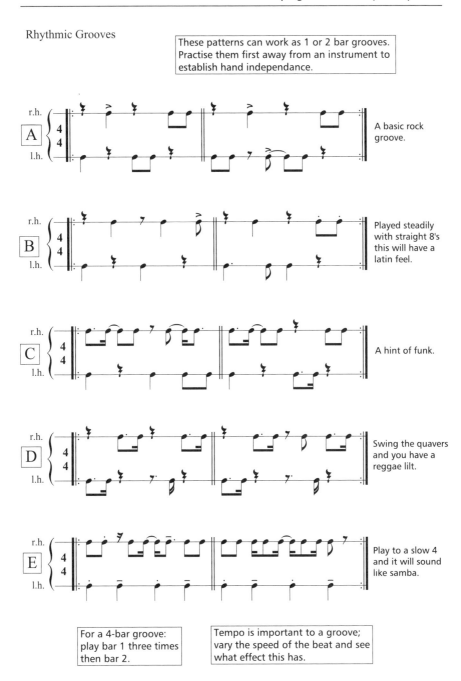

A basic rock groove.

Played steadily with straight 8's this will have a latin feel.

A hint of funk.

Swing the quavers and you have a reggae lilt.

Play to a slow 4 and it will sound like samba.

For a 4-bar groove: play bar 1 three times then bar 2.

Tempo is important to a groove; vary the speed of the beat and see what effect this has.

Figure 12.9 Rhythmic grooves.

AMAZING GRACE

Arranged by Julian Raphael

There are many creative possibilities when harmonising a simple, well-known pentatonic melody. Section A allows space for the melody to breath its natural line with pedal points and held notes giving a subtle resonance. Section B, while still relying on diatonic harmonies, offers inner movement and counter-melody and some chords that are not, at first, obviously consonant with the tune. The final verse provides some altered harmonies that are commonly associated with modern gospel arrangements and help provide interest and surprise.

It is good practice to keep the lead melody out of the accompaniment but find ways of supporting and enriching the vocal line through sensitive use of space, movement, dynamics and colour.

Take some familiar folk-style melodies and experiment with accompaniments that offer changes of mood and texture. Breathe new life into old friends.

Figure 12.10 Exploration of song and accompaniment style: 'Amazing Grace'.

Table 12.1 Opening bars of the Marcello example

Analytical focus	Metaphorical focus
3/4 time: solo oboe and strings; c minor. A single stream of six slow, repeated string quaver C's joined in the next bar by the D above for six more pulses. The dominant 7th chord is spelt out around the next six quavers. Expectations are set for the arrival of the solo oboe. It enters above the continuing pulsating string texture. The rising melody starts out from the home tonic grouped in paired quavers. It climbs in thirds before coming to rest after a semiquaver embellishment. This longer sound is supported by slower crotchet movement downwards in the lower strings. The oboe starts out again one tone lower and in sequence. There are two further sequences, each starting one step lower, the second with quick demisemiquaver figurations. All the melodic material is related to the opening musical gesture and so on.	The opening string pulses feel like a heartbeat and there is a sense of being cradled and supported. But from the outset this threnody is not comforting. There is also a sinking feeling. There are pulls at the heart as the steps and layers of sound are added. The oboe solo feels very poignant. It feels very alone as it weaves its sad story line. There is some consolation with the support of the strings and you feel safe because the bass is always there. This story appears in different versions. It is repeated and elaborated as more depths, details and complexity are added. The addition of quicker notes above the string threnody adds to the feeling of the emotions being quickened and intensified. It feels that you can almost get inside the oboe and sing your own story and version of this sad song.

ON LISTENING TO MUSIC

Open listening as part of training

A music therapy training provides many opportunities to reappraise our approach not only to our playing but to listening to music. Some students might have graduated recently from university courses that stressed an analytical approach to music listening; others may have experienced many years of performing or teaching with little sustained spare time for private listening. We wish to encourage a similar flexible attitude to listening as we have been doing for the practical exercises. One approach is to start with two kinds of listening, one analytical and one more metaphorical and feeling-based (with thanks to Kenneth Bruscia who introduced Leslie Bunt to this approach). This approach is used here to describe the opening of the famous slow movement of Marcello's *Oboe Concerto in C minor* (see Table 12.1).

Doubtless we would have failed our music degrees if we presented a version of the right-hand column in our exams and even the left is far from an in-depth analysis. But we do learn from our patients that it is very common to speak about the effects of listening with more of these feeling-based comments. It is refreshing to find ways of integrating both listening styles. One way is to use this kind of open listening as a stimulus for an improvisation. Take another Baroque example, this time the slow movement from Vivaldi's *Guitar Concerto in D major*. If we listen analytically we hear a slow, dotted, unfolding guitar melody, decorated on the repeats, with long sustained chords (usually one change of harmony per each bar – simple quadruple time). The form is a simple binary with repeats. If we listen with less analysis we are aware of an overriding gentle mood, the guitar weaving its melody as a kind of 'personal gestalt'. There are few obstacles en route; everything is calm and serene. The mood is supported by the accompanying strings that act as a kind of holding cradle, and more so than the Marcello. Students can then be invited to recreate their own version of this unfolding foreground melody supported by a gentle slow-moving background with the intention of creating the same warm and comforting atmosphere.

Other pieces can be used to explore different moods and musical frames. Here are two different examples.

• *Mother and Son* from *Trisan* explores interactive dialogue between two main contrasting elements. The piece starts with sampled wind sounds before a bamboo flute enters in solitary mood (repeated hearings create isolated images of deserts or mountainous places). A drum introduces a heartbeat pulse that provides a sense of holding and grounding. The speed suddenly increases (listeners often have images here of birth itself) as the flute and drum 'fly' together with the odd splash of keyboard harmonies. The various elements are entwined together.

• *Vocalise* from Messiaen's *Concerto for Four Soloists* (flute, oboe, piano and cello) is an interesting exploration of how four voices can maintain their own identities, yet work together with the support of strings. This is part of Messiaen's last work and was composed as a homage to Mozart. The instruments enter in turn: flute, piano (mostly playing accompanying arpeggios throughout), oboe, cello before working together exchanging fragments of melody. There is central flute/oboe imitative exchange; the cello and piano then lead off the final section with the oboe melody and piano decorations, this time with the celesta adding further colours to the orchestral texture.

Both simple yet carefully crafted structures provide frames for improvisations.

On working with individuals and groups

There are many imaginative ways that short pieces of music can be listened to with individuals and groups including:

- as an aid for relaxation at the end of a session;
- inviting patients to bring in favourite music to share and to stimulate discussion;
- to provide a stimulus for movement;
- to provide a stimulus for drawing or creative writing, either during or after listening;
- to be a stimulus for further improvisation as outlined above;
- as a focus for some therapist-directed listening based on such themes as: a meadow, a doorway, following the course of a river, exploring a house, climbing a mountain, meeting a wise old person (for practical suggestions on choice of music and further guidance on the use of directed listening using such archetypal topics, see Assagioli 1965; Bonny and Savary 1973; Leuner 1984).

If the therapist chooses to include a listening approach it is important to be familiar with the music and we recommend listening in both ways detailed above. There is further discussion on the specific approach of Guided Imagery and Music (GIM) in Chapter 15 and the results of some research including listening in a relaxed state in Chapter 14. We note that there is a predominance of classical and instrumental music recommended in GIM and in the suggested texts above. Such music has survived through various shifts in popular taste and avoids the highly personal associations of much vocal music. Doubtless as modern recording techniques bring easier access to music from all corners of the globe, GIM practitioners and other therapists using listening in their work will be increasingly challenged to explore whether such music can be integrated into their work.

SUMMARY

This chapter has extended in practical terms some of the very basic exercises included in Chapter 11. Both chapters offer the music therapist trainee an introduction into exploring musical and personal resources for use in practice. We have needed to be highly selective with the intention of presenting a wide range of options from different musical traditions. We hope that the suggestions will be used imaginatively and with enjoyment. We end with a short list of other publications that include practical resources and that we have found useful:

Pied Piper: Musical Activities to Develop Basic Skills – John Bean and Amelia Oldfied, Cambridge University Press (1991).
Creative Music Therapy (pages 215–225 and Appendix I) – Paul Nordoff and Clive Robbins, New York: John Day (1977).

Healing Heritage: Paul Nordoff Exploring the Tonal Language of Music – edited by Clive and Carol Robbins, Gilsum, NH: Barcelona (1998).

Making Music with the Young Child with Special Needs: A Guide for Parents – Elaine Streeter, London: Jessica Kingsley (2001).

Creative Jazz Improvisation – Richard Michael and Scott Stroman, London: Stainer and Bell (1990).

Creative Music in Group Work – Christopher Achenbach, Bicester: Winslow Press (1997).

Postscript to Part III

Leslie Bunt and Sarah Hoskyns

We add the voices of our interviewees as a postscript to this section and a bridge to the next. All four are trainers themselves and here are some of the themes introduced during their interviews.

Jean Eisler contributed a great deal in the early days of the profession in setting up clinical placements for students. In this way she felt that she was supporting Sybil Beresford-Peirse who was directing the Nordoff–Robbins course at that time.

> *I was so convinced by the rightness of this approach that I felt that what was important was to develop as a music therapist myself, but also to support Sybil in the work she had started with students. We needed placements. Places where they could develop in their own way. In fact, one of the last things Paul Nordoff said to me the week before he died, when I visited him in hospital, was: 'I've done my work here. It's up to all you people to carry it on and develop it'. He was giving us the freedom to do it. It was important to be told this. There were to be no frozen idols and theories, however inspiring.*

Helen Odell-Miller referred to the central importance of the music in music therapy.

> *Although I've been committed to using psychoanalytic theory to inform my work there might have been a danger up to the last couple of years of the music getting lost. . . . When you are training students that has to be central. . . . I think that music has something quite particular to offer where other things don't. . . . To give an example one might learn in one's training that you should always follow the client's music. What do you do when you go into a room and there isn't any music? There is the idea that you have to wait but you could wait for ever for one sound. My feeling is the work is through the music and it is also about the therapist using their own music.*

One of **Elaine Streeter's** strong concerns is the importance of experiential music therapy for music therapy students.

How can you know about the client's point of view in music therapy unless you've tried to express yourself in your own way with a music therapist supporting you? ... Students come out of a music therapy musical experience and begin to understand how this could be important for somebody. It's something about valuing the profound nature of your own work, not just that it's a good thing to do or it might help, but actually experiencing something for yourself through music in music therapy.... When students go through this process they may be able to get to a moment or a music that helps them to understand themselves or to help them express something. It takes them on a journey of self-expression or self-discovery. Once you've been there with people and done that then you have a tremendous belief in it... But if you don't know who you are in music, I mean in improvisation, then you cannot know what influence you are having on your patients. If you don't know the parts of yourself that are problematic – the obstacles in the path of expression within music – if you don't know what those obstacles are that you put in the way of expression then when you get to improvise with your client there may be potential difficulties.

Tony Wigram has experience of both the British training courses (as placement supervisor, guest lecturer and external examiner) and of many courses in other countries, in particular his work at the University of Aalborg in Denmark. While he recognises the importance of training people later in life, as commonly practised in the UK, he does view the shortness of UK postgraduate training as a current weakness.

... one or two years is a very short time in which to pack in all the elements required. And I have become very aware of that since working on a five-year training course in Denmark.

SUMMARY

These comments from our four interviewees stress some of the important themes of this section: the central aspect of music within training; the importance of the clinical placement to which all aspects of any training must relate; the need for time to integrate all the diverse elements and for some kind of sustained personal therapy during training (ideally music therapy), which is now a mandatory requirement of state registered training courses.

In the next section of the book we begin to explore areas that are important to the emerging music therapy professional.

Part IV

Professional life

Introduction

Leslie Bunt and Sarah Hoskyns

Our four interviewees were asked for their opinions of the current status of British music therapy both nationally and internationally.

This is **Jean Eisler's** reply.

> I think it's come a long, long way but we still have far to go persuading everybody that music therapy can play a vital part in a child's development. We can now get music therapy included in a child's Statement of Special Educational Needs, but by now it should be a more automatically promoted form of therapy when needed. In my experience music therapy has often profoundly helped children and sometimes this has led to schools setting up their own music therapy post.
>
> I think in general, we have a very good name internationally. I wish people would include more of the music in conference presentations, because that is what convinces people of its effectiveness. On the whole it seems to me that there is an overbalance of theoretical and written material and that it really needs to be backed up with the music and the music-making.
>
> There is a very wide spectrum of music therapy approaches now. Also many of the children we work with are from various ethnic groups. We need to draw in a wider range of ethnic musicians to come and join us in the work.

Helen Odell-Miller thinks that:

> Politically it's in a good state with the state registration of music therapists coming together with other arts therapists, joining the Council for Professions Supplementary to Medicine (CPSM).

Elaine Streeter feels it difficult to judge the real status of music therapy in the UK since she is free to work in areas that interest her. She thinks the situation would be different if she had just emerged from a training course.

Some graduates find it difficult to survive on music therapy work alone, although that, of course, may be a good thing. Doing too much too quickly can be overwhelming. There are just not enough jobs. I can see from our professional perspective that things are getting better – state registration, supervision schemes and all these things . . . but out in the workplace, it is still very hard . . . I think that we're refining and deepening our professionalism through extended training but I'm not sure that our culture as a whole is moving on. I think it's pretty much that we need to identify what already we know is effective in music therapy and push for further provision nationally – one area is pre-school children. There are many other areas where research is beginning to show effectiveness in statistical terms. Good research is essential in moving the profession forward.

Tony Wigram considers that:

Our status is in many ways strong but in many ways weak. We accept good musicians and try to help them apply those skills. We have a career structure and state registration, therefore we have a good status and potential for people to see there is a good career in music therapy. Our methods are based in improvisation and psychotherapy and these give us great flexibility in our approach. Also there are some diverse approaches used and a wide range of applications clinically.

We haven't developed enough methods of assessment compared to other professions. We would be much stronger if we had some standardised forms of assessment. To determine if somebody is indicated for intervention is very haphazard and individual in music therapy. Evaluation and research is another big area of weakness. When people describe their work they don't give enough information about the data from which they are drawing their interpretations. They don't give enough detail about their music material to give an idea about how they came to the conclusions they came to about the clients.

Internationally, I observe different impressions from different places. In Europe a lot of countries regard our work at a high level because it is a postgraduate profession. We have a long history, run successful conferences and produce good publications. Perhaps we are regarded as one of the leaders in music therapy because we have eminent and pioneering spirits like Priestley, Alvin and Nordoff and Robbins. In the USA perhaps there is the feeling that we don't have enough research or a *strong enough theoretical base for our work but American colleagues may be coming from a very different point of view. However, I think people are attracted by our psychotherapeutic approaches. Many courses in the USA are more 'method'-based. Perhaps British music therapists should be more aware of the work that goes on in other countries. It's noticeable in British publications that there is not enough reference to international writing. But I think it's getting a lot better now.*

This section of the handbook focuses on the life of the professional music therapist after training. We shall discuss the practicalities of job creation, referral and assessment, supervision and further training (Chapter 13); introduce some current debates in research (Chapter 14) and explore the processes of transformation that occur in Guided Imagery and Music – one possible option for further training (Chapter 15). We shall end by tying up some loose ends and looking forward to music therapy's development.

The professional music therapist

Leslie Bunt and Sarah Hoskyns

INTRODUCTION

What happens after our student music therapist has successfully completed training? What are some of the issues out there in the rather more independent and risky atmosphere of the working environment? Gone is the intensive support of course tutors and the student group. Some of the challenges involve finding enough suitable work, learning how to sustain a therapeutic relationship over a longer period and how to bring established work to a suitable close. We begin this chapter by exploring some questions that often arise during the newly qualified therapist's early employment. We review some issues relating to referrals, assessment and report-writing and discuss the importance of regular supervision in learning to manage the therapeutic relationship. Continuing education protects the therapist against 'burnout' and some common routes for further training and support are identified. We conceived this chapter as a transition from training to work: some sections are geared to new professionals; others to more seasoned practitioners and supervisors.

SOME COMMONLY ASKED QUESTIONS

Q: *Where can I find out about music therapy jobs?*

A: Your best route is the professional association's regular job list (see address of APMT in Appendix I). There may be some general therapy posts advertised regionally either through local press, health or social service channels. Sometimes posts in schools requiring qualified teacher status and a therapy qualification will be advertised nationally. Other advertised positions will be either contracted employment within the Whitley Council Career and Grading Structure (Senior I, Senior II and so on) or freelance work at a sessional rate. The APMT can advise on all current rates of pay and scales of employment.

Q: *What happens next?*

A: Read the advert carefully, it will give you procedures to follow. Some employers use standard application forms; others invite letters of application. You will probably be asked for a curriculum vitae and to supply names of referees. If you have just trained, one referee could usefully be a course tutor or supervisor, and the other someone who has known you personally or professionally for a longer time. Be prepared to give reasons for your interest in the job and to describe what you could offer to the post. It is very important to check the job description carefully and to ensure that you cross-reference it with your own statement. Take time with this. The points you make are likely to be explored should you be short-listed for interview. Prepare the application in a thorough and professional way, keeping a photocopy of your final version. You may need to make several rough drafts and consult colleagues. In the present job market there is a great deal of competition and both the content and the way the application is presented go a long way to secure you an interview.

Q: *What can I expect to happen in an interview?*

A: This varies. It is becoming common practice to be asked to give a short audio or video presentation of your work (for which you must have consent). Standard questions for all candidates often focus on: personal background; analysis of strengths and weaknesses relating to the particular post; your estimation of music therapy's contribution to the client group including assessment and review procedures (you could also refer to relevant research or evidence from colleagues' practices); your own relevant clinical experiences and knowledge of institutional practice. Here are some practical tips:

- only take up an interview if you are genuinely interested in the position;
- find out as much as you can about the post by going on a visit, talking to other staff, consulting webpages and so on so that you can talk with assurance;
- be enthusiastic;
- imagine what the interviewers might want from you: to interact with you, to feel confident that you fulfil the criteria and could do the job;
- gauge your responses: be communicative but do not bombard; keep a balance between personal feelings and a professional stance;
- be mindful of the kind of person needed for this job, for example someone who is reliable, consistent, a good communicator and teamworker.
- make sure you prepare some questions to ask.

Q: *How do I go about creating my own job?*

A: This is quite a common route in the UK and, if you are used to the life of a freelance musician or teacher, you should know that this will take time and require determination and persistence. Ask yourself what work really excites you, your interests may have shifted since training. As the mythologist Joseph Campbell so often suggests 'Follow your bliss'. It may be possible for one of your training placements to develop into a professional position, particularly if you have set up the placement yourself with the support of the course team. Otherwise we assume that you will want to set up some work near to where you are living. Here are some practical pointers:

- introduce yourself to local music therapists and your APMT area group;
- your colleague(s) can give you introductions to helpful sources of work or potential openings;
- make use of any personal contacts, always preferable to blind approaches;
- a short phone call can help you establish whether an approach would be welcomed, to whom and at what level of management it should be addressed;
- offer to visit to explain briefly about music therapy and to get a feel for the setting;
- could you imagine yourself working there?;
- if so, offer to facilitate a staff workshop or present some case material;
- think about preparing some promotional material but also look at existing handouts from other centres, colleagues and the APMT.

Q: *If I get as far as an invititation to speak to staff and run a workshop, what do I do?*

A: You could call on a more experienced therapist to assist you and this can add more weight. If this is not possible try to enjoy the challenge. The staff should be curious to learn but will not want a long-winded and jargon-based lecture (any supportive or research-based material could be included in a hand-out). Put yourself in their shoes to imagine the kind of material that would be of interest. You probably will be given a precise time slot during a busy working day so do respect the time boundaries. Make sure you have consent if you are presenting video or audio material and check the availability of equipment. We suggest you aim to make your presentation lively, breaking up any talk with examples and overheads to clarify your main points. Your enthusiasm for the work will go a long way in convincing your potential colleagues of the importance of the work. Use musical instruments and encourage the staff to explore so that they can imagine their clients playing. Supportive group skills and some simple structures will promote security in the workshop group (see examples in Chapter 11). Remember to leave time and space for questions and discussion.

Q: *If I get to the stage of having some work, what must I sort out?*

A: Consult the information supplied by your professional association about contracts, rates of pay and insurance. If you are to become an employee make sure you are given a contract (however part time or short term) and study the small print carefully in relation to terms and conditions of pay, sickness cover and holiday allowance. Ask about any pension scheme that you may be entitled to join. Are the lines of management clear both clinically and administratively? Is regular clinical and managerial supervision built in to your contract? If not, can it be? Make sure you are satisfied with all of these arrangements. Take responsibility for checking your state registration.

If you are self-employed ascertain that the agreed fee is within the range recommended by your professional association. If not then it is your personal decision whether to accept the position or not. Check the lines of management and the referral procedures. Ask for a letter of engagement outlining the agreed terms or a self-employed contract. Seek an accountant to help you with your tax and financial returns. Set up an income and expenditure book, either by hand or electronically. Keep receipts for everything connected with your music therapy sessions including instruments, travel, training courses, stationery and professional memberships (state registration, APMT and so on). Ask your accountant whether you could get any tax allowances for using your home as an office.

Whether employed or self-employed you will need to check insurance cover, in particular professional indemnity. This will protect you in the unlikely event of any legal case being brought against you for an accident occurring during a session. You will need to insure your own instruments and any other equipment if you use it for work purposes.

Q: *I only have a day a week at this centre and already have far too many referrals. How do I prioritise?*

A: Look seriously at the amount of time available and number of people you can comfortably see in the time. Conveyor-belt music therapy is not a productive experience for either patient or therapist. Make sure you build in sufficient time in between sessions for taking notes and preparing the room and yourself for the next session. Remember that as a therapist you are also being paid to observe, think and discuss with other staff. Have proper, regular breaks and try to really use them. To avoid further pressure, create some criteria for prioritising referrals. You can back up your criteria with research that provides supportive evidence, so keep up with your reading of the journals and other literature. Agree on the number of individual and/or group sessions you can manage comfortably in a day. How many people do you want in a group? Be aware of the support that working with a co-therapist can offer.

Q: *How can I protect myself against future 'burnout'?*

A: David Stewart carried out a survey that included questions relating to job satisfaction. There were 126 respondents, representing over half of the number of music therapists in the UK in 1997 to his survey about the state of the music therapy profession. He identified the following factors that helped keep people happily in employment: peer contact (46 per cent), organisational context (40 per cent) and personal and professional development (14 per cent). The top eight ranked support networks were: individual supervision; good communication with parents and carers; informal opportunities to share work with music therapists; further training; attendance at conferences and workshops; reading; meeting with others from related professions and formal opportunities to share work with other music therapists (Stewart 2000: 19).

A further pattern confirmed by Stewart's survey is for music therapists to combine different positions or to continue with instrumental teaching and performing. Only 16 per cent of Stewart's respondents worked full time with the average number of days per week being just under three and a half. What is encouraging was that 82 per cent of respondents had been able to secure sufficient work for themselves since training.

We hope that this series of general questions and answers will help to raise awareness and set up good habits for practice (for further information, see the APMT Information Handbook). We now need to discuss in more detail some managerial and administrative aspects of the work before considering the management of the therapy process itself.

REFERRAL, ASSESSMENT AND REPORT-WRITING

We are now assuming that our new therapist is in a post. Referral and assessment now become important issues.

Referral to music therapy

Music therapists often create their own referral forms. They share some general features: factual information about the client; means of contact for parent, next of kin, significant other, care worker and so on; relevant medical information and name of GP/medical supervisor; reasons for referral; and note of any other agencies involved. Some therapists also include some general guidelines about music therapy and some criteria for referral. We include an example of a referral form for adults (Figure 13.1). A form for children might also include details of the child's position in the family, any recent family changes and nursery or educational provision. A self-referral form might be similar to Figure 13.1 listing the person's doctor and any other professional involvement rather than ward or centre contacts. It is common

Name ....   Date of birth.................................

Address.......................................   Next of kin..................................
....   Daytime telephone number...............
....
Telephone number..........................

Hospital ward/community centre etc...
Key worker.................................   Telephone number........................
Medical supervisor (e.g. psychiatrist).............................

Reasons for referral

Referred by.................................   Relationship to patient/client..............
Contact telephone number...............   Date of referral............................

Has the patient/client been consulted?.................YES/NO
Name and address of general practitioner...
....
Telephone number...

Brief medical history

Other relevant information
(e.g. history of epilepsy, diabetes, sensory impairment, challenging behaviour, current
medication and any recent changes)

Other professional involvement (e.g. speech therapy, physiotherapy)

Current life situation

Name of contact for sharing of any confidential information.......................................

Funding source: health service, education, social services, private, charity, grant, research
etc.

Number of sessions contracted........................

Figure 13.1 Referral form for adults.

practice to inform the doctor of any self-referral. The person making the self-referral is invited to sign the form and to agree the fee and length of initial contract. A further form is included regarding consent for audio and/or video recording of sessions (Figure 13.2). It is advisable also to prepare a withdrawal of recording consent form.

Assessment in music therapy

Following referral, normally there is a period of assessment to ascertain the appropriateness of music therapy. This is only one kind of assessment: procedures can also be used to evaluate a particular stage in the work, to gather evidence as part of a research project and for reports for other professionals, or to examine the conditions for ending therapy. In 2000 the Spring/Summer issue of the *Journal of Music Therapy* was published alongside *Music Therapy Perspectives* as special issues on this important area of assessment. In this section we begin to introduce this complex field and review some of the themes raised in these publications.

The art therapist Linda Gantt in her special feature 'Assessments in the Creative Arts Therapies: Learning from Each Other' raises these key questions:

- What are we assessing that other related fields are not or cannot?
- What can we devise that would be a creditable addition to the battery of existing psychological and psychiatric tests?
- Are there generic assessments that could be applied to any population or setting?
- Are we able to demonstrate that we have reliable and valid instruments?
- Do our assessments mean anything to others besides those of us in the particular discipline?

(Gantt 2000: 42)

Gantt points out that these questions are similar to those raised previously in music therapy publications by Isenberg-Grezda (1988) and Bruscia (1988). What seems to be underlying these questions is a need to devise more of our own specific assessment tools and ones that are reliable and valid (points highlighted by Wigram in the Introduction to Part IV). For many years music and the other creative therapies have relied on standardised assessment procedures from outside our disciplines, as observed by Gregory (2000) in her review of 'Test Instruments Used by *Journal of Music Therapy* Authors from 1984–1997'. Non-musical behaviours were more readily assessed than musical ones with the adaptation of standardised checklists to include some music-based features occurring in some studies.

Gantt infers that a first priority is to be clear what we are exploring if we are to create our own assessment tools. Some of the issues in compiling

Statement of Intent

It is the policy of (enter name of centre or therapist here) to seek consent to record music therapy sessions on video or audio. This is to enable the therapist to monitor and evaluate sessions and to use them for further study and supervision. Consent is also being sought separately to use the recorded material for student teaching, research and presentations at professional meetings and conferences.

The video/audio material will be kept in a locked cupboard and will not be made available within the general public domain (e.g. media, the Internet).

Name of patient/client...
Address and telephone number..,..................................
....
....
....

Consent for audio/video for monitoring sessions by therapist   YES/NO
Consent for audio/video for further study and supervision   YES/NO
Consent for audio/video for teaching, research and presentation   YES/NO
                                        (please delete as appropriate)

Signed..

Please print name.....................................

If signing to give assent* on behalf of the client/patient please indicate relationship
....

Address and telephone number (if different from above)
....
....
....

Countersigned by therapist...

Please print name.....................................

Date................................

* Where it is difficult for the client/patient to give personal consent it would be necessary to obtain assent from a person close to the client/patient.

Figure 13.2 Audio/video consent form.

standardised assessments outlined by Gantt and others in these publications include:

- the rare cases of autistic savants and people with neurological damage with exceptional musical or artistic talents (for example Sacks 1985);
- the notion of musical intelligence as developed by Gardner (1985);
- further individual differences in music creating notorious difficulties in creating any developmental profile in music;
- the lack of any standardisation and difficulties in using musical behaviours to evaluate so-called non-musical behaviours such as motor control and self-expression, although Wilson and Smith (2000) found some evidence of their use;
- the intuitive kind of assessment used by experienced clinicians, tuning in to areas of clinical importance;
- the reluctance of many practitioners to reify and put into boxes aspects of the musical and therapeutic process;
- the challenge of using any preset categories in both open-ended and rigorous ways;
- the overriding question of whether to concentrate on the non-musical behaviours as manifest in the music or to focus on the specific contributions of music for aiding further understanding.

A few assessment procedures that have evolved from within music therapy have been published and are therefore available for other colleagues to use, even if they fall short of the rigours needed for standardisation. Early examples are the two scales charting a child's communicative responses and relationship with the therapist published by Nordoff and Robbins in *Creative Music Therapy* (Nordoff and Robbins 1977) and Edith Boxill's 'Continuum of Awareness' designed for work with the developmentally disabled (Boxill 1985). One of the most commonly cited references relating to music therapy assessment, is the Improvisation Assessment Profiles (IAPs) devised by Kenneth Bruscia and included in *Improvisational Models of Music Therapy* (Bruscia 1987). The IAPs can be used generally in different contexts and can be adapted for both individual and group work. They are extremely comprehensive with six overall profiles itemised by Bruscia: integration, variability, tension, congruence, salience and autonomy. Tony Wigram has adapted the two profiles of autonomy and variability to develop a specific assessment tool for his diagnostic work differentiating between those children on the autistic spectrum and those with some other pervasive developmental or communication disorder. In reference to the two profiles Wigram states:

> Autonomy helps one look closely at the interpersonal events that are going on, particularly the readiness of a child to work together with a therapist, take turns, share and act as a partner, or their propensity

for resisting suggestions or becoming overly dependent. Variability can illustrate at an inter- and intra-musical level the child's capacity for flexibility and creativity, or evidence of a child's rigid or repetitive way of playing that might support a diagnosis on the autistic continuum.

(Wigram 2000: 17)

Wigram uses this method clinically in diagnostic assessment. There are limitations and he refers to the inherent subjectivity, potential observer bias, lack of any real inter-observer reliability and external validity. The richness of the music therapy interaction is reduced to a few manageable areas. Again this introduces more individual bias and subjectivity. To return to one of the opening questions – what material is selected?

Descriptive analysis using narratives rather than checklists or charts is the focus of a model of music psychotherapy assessment proposed by Joanne Loewy. 'Essential to the understanding of a music therapy experience is the recognition of how one assigns meaning to an experience through the process of translation and interpretation' (Loewy 2000: 47). She outlines the ongoing conundrum that using purely musical terminology to describe a music therapy process does not include the psychotherapeutic context and vice versa, using the terminology of psychotherapy precludes the details of the creative musical experience. She recognises the dearth of music therapy description from within the clinical music therapy experience. As we discussed in Chapter 1 there is still this polarity between viewing the work through other theoretical and psychological lenses or focusing on the music. We still need to find a language or languages to describe the music therapy experience from within our own discipline, an experience that integrates both the musical and other perspectives.

In her work on assessment Loewy itemises 13 areas of enquiry that form part of both structured and free-flowing music therapy experiences in a variety of different clinical settings. The selected areas are: awareness of self, other and the moment, thematic expression, listening, performing, collaboration/relationship, concentration, range of affect, investment/motivation, use of structure, integration, self-esteem, risk-taking and independence. These particular constructs, which seem to include both musical and more psychological and therapeutic perspectives, evolved over extensive periods of study, research and wide clinical experience. They are nevertheless still very subjective and, as Wigram commented on his own assessment procedure, lack reliability and validity. Each area could be construed differently by different therapists.

Colin Lee attempts to bridge the gap between clinical issues and the musical content of a session by a detailed analysis of the 'musical building blocks of improvisation as a means to better understand the intricacies of the process' (Lee 2000: 147). His nine-stage method of assessment includes listening to recordings of music therapy improvisation by the therapist, patient and outside observers, such as a musician or psychotherapist. In various stages holistic and very specific listening approaches are used, followed by notation and identification of significant moments, before all areas of the process are brought together and discussed. (Chapter 8 by Sloboda and Bolton uses an approach akin to Lee's scheme.)

We end this section where we began by referring to Gantt's study. She concludes by advising her readers to work towards validating various assessment tools. She proposes we move from a personal and subjective choice of what we assess to a more objective viewpoint. We can start by still being intrigued by the kind of significant clinical material highlighted in Lee's approach. We can then explore whether such behaviours are unique to that individual or could correlate or not with other individuals within a similar clinical population or in other areas. Gantt suggests starting with designing assessments for specific clinical populations and then carrying out some correlation studies with more general ones, although we still see this as being fraught with methodological problems. Can we work from within music therapy itself? Can we observe different behaviours across the lifespan? Can we always be open to change and inspiration while respecting the need for external reliability and validity? Such complexities have prevented us from including any examples of generic assessment forms at this stage in the evolution of music therapy.

Some pointers on writing reports

Institutions such as hospitals and schools have different needs and traditions in the writing of reports and arts therapists need to be aware of how the clinical team manages reports in general. It is good practice to make sure that we write reports in time for all reviews of treatment and to provide a report of assessments undertaken. If there are no formal requests for reports by managers we need to make our own policies on the regular evaluation and appraisal of our clinical work. We can ensure, for example, that we issue annual or six-monthly reviews of treatment and pass on a record of our work if a patient is moved from our service or leaves under natural conditions.

This kind of report for institutional records is different from the detailed in-depth case studies that students often undertake while they are training, or for presentation at a conference when qualified (see Chapter 10 for discussion of case studies). Such a case study is perhaps as much for the practitioner (to process their thinking, to study in depth their approach, to collect together notes, to share with tutors or members of the music or arts therapies profession) as for the reader. The report for the patient's notes or files is usually for a multidisciplinary team, and perhaps for the family or patient to see and therefore needs to be written accordingly, minimising jargon and technical terms and perhaps including some brief material that explains the nature of music therapy.

Watchpoints

- Be aware of who will read the report, for example: nursing or teaching staff, clinical psychologist, social worker, head teacher or parents.
- Be sensitive to issues of confidentiality, and consider what is appropriate to write (put 'CONFIDENTIAL' at the top of the report particularly if using the patient's name and identification details).
- Be concise – ideally a file report should not be more than two sides of A4.
- Use short clear sentences where possible, with a minimum of technical terms. The aim is to be lucid and communicative in writing.
- Try to prepare the report in advance of a meeting so that everyone has a chance to read it.
- Attach a department brochure explaining the aims and procedures of music therapy or include a short paragraph for readers who are new to this work.

General suggestions for areas to include in a report are:

1   name and age of child or adult and date of report;
2   number of sessions, their frequency and time of day;
3   minimal background, for example referral, previous treatment, any pertinent issues for the patient;
4   aims of treatment;
5   how the patient presents – aiming for clarity and including some description of the sounds within the music room;
6   an evaluation of the period of work;
7   recommendations.

The following example of a final music therapy report was written for a dual purpose:

(a) to be part of a review of a child's future educational provision;
(b) to form part of a clinical review to aid diagnosis.

CONFIDENTIAL

Name: Jane Robson

Age at time of report: 8 years 6 months

Date of report: 11 June 2001

Final Music Therapy Report

Jane was referred to music therapy by her consultant paediatrician when she was 5 years 4 months for exploration of her complex communication and emotional difficulties. She has attended a local music therapy centre for weekly individual music therapy after school for eight blocks of twelve sessions.

Jane has been highly motivated to make music, concentrating for extended periods with sessions lasting up to 45 minutes. She handles the various musical parameters with sensitivity, flexibility and sustained attention to detail with particular curiosity in soft and low sounds. She does have an acute hypersensitivity to sounds with problems filtering sounds that can create extreme anxiety, high arousal levels and at times physical rigidity. She has a vivid imagination and a highly developed idiosyncratic language that can create isolation and misunderstanding. She has difficulties at times reading the responses of others, making social interactions problematical, often approaching adults in an overfriendly and uninhibited way. She is emotionally hypersensitive often creating a misrepresentation on how people view her, particularly if she does not have full sight of faces. Jane appears to have a poor self-image and lack of confidence, particularly in areas where she fears failure.

The initial aims of music therapy were to:

*   help to reduce anxiety;
*   encourage imaginative play;
*   boost her self-esteem;
*   provide an outlet for emotional expression.

Jane has achieved a great deal in her music therapy and appeared to gain much pleasure from her creative work. She developed a very close and trusting relationship with her music therapist. She began to find ways of monitoring her levels of at times quite disempowering anxiety when she understood that she could be in control of the levels of sound and nature of the musical activities. This included predicting changes in her own sounds and those of the therapist. Creating stories in music, her own songs and theme-based improvisations built on her rich imagination, private language, symbolic play and musical intelligence. This all helped to boost her self-esteem. She was aware that the time and space were for her, a safe place for her feelings to be externalised and acknowledged. She brought a wide range of emotions to the sessions. At times her music was lively, joyous and excited; at other times she articulated themes of fragility, fear, abandonment and isolation in the music.

Her mother noted her progress towards the aims of the therapy. She observed the growth in Jane's sense of play, fun and use of imagination. These developments were beginning to be transferred to areas of her life outside of the sessions.

Recommendations

Music therapy has been beneficial for Jane in building on her strengths, boosting her self-esteem and providing a safe place for expressing her needs and complex emotional world. Clearly her whole self is very present in the music. Besides the specific benefits of any future period of individual music therapy, more regular exposure to individually tailored music-making is recommended to her teachers as a means of developing her general learning. Regular music sessions would be advantageous to a child with Jane's range of strengths and difficulties. Such a strategy may be more beneficial than to continue in a social environment where the main day-to-day emphasis is on numeracy, literacy and other spatial tasks, the very areas and difficult tasks she finds confusing.

This report was used in making recommendations for future schooling, the ideal being a school for exceptional children like Jane with small classes and regular one-to-one adult support. The report was also used as an aid for diagnosis when it was considered that Jane's particular constellation of difficulties resembled the behavioural characteristics of Williams Syndrome (WS). She does not have any of the physical features associated with WS but does appear to share some similar psychological features.

ENDING THERAPY

'Jane', described in the report above, was being reassessed for her educational provision. Views from everybody involved in her care were being sought in order to gain a full picture of her development. She had received music therapy over a three-year period and the music therapist was beginning to feel that they had met some important goals and that a review of the way forward was needed. In this way, both an external reason (the possible school move) and the therapist's own appraisal suggested that it was relevant to consider bringing the work to a suitable ending. The preparation of the above report was an important stage in the process. The therapist felt the need to appraise the work and to review how far general aims in music therapy, such as developing imaginative play, confidence and communication had been realised. In fact the therapist was able to arrange for a transitional stage when Jane began to build on her musical curiosity with a series of therapeutically oriented piano lessons with a colleague trained both as a teacher and therapist.

In *An Introduction to the Therapeutic Frame*, Gray makes a link between evaluation and ending in verbal psychotherapy. She notes that the therapist needs some objective measures to assist in deciding to bring therapy to a close.

We can look for evidence that our clients are overcoming some of the difficulties they have told us of: the relationship with the therapist may be the crucible for change but it is when our clients report improved relationships in the world outside that we begin to know that they are truly helped by their affiliation with us.

(Gray 1994: 135)

In 'Jane's' case developmental goals had been achieved at the end of the three-year period as well as progress in communication and relating and this helped the therapist to decide about the appropriateness of ending. Gray also gives emphasis to the therapist's role in containing anxiety, both one's own and the patient's, particularly in the move towards ending. She discusses 'having to manage my own guilty feelings regarding abandonment and broken promises, and not avoid them', and notes that her patient valued being told directly and honestly the therapy would end. If we leave a post in order to move on to other work, we have a responsibility to be thoughtful, to try to give our patients time to adjust and most of all to be honest about partings; that is, not avoiding 'the reality of leaving someone by taking refuge in rationalization or reassurance' (Gray 1994: 136)

Gray discusses the preparation of ending for verbal clients. Music therapists often have the challenge of trying to communicate about an ending to clients with few or no verbal skills. This brings a new area of anxiety; how far does the client understand that this will happen? Perhaps the most important issue here is our own intention, that is trying to make the best attempt possible to get the meaning across that there are only a limited number of sessions left. Many therapists use physical counters (a chart or calendar with stars/stickers or photos) or colour in squares to count down each session, and ensure that other staff are aware of difficulties that might be encountered after the work has finished.

In summary here are some general implications for ending a period of music therapy:

- We need to have a thoughtful approach to this process and to think about how to communicate as clearly as possible to non-verbal patients.
- We need to take into consideration the patient's experience of loss and to imagine how ending the work will be received by the patient.
- We stressed in Chapters 1 and 2 the importance of 'relationship' in music therapy. Ending relationships involves anxiety and pain, on both sides. We must bear this in mind and provide a safe frame for managing the parting.
- How far is this decision on our terms? Can the patient be consulted or involved in the decision appropriately? It is our ethical responsibility to work in the best interests of the patient.

- A careful appraisal of the period of work, considering whether issues have been worked through or resolved and some aims (if applicable) have been met should happen before the decision is finalised.
- Appropriate time should be allowed to prepare for a thoughtful ending. This allows a range of feelings to be expressed and for the patient to have an opportunity to react. Be aware that sometimes circumstances are beyond our control (a patient is moved hurriedly) and we may just need to do the best we can.
- How does this possibility link with the patient's other experiences? Is there a natural set of breaks (as with the school change); if so does this make it easier for the patient or will it mean losing everything at once?
- How does the patient's whole 'package of care' work? Negotiation with other staff and carers will be important to get the balance right.
- Endings can be good, appropriate and an opportunity to move forward and to have new experiences.

THE NECESSITY OF REGULAR SUPERVISION

At the end of the question and answer section above we noted how Stewart's survey itemised individual supervision as the most valued system of support. When we first qualified there was no supervision scheme in place. We needed to seek out colleagues from other disciplines such as psychotherapy. As the profession has matured so has the growth of a group of experienced clinicians to act as supervisors. Before turning to some different models of supervision now available to the music therapist we can chart the development of the supervision scheme in the UK by turning to the voices of our interviewees.

Jean Eisler talked of early support groups (in the 1970s) organised at the Nordoff–Robbins Centre by Sybil Beresford-Peirse and of her work guiding newly qualified therapists at her places of work. She does not describe this guidance as supervision *per se* but we can regard it as a kind of mentoring or apprenticeship.

From very early on Sybil Beresford-Peirse insisted that we had regular groups. It was not a therapeutic group but it was run by a psychotherapist and we brought problems we had experienced in our work and how it affected us. Sybil ran the development of those years very soundly... I felt that my job during all those years was to support her to enable it [the Centre] to grow... I stayed in charge of the work at Goldie Leigh [the setting for the first Nordoff–Robbins course in 1974] at Sybil Elgar and later at Queen Mary's, Carshalton. Over the years, we had the

> *opportunity to have about 25 students for their clinical practice and observation work there. We didn't call it supervision then and it wasn't really. I think quite an important thing was the fact that we weren't so close to the course and that we were working outside. That made it possible for us to develop ourselves and to be free, in a sense, to move on from what we learnt strictly on the course. We needed to learn to apply it.*

Helen Odell-Miller also needed to look to other disciplines for influence and supervision.

> *A major influence was Dr Graham Davis who was the first psychoanalytic supervisor that I had. He was a biodynamic therapist as well as a Freudian analyst and he loved music. He could listen to improvisations and tapes and have quite a good notion of what was going on, coupled with the fact that we set up an arts therapies supervision group. The other music therapists in the group could help him inform the musical part of the work but also I learnt a lot from other arts therapists. I think that's been crucial.*

A travelling scholarship in 1984/85 gave **Elaine Streeter** the opportunity to study supervision schemes in other countries. At that time she was director of training at Roehampton Institute and was concerned to find ways of developing specialist music therapy supervision for newly qualified therapists in particular. When asked about her contributions to music therapy Elaine replied:

> *I think the supervision issue is an ongoing contribution. That came from my Churchill Fellowship in the USA and Canada on supervision for music therapists. On my return I decided to try to instigate a post-diploma supervision scheme. I took this idea to the APMT where it was met with a lot of interest. Helen Odell, who was the chair of the APMT at that time, was keen to work with me on this. We decided to form a sub-committee and came up with a number of different suggested schemes. Each one was met with a wave of resistance from the professional members. We continued on our surfboards until finally we managed to get it across that the introduction of a supervision scheme was not intended to make people feel undermined but to help the profession grow. That's something I'm proud of and is now really pretty much established.*

In his interview **Tony Wigram** considered post-diploma supervision as a strength of current music therapy practice in the UK. He compared this with similar developments in the USA.

> *Another real strength is the development of post-diploma supervision. There is a lot more emphasis in this country on therapists continuing to seek guidance and support for their work. In the USA you can't sustain your Board Certification if you can't prove that you are having 'Continuous Music Therapy Education' – this is very good. That is not so typical in other countries.*

Hopefully students will have had a positive experience of supervision during training both from placement supervisors and within the course in small group and individual sessions. There may also have been some experience of peer group supervision.

During training supervision will have been both supportive and educational, for example a supervisor supplying some information about a patient's condition or teaching a specific musical intervention. It is likely that there will now be a transition to a model that has less emphasis on the educational and more on 'thinking with' the supervisor. The focus may develop more towards independent thinking and consideration of managerial and team dynamic issues. We define music therapy supervision so:

> Supervision in music therapy is an interactive process between a practitioner and a more experienced colleague, concentrating on musical, practical and dynamic issues. There is a mutual shared interest in the work with the central emphasis on the practitioner becoming more effective in working with clients. Through the establishment of a clear frame of meetings, the supervisor facilitates open and honest articulation of material arising from the work. The process takes place within a context that is both supportive and critically reflective.

We focus more now on the supervisory process and a supervisee can expect:

- confidentiality;
- to be supported in a safe, consistent and boundaried space;
- to be given focused attention;
- to be given reassurance and encouragement to explore reactions to the work including difficult feelings and areas of vulnerability associated with helping people: fear, inadequacy, distress, prejudice, over-identification and so on;
- to be given any appropriate information or recommended reading;

- to be assisted and inspired with the musical 'nuts and bolts' including the practical management of the setting;
- to explore the musical process in practical and imaginative ways;
- to help further our own personal style of work;
- to be challenged over any preconceptions or rigidly held beliefs;
- to explore our reactions to the setting and interpersonal dynamics with team members;
- to further the development of our own 'internal supervisor' (Casement 1985);
- clear boundaries on the difference between supervision and personal therapy;
- clarity regarding financial and contractual arrangements.

As we continue our discussion of supervision we shall be drawing substantially on the process model of supervision in *Supervision in the Helping Professions* (Hawkins and Shohet 1989) and be referring to the work of Casement (1985), Dass and Gorman (1985) and some thoughts on music therapy supervision by Brown (1997) and Dvorkin (1999). We concentrate here on the one-to-one encounter centred on clinical work, while being aware of the existence of other kinds of supervision such as managerial support.

Our newly appointed therapist needs to be familiar with the therapeutic orientation of the supervisor. It is likely that a supervisor who works, for example, within a humanistic or psychodynamic framework as a therapist would use this frame as a supervisor. The particular orientation of supervisor should be common information; the APMT, for example, publishes a list of approved supervisors with details of each supervisor's style of work and range of experience. It is in our interests to be open to new approaches. This is particularly useful in exploring what Hawkins and Shohet describe as our 'blind spots, deaf spots and dumb spots' (ibid.: 48). Their process model of supervision can be divided into three main areas:

(a) a case-centred approach when supervisees bring material that focuses on the detail of sessions and the content of the work;
(b) a therapist-centred approach when supervisees focus on their own feelings, interventions and processes;
(c) an interactive approach when there is a detailed exploration of processes in the relationship between patient and therapist as possibly mirrored in the relationship within the supervision process.

Hawkins and Shohet describe this process model as involving two interlocking systems: the system that connects therapist and client and that of the supervisor and supervisee. A music therapist might start by concentrating on what happens in sessions: the music played by the patient and the presenting problems. Attention here could be drawn firstly to the interventions made by the therapist, what music the therapist played or how any words were managed, and secondly to the dynamics of the therapeutic relationship including both conscious and unconscious processes. Shifts can be made between these different worlds of client and therapist. The supervisor can also help the supervisee to begin to explore counter-transference issues.

We are fortunate as musicians in being able to explore a musical solution to a psychological or therapeutic obstacle. Some examples are:

- the supervisee is invited to improvise around the feelings about a particular client or stage in the relationship;
- the supervisee explores what it feels like to be in the client's shoes by playing as if the client, with the supervisor taking on the role of therapist;
- using flexible exercises to allow the supervisee to shift position from client to therapist, playing the kind of music typical within each role and gaining insight into how the roles relate from a number of perspectives;
- exploring alternative methods for handling personal dynamics or specific incidents within the therapy.

The process model unfolds to include an exploration of the relationship in the supervision as it might mirror the happenings on an unconscious level within the therapy. This can provide very useful insights, as can supervisors being open and honest with their own counter-transference feelings and images. Hawkins and Shohet consider that good supervision shifts between these different levels using a technique they define as 'helicopter ability':

> This is the ability to switch perspectives; to be able to focus on the client that the supervisees are describing; to focus on the supervisees and their process; to be able to focus on your own process and the here and now relationship with the supervisees; to be able to see the client within their wider context and help the supervisee do likewise; and to see the work within the wider context of the organisation and the inter-organizational issues.
>
> (Hawkins and Shohet 1989: 37)

Hawkins and Shohet place their process model within larger organisational, professional, social, cultural and ethical constraints. There are broader economic, religious, political and cultural backgrounds of both patient and therapist to consider. In undertaking any form of supervision we come face to face with our own flaws, weaknesses and issues, some of which may overlap and be explored in our personal therapy. This brings us to consider the notion of the 'wounded healer' (for further exploration, see Pavlicevic 1997 and Priestley 1994 in particular).

The most familiar models of who we are – father and daughter, doctor and patient, 'helper' and 'helped' – often turn out to be major obstacles to the experience of our caring instincts: they limit the full measure of what we have to offer one another. But when we break through and meet in spirit behind our separateness, we experience profound moments of companionship. These, in turn, give us access to deeper and deeper levels of generosity and loving kindness. True compassion arises out of unity.

(Dass and Gorman 1985: 20–21)

This example taken from a training-level supervision group demonstrates the three areas of the process model proposed by Hawkins and Shohet.

During group supervision two students presented an assessment session when they worked as co-therapists with an elderly patient.

Case-centred level

One of the students placed the work in the context of the patient's life and institutional setting. The patient was described as very withdrawn and non-communicative; these were the main reasons for the referral. The supervision group watched the first part of some video film when the initial focus was on the musical material and musical relationships between the patient and the student therapists. The group realised quickly that the musical preference of this so-called withdrawn patient was in fact very lively and loud. There was sustained drum-playing, which one of the students supported at the piano. The supervisor asked how the students negotiated the roles of co-therapist. In this stage of the assessment session it was clear that one student acted as the main musical support with the other student working along-side the patient. This dynamic was altered quickly by the patient who pointed to each therapist in turn to indicate when she wanted to hear their music, either harp or piano. Each adult in the room played in turn. There were few words but much exchange of gestures.

Therapist-centred level

The supervision moved away from preoccupation with the content into more reflec-tion on how the two therapists felt within this dynamic. It was clear to the group that the dynamics were shifting and that the patient was having a powerful influ-ence on the therapists. This was made more apparent when the patient accepted the invitation to join one of the therapists at the piano and then eventually to play there by herself. The unfolding of this elderly patient's personality was clearly felt *and acknowledged by the two therapists. They were very moved by the speed of this process. They were excited and felt warm feelings towards this elderly lady who could have well been the age of one of their well-loved grandmothers. What was also of note (and linked to the process model outlined above) was that the dynamic within the therapy room began to influence the atmosphere within the supervision group.*

Interactive level (therapy/supervision)

The group was meeting in the evening at the end of a tiring day. The mood shifted with the level of excitement almost palpable as this mirrored the emerging feelings of this patient coming alive in the music. There was a rapid increase in the number of comments and reactions, with at times many people speaking at once. Clearly the relationship between the students and patient had become transferred into the supervision process. The group left in an uplifted mood, full of enthusiasm to observe that music can act in such a transforming and powerful way.

Sandra Brown's 1997 paper provides a thorough discussion of perspectives from Hawkins and Shohet integrated within Casement's notions of the holding frame and containment. She presents a multidimensional picture of the work in music therapy supervision ranging from an emphasis on the musical relationship in the therapy room, through practical issues of management, interpersonal dynamics in both the therapy room and the working environment to the dynamics within the supervision process. Brown emphasises the multifaceted and flexible nature of the music therapy supervisor and regards musical tools of being of high value in gaining insight. Dvorkin also highlights these two areas as being helpful to restore confidence in rather demoralised and overworked clinicians and those who are not so familiar with a more analytical approach to supervision (Dvorkin 1999). Like Dvorkin, Brown points out that as music therapists understand more about therapy, often through their own personal therapy journeys, there is an increasing focus on dynamic issues within supervision. While being aware of professional boundaries, Brown encourages a delicate approach to the diversity of roles within a small profession. She is not averse to seeing a close colleague or offering a cup of tea but carefully thinks how to manage this with integrity and professionalism.

Flexibility, containment, musicality and imagination: these are features in the supervisor's approach that can help the young professional to feel understood and foster confidence, growth and change. A good experience of supervision can help develop Casement's significant concept of the 'internal supervisor'. There is a growing internal process with the voice of the supervisor being merged with the therapist's own reflective and independent observations.

The growing importance attached to music therapy supervision is indicated by the recent publication of a specific text edited by Forinash (2001).

FUTURE ROUTES FOR EDUCATION AND TRAINING

Further training was itemised as the third most important factor contributing to job satisfaction in Stewart's survey (2000). At present there is no advanced specialist clinical training after basic diploma and Master's qualifications in the UK, although there are moves to do this at the centres where the courses are based, for example the recent validation of a Master's in supervision at Anglia Polytechnic University. Until advanced music therapy training becomes established colleagues will continue to seek out varied additional training elsewhere. There are several common patterns in the UK.

One group of colleagues, after a period of general practice in a variety of contexts, have gravitated towards a specialist field, for example: autism, neurology, palliative care, sexual abuse and forensic psychiatry. They have become associated with making a contribution within that area and become known both nationally and internationally through their teaching, presentations and publications (see Chapter 1 for examples). Further education options present themselves within that particular speciality through attending conferences, extra training and more personal study and reflection. Some of this group may move into the next pattern that we have observed.

This second group is a smaller one of those music therapists who have decided to embark on some research in relation to their chosen area of speciality within the field. The work may develop into a research degree or form part of a collaborative project with colleagues working within the same field but from different professional perspectives. A rapid learning curve has been necessary here as to date, with the exception of the bolt-on Masters' courses, there are no courses in the UK specifically related to teaching research methods in music therapy. We have both had to seek out specific research supervision for our own work as music therapy researchers. There are some moves to address this lack with research seminars and conferences being delivered at City University, London, the Nordoff–Robbins Centre and the University of the West of England to list three recent developments. The tradition is much more highly developed in the USA (Wheeler 1995) and also elsewhere in Europe with research centres at the Universities of Aalborg, Denmark, and Witten Herdecke, Germany and in Nijmegen, The Netherlands, for example. Once again this group of therapists has become associated with their research through publications and presentations both nationally and internationally.

A third group is made up of those music therapists who have chosen to find additional training from outside music therapy. After an initial period of work a need for further learning becomes a prerequisite and colleagues have sought further insight into their work from other perspectives. Some music therapists have embarked on extensive and costly additional training in, for example, child psychotherapy, counselling, psychology or adult psychotherapy. There have been many professional advantages to this trend both for the individual therapist and for the profession as a whole. Both Streeter and Wigram commented in their interviews about the nourishment of their training in other disciplines, psychotherapy and psychology, respectively, as well as keeping their musical selves alive. Streeter commented:

> Once you start thinking about the person as well as the music in a big way then you've also got to think about yourself, you as a person, you as a musician as a creative artist. Equally important have been my own adventures into creative work outside of music therapy, in the live theatre, in the dubbing theatre, in the film editing room, as a writer and currently as a student of architecture. These experiences keep me thinking about creative processes and hopefully keep my teaching fresh.

And Wigram:

> There are also the continuing influences from musical life outside music therapy, for example my church choir influences. Music therapists should always sustain their musical influences and their music experiences. I have always done that by playing in opera orchestras and being a church organist. These areas are a big part of my life.

One fundamentally music-based further training route is Guided Imagery and Music (GIM). GIM was created by the music therapist Helen Bonny and involves listening to specific programmes of recorded music in a deeply relaxed state. Some of the transformation processes of GIM are discussed in Chapter 15.

SUMMARY

In this chapter we have introduced areas that need to be addressed as the recently trained therapist moves out into the profession. We have looked at some practical questions and discussed referral and assessment procedures and report-writing. We have particularly stressed the importance of supervision. We have indicated some opportunities for further training, development and education in the UK. In the next chapter we now focus on one of these areas, namely research.

Chapter 14

Some reflections on music therapy research: an example of collaborative enquiry

Leslie Bunt

INTRODUCTION

> Medicine comprises science with handicraft, art, and often, with spirituality. We are talking here about the healing arts . . . Without intuition, fantasy, emotions, reverence, and aesthetics, a scientist would be blind; without logic, discipline, and ratio, an artist would be only a dreamer. As physicians and therapists, we need a synthesis of these. Music is the most intense means of emotional communication and it facilitates such a synthesis in many ways.
>
> (Spingte 1998a)

Music therapy is witnessing a steady rise in its acceptance as a paramedical discipline, blending both artistic and scientific processes into a 'healing art'. This rise was charted in Chapter 1 and examples of various clinical applications were included in Part II and elsewhere. Alongside this growth in the range of clinical material have emerged different research traditions, each contributing to the discipline's further acceptance. Some current patterns in research are outlined in this chapter and some historical, philosophical and practical reasons for differences between the emergent traditions discussed. The chapter's main contention is that there is room in music therapy for a wide variety of research approaches. Flexibility, tolerance and common sense are essential if we are not to find ourselves becoming too far removed from the very people music therapy is aiming to help. The themes of synthesis, balance and integration, introduced above by the medical practitioner and music medicine specialist Ralph Spingte, influence how this chapter unfolds. The second half of the chapter illustrates some of these themes by charting the stages in some collaborative research at the Bristol Cancer Help Centre.

SOME CURRENT PATTERNS IN MUSIC THERAPY RESEARCH

Note Key research terms, defined briefly here and in more detail in other texts, appear in bold (for their further elaboration see, for example, Aldridge 1996; Ansdell and Pavlicevic 2001; Gilroy and Lee 1995; Langenberg *et al.* 1996; Ruud 1998; Smeijsters 1997; Wheeler 1995; Wigram *et al.* 1995).

There are external pressures from employing agencies for therapists to justify and evaluate their work. The 'business speak' of audit, cost-effectiveness, quality assurance, appraisal and monitoring has created a purchaser/provider and marketplace atmosphere in the delivery and evaluation of therapeutic services. Penny Rogers has discussed the concept of **evidence-based practice (EBP)** in relation to music therapy. She cites one definition of EBP, namely: 'The conscientious, explicit and judicious use of current best evidence in making decisions about the care of individual patients' (Sackett *et al.* 1996; see Rogers 2000: 11). Rogers cautions against the overemphasis on the 'gold standard' of **randomised control trials (RCTs)** in indicating evidence of good practice, such approaches not linking easily with more individually based therapeutic practices. Nevertheless, carefully organised studies demonstrating the efficacy of the work are still required; we owe this to our patients, employers, as well as to ourselves. Questions that arise from clinical practice can be tested through research – these thorough journeys of searching or searching again. Studies can be set up that research links between stated objectives for a piece of work and the resulting effects of the intervention. Results can then inform further practice.

Studies that explore causal links between intervention and resulting effects are often described under the generic term of **outcome**. Here the emphasis is on recording the effects/outcomes of the work, usually in a language accessible to all, over and above any detailed descriptions of the specific therapeutic **process** by which any outcomes are reached. Here are some examples of outcome-based questions:

(a) When working with children with communication problems are there any measurable changes in the number of vocal sounds over a period of time in music therapy when compared to a similar period without therapy?
(b) In what measurable ways can music therapy contribute to the individual therapeutic aims devised by the multidisciplinary team for adults with profound learning difficulties?
(c) When working with a group of elderly patients what is the amount of engaged contact time in music therapy when compared to another group activity such as reminiscence therapy (see Odell-Miller, 1995; Chapter 9)?

Outcome studies stress an objective stance generally employing a research **method** (ways of gathering and analysing the data) that records externally observable and measurable behaviour. A series of **hypotheses** and **research questions** are set up before the project begins. In example (a) above what is called the **null hypothesis** would be that there are no changes in the number of vocal sounds when two similar periods are compared. The project can then be constructed to prove or disprove this hypothesis. The researcher, who often sets out with a particular hunch, places the developing questions within the context of previous published research in the area or specific theoretical background. These initial surveys are then included in the **literature review**. From where do the questions emerge and why are they needed? Criteria for the research project are selected; in the above example the children could all be under 5 years old and non-verbal. A group of individuals are then carefully selected that fit these **research criteria** and this group is commonly referred to as the **sample**, the question of sample size always being a source of much debate as it influences the kind of statistical analysis that is possible. An element of **control** is important, both in setting up of **control or comparison groups** (the same number of people either not having the particular intervention or a comparable one, as in example (d) above) and controlling and **matching** for **variables** such as age, sex and any specific diagnosis. A very robust control is to allocate individuals to the treatment and control or comparison group in a random fashion, as in a traditional RCT.

Variables are also labelled as being **dependent** or **independent**; in example (a) the dependent variable would be the vocal sounds with the music therapy intervention the independent variable. Can any causal links between these two variables be established? **Measures** and **procedures** that can be **quantified** numerically are generally employed in these kinds of studies. Numbers are used to quantify the existence, strength or **frequency** of the observed phenomena. If the **raw data** resulting from the measures and procedures meet certain prescribed conditions then statistical tests can be applied. Space precludes discussion of the various criteria for **descriptive or inferential statistics, parametric or non-parametric tests** and the reader is referred to such standard texts as Siegel (1956) and Snedecor and Cochrane (1980) and to the advice of a statistician. As pointed out by Ansdell and Pavlicevic in their very approachable text *Beginning Research in the Arts Therapies: A Practical Guide* (2001) it is important to be mindful of what kind of statistical analysis is to be used before starting a study. What level of **probability** is to be set so that any results can be given a **level of significance** beyond mere chance occurrence? It is usual to set at least a 0.05 level, that is a guarantee of up to a 95 per cent that results are not due to chance. If the measures and procedures are sufficiently **valid** and meet the criteria for specific statistical tests then **generalisation** of effects is possible – what applies to this sample population could generalise to a larger group. Measures also need to be sufficiently robust to enable other researchers to **replicate** the study by testing the same hypotheses with the similar method using a different sample.

There is a further range of internal pressures from within the profession itself. During the last decade many questions have focused on discovering more of the meaning of the music therapy **process**. Such knowledge can enrich the development of our practice; the knowledge gained can be passed on to our students and colleagues. Here the emphasis is on an internal enquiry, an exploration of the processes that are regarded by many to be at the heart of music therapy. **Quality** is often diametrically opposed to **quantity**, an individual's evolving response to the music therapy process given more emphasis than the more quantifiable outcomes to the work. The subjective worlds of both patients and therapist are regarded as having validity in their own right, their voices often being very much part of the research. There is not a striving for external objectivity as in the harder more quantifiable outcome-based studies. There is not a search for any one objective truth; on the contrary there is a celebration of multiple perspectives. In approaches within this softer process-based tradition the research questions emerge as the work progresses; the questions are **grounded** in the practice. Process-based research still demands attention to notions of validity and scientific rigour. A literature review is still necessary. The data from this kind of research can be presented as musical or verbal transcriptions and narratives, or using other 'maps' (images, metaphor, journals and so on) illustrating the detailed processes, themes and constructs embedded in the work.

There is certainly a heightened emphasis on the music and its interpretation in this line of exploration, with researchers often including documentation of the musical material as central evidence. There is much discussion of the role of the researcher as therapist and/or observer. Other members of the clinical team or observers are often included in the research, their voices being included alongside the clients and therapist (Reason and Rowan 1981). This is the basis of evaluation from different viewpoints, often referred to as **triangulation**. Here are some process-based questions:

(a) What are the 'critical moments' in a period of therapy as identified by significant adults in a child's life – parent, teacher – alongside the views of the therapist?
(b) How are the 'critical moments' in a period of therapy defined by a depressed adult patient, the therapist and external observer?
(c) When is it appropriate to use group improvisation techniques and when pre-composed music when working with elderly patients with dementia?

In addition to outcome and process-based studies there are also smaller research traditions of a more philosophical or historical nature (see reviews by Aigen 1995; Solomon, 1995).

In their interviews Helen Odell-Miller and Tony Wigram referred to some of these emerging patterns. Helen completed her M.Phil. at The City University based on an evaluative study of music therapy with older people with dementia (see Chapter 9). She is currently planning research with people under 65 years old and is concerned that research be linked to clinical practice.

> I think that more than ever music therapists are going to have to relate what they are doing to the clinical context of the people that they are working with. I think if they can't demonstrate outcome and that in some way this work is contributing to the overall life of the person relating what they are doing back to the original difficulty, diagnosis or problem then it won't develop.... I am very interested in process, for myself, and for my clients I know that's also very important.

Tony completed his doctorate based on his work in vibro-acoustic therapy (see Skille and Wigram 1995) and his current position in Denmark as head of an international Ph.D. programme equips him well to observe some current patterns. He shares Helen's concern to relate research to practice.

> I still feel strongly about trying to quantify the effects of music therapy. To find out what the outcome of our interventions is and to argue based on the evidence of good data that music therapy works.

SOME ROOTS OF THESE PATTERNS: FURTHER THOUGHTS ON QUANTITATIVE AND QUALITATIVE METHODOLOGIES

> Approaching musical applications in medical settings with scientific means that include both qualitative and quantitative measures does not diminish the scientific reputation of either Music Therapy or Music Medicine. The artificial dichotomy between qualitative and quantitative research is identified as such in medical science nowadays.
>
> (Spingte 1998b: 9)

Clearly certain kinds of questions demand certain kinds of research strategies. If we are interested, for example, in finding out how music therapy can be effective in helping to organise the control of movements for an adult with Parkinson's Disease then some form of external, quantifiable and outcome-based measures may be appropriate. The goals of the research relate to charting externally measurable and objective changes. Obviously such a one-faceted approach is only able to answer one narrow band of questions. Alternatively if we were interested in exploring how music therapy contributes to the same person's inner feelings of self-worth we would then be looking at a completely different set of questions and approach. We would most likely be setting up questions and methods based in the narrative flow and interactions between both parties in the relationship. The specific processes of that particular therapy for that particular person would become more the focus. Obviously the personal motivation, philosophical and value system of the therapist will influence the choice of research method (Gfeller 1995). Each researcher will bring to each project their own frame of reference or **paradigm** through which to view the work and, according to Lincoln and Guba (1985: 15), 'Paradigms represent a distillation of what we *think* about the world, (but cannot prove)'.

As discussed in Chapter 2 in any music therapy encounter we can never overlook the therapist's clinical orientation and the connections between values, norms and interests in relation to how we perceive and act in the world (also see Ruud 1998). Further to this discussion Jane Edwards has surveyed **ontological** (nature of being) and **epistemological** (nature of knowledge) issues in relation to the various paradigms and traditions at the root of music therapy research (Edwards 1999). She indicates that specific methodological issues emerge from questions relating to paradigms, including in her review succinct background to **positivism, post-positivism, constructivism and critical theory**. At a rather more pragmatic level we should also not overlook the question of who is paying for the research, the particular clinical setting and general working conditions. In all the intricate debates over which method is more appropriate, and much has been written and discussed in recent years, we must continually bear in mind our prime responsibilities to our clients and patients. As Bruscia states:

> It bears repeating that the primary mission of music therapy, as both discipline and profession, is to help clients to achieve health through music. To limit music therapy research in any way is to limit this mission in a corresponding way. If the client's health is conceived only in physical or behavioural terms, then quantitative research might be sufficient; conversely, if the client's health is conceived only in internal, covert, or experiential terms, then qualitative research might be sufficient. The problem is that to define health in such either-or terms, and to limit the goals of music therapy practice to either overt or covert goals, physical or social realities, or objective or subjective phenomena is essentially a violation of the rights of our clients to comprehensive treatment, and thus to complete health.
>
> (Bruscia 1995b: 73)

It is clear that there are many different and valid methods of research in music therapy. The early research work, particularly in the USA and more recently at the beginning of the research tradition in the UK, employed established methods from the worlds of psychology, the behavioural sciences,

Table 14.1 Some implicit assumptions within quantitative and qualitative approaches

QUANTITATIVE	QUALITATIVE
• Positivistic	• Non-positivistic
• Hypotheses derived from previous theory and practice	• No a priori hypotheses – emerge from process
• Replicable questions	• Context-based questions
• Representative sample	• Unique individuals
• Reductionist	• Non-reductionist
• Mechanistic	• Narrative/discursive
• Causal (independent and dependent variables)	• Non-causal (continuing process of interrelationships in the research)
• Measurement	• Interpretation
• Prediction	• Non-predictability
• Search for objective truth	• Value for subjective perspectives
• Search for external evidence	• Voices of client/patient, therapist
• External observations	• Internal observations
• Outcome	• Process
• External controls	• Internal controls
• Valid and reliable measures	• Internal validity and reliability
• Can generalise results	• Cannot generalise results

medicine and other clinical practices to account for the efficacy of the work. The emphasis was on behavioural, physiological and outcome measures that could be quantified. Interestingly, while some of the early research was laboratory-based there was a move to develop studies of a more natural-istic stance with research soon moving out of the laboratory into the therapy room. It is of no doubt that this early research (well documented in such journals as the *Journal of Music Therapy*) made enormous contributions to the growth of the profession. Posts were created on the evidence of the 'proven' effects of intervention. However, studies were becoming full of complex test data and statistical analysis and many music therapists found it difficult to access the material. Therapists with an extensive musical background often felt more comfortable with research material rooted in artistic, social, aes-thetic, cultural, musical or therapeutic perspectives. There was a call for more consideration of the art rather than the science of music therapy. Gradually there was a move to create studies with more musical/therapeutic processes at the centre. This more qualitatively based approach has gained much ground recently and is seen by many influential researchers as the approach more suited to the inherent nature and meaning of music therapy. Today the pendulum has certainly swung over in favour of qualitative research.

There are major philosophical issues at stake here and before moving on some of the key issues in both quantitative and qualitative approaches are summarised in Table 14.1. These issues are explored extensively in the references cited above.

HOW CAN DIFFERENT APPROACHES EXIST SIDE BY SIDE?

While clearly not wanting to limit research in any way Bruscia is one of many researchers who views the quantitative and qualitative approaches as arriving from completely different world-views and not part of any connected continuum. What does seem appropriate, however, is for these two approaches to be used selectively to address different questions, as in the example of our Parkinsonian patient above. Besides the possibility of linking a particular project to the appropriate approach Bruscia also proposes two further options. One is to look at different aspects of the same phenomenon in different and independent studies. This relates to the notion of viewing clinical work through different 'lenses' be it psychodynamic, developmental or physiological as discussed by Pavlicevic (1997). The second option is to combine different procedures and kinds of data in the same study but to stay firm to one of the two philosophical positions (Bruscia 1995b).

Ken Wilber has been a source of inspiration in other chapters and this passing reference to using various 'lenses' through which to view the work links to his explorations of the different ways we access knowledge. In *Eye to Eye* Wilber recalls St Bonaventure's teachings concerning three basic ways of knowing, namely: 'the *eye of flesh*, by which we perceive the external world of space, time and objects; the *eye of reason*, by which we attain a knowledge of philosophy, logic and the mind itself; and the *eye of contemplation*, by which we rise to a knowledge of transcendent realities' (Wilber 1983: 3). Traditionally the world of empirical science belongs, for the most part, to the 'eye of flesh', psychology and all internal philosophical exploration to the 'eye of reason' and meditative and religious experience to the 'eye of contemplation'. According to Wilber the dominant world-view of contemporary science tends to link the 'eye of reason' to the 'eye of flesh' taking account of evidence from rather narrow bands of empirical investigation. There is no place in this world-view for the 'eye of contemplation'. If we look at music therapy research through these three 'eyes' we can see how, for example, that a quantitative exploration of basic physiological changes while listening to or playing music could link to the 'eye of flesh' (a search for evidence at a sensory level).

We could research the more rational and mental aspects of the work linked to the 'the eye of reason' – how the music helps to organise thinking or to release a range of feelings, for example. We are then moving from an external search for evidence of what can be observed happening to a more internal and qualitative search for evidence of meaning. The more ineffable aspects of our work move us even further (deeper or higher depending on our choice of metaphor) into more internal (those perennial and existentially based questions) and spiritual worlds ('the eye of contemplation'). Now can these three 'eyes' of knowing ever become more integrated, the worlds of empirical investigation existing on more equal terms with the worlds of mental investigation and transcendental exploration? In a later text *The Marriage of Sense and Soul* Wilber proposes that a major challenge for today is to find some way of integrating the 'eye of contemplation' with the other perspectives, while still upholding their differentiation (Wilber 1998 and also see Wilber 2000).

The three 'eyes' can be defined further. Wilber describes the external 'eye of flesh' as 'monological' – in our context of music therapy we can investigate physiological responses to sound without ever having to interact with the person. We can view the person from outside with one-way monologues. The internal 'eye of reason' involves engaging with and trying to understand the person and is described as 'dialogical'. Wilber describes the 'eye of contemplation' as 'translogical,' transcending the logical, rational and mental. We can see how these further descriptions apply to some current themes in music therapy research. There is a concern to move away from a monological view of the work and to engage with the people involved in the research in some form of active dialogue. 'We are not subjects staring at objects; we are subjects trying to understand subjects – we are in the intersubjective circle, the dialogical dance. Monological is to describe; dialogical is to understand' (Wilber 1998: 118).

Wilber takes us even further; the worlds of art, science and morals all being described in different kinds of language. Art and all personal, aesthetic and expressive experiences are highly subjective and described in 'I' language. The monological world of science is objective and described in 'IT' language. The world of shared morals is very much the collective 'WE.' The trap of today's world-view is that the world of 'IT' seems not only confined to empirical science but has also attempted to move into the worlds of 'I' and 'WE,' a world-view referred to by Wilber as 'flatland.' It is invasive and all encompassing – all 'Is' and 'WEs' reduced to 'ITs'. There is not much space in this 'flatland' for artistic expression or the worlds of soul and spirit. Here are further reasons for some of the current concerns in music therapy research. The overemphasis on quantitative (monological) research for so many years goes some way in explaining the more recent swing to more qualitative (dialogical/translogical) research. We can externally measure changes, for example, in brain patterns ('IT') while listening to music but they tell us little about the mind/psyche ('I') or the individual's unique response to the music. But the question remains – does a qualitative approach by itself take us any closer to understanding the whole picture?

In tracking the development of some of Wilber's ideas in relation to music therapy research it now seems possible to propose an integration of the different worlds, while tolerating and respecting their differences. A broad approach to empirical exploration can include evidence from the external 'ITs' and the internal worlds of 'I' and 'WE'. Each area can stand on its own with its own internal validity, form, content and relevance. Each research tradition can contribute its perspective to a larger whole. The notion of a continuum is being advocated here, keeping as open an attitude as possible to working within multiple perspectives. Wigram also welcomes a balance between quantitative and qualitative research and looks forward to more joint research.

> Collaborative research would be very beneficial. Joint research with psychotherapists, with psychologists, teachers. The balance has perhaps swung too strongly towards qualitative research. This has been very valuable but I would still like to see quantitative studies done, to actually make deeper investigation, to make us sure that what we are doing and how we do it are effective. The future will depend a lot on all of those factors. We can't rest on our laurels. You can have a very good team valuing your work but just down the road may be an institution who have never heard of music therapy and you have to start again.

EXAMPLE: A COLLABORATIVE STUDY OF THE MUSIC THERAPY PROGRAMME AT THE BRISTOL CANCER HELP CENTRE (BCHC)

Introduction

The arrival in Bristol of a visiting music therapist/researcher (Sarah Burns) created the opportunity to further some collaborative research into the music therapy programme at the BCHC. The two music therapists (SB and LB) agreed to work within a broad perspective, enabling any collaboration to develop as a bridge between some of the patterns in research outlined above. The key collaborators in any research were to be the cancer patients and we wanted their voices and needs to remain the central theme. So as to broaden the potential of the collaboration two other researchers from different disciplines were invited to join the team: a neuroendocrinologist (Mike Harbuz) and a psychophysiologist (Frank Hucklebridge). In collaborating together we were interested in how the music therapy programme could be studied from different viewpoints with each researcher remaining true to their research orientation and particular world-view. This part of the chapter will focus on procedural issues and features of the collaboration; supporting references and interpretations of results are published elsewhere (Bunt et al. 2000; Burns et al. 2001). Firstly, it was important for the members of the group to be familiar with the philosophy of the BCHC and the place of music therapy within the overall service.

The context and some background

The BCHC offers a holistic programme addressing all aspects of patients' needs with an emphasis on the integration of mind, body and spirit. The centre receives some referrals from health-care practitioners but mostly self-referrals. Since the mid-1980s music therapy has been a well-established part of the weekly group residential programme that includes meditation, guidance on nutrition, spiritual healing, therapeutic massage and counselling. The researchers were aware of evidence that these kinds of interventions contributed to overcoming the sense of powerlessness that people often experience when faced with a diagnosis of cancer. The music therapist researcher (SB) also documented the existing literature on the effective use of music therapy in cancer care.

The current music programme combines a one-hour listening experience (live or recorded music) on the Monday or Tuesday evening with a one-and-a-half-hour music therapy group on the Wednesday afternoon. This is a one-off therapy group with very clear boundaries. In general each group (averaging between 8 and 10 residents and a small number of supporters) starts with an emphasis on establishing feelings of trust and security. This is achieved by encouraging music-making that gives a sense of freedom within clear structures, for example instrumental free exploration, pulsed-based or call and response activities. As the members of the group feel more at ease with the various 'players' in the setting the therapist is less directive. Free improvisation usually forms the central part of the session with themes emerging from the spontaneous music that are further articulated through more playing or sometimes through some selected listening (with or without guidance). There is flexible blending of words and music as the members of each group begin to work on issues that have arisen during the week to date or have been sparked off by the music. The therapist (LB) makes sure to bring the work to a clear closure. The work is very music-centred, framed within a humanistic/transpersonal perspective. As a trained practitioner in Guided Imagery and Music LB brings aspects of this approach to the work. A further containing feature is the pre- and post-briefing with the resident counsellor, nurse and any other relevant staff.

An earlier 'pilot' study

The music programme generally created much spontaneous feedback from the residents and supporters. The staff at the Centre had reported anecdotal comments indicating that the music therapy session was viewed mostly as a positive experience. This was verified by an earlier 'pilot' study when spontaneous answers to the statement 'Music and Us' made before and after the music therapy group were collated and codified by a psychologist/counsellor. Key elements to emerge from this earlier study and first collaboration were: constructs that shifted from the individual to the collective; passive to active feelings; shifts in energy; temporary relief from preoccupation with pain and gaining new insights (for detailed results see Bunt and Marston-Wyld 1995; Bunt 1994: 151–157).

This earlier collaboration was safe and friendly. The researcher's humanistic approach to counselling was comparable to the music therapist's approach. Her therapy skills enabled her to feel comfortable conducting semi-structured interviews and informal discussions with the patients. We were aware that her previous knowledge and support for music therapy could have led to bias in her selection of the various 'constructs'. As in similar descriptive work there were also issues of 'translation' with several aspects of the musical experiences being difficult to record in words. Gary Ansdell aptly describes this as the 'Music Therapist's Dilemma' – 'the core problem in music therapy of having to use words and verbal logic . . . to represent complex musical processes in music therapy (and the therapeutic processes which are seen to occur within these)' (Ansdell 2001: 23).

Identifying the strengths and interests of the members of the research group

The members of the new research group were able to observe from the earlier study how the constructs subdivided into external and internal areas, individual and collective experiences and comments that could be linked to Wilber's three eyes of knowledge. Would it be possible in a new project to look at the different phenomena with the 'eye of flesh' (a physiologically based study), the 'eye of reason' (a psychological and more internal study) and the 'eye of contemplation' (a more process-based study, respecting the more meditative aspects of the work at the centre)? Could a new project be set up with different sections that maintained their own differentiation but also contributed to a holistic and larger integration? Could different parts of the project use separate yet sufficiently rigorous research methods? Would a larger picture be built up by using a range of both external and internal measures? Could then the results from the different smaller studies be integrated to inform the direction of future work?

The members of the research group wanted to use different ways of exploring some of the effects and the processes at work during both the listening and the playing experiences. Each researcher brought to the project their personal philosophical orientation, values, interests and preferred mode of research. For this collaboration to be effective and for mutual trust and understanding to evolve, it was important that these orientations were transparent and open from the outset of the project. Discussions at this stage were concerned with respecting and tolerating the different approaches. We were aware of the current divisions (outlined above) between research into the effects of intervention (quantitative) and the processes (qualitative) whereby the effects were reached. We felt that there were gradations between these two positions and agreed with Smeijsters' stance that 'It is also true that "effects" are part of the process' (Smeijsters 1997: 44). The group of researchers wanted also to:

- respect the wishes and needs of the patients at all times;
- keep the project as naturalistic as possible with as little interference to the customary pattern of the sessions;
- respond to the rigours of EBP;
- respect the complementary and transpersonal ethos of the centre;
- explore what was happening from multiple perspectives;
- maximise the strengths of the different members of the research group.

Opening questions

After a series of meetings a range of questions emerged that could be approached using both quantitative and qualitative procedures. The meetings were not always easy and straightforward with the various conflicts between different research traditions and world-views being welcomed as a means of making the various assumptions explicit (Torbert 1981). Four main questions and a supplementary question emerged:

1   Are there any individual psychological changes during the experience of listening to music in a relaxed state?
2   Are there any individual psychological changes during the active music therapy?
3   Are there any individual physiological changes during the listening experience?
4   Are there any individual physiological changes during the active playing session?
    Supplementary question: Are there any reported differences between listening to the same music played either live or recorded?

We wanted to give equal validity to both psychological and physiological measures. There was a particular interest in any potential correlation between the results from the psychological and physiological measures, staff at the BCHC being very interested in the recent work on psychoneuroimmunology.

Formulating the methodology, further consultation and background

Firstly, the two music therapists wanted to use focus groups as a qualitative method of research. Using this method data emerge from group discussions and interviews that 'focus' on a certain topic. The music therapists were keen for the focus groups to be a time for patients to compare and contrast their experience in both the listening and playing sessions. Secondly, after consultation with an experimental psychologist, the research team decided to use a mood adjective checklist (the UWIST test, devised by the University of Wales Institute of Science and Technology). This standardised pre- and post-test can be used to measure changes in levels of tension, energy and hedonic tone (feelings of well-being), some of the areas noted in the earlier 'pilot' study. Thirdly, the two scientists in the group proposed initially to measure variable heart rate responses as potential indicators of any physiological change. After lengthy debate it was decided that saliva testing would be a less intrusive method. Collection would be made by the patients placing a salivette under their tongue for a period of three minutes prior to and after each session. This test was identified to measure for salivary immunoglobulin A (sIgA) and cortisol, research evidence positioning sIgA as a marker of immunity and changes in salivary cortisol as an accepted and validated measure of stress. The music therapists were aware that combined music and imagery interventions with college students had produced significant increases in sIgA and that within music therapy there had been some work indicating changes using sIgA as a marker. The group knew of no studies that investigated the relationship of these physiological parameters in cancer patients.

Hypotheses and hunches

We created some hypotheses for the physiological and psychological-based questions. We hypothesised that:

(a) during the listening session people would become increasingly more relaxed, less tense and have an increased sense of well-being;
(b) during the music therapy session group people would become more energised, have an increased sense of well-being and feel less tense;
(c) during both listening and playing experiences the levels of sIgA would increase and levels of cortisol decrease;
(d) the presence of live musicians would contribute further to the hypothesised changes in (a).

For the more qualitative aspects of the study we wanted the questions to evolve more from the processes, from the reporting, observations and focus groups.

Further practicalities and setting up the procedures

The research protocol was written by the music therapist researcher and submitted for funding. The research committee at the BCHC approved the protocol. The project began in earnest with initial funding in place.

It was decided to adopt three different kinds of procedures:

1   the UWIST test (pre- and post-session);
2   focus groups;
3   saliva tests (pre- and post-sessions).

If we look at these procedures within the frames of reference proposed by Wilber, it is clear that the saliva tests sit within the external, quantitative, objective, monological ('eye of flesh') frame (IT). The mood checklist, although using a numerical rating scale and available for statistical analysis, needs to engage more internal exploration, a more 'I'-based and 'dialogical' injunction. The discussions in the focus groups provided data that flowed very clearly from a definitely 'I'-based perspective ('eye of reason' with some features of the 'eye of contemplation').

Participation in the project

We approached each member of each residential group within the time period of the project to inform them of the project and request their participation. All agreed to take part and signed consent forms, a total of 29 cancer patients (21 female and 8 male) with the average age of 49. We would be focusing on the cancer patients although the groups would function in the usual way including both patients and their supporters. There were two stages to the project.

Stage 1 comprised:

•   20 people (15 women and 5 men) in three consecutive weekly groups;
•   Tuesday evening one-hour session of listening (recorded) facilitated by the music therapist (LB) – a short relaxation induction followed by the music;
•   Wednesday afternoon one-and-a-half-hour music therapy group facilitated by LB;
•   pre- and post-UWIST tests for both listening and music therapy sessions administered by the music therapist researcher (SB);
•   Friday morning one-hour focus group meeting facilitated by SB with the resident group counsellor in the role of observer and recorder.

Note The music for listening was composed by Celia Harper for 'Sulís' (a group of distinguished concert artists) for use in such contexts as the BCHC. The music is meditative, mostly using ancient Latin texts, and is scored for various combinations of soprano, male alto, violin and baroque harp.

Stage 2 comprised:

•   one group of 9 people (6 women and 3 men);
•   presence of live musicians from 'Sulís' for listening to the same music as in Stage 1 and performed in the same order;

- music therapy group as in Stage 1;
- pre- and post-UWIST tests as in Stage 1;
- saliva testing for sIgA and cortisol in both listening and music therapy sessions.

Note Two further weeks were scheduled for Stage 2 that would have increased the number of patients to bring numbers closer to those of Stage 1. Unexpected circumstances, beyond the researchers' control, resulted in these plans being curtailed.

Collation and analysis of the data

Only data from the patients were used in the analysis. The music therapist researcher (SB) collected and collated the psychological tests. The raw data were sent to a statistician for analysis using descriptive statistics and a series of paired *t* tests. SB transcribed all the recorded data from the focus groups. The salivettes were frozen after collection and sent to the psychophysiologist for analysis. SB acted as the overall coordinator of the data.

Summary of results

The statistically significant results were:

(a) from the UWIST test:

- less tension at the end of the listening group;
- less energy at the end of the listening group;
- increased sense of 'well-being' (hedonic tone) after the music therapy group;
- increased level of energy after the music therapy group;
- less tension after the music therapy group in three of the four weeks.

(b) from the saliva test (based on samples from eight patients):

- increased concentration of sIgA in the saliva after listening;
- increased secretion rate of sIgA in the saliva after listening;
- reduction in salivary concentration of cortisol between the Tuesday and the Wednesday sessions.

The other non-significant results were:

- increased sense of well-being after the listening;
- more pronounced psychological changes in the presence of the musicians (Stage 2) than when compared to listening to the same music on their CD (Stage 1).

Some of the earlier hunches and observations regarding feelings of well-being, changes in energy and tension level were confirmed. It was clear, for example, that there was a significant decrease in the level of tension after listening and a significant rise in energy after the music therapy group. Patients felt better about themselves after playing. The more internally observed mood changes with the decrease in tension level after listening were matched by the physiological changes. However, there was no significant correlation between the two groups of physiological and psychological results.

These results were further supported by the qualitative data from the focus groups originally analysed by recording recurring themes and allotting them to each of the three tones (hedonic, tense arousal, energetic arousal) of the UWIST test. The presence of the live musicians appeared to increase the effects.

Note For more detailed discussion of the results, see Burns *et al.* (2001).

Further analysis of the themes from the focus groups

Some comments focused on describing a sensory response ('eye of flesh'), some a more internal and mental reaction ('eye of reason') and others a more spiritual perspective ('eye of contemplation'). A group of music therapy students helped to code the comments using a frame derived from Wilber's differentiation. The main features to emerge from this first analysis by the students were:

- the large proliferation of **M**ind-based ('eye of reason') comments;
- the very few specific **S**pirit-based ('eye of contemplation') comments;
- the large number of comments that overlapped across the three codes (**M**ind, **B**ody, **S**pirit).

It was decided to add further overlaps to the codes: **B/M**; **M/S**; **B/S**; and the fully integrative **M/B/S**. SB and LB coded each of the 174 comments from the four weeks of focus groups. This second attempt at coding confirmed:

- the supremacy of **M** comments;
- the high ranking of **B/M** and **M/B/S** comments;
- taken together the more integrated comments (**B/M**; **M/B/S**; **M/S**; and **B/S**) making up the second largest grouping of comments;
- the larger number of **B** comments relating to the listening;
- the very few **S**, **M/S** and **B/S** comments.

To provide a flavour of the comments here is one from each code:

M   *freedom of choice; freedom to express* (playing)
B/M   *the change of mood within the music had a 'knock-on' effect both emo-
         tionally and physically* (listening)
M/B/S   *feeling immersed in the sound of the Tibetan bowl, went off somewhere
         – very calming* (listening)
B   *felt the immune system had a boost* (general comment)
M/S   *inspired (!) to take up the playing of an instrument* (playing)
B/S   *felt more relaxed and uplifted towards the end of the session*
         (listening)
S   *felt more whole and harmonious* (listening)

Flaws and pointers for future study

There were obvious methodological flaws in the project. Patients were self-selecting, being drawn to the BCHC and its philosophy and ethos, creating a bias. Rigorous controls and comparisons were lacking and the patients exhibited both different types and stages of cancer. Patients were also at different stages in their treatment process.

This collaboration is being developed further into a larger study to:

* focus on one physiological measure;
* explore subjective experiences and influence on mood using not only standardised tests but semi-structured in-depth interviews and journal-keeping;
* focus on one cancer population and a limited age range;
* select groups of patients that are not undergoing chemotherapy or radiotherapy or any other intensive intervention;
* include pre- and post-observation periods and a comparison group;
* provide courses of ongoing music therapy;
* allocate patients randomly to one of two therapy groups or the comparison group;
* explore a wider range of musical styles and personal preferences for the listening experience, both live and recorded.

The protocol for this new study is being written up with a view to seeking funding and approval by the various ethics committees. Sarah Burns has left the Bristol team to pursue her own doctoral work researching music therapy with breast cancer patients in Australia. The group has been joined by three additional members: the BCHC's Director of Education (Pat Turton) and two university colleagues (Norma Daykin and Stuart Mclean) specialising in health and social care issues from fundamentally qualitative perspectives and whose input into this ongoing process is hereby acknowledged.

A musical metaphor

The musical form of theme and variations was used metaphorically to describe the stages in this collaborative process when this work at the BCHC was presented at a music therapy research convivium (included in Robarts, forthcoming). The third movement of Benjamin Britten's second string quartet (a string quartet in itself a superb example of subtle negotiation and collaboration) employs one of his favourite forms, a Chacony. Britten begins with a unison treatment of his theme and during the ensuing 29 variations this theme is subjected to various treatments. Different voices are introduced to comment on the theme; the theme moves between foreground and background textures. It is extended, rhythmically altered or heavily disguised. The movement also includes three solo cadenza-like passages. If we extend the metaphor to the work at the BCHC, the opening questions relating to the needs of the cancer patients could be regarded as the central theme. The 'players' in the collaborative enquiry each had their own views and perspectives on the theme. Sometimes a particular voice was very prominent and would move a different point of view into the background, albeit temporarily. As in the Chacony there was constant debate, ideas being exchanged and elaborated and with at times conflicting views – all eventually moving to a resolution. Throughout the process it was possible to return to the opening questions (theme) if any discussion was moving too far away from the initial ideas. Space was even provided for the occasional cadenza-like flight of fancy.

CONCLUSION

The work at the BCHC provided rich sources of data that were analysed using different approaches. Each individual approach was differentiated, considered as important as the others and yet able to contribute to a larger perspective. Some research based within one context was interpreted with this emphasis on multiple perspectives. This attitude was in line with the complementary and holistic philosophy of the BCHC. We attempted to demonstrate how internal and more subjective comments have as much validity as the more objective and physiological measures. Changes in sIgA levels are interesting to record but more meaning is added once participants are asked to reflect about their internal states and level of tension arousal. Comments of a more contemplative nature were also given much attention. Some of the analysis focused on individual responses; other results were presented as group scores. Varied ways of describing the work, drawn from the traditions of different disciplines, were integrated into the final report for the Centre and subsequent publications. Art and science appeared to be well integrated in this study.

The researchers approached the study from these different perspectives. We adopted the broad approach to empirical investigation as advocated by Wilber. We tried to explore each area with the same amount of rigour and discipline; for example there was as much care taken with the setting-up of the procedures for the focus groups as for the saliva test. All the areas were concerned with systematic enquiry, data collection, analysis and interpretation. Connections were made both within and across each area of investigation. The participants did not appear confused by the different ways with which we approached this study. There was unanimous agreement to be involved in the project. At the start of the project the two music therapists were most interested in how to manage the focus groups, being intuitively drawn to a more qualitative approach within this particular context. We were worried that even the few minutes demanded by the saliva test would be too intrusive and damage trust and feelings of safety. Paradoxically there was a great deal of interest shown by the participants in the saliva test. They seemed keener to know the harder results from this quantitative analysis than a summary of the focus group discussion and the results from the mood checklist. The music therapists may have been worried but the participants convinced them that these anxieties were unfounded. This was a change in viewpoint that resulted from carrying out this study.

In concluding her paper 'Our Own Kind of Evidence' the art therapist Andrea Gilroy writes:

> But in establishing research in art therapy I hope we will use both qualitative and quantitative methodologies to ask questions *which matter*, which will be of direct benefit to patient care and which make sense to us and to our patients. This is where experience and common sense speak loudest – that we conduct research that builds on clinical experience and skills rather than neglecting or diminishing them. This is an immensely exciting prospect and one which must *not* be curtailed by externally imposed 'rules of evidence.' We have our own kind of evidence.
>
> (Gilroy 1996: 59)

Only one change is needed to substitute the word 'music' for art.

5

ormation, Ovid and
d Imagery and Music

Leslie Bunt

INTRODUCTION

> We cannot help but transform our experience – Freud's emblem for this
> is dream-work – and we cannot help but express ourselves.
>
> (Phillips 1998: 11)

Guided Imagery and Music (GIM) was presented at the Ninth World
Congress of Music Therapy (held in Washington in 1999) as one of five specialist approaches in music therapy. The lengthy training in this approach
is one of the options available to a music therapist seeking new and exciting
challenges. This chapter presents some perspectives on the transformational
potential of this powerful approach.

To echo Adam Phillips, GIM therapists clearly witness clients transforming their experience and expressing themselves. It is as if the world of
dreams can be glimpsed while the music lasts. In GIM a complex matrix of
transformations continually takes place through changes in levels of consciousness, in the images and in the structural aspects of the music. Clients
appear to seek out deep transformational processes in coming to GIM and
these various changes often develop into a pattern unique to each person's
journey through therapy. This chapter includes an example from one
client's journey, including themes from the GIM sessions and their outward
expression in interlinked sessions of active improvisation, the most common
approach described throughout this handbook. Reference is made to the
Roman poet Ovid and his collection of stories *Metamorphoses* in connecting the nature of transformation in GIM with deep and collective processes
at the root of our humanity. It is rather inspiring that these very ancient
and mythical stories continue to have such a deep resonance for us today.
It is as if they demand to be articulated in their various guises at different
times in history.

> Nor does anything retain its own appearance permanently. Ever-
> inventive nature continually produces one shape from another. Nothing

in the entire universe ever perishes, believe me, but things vary and adopt a new form. The phrase 'being born' is used for beginning to be something different from what one was before, while 'dying' means ceasing to be the same. Though this thing may pass into that, and that into this, yet the sum of things remains unchanged.

('The teachings of Pythagoras' from Ovid's
Metamorphoses: Book XV)

Ovid used the character of Pythagoras to articulate these aspects of changing form, of transformation. We may resist these ideas in our human striving to cling to some sense of permanency but we know deep down that nothing in the universe is rigidly static or lasts for more than a fraction of a second in a similar form. Everything is in a state of flux. In discussing Plato's distinction between being and becoming, Richard Tarnas writes:

All phenomena are in a never-ending process of transformation from one thing into another, becoming this or that and then perishing, changing in relation to one person and another, or to the same person at different times. Nothing in this world *is*, because everything is always in a state of becoming something else.

(Tarnas 1991: 9)

WHAT IS GIM?

GIM involves listening to specific programmes of recorded music in a deeply relaxed state. The Association for Music and Imagery describes GIM as 'a music-centered, transformational therapy which uses specifically programmed classical music to stimulate and support a dynamic unfolding of inner experiences in service of physical, psychological and spiritual wholeness' (AMI 1990). The form of a classic GIM session is divided into five clear sections, lasting between one and a half and two hours:

1   *Prelude* This is generally verbal in nature, as at the start of any psychotherapeutic encounter, but may also include the use of journal, mandala drawing, improvised music-making or other artistic expression.
2   *Induction* The guide/therapist invites the 'traveller' to lie on a couch and induces a deep state of rest using a variety of relaxation techniques, the client moving from the upright position in the 'here and now' to an altered state of consciousness (ASC). As the induction draws to a close there is a transition to the next section when the therapist suggests a starting image to the 'traveller' (the choice of image often emerging from themes aired during the Prelude). This interaction of concentrated focus while in a state of deep relaxation is one of the key elements of GIM.

3 *Listening and imaging* This is the heart of the session when the traveller is invited to share the experiences of listening to the music and to report any images to the therapist/guide. The term 'image' is used generically to refer to all body-based sensations, feelings, intuitions, memories, associations, symbols, visual images or any other inner experiences. The role of the therapist is to witness and help deepen the client's elaboration of these experiences using appropriate interventions including reflective questioning and non-verbal support. The therapist is attentive not to direct any images.

4 *Return* The traveller is assisted by the therapist to return to the 'here and now.'

5 *Postlude* The traveller processes the experiences with the support of the guide, making any connections with the Prelude and the stage in the therapeutic process. The images develop a life of their own and a client may gain insights some time after the session as the images continue to resonate.

TRANSFORMATION IN GIM

It is significant that the AMI describes GIM as a 'transformational therapy'. One of the therapeutic strengths of GIM is this rich interplay between the 'unfolding of inner experiences' that can lead to wholeness and the deep listening to music within an ASC. It is a therapy that moves and has its resonance through a complex web of transformations. There are at least three aspects of the GIM session where transformations can be located. Firstly, the images, symbols and feelings experienced in GIM sessions occur while in an ASC. During the induction the therapist invites the client to move to a different space and time, from the therapy room to 'various realms of the imagination' (Bruscia 1995a: 181). This moving of consciousness is in essence transformational. There is a changing of the form of consciousness from an everyday waking state to an ASC. Secondly, the images, symbols and feelings themselves undergo continual changes in form, shape and meaning within each session and from one session to the next. The images transform as the person moves through the therapeutic process, shifting from preconscious to pre-personal through the fully differentiated personal levels of development to those of transpersonal consciousness (see Clark 1999; Lewis 1999; Wilber *et al.* 1986). Thirdly, there are complex transformations constantly unfolding within and among the many layers of the music itself, with simultaneous and sequential organic changes occurring in melody, harmony, rhythm, form, timbre and so forth. If we take modulation as an example of a process of transformation we can observe how in Western classical music, for example, there are significant shifts and transitions between one key and the next. Music is also able to be in more than one key at any one time or even to have no sense of key at all. So many of the musical forms and structures that have survived through the centuries have organic growth and transformation at their core, for example: theme and variations, fugue, sonata form and the whole edifice of Western classical symphonic writing. As implied by Ovid, music, like everything else in the universe, is continually producing one shape from another, is constantly in a state of becoming something else.

These three transformational aspects of GIM – changes in consciousness, images and the music itself – are seen to be all closely interrelated in a dance-like matrix. Transformations in the levels of consciousness can link with changes in the music. Close study of the various musical programmes used in GIM from both practical and theoretical standpoints reveals both how these shifts and transformations occur and also the great care needed in creating programmes to enable the client to make full use of the various levels of the altered state. For example, the GIM programmes, particularly the more advanced ones, place the most intense music or music with the most sustained mood or length at central points within the programme. This allows sufficient time for the client both to reach a deep altered state and to emerge from it during the music that precedes and follows. There is also a rich interplay between image and music. Musical transformation can be a metaphor of psychological transformation; Bernstein going further to say that 'All musical transformations lead to metaphorical results' (Bernstein 1976: 153).

During a series of GIM sessions we can observe similarities between different musical structures and processes and certain structures and processes in the imagery. While hearing the music the client is also creating an instantaneous link between image and music. It is as if the client is experiencing the music at different levels, from the surface to the deep structural, reaching into the music to find the level that matches and resonates with the image. Sometimes the music is very much to the foreground in this process, the musical structures influencing the way in which the images are evoked and transformed. This does not happen in any simplistic one-to-one symbolic or causal correspondence between one musical gesture and the creation of an image but in an ongoing organic and interactive way, which is in itself another process of transformation. At other times the images tend to ride on the music with the music being present as a container in the background. Here the images seem to take on a life of their own with threads of connections to the musical containment.

Music shifts and transforms. As implied above we also know that this shifting process is 'true of our internal universe of images, thoughts and sensations' (Engler 1986: 18). We are continuing to learn more about these shifting patterns of transformation from the physical sciences and from researchers creating bridges between Western psychology and ancient systems of Eastern religion (for example see Wilber 2000). In this way the whole notion of transformation links the ancient philosophers from both East and

West with contemporary explorers of consciousness and the very central mystery of music. We remain intrigued by this notion of continually changing form yet the sum of things remaining unchanged. We are moved and inspired by this great paradox.

A FURTHER NOTE ON EMOTION AND MUSIC

Music has been viewed as being composed of the very gestures, dynamic forms and changing shapes of our emotions (Pavlicevic's elaboration of 'dynamic form' was discussed in Chapters 1 and 4). Changes and transformations in our lives can likewise resonate in the symbolic forms of music; in this way, music acts as a 'transformer of shared meaning' (Bunt 1994: 73). We hear and recognise ourselves in the music. Working in GIM brings us in constant contact with these various meeting points between music and emotion. Firstly, there are the associative connections: the 'Darling, they're playing our tune' notion (Davies 1978), which can also be observed in other forms of receptive music therapy. In GIM a particular piece of music or fragment of melody, rhythm or harmony can trigger a whole range of highly personal associations with specific events and places, images, memories of certain people, particularly if the experiences or people have been significant in the person's life. Secondly, listening to music can create links between particular musical characteristics and some external natural event or human feeling. We can describe these connections as 'iconic', in GIM observing clients making connections between aspects of the music and non-musical events and feelings. A third area focuses on more intrinsic connections. Here connections can be observed between the internal emotional experiences and both surface and deep structural aspects of the music. In many ways GIM allows for an interaction between these three kinds of connections (for discussion of all three – associative, iconic and intrinsic – see Juslin and Sloboda 2001).

EACH CLIENT'S UNIQUE JOURNEY AND PATTERN

It seems that people come to GIM seeking some kind of transformation. As a therapy GIM enables people to explore the transformational processes described above. They appear to do so at deep internal levels rather than in seeking transitory solutions or surface changes to their lives – the notion of deep structural transformation appears more the focus of the GIM than temporary change and solution (Zackey 1999). This tends to happen regardless of any resistance to the process of therapy. A part of each person seems to be seeking, often unconsciously, a process of transformation at some level. Clients use the GIM experience to explore their own process, their own personal way through the journeys. This makes every process a unique and highly subjective experience. Very often a pattern to the images begins to become established over the sessions with repetitions and variations; a musical parallel could be the formal device of theme and variations, each variation bearing some relation to the main theme. Different images are often elaborated over the sessions in relation to this overall pattern, which is on one level highly personal but also often contains archetypal material that can help the client and therapist place the individual experience within a more collective context. In GIM any pattern that continues to occur as a sequence often surfaces in different sessions and with very different music. This is another example of potential transformation, the music again seeming to serve as an agent of transformation. It also contributes to making the whole GIM experience such a highly active and creative process.

A main contention of this chapter is that people will find within the form of GIM – within this complex matrix of the ASC, the images and the very music itself – those ever-changing processes of transformation that they are seeking. This may be done consciously, subconsciously or even superconsciously. Any particular pattern often develops an organic life force of its own with unique shifts of rest and change, mini-births and deaths. The transformational aspects of these patterns bear some relationship to Erdonmez Grocke's notion of pivotal moments in GIM. She describes these moments 'as meaningful because they transform some aspect of the person's life' (Erdonmez Grocke 1999: 209).

AN EXAMPLE OF A PATTERN IN A SERIES OF GIM SESSIONS

The opening quote from Ovid refers to dying and being reborn; it is these mini-deaths and rebirths that are so common in therapeutic work. The journey from loss and dissolution, through fragmentation and final transformation as a rebirth became a central pattern of Kay's GIM sessions. Reflecting on her series of sessions it is possible to observe how the images related to each part of the overall progression from loss to rebirth. Time and time again this overall pattern emerged with different music and through different imagery scenarios. Ovid will continue to be an inspiration as parallels are drawn between Kay's personal exploration of this pattern and more archetypal features. The intention is not to present a case study or the minutiae of her therapeutic process as such but to bring material from a series of sessions to explore the transformational aspects of her main pattern. A further aim is to explore parallels and links between structures in both the images and the music. A closer study of aspects of one session will be used to unravel some of the links between the music and the images.

Kay was in a transition stage in her life. She was changing careers and during the series of sessions was involved in an arts therapies training course. At the time of the therapy she was in her mid-40s. Her private life was in a state of flux and transition. She felt very alive in her new training course and with the members of her training group. She was discovering a new identity for herself, which was giving her a deep sense of contentment and fulfilment.

Very often the first GIM session presents an overview of a pattern and images that evolve and are evoked during subsequent sessions. At the start of her first session Kay quickly shifted away from the given image of a meadow to the entrance of a rocky scene (the music was the sunrise sequence from Ravel's *Daphnis and Chloë* – the start of Bonny's *Exploration* programme). She felt lonely and unsure from the very first moments of this initial session. The rocks were comforting but she felt frightened being 'on the edge', the ground falling away to one side revealed a huge expanse. Her subsequent shifts in images were connected to the different moods of the music – looking onto another world of an old-fashioned busy street scene during Brahms' First Symphony's *Allegretto* and moving to a formal garden during Resphigi's *Gianicola*. It was late summer and this garden was full of rocks, water, ferns and pine trees. She felt stronger and rather wild while putting her back to the trees. These trees linked to pines on a small island where there was more water and lakes. There was a brief flying interlude during Debussy's *Sirènes* before feeling cut off on the side of a hill, not knowing where to go. She merged with a rock, dissolved, broke up the rock into sand and then edged out of it in the form of a stone creature. She became very fluid sliding in the mud and she felt this in her stomach. She became the side of the hill, felt on the outside again as she observed a village below and listened to the church choir singing (during a choral piece by Tschesnekoff). Her final image (during Pachabel's *Canon*) was of becoming a very young child, being on her own in a playpen and feeling trapped and sad.

The elements of air, water and earth were all featured in this opening session; the fourth transforming element of fire was to come much later in the series of sessions. Being 'on the edge,' merging with natural objects, transforming into creatures before being changed into younger or different aspects of herself were part of a pattern that permeated this and each of the other 13 sessions. Reflecting on this session it is possible to observe how her main progression (loss through metamorphosis to rebirth) appeared from the very outset.

Kay's particular metamorphosis seems to correspond to the final stages of the 'Great Round of the Mandala' as described by Kellogg (1978; also see Fincher 1991). Stage Ten, 'The Gates of Death', is associated with a descent into the unconscious to seek renewal. The stage 'represents the death of out-moded conscious contents and the pain of change' (Fincher 1991: 126). This is often a feature of middle life and, as with Kay, can be seen as a need to reassess both professional and personal aspects of one's life. It can be an anxious, depressing and difficult phase and one that seems to be very much at a crossroads.

The start of this initial session was difficult for Kay. Her descent into the unconscious was via an entrance into a rocky and very isolated scene. She was 'on the edge' from the start with the opportunity to move across into other domains if needed. There was much looking on these different domains from outside as she shifted between different time frames and spaces. This position of being 'on the edge' was apparent from this first session. It would permeate much of the ensuing work, very much a place of difficult transition and yet one later described by Kay as 'the enlivening edge' (see Introduction and the discussions of threshold and 'liminal' experiences).

In the next Mandala stage of 'Fragmentation' there is no central core or unity for the person. Rather there is a loss of physical and psychological boundaries. This stage can be observed in Kay's initial session with the close contact with the natural world when feeling strong against the trees and more clearly in the image of merging with the rock, when she lost all sense of her physical self. The former order needed to collapse and to disintegrate. In Ovid's *Metamorphoses* an example of turning into stone is the outcome of Niobe's grief for her dead children and husband.

> The breeze could not stir her hair, the blood drained from her colour-less face, her eyes stared in an expression of fixed sorrow. There was nothing to show that this image was alive. She could not turn her head, nor move her arms or legs: even inside her, her tongue clove to her palate and froze into silence, there was no pulsing in her veins, and her internal organs were turned to stone: yet still she wept.
>
> (Ovid, *Metamorphoses*: Book VI)

At these times of disintegration it was very difficult to have any sense of where, what, or who Kay was. In later sessions Kay, the other elements of water, air and fire would be part of this breaking-up of boundaries.

In 'Transcendent Ecstasy,' Stage Twelve, the process continues with the transformation of energy into a bursting out and renewal. While there was a feeling of being overwhelmed in the previous stage, here the converse is often the case, with joyful feelings of liberation and release. The stage of 'Transcendent Ecstasy' . . . 'can herald a new integration . . . the space reflects a coming together of the earlier fragmentation through a lustrous eruption' (Fincher 1991: 132). Kay felt a need to move and climbed out of the rock as a stone creature. She needed this kind of strong energy to move outwards and to explore a new form of her image. In this very opening session the new integration then shifted her back in time into an image of herself as a very young child, thus completing the circle and beginning anew – 'death and birth are often more closely alike than different' (Fincher: 132).

SOME CONNECTIONS BETWEEN MUSIC AND IMAGE IN ONE SESSION

Bonny's *Comforting* programme was used for session seven. Clear shifts relating to the overall pattern described above could be linked to both surface and deep structural aspects of the music. Some of the changes in the images are presented here in relation to what was happening in the music. The main focus will be on the overall pattern already observed.

Haydn's *Cello Concerto in C: Adagio*

Kay moves into an elegant hall full of mirrors. This opening image resonates with the classical simplicity and formal clarity of Haydn's orchestral introduction. The pace is slow and the simple walking bass line accompaniment supports the rise and fall of the opening melody. In a similar manner, Kay slowly peruses the hall. Rhythmic patterns are repeated and elaborated as doors lead off into different rooms. Just after the cello's entrance Kay has an image of Ophelia moving through the hall. The cello's line/Ophelia's meandering evokes feelings of being trapped in circumstances, confusion, sadness and a tragic sense of the inevitable. At the harmonic shift to the dominant and the transposition of the opening material the scene shifts to the gardens outside. Kay is not sure if she is watching or wanting to be Ophelia.

As the tonality shifts to the minor and back again to the major with further melodic decoration, Kay has the sensation of not being able to reach Ophelia. In parallel with the deeper harmonic and melodic shifting structures Kay is not sure where she is going. Is she reaching deeper into the unconscious? Where is the music going? Where is Ophelia going? At the clear reprise of the opening material Kay reports a more focused image and states clearly that she is not Ophelia. In the image she does however still feel rather lost like Ophelia. She follows the cello as it moves into its solitary cadenza and this does little to alleviate these feelings of being lost and rather stuck. This transition phase feels difficult for Kay. There is a final and crucial shift in this movement (part of her usual pattern) when she begins to give up her form and becomes part of the tree in the garden, rooted to the spot with the roots extending outwards. The full string four-bar coda seems to accentuate this rooted sensation. The music comes finally to rest, as she does in the image of being rooted under the ground.

Sibelius' *Swan of Tuonela*

The image of spreading outwards continues with the slow and flowing melody of the opening cor anglais solo. The upward climbing phrases on the ensuing solo cello and viola seem to connect with more extending, the roots creeping out and through the earth. The images are beginning to move through this commonly observed pattern of fragmentation. As the music moves to the first loud and intense climax there is a further letting go as the tendrils and roots grow over the edge of a cliff. Letting go into the earth feels comforting. Kay has come to an edge again, described by her as the end of something. It is a long way down; there are no lower supporting strings. It is sometimes light and sometimes dark. Some severe horn calls create more foreboding and a pull into further darkness. Kay appears to go deeper into the ASC and darker images. The return of the cor anglais melody creates a further shift and she momentarily re-forms as herself as she recalls the recent death of her partner's father. Kay relives seeing him, his breathing and being with him as he dies, the long drawn-out final chords of this desolate piece entraining closely with her breathing, tears, sighs and these images of finality. A great deal of sadness is evoked by the memory of her recent loss.

Villa Lobos' *Bachianas Brasilerias: Number 5*

Kay appeared to use this music as a container for a further exploration of the recollection of the death she was rewitnessing. As words are added to the melody in the middle section of this piece she notices that her partner is also present in the scene. In her images no words needed to be exchanged.

Boccherini's *Cello Concerto in B flat: Adagio*

There are further shifts and transformations in this movement. She moves from images of the hospice to seeing herself as a child ill in bed. Her mother attends her. The cello melody is full of long sustained notes. There is a certain timeless and suspended feeling to the music. She recalls the faces of her parents who currently live a long way away. Expansive phrases in the music, a crawling bass line under sustained cello notes and an implied quickening in the music all occur at the same time as a further transformation in the images. She imagines herself crawling, not in the current image of a child but by transforming into a tiger. She enjoys the sensation of running on all fours up the motorway to her parents' house. There is more energy about. She is moving through the final stages of her usual pattern. The music feels stronger and she feels cheerful. There is a further quickening of the rhythmic patterns as the cello continues to weave its changes. The phrases fall towards the end of the movement. Kay's elevated mood shifts, as the tiger is not made welcome at her parents' house. The door is closed; the parents do not understand. Kay feels her parents will try to capture the tiger and put her into a cage. The tiger withdraws to hide in the woods and mountains.

Susanin's aria from Glinka's *A Life for the Tsar*

The Russian atmosphere of this bass aria connects with a second animal meta-morphosis. The tiger turns into a snow leopard, standing on the rocks in the mountains. The leopard imagines hearing an old man singing with his voice becoming more prominent as more is communicated to the leopard. There are deep connections here. The leopard hears the old man singing about loss and sadness (whose loss?) and his hard and poor life living in the mountains. There is poignant synchrony between the actual words of the aria, even though sung in Russian, and this part of Kay's journey. Susanin sings about his torment and grief as he prepares to surrender his life for his country. He is far from all he loves in a dense, dark and inhospitable land of forests and bogs. He imagines his mutilated corpse lying next morning in this desolate place with both a crow flying past and (more significantly for Kay's images) a soli-tary wolf running by. In Kay's images the leopard makes friends with the old man (he is not alone) and there is a warmth and affection between them.

Der Neuierige from Schubert's *Die Schöne Mullerin*

Here, another male sings about longing and the romantic juxtaposition of bliss and despair. 'Does my love love me?' the singer asks the brooklet. The leopard and elderly singer share a respectful distance and understanding. They respect each other's strengths and differences including a kind of wildness and independence. Kay moves up into the sky and looks down over the scene. The snow leopard disappears. The organum-like chords in the accompani-ment (at the phrase beginning 'die beiden Wortchen . . .'/'each small word comprising my world of bliss or despair') coincide with this movement and shift in level. Will the answer to the lover's question be yes or no? There seems to be another synchronicity and deep resonance, this time between the questioning aspects of the song and the tender, respectful but curious connections between the leopard and the elderly man.

Debussy's *The Girl with the Flaxen Hair* from *Preludes: Book One*

One final shift and a sense of coming home occur. The previous transfor-mations have helped Kay, as was her customary pattern, to find a new energy and perspective. She returns to her present self and time frame and enjoys being with a friend in a café at the top of the mountain. They look out over the snow together. Eventually Kay feels held and safe in her friend's house back in her own town. This final shift seems very connected to the musical flow of ideas in this succinct and quintessential piece of Debussy. The deceptively simple strand of melody is held in rich slow-moving chords. The rhythmic shape of the opening melody is never far away even when it is most elaborated. It returns with a feeling of predictability and security at the end. At last the images now for Kay are those of safety, support, being held and returning home.

EXAMPLES FROM OTHER SESSIONS

During other sessions the various images that were evoked could be grouped according to the same stages described above. Examples of the whole or a major part of her overall pattern were found in all of the sessions.

Stage Ten – Gates of Death

Kay would often find herself in a state of transition, being on the edge between different worlds, for example on the edge of a wood or river. As one supervisor noted, each GIM session can be viewed as being on an edge, shifting between different states of consciousness and moving in and out of the different images. Kay's descent over the edge into the unconscious to seek renewal was typified by journeys through the four elements of the universe: earth, water, air and fire. At the beginning of the series of sessions this would mainly be via the element of earth in the form of rocks, mud, sand, trees and leaves. This extended in later sessions to moving through walls and parts of buildings. She would often be held in water, let go through lakes, or move through rivers or underground waterways. In many instances she explored the journey through the wind and air, sometimes moving through shafts of different colours. Sometimes she would move among different elements within one session: moving through the earth, into water and eventually soaring into the air, often to create a sense of distance from the image. In later sessions, the transforming power of fire completed Kay's exploration of all of the elements. The fire images usually began by being external, for example being beside a fire or in a fire pit. They became more internal as she explored and began to recognise and welcome her fire within.

Stage Eleven – Fragmentation

In her images Kay would often quickly lose all sense of boundaries and give up her previous form. When she moved through the element of earth this would often involve spreading out through earth and mud; being pulled down through rocks; breaking up into sand particles or becoming the trunk, branches and leaves of trees. This spreading-out through trees was a very common image. In Ovid's *Metamorphoses* both Daphne and Myrrha also move into trees. There are no parallels to be drawn between Myrrha's and Kay's personal stories but Ovid's descriptions are similar to the way Kay found her images developing in more than one session.

Earth heaped itself round her legs as she spoke and roots, breaking out through her toenails, stretched sideways, forming foundations for a tall trunk. Her bones were changed into hard wood and through the marrow, which survived in their interior, flowed sap instead of blood. Her arms became large branches, her fingers smaller ones, and her skin hardened into bark. . . . Impatient of delay, she sank down to meet the wood as it rose, and buried her face in the bark. Though she lost her former feelings when she lost her body, yet she still weeps, and warm drops flow from the tree.

(Ovid: Book X)

Kay often found comfort in the early earth-bound images. The fragmentation became more disquieting when she later found herself blown about as sand or trampled underfoot as bits of leaves. Similarly, water also created mixed feelings. During the early sessions she would often find a sense of release from letting go into rivers and lakes. Again there are examples from Ovid as in the story of Arethusa:

A cold sweat broke out on my limbs, when I was thus trapped, and dark drops fell from my whole body. Whenever I moved my foot, a pool flowed out, moisture dripped from my hair. More quickly than I can tell of it, I was changed into a stream.

(Ovid: Book V)

Later disintegration into water found her formless, dizzy and frightened, swirling around in a dark underwater passageway. She would find herself initially merging with various colours and then completely losing her sense of self and breaking up into shafts of light. She often described her move through these various elements as being both formless and yet highly formed. In later sessions she used fire images to embody some of the formless images, seeking fire to take her away from air- or water-based images. As noted above there were many shifts between the elements, for example moving between the sky and woods or moving like a chameleon in and out of trees. At times she would spread out and fragment across an entire scene, embracing many of the elements.

Stage Twelve – Transcendent Ecstasy

After becoming disembodied Kay often searched for a new form. This new freedom and identity would often manifest itself in the form of such powerful animals as tigers and leopards, as in the session described above. The appearance of animals is often linked to the more instinctive, primitive and non-rational aspects of our psyche; these appearances were always helpful for Kay. She allowed their presence to help her move forward and make significant shifts. They never appeared as terrifying or overwhelming to her. She would also transform herself into brightly coloured birds or fly on the top of them. During one late session a bird burst out of the top of a fire (she sensed she was also on fire), burning away the old as she flew ecstatically into the air. The bird transformed into a huge and powerful eagle, eventually breaking out of itself and leaving Kay wrapped in a feathered cloak as she flew back to the fire. Again it is interesting to read of parallels in Ovid. He describes the transformation of Daedalion thus:

> There Apollo took pity on him and, when Daedalion threw himself from a towering rock, turned him into a bird and bore him up, to hover on the wings which he had suddenly acquired. The god gave him a hooked beak, and curving crooked talons, but left him his one time courage, and strength greater than his body.
>
> (Ovid: Book XI)

Kay's images also included transformations into fish, badgers, a she-wolf, chimpanzees and more mythic characters including a winged horse, a dragon, a mermaid and a green man/woman. These new transformations always brought with them some insight and connections were made with her life; for example we saw above in session seven that Kay felt very independent, alive, powerful and free as the tiger. She recognized the strong and powerful parts of herself. The water-based transformations were often connected with feelings of renewed self-acceptance and rebirth. There were also playful and more social images such as the colleagues from Kay's training group all turning into chimpanzees dancing and having fun together.

ARTICULATION OF THE PATTERNS IN IMPROVISED MUSIC

During the first meeting Kay had asked about the possibility of incorporating some improvisation-based sessions into the overall process. She played the piano. How could the instruments be used to articulate in a different expressive form some of the patterns explored during the GIM sessions? There were a total of seven improvisation-based sessions at various stages during the process of therapy. Each lasted for an hour with a standard format of:

(a) opening discussion;
(b) emergence and selection of a theme on which to base the improvisation;
(c) a central period of sustained improvisation using piano and a range of large tuned and untuned percussion instruments (this part also gave Kay opportunities to explore movement and dance); and
(d) closing reflection.

The improvisations were recorded and Kay would take away the recording for private listening before the next GIM session. These playing sessions took place in a different physical setting than the GIM.

After the first three GIM sessions Kay requested to experience one of these improvisation sessions in order to play out some of the feelings evoked by the GIM. In this first playing session Kay explored images and themes that had been evoked during the early GIM sessions, in essence a series of polar opposites: holding/being held; darkness/light; responsibility/letting go; and intimacy/separation. She started with a series of quiet repeated C's then moved outwards to a climatic, pivotal and central point on large drums and cymbals before returning to the opening mood. She was held and contained by the therapist's musical presence on various instruments yet felt free to move outwards and to explore; there was both a feeling of intimacy, connection and separation; the music was full of a rich contrast of dark and light timbres and textures. There was a feeling of some transformation having taken place.

Two more GIM sessions occurred before the second of the improvisation sessions. Kay requested to use the music to explore some aspects of her relationships with male figures in her life. She wanted to explore the dynamic of expressing anger and the various responses that could meet this, including a somewhat dead response when she wanted a strong one. During the music-making the therapist started by representing a more passive role to Kay's more assertive playing. She wanted to explore how these two contrasting worlds could meet, change and move potentially to a more balanced integration. This approach resembled the 'splitting' technique described by Priestley (1994) when both therapist and client explore the feelings behind the articulation of polar opposites with both client and therapist taking on different roles. In this session Kay's music started softly on the piano before moving to a loud outburst. The therapist stayed playing soft music and met Kay's outburst by retreating further into this dead response. The music became tense and Kay sensed this in her stomach (as she had done when exploring this dynamic in a previous GIM session). Kay played more loud outbursts and invited the therapist to meet her at this level. Eventually both worked at the same level of loudness and intensity. There was an increased sense of being equal partners in the music. Kay listened to the recording and reported at the next GIM session that she had felt calmer after the playing session, finding parts of the co-created music very beautiful. She added that she had gained an insight into her need to allow other people to deal with issues at their own pace.

The pattern developed of interweaving a playing session between the GIM sessions. During the ensuing four sessions of improvisation she explored aspects of these following constructs: being met/not being met; in/out; being held back/feeling authentic; feeling safe 'on the edge' and intimacy/solitude. She explored the space in the music therapy room, moving and dancing as she played when the mood and the music inspired her. She used the improvisation sessions to explore feelings relating to the future of her relationship with her partner. She played out her feelings associated with being the tiger (see above) when her playing was vital, highly charged; she vocalised spontaneously with strong and loud sounds. At the end of this particular session there was more colour in her features and she reported the sense of getting in touch with her real sense of self and feeling very alive.

There was one last improvisation session before ending the final sequence of GIM sessions. She was tearful during this session. Making music in a safe setting had evoked feelings of sadness and isolation. She felt moved being heard and responded to, particularly by a man. In this session she used the form of one of Satie's *Gnossiennes* (a favourite composer) as a framework for the improvisation. She started by playing the first section of the piece and used the harmonic, rhythmic and melodic features as a springboard for the improvisation, returning to the theme as a point of reference in the manner of the musical form of theme and variations. This structure seemed apt for articulating some of the variations of the themes evoked during the GIM process.

SUMMARY OF KAY'S PATTERN

Most sessions could have been used to explore this overall pattern of loss, fragmentation, re-forming and eventual rebirth. It was linked to this pattern that she chose to bring one of Strauss' *Four Last Songs* for some joint listening in the very last session.

Images of transformation were very creative times for Kay. After a loss of self and her physical boundaries she would often, in her images, transform into animals to move from one level to the next. This meant a move from a difficult situation to one where she felt more alive, independent and free and where almost anything was possible. The energy and power given to her by these transformations helped her in the transition to move into a new stage in her professional life and the eventual break with her partner. These were edges over which she had sufficient confidence and energy to both look and move. The transition was not always straightforward, as the independent tiger within her has also caused her problems, for example in trying to set up new work. Is there a place for strong, independently minded and creative people within her team at work? She said after one session 'Who would want a tiger in the house?'

As in Ovid's *Metamorphoses*, in Kays' sessions there were frequent images of transformation into animals. She also moved through the natural world of all the elements during the series of GIM sessions.

> The everlasting universe contains four elements that give rise to bodies. Two of these, earth and water, are heavy and, by their own weight sink

down, while the other two, air and fire, which is more rarefied than air itself, are weightless, and soar upwards, unless something holds them under. Though these four elements are distinct from each other in space, yet they are all derived from one another, and are resolved back again into themselves. Earth is broken up and refined into liquid water, water becoming still less substantial changes into air and wind, and air too, being already of the finest texture, flashes upwards when it loses weight, into the fiery atmosphere above. Then the process is reversed, and the elements are restored again in the same order: fire condenses and thickens into air, air into water, and water, under pressure, produces earth.

(Ovid: Book XV)

The whole transformational cycle begins again.

CONCLUSION

The observable pattern that permeated Kay's GIM journey has been used to reflect on some of the transformational aspects of GIM. Clearly Kay was able to use the sessions to move through a transitional stage in her life, one with both personal and professional implications. She sought out those aspects of transformation that resonated for her. This series of sessions has been used to highlight some of the complex interactions between the transformational potential of the ASC, the images and the music in GIM. Working with music as co-therapist a GIM practitioner is able to witness profound and potentially life-enriching transformations for clients. As the Scottish composer James MacMillan has suggested: 'After all, music has the potential to change our lives, but only when we are totally open to its transforming power' (Interview in *The Independent*, 26 March 1999).

Chapter acknowledgements

To Kenneth Bruscia for his encouragement and advice in the preparation of this material and his inspirational teaching during the GIM training. To fellow trainees, a remarkable international group of music therapy teachers. To supervisors, Catherine O'Leary and Georgette Zackey, who added their reflections on the material from Kay's sessions. To Denise Grocke for further insight into the meaning of Susanin's Aria. To the editor of *The Journal of the Association for Music and Imagery* for permission to reproduce this material from a previously published article. Above all to Kay for providing opportunities to witness her many transformations during her GIM process and for giving permission for the material to be used again as the basis for this chapter.

Plate 15.1 Thetis escaping Peleus – transforming into fire, water, a lion and a serpent (from the base of a Greek cup signed by Pethinos – late sixth century BC)

Endnotes

Leslie Bunt and Sarah Hoskyns

INTRODUCTION

As we near the end of this journey we return to the Introduction's image of a threshold. Here we round off some themes and raise some ideas for the future. During this writing project we have shared hopes and concerns, some different preoccupations evoked by our own interests and the fact that we bring our experiences as a woman and a man working in different ways in this female-dominated profession. We include some pictorial images and reflections on music to accompany these notes. There are also some final thoughts from our colleagues. We have attempted to cover a range of material in this handbook in as comprehensive a way as possible. We appreciate the ambitiousness of this task and that obvious omissions have occurred but hope that in these closing pages there may be some challenges to offer both ourselves and other colleagues in the coming years.

ON OUR LINKS WITH MUSIC

> A candidate comes to the audition for a music therapy course and plays the panel some music before being interviewed personally. The choice is a very technically demanding study by Chopin played from memory. Finger control is flawless, the scalic passages evenly controlled and Chopin's precise instructions observed. Why is it that the performance leaves us cold and the main music examiner whispers: 'Where is the music?' Somewhere, the instinct to communicate in music has been lost, presenting a problem to someone wishing to train in music therapy.

Perhaps a part of the answer to the examiner's question lies in the fact that this candidate failed to understand the true nature of performance in the sense of *per-formare*, to bring into form. There were no fluid connections between the inspiration of Chopin and us, the three listeners in the room. Had the candidate's emphasis on technical perfection got in the way, placing the performer at the centre? In *Performance: Revealing the Orpheus within* Anthony Rooley reminds us that:

> The true task of the performer is to bring into our sensual world those things (power, energy, inspiration) which already exist in an un-formed stage – literally to 'bring into form'. The performer is then seen as a porter, a carrier, a transmitter, dipping into the subtle non-formed world and manifesting it in the tangible world of form.
>
> (Rooley 1990: 25)

Rooley refers to earlier concepts of performance including the sixteenth-century balance of *decoro*, *sprezzatura* and *grazia*. *Decoro* focuses on all that can be studied and prepared, all that is technically correct (there was rather an overdose of *decoro* in our candidate's playing of Chopin). *Decoro* is balanced by *sprezzatura* that cannot be rehearsed and is 'a lightning-like energy which carries courage, boldness, even rashness, and excitement' (ibid.: 11). This was definitely missing from the performance of the Chopin. *Grazia* is harder to define and is a gift, being more connected with numinous influences, 'noticed first in the spaces between the notes, in the silences rather than the sounds' (ibid.: 13).[1] In fifteenth-century Florence the physician–musician Marsilio Ficino (described by many as a second Orpheus – see Voss 2000) was certainly aware of this influence of the divine in creating both moments of frenzy and blissful tranquillity in his playing. Ficino was a true musician therapist and 'knew intuitively and in theory that psyche needs imagination' (Moore 1990: 203). Perhaps it is time for a reinvention of Ficino's notion of 'musicus' or 'musician of the soul' (Gaggero *et al.* 2001). We could also explore his emphasis on *musica humana* (music of the soul represented in shifts in human feelings, moods and thoughts) linked with *musica mundana* (the inherent patterns in nature and movement of seasons and planets) (Moore 1990).

Orpheus, Ficino and Rooley can be inspirations for both the performer and musician therapist. Some of these earlier principles regarding performance go some way in clarifying what is often considered problematical if performance and therapy are linked in any way. As musicians we can employ the rigour of *decoro* balanced with the risk-taking of *sprezzatura* in order to reveal the Orpheus within. 'When Orpheus steps forward singing new songs of divine inspiration, then Euridice is enticed out of the audience and the oldest reactions of the myth are re-enacted – Orpheus and Euridice are united

---

1 Ansdell has also alluded to music therapy's connection with Rooley's ideas in his chapter on 'Connecting' in *Music for Life* (Ansdell 1995: 217).

in love and harmony' (Rooley 1990: 115). As therapists we can draw on a similar balance: patients rely on us to be consistent, effective and well practised yet able to be imaginative, intuitive and to take risks. We need to be at the same time highly focused and in tune with our patients yet have the humility to stand aside and to realise that our responsibility is to serve our patients and help channel connections between musical inspiration and their needs.

In the first of the two illustrations from Blake's *Book of Job* (see Plate 16.1) the 'music' is still in an unformed state, in fact not even there. It is waiting to be sounded with the instruments nestling in the tree. There is active playing – music coming alive – in the second illustration (see Plate 16.2, which is the final illustration to the story) although father Job still looks rather miserable. We can relate this transition from no playing to playing to Small's notion of 'musicking' (see Chapter 1). We can also recall, in relation to therapy, Sacks' description of the loss of a natural 'musicalness' in a Parkinsonian patient's movements and her comment that 'as I am unmusicked, I must be musicked' (Sacks 1991: 60). The members of Job's family become 'musicked' by the end of the story, even if he still seems unable to smile.

SOME GENDER ISSUES IN MUSIC THERAPY

Blake is a male artist portraying Job, a male prophet. We have celebrated Ficino and Rooley as male performers who are in touch with ancient traditions. We have acknowledged the presence of Euridice to create the complete performance (see also Bunt 1994) but it is Orpheus in the quote from Rooley who does the enticing. To redress the balance immediately at the start of this short discussion on gender issues we invite our readers to explore the music and inspirational writings of the great female mystic, artist, writer and musician Hildegard of Bingen (1098–1179). Listen, for example, to *A Feather on the Breath of God: Sequences and Hymns* performed by Gothic Voices (Hyperion A66039) and her Play of the Virtues *Ordo Virtutem* performed by Sequentia (Harmonia Mundi 77051-2-RG). For selected readings see editions by Fox (1987) and Hozeski (1987) and for her visionary illuminations (Fox 1985). Her timely rediscovery has been instrumental in further assessing the historical and social position of the female composer.

We feel the time is right to bring a debate on gender issues more into view. Within the music therapy literature we have only been able to find some concluding comments to Brusica's chapter on 'Modes of Consciousness' (Bruscia 1995a). In these couple of pages Bruscia cites female therapists such as Alvin and Kenny who write about creating safe 'nests' (Alvin) and 'musical spaces' (Kenny) and his own work as a male therapist of moving levels of consciousness across various boundaries and spaces. This is how he ends:

Plate 16.1 'Thus did Job continually'. Plate number 1 from *The Book of Job* by William Blake (Copyright The British Museum)

The importance of examining and admitting to gender orientation is three-fold. First, it helps therapists to acknowledge the unavoidable biases that gender brings to their theories, research projects, and clinical practices, either unconsciously or unintentionally. This is especially important in professions such as music therapy, and with techniques such as GIM,

Plate 16.2 'So the Lord blessed the latter end of Job more than the beginning'. Plate number 21 from *The Book of Job* by William Blake (Copyright the British Museum)

which have a predominance of one gender (viz., females). Second it adds to our understanding of the conditions under which male and female clients need male or female therapists. And third, it points to a real need for therapists to be able to function from the opposite gender's point of view. Male therapists must have free access to their female sides, and female therapists must have free access to their male sides.

(ibid.: 195)

The themes raised by Bruscia are demonstrated in the following example of a training exercise.

'Our identity as therapists' was the theme of a residential weekend for a group of music therapists (75 per cent female, 25 per cent male). The group had previously read Bruscia's comments and began the session by listening to Elgar's 'Dream Children' to focus attention on the theme. There were two trainers, one female and one male. The music brought up a lot of material relating to parental influences and the holding and boundary issues raised by Bruscia. The men and women divided into two groups. The men jostled for solo limelight in the music with a tension between being part of the group and craving independence. They introduced the myth of Narcissus quite spontaneously and explored the shadow side of male energy especially domination and control. There was a discussion on the integration of strength and mystery after listening to Holst's 'Uranus' from The Planets. The group had a strong desire to intrude into the female group. The women had been discussing maternal style in therapy, being strong without taking on the negative attributes of saturating the space (the myth of Echo – in polarity to Narcissus – arose quite spontaneously). They had just started to listen to the beautiful slow movement of Ravel's G major Piano Concerto when the men returned and demanded entry into the space. The way was blocked by the leader but this did not prevent the guitars, double bass, clarinet and drum and drum sticks (all that phallic energy) from entering. Some of the women resisted, some improvised music alongside or with the men, some echoed, some withdrew. The Ravel was still playing and at the return of the main theme in the cor anglais all the men stopped their loud playing and knelt down (as if at a signal) in a circle behind the women's circle. It felt quite a bizarre, uncanny yet totally natural moment. The music of Ravel and the female group had contained the noisy male intrusion. There was no need for any verbal explanation for this dramatic and metaphoric enactment.

The example provides vividly articulated evidence of the containing and holding energies of female therapists and the penetrating and invasive energies of the male therapists. Can only a female therapist know what it really feels like to offer a client a safe space with clear boundaries? Is a male therapist, in his very nature, always interested in pushing against the boundaries, wanting to get out of the contained space and eager to show clients different routes out of the situation? In a nutshell are male therapists over-concerned about provoking and directing and females in nurturing and supporting? Do male therapists have to work hard on accessing their nurturing sides and female therapists on pushing against the boundaries? Can we only imagine what it might be like from the other perspective? Or alternatively do most therapists just 'get on with the job' and draw on whatever energies are required from within the complexities of their personal make-up depending on the context and needs of the people with whom they are working?

It is interesting that, allied to these themes of holding and containment, there is the prominence of theories of mother–child interaction as points of reference for much recent music therapy practice in the UK. In spite of the fact that the profession is predominantly female, these references are adopted by both female and male therapists alike. In countries where music therapy has emerged from a predominantly medical background many male doctors often head the profession. Here it is usually harder for the predominantly female-based new generation of trained music therapists to break into the male group and to be heard and given positions of leadership and responsibility. Splits sometimes arise, particularly if the group of female therapists comes from a musical background. Perhaps we need to acknowledge more the strengths given to the work by both female and male therapists alike. We can look at these gender issues and themes of containment and penetration as belonging more to a flexible continuum. The situation is more complicated when we bring issues of sexual orientation into the discussion.

To conclude this section we indicate how we both perceive the drawing of the house in Plate 16.3. The image of a house is often considered as a symbol of self and takes us beyond gender issues to other themes of this book.

SH: On a first look at this little house, I think it seems a peaceful and certain sort of place. But my strongest association with it is a kind of *Hansel and Gretel* Gingerbread or Sweet House – intriguing, twinkling, inviting but with the possibility of being rather dangerous. It is set in a forest – or so it seems to me – so is there a witch there? I might have to outwit or fight her if there is. It makes me think of *Into the Woods* by Sondheim – fairy tales that take you on a path into the unconscious. It's a mixture of safe (its construction and clean lines) and risky (I don't know what is going to happen there).

LB: I notice the half-open door and can make out the image of a female figure from the odd lines on the threshold. This attending female figure seems to be providing an invitation into the inner space. This interior has some sense of the unexplored, the unexpected and possibly mysterious – there is

Plate 16.3 West Entrance to St George's Asinou Church, Kakapetria,
Cyprus (Jonathan Barnes)

an inner arch – yet the little house or chapel as a whole feels very strong
and safe, a real sense of a sanctuary. This house could provide clear boundaries for work. It is also boundaried by trees providing a sense of isolation
but also of protection.

In reality this is another entrance to the very first image in the Introduction to the book. To go forward we return to our beginnings. As in music
our journey has been cyclical, dipping in and out of the various stories of
the patients, clients and colleagues who have accompanied us. Some themes
recur and we conclude with final pointers and reminders of some central responsibilities of our work.

SOME POINTERS ON THE FUTURE DEVELOPMENT OF MUSIC THERAPY AS A PROFESSION

LB: I think that music therapists will continue to work within the areas where there is growing evidence of our efficacy, for example with autistic children, the profoundly disabled and the very depressed and anxious. It is here that the non-verbal nature of music can be seen as a very powerful and effective intervention. State registration has clearly given the profession a boost but I am concerned that we avoid any moves to rigid standardisation and over-bureaucratisation, so much the antithesis to the creative spirit at the root of our work. What I would like to see in the future is more work in areas that ten years ago would not have been considered as top priority. We included some of these areas in Part II such as neurology and forensic psychiatry. I am also thinking about, for example, work with children and adults who are living with cancer and other life-threatening diseases, more work in the acute medical field and with children in mainstream schools. I was quite stunned recently to learn from a survey carried out by MusicSpace West Midlands that the majority of their urgent referrals were from mainstream schools with a large proportion of boys. Here were children whose emotional and behavioural problems were denying them access to the school curriculum and causing huge problems in class.

Helen Odell-Miller would like to see '*a music therapist available for everybody who needs one*'. **Elaine Streeter** feels that '*until we begin to look at how music therapy can work for people with fewer severe difficulties we're going to remain a small profession*'. She sees music therapists working with similar groups that are seen by counsellors and psychotherapists.

SH: Drawing on some of my experience as parent, being a consumer of early years' services I have been very affected by being alongside families' difficulties in getting early intervention for young children with disabilities. I have been shocked by the lack of services for diagnosis and support of the whole family. This seems to tie in with your points about possible development in mainstream schools. Likewise it would be extremely valuable to have more therapists attached to mainstream nurseries (see comments made by Hugh Jolly in Chapter 1 about the value of music therapy contributing to the early assessment of developmental needs). We also have tremendous support and interest from allied professions such as speech and physiotherapy in the 'warming-up' holistic, communicative approach of music therapy. Music therapists are developing extra training in family services and our recent conferences have indicated excited interest around the country from young and keen workers and very experienced professionals. It was clear in Chapter 4 how much support Suzanna's mother gained from her involvement in your work with her child: it would be good to see the families of highly dependent adults getting similar attention. On another track, I have some concerns about the specialisation of music therapy services in dedicated music therapy centres (this is rather ironic given both of our involvement in MusicSpace). How do we preserve the significant principle of multidisciplinary work and arts therapies teams while still raising awareness and funds for the particular gifts of music therapy?

We both appreciate these optimistic comments from **Jean Eisler's** interview that predict a huge growth in music therapy because of its vitality and human qualities.

> I was at a therapy conference in America recently and there was a splendid chairman who summed it up and said: we have all got to realise that within the next ten years the chief therapeutic input to people will be music therapy. It's not only got to be but it will be, because it is so vital. It's based on every human being's vital energies.

Other pointers that we feel need our future attention include:

- training of people from different musical backgrounds, particularly non-classical;
- a real effort to bring musicians from other ethnic backgrounds into the profession (music therapy is still very much a white, middle-class profession) but this opens up a debate on the very European and Western roots of the whole notion of therapy;
- the development of advanced clinical trainings to bring us more in line with directions in Europe, other clinical professions and to safeguard the future of our state registration through our continued professional development;
- increased access to the Internet both as a means of international contact and of collating evidence of effective practice across different client and patient groups, for example David Aldridge's creation of the international Website Musictherapyworld.net;
- the balancing of these technological advances with keeping alive all of the personal support, challenging debate and dialogue that takes place when music therapists meet together, a reflection of the very human meeting points at the root of our encounters in music therapy with people of all ages.

In his views on the future **Tony Wigram** stressed the need for a larger public profile through attending conferences and publications. He also was realistic about the problems in creating work.

> *The big crisis that's developing is how we get work? Increasing pressures on the money for services and with the development of new management systems it becomes increasingly difficult for clinicians to enlist other clinicians as was happening in the 1970s and 1980s. You have to present a very good profile. People have to know about this at all levels, how to present music therapy as an intervention that has its unique qualities. We have to be able to answer specific questions particularly about methods and evaluation. We should have another big international congress here. It attracts publicity and builds up the stature of the profession.*
>
> (Note The Tenth Music Therapy World Congress, Oxford – July 2002.)

A FINAL RETURN TO OUR KEY RESPONSIBILITIES: TO WITNESS AND TO LISTEN

There are times in our work when all words seem useless, they drag us all down. There are even times when, dare we say, all sounds and music seem inappropriate, an intrusion and completely out of place. At such times resting quietly in the silence, not thinking, not doing, all provides the appropriate and very open space for so much to happen. A member of a group may begin to say something, a child may start to play, some music or sounds may emerge from somewhere. The atmosphere may lighten and there may even be some laughter. Dorit Amir has recently beautifully reminded us of the role of humour in music therapy (Amir 2001) and this is echoed in *The Tibetan Book of the Living and the Dead* by Sogyal Rinpoche.

> I have found that, as in all grave situations of life, two things are most useful: a common-sense approach and a sense of humour. Humour has a marvellous way of lightening the atmosphere, helping to put the process of dying in its true and universal perspective, and breaking the over-seriousness and intensity of the situation. Use humour, then, as skilfully and gently as possible.
>
> (Rinpoche 1992: 174)

We can attend and witness to all that is not only beyond words, but also beyond music. We turn to the prize-winning author Ben Okri for some final words and to Plate 16.4 by Jonathan Barnes.

> When things fall into words they usually descend. Words have an earthly gravity. But the best things in us are those that escape the gravity of our deaths. Art wants to pass into life, to lift it; art wants to enchant, to transform, to make life more meaningful or bearable in its own small

and mysterious way. The greatest art was probably born from a profound and terrible silence . . .

I think we need more of the wordless in our lives. We need more stillness, more of a sense of wonder, a feeling for the mystery of life. We need more love, more silence, more deep listening, more deep giving.

(Okri 1997: 5–7)

We wonder how will you reflect on these words as you contemplate a final threshold in the last drawing?

Plate 16.4 Entrance to St Gabriel's Chapel, Exeter Cathedral (Jonathan Barnes)

Approved postgraduate music therapy training courses in the UK

1 The Academic Register
  Guildhall School of Music and Drama
  The Barbican
  London EC2Y 8DT
  Tel: 020 7628 2571
  www.gsmd.ac.uk

2 The Administrator
  The Nordoff–Robbins Music Therapy Centre
  2 Lissenden Gardens
  London NW5 1PP
  Tel: 020 7267 4496
  admin@nordoff-robbins.org.uk

3 The Academic Registrar
  University of Surrey, Roehampton
  80 Roehampton Lane,
  London SW15 5SL
  Tel: 020 8392 3000
  www.roehampton.ac.uk

4 Music Therapy Administrator
  Department of Music
  University of Bristol
  Victoria Rooms
  Queens Road
  Bristol BS8 1SA
  Tel: 0117 9545032
  www.bris.ac.uk/Depts/Music

5 Director, MA in Music Therapy Training Course
  Anglia Polytechnic University
  East Road
  Cambridge CB1 1PT

Tel: 01223 363271
www.apu.ac.uk

6 Postgraduate Admissions
Welsh College of Music and Drama
Castle Grounds
Cathays Park
Cardiff CF1 3ER
Tel: 02920 342854
www.rwcmd.ac.uk

7 The Administrator
Postgraduate Diploma in Music Therapy (N-R)
Moray House School of Education
University of Edinburgh
Chessel's Lane
Holyrood Lane
Edinburgh EH8 8AQ
Tel: 0131 651 6636

Other useful addresses:
The Administrator
BSMT
61 Church Hill Road
East Barnet
Hertfordshire EN4 8SY
Tel: 020 8441 6226
Email: info@bsmt.org
www.bsmt.org

The Administrator
APMT
61 Church Hill Road
East Barnet
Hertfordshire EN4 8SY
Tel/Fax: 020 8440 4153
Email: APMToffice@aol.com
www.apmt.org.uk

Resources

The following list shows some recommendations for instruments:

- a range of drums on stands for stick drumming (for example roto-toms, tom-toms, tuneable rotary tympani); and for palm drumming (for example djembes or congas);
- bongos (lightweight or on stand);
- tambourine;
- a range of tambours and/or hand-held drums;
- a range of gato drums (also known as tongue drums);
- claves;
- wood blocks;
- castanets;
- temple blocks;
- maracas;
- rainstick;
- guiro;
- cymbal (14-inch) on a stand;
- cabasa;
- Chinese gong;
- flexatone;
- large wind chimes on a stand;
- small hand-held wind chimes;
- a range of bells: hand bells, Tibetan bells, Indian bells and so on;
- xylophone (tenor/alto plus soprano for children and bass if budget allows);
- metallophone (tenor/alto plus soprano for children and bass if budget allows);
- glockenspiel (tenor/alto plus soprano for children);
  (if possible we recommend chromatically tuned percussion but if outside budget then with F#s and B flats to allow for some work in different keys and modes);
- some kind of plucked instrument, for example a guitar, lyre, cimbala or autoharp.

We recommend a balance between tuned and untuned percussion. When working with children (and for some adults) these extras are useful:

- swanee whistle;
- bird calls: duck, nightingale, cuckoo and so on;
- ocean drums;
- Nordoff–Robbins reed horns and a set of reeds;
- individual tone bars.

For choice of keyboard, we make two suggestions:

(a) For experienced players: look for a digital piano of professional quality with an action-weighted keyboard. Some models can also be equipped with a sequencer and rhythm machine. Price: between £800 and £1,500.
(b) For occasional use by less experienced players: you could choose a 4-octave portable home keyboard with lightweight but touch-sensitive plastic keys. This should have general *MIDI* capability (about 128 high-quality sounds plus accompaniment styles). Price: between £200 and £400.

Use of technology

- Compositional and sound-producing programmes like *MidiGrid* have been used effectively in music therapy, particularly for client groups with severe physical and sensory disabilities. For further information and advice, we recommend contact with the Drake Music Project, 79 East Road, London N1 6AH, telephone 020 8692 9000, website: www.drakemusicproject.com
- *Soundbeam*: an exciting instrument that produces a wide range of controllable sounds by interrupting an infrared beam through movement. For information about Soundbeam contact: The Soundbeam Project, 463 Earlham Road, Norwich NR1 7HL, telephone: 0160 356 7788, fax: 0160 350 7877, email: 100530.3530@compuserve.com
- Music-writing programmes such as *Sibelius* and *Cubase Score* are very helpful tools for presenting notated examples for professional presentations.

Association of Professional Music Therapists (APMT): Code of Professional Ethics and Discipline

1. Code of Ethics

   A member of the APMT in the United Kingdom shall agree in writing to and thereafter abide by the following code of ethics:

   (i) A Music Therapist shall always act in the best interests of the client. Among other things this should include:

   a) Refraining from disclosure of confidential information obtained from or about a particular client except within the multi-disciplinary team responsible for treatment. Confidential information may be disclosed to students on placement, but only with the agreement of the relevant authorities (e.g. hospital, school).

   b) Music Therapists should be aware of and agree to abide by their relevant Area Child Protection Committee (ACPC) Inter-Agency guidelines, as Child Protection is an important issue for all music therapists regardless of whether their work routinely brings them into contact with children. Music Therapists have a duty to pass on information relating to suspected adult to child, or child to child, abuse and therefore should ensure their adequate training in its recognition. Music therapists should read the relevant literature in the APMT Information Book.

   c) Before using any verbal, written or recorded information acquired within the therapeutic relationship, for the purposes of publication, public presentation or broadcasting, the nature of the use of such material should be explained to the client (and/or guardian), and his/her permission obtained. The use of case material for articles in professional journals would not fall under this clause. In all cases anonymity should be respected.

   d) Maintaining the client relationship on a strictly professional basis.

e) Maintaining communication with doctors and other relevant professionals and advising them of the nature and progress of treatment.

f) Seeking advice as necessary from other appropriate professionals.

(ii) A Music Therapist shall ensure that a satisfactory standard of professional competence is maintained. Among other things this will involve responsibility for:

a) Restricting his/her practice to within the limits of his/her own training and competence.

b) Undertaking when possible to attend any courses, conferences, lectures etc., offered by appropriate organisations in order to extend his/her range of skills and knowledge.

c) Maintaining his/her own musical skills at the highest level of professional competence.

(iii)

a) When undertaking private treatment, a Music Therapist should ensure that a referral from a medical practitioner or from other professional involved in the treatment of the client is obtained, unless this is judged to be inappropriate. In all cases, whether in private practice or other, the therapist should liaise as closely as possible with those involved in the treatment of the client and a case history should be obtained.

b) Department of Health circular hc77 33 September 1977 reads as follows:

In asking for treatment by a therapist, the doctor is clearly asking for the help of another trained professional, and the profession of medicine and the various therapies differ. It follows from this that the therapist has a duty and a consequential right to decline to perform any therapy which his professional training and expertise suggests is actively harmful to the patient. Equally the doctor who is responsible for the patient has the right to instruct the therapist not to carry out certain forms of treatment which he believes harmful to the patient. (Summary Para.2 (ii)).

(iv) A Music Therapist shall conduct his/her affairs in a satisfactory manner. Among other things this will include:

a) Maintaining a fitting level of inter-colleague relationship, both within the profession, with those in other professions and with his/her employer.

b) Refraining from giving treatment whilst under the influence of alcohol or drugs unless prescribed by a medical practitioner.

c) Refraining from giving treatment unless mentally and physically fit to do so.

d) Refraining from delegating duties to unregistered persons, except in the case of Music Therapy students in training, in which case full responsibility must be assumed by the therapist for that delegation.

e) Refraining from committing any criminal act in the practice of his/her profession.

f) Providing suitable premises and conditions for the treatment of clients.

g) Insuring the clients against all risks while on the therapist's premises. Therapists working in private practice should have malpractice insurance.

h) Acceptance of the minimum current rate recommended by the APMT for private sessions.

i) Ensuring absolute hygiene of instruments and equipment, both for the therapist and client's benefit. Advice about current hygiene practices should be sought from the APMT, hospital pharmacy or other appropriate source.

j) *Legacies and Gifts*: Music Therapists should not solicit for personal financial gain. They should neither offer nor accept tokens such as favours, gifts, legacies or hospitality which might be construed as seeking to promote undue influence. Where relevant they should adhere to guidelines or procedures published by Employing Authorities.

2. Disciplinary Procedure
    Breaches of the code of conduct may be dealt with by a disciplinary sub-committee of the Executive; this committee will include the Chairperson of the APMT. Membership of the APMT may be terminated.

August 1999

BIBLIOGRAPHY

Aigen, K. (1995) 'Philosophical Inquiry', in B. Wheeler (ed.), *Music Therapy Research: Quantitative and Qualitative Perspectives*, Phoenixville, Philadelphia: Barcelona.

Aigen, K. (1996) 'Being in Music: Foundations of Nordoff–Robbins Music Therapy', *The Nordoff–Robbins Music Therapy Monograph Series 1*, St. Louis, MO: MMB Music.

Aigen, K. (1999) 'The True Nature of Music-centred Music Therapy Theory', *British Journal of Music Therapy*, 13, 2: 77–83.

Alajouanine, T. (1948) 'Aphasia and Artistic Realisation', *Brain*, 71: 229–241.

Alan, T. (1969) *The Aesthetics of Robert Schumann*, London: Peter Owen.

Aldridge, D. (1996) *Music Therapy Research and Practice in Medicine: From Out of the Silence*, London: Jessica Kingsley.

Aldridge, D. (1999) *Music Therapy in Palliative Care*, London: Jessica Kingsley.

Aldridge, D. (2000) *Music Therapy in Dementia Care*, London: Jessica Kingsley.

Alvin, J. (1975) *Music Therapy*, London: Hutchinson.

Alvin, J. (1977) 'The Musical Instrument as an Intermediary Object', *British Journal of Music Therapy*, 8, 2: 7–13.

Amir, D. (2001) 'The Place of Humour in Music Therapy', Paper presented at the Fifth European Music Therapy Conference, Naples, Italy.

Andrews, R. (ed.) (1998) *Dictionary of Contemporary Quotations*, London: Cassell.

Ansdell, G. (1995) *Music for Life: Aspects of Creative Music Therapy with Adult Clients*, London: Jessica Kingsley.

Ansdell, G. (1997) 'Musical Elaboration: What Has the New Musicology to Say to Music Therapy?', *British Journal of Music Therapy*, 11, 2: 36–44.

Ansdell, G. (1999a) 'Music Therapy as Discourse and Discipline: A Study of Music Therapist's Dilemma', Unpublished Ph.D. thesis, City University, London.

Ansdell, G. (1999b) 'Challenging Premises', *British Journal of Music Therapy*, 13, 2: 72–77.

Ansdell, G. (2001) 'Musicology: Misunderstood Guest at the Music Therapy Feast?', in D. Aldridge, G. di Franco and T. Wigram (eds), *Music Therapy in Europe*, Rome: ISMEZ/Onlus.

Ansdell, G. and Pavlicevic, M. (2001) *Beginning Research in the Arts Therapies: A Practical Guide*, London: Jessica Kingsley.

APMT (2000a) *A Career in Music Therapy.*

APMT (2000b) *How can Music Therapy Help People with Learning Disabilities?*

Asbridge, D. (2001) Personal Communication.

Assagioli, R. (1965) *Psychosynthesis: A Manual of Principles and Techniques*, Wellingborough, Northamptonshire: The Aquarian Press.

Association for Music and Imagery (AMI) (1990) P. O. Box 4286, Blaine, WA 98231-42286.

Axline, V. (1964) *Dibs: In Search of Self*, London: Penguin.

Bailey, D. (1992) *Improvisation: Its Nature and Practice in Music*, 2nd edn, London: The British Library National Sound Archive.

Bailey, N. and Cooper, S. (1999) 'Community Care for People with Learning Disabilities', *British Journal of Learning Disabilities*, 27, 2: 64–69.

Barham, M. (1999) 'The Arts Therapy Profession Comes to the Edge', in A. Cattanach (ed.), *Process in the Arts Therapies*, London: Jessica Kinsgley.

Baron-Cohen, S., Tager-Flusberg, H. and Cohen, D.J. (1993) *Understanding Other Minds*, Oxford University Press.

Bartram, P. (1991a) 'Aspects of Psychodynamic Music Therapy', Paper presented at the Scottish Music Therapy Conference.

Bartram, P. (1991b) 'Improvisation and Play in the Therapeutic Engagement of a Five Year Old Boy with Physical and Interpersonal Problems', in K. Bruscia (ed.), *Case Studies in Music Therapy*, Phoenixville, Pennsylvania: Barcelona.

Basso, A. and Capitani, E. (1985) 'Spared Musical Abilities in a Conductor with Global Aphasia and Ideomotor Apraxia,' *Journal of Neurological and Neurosurgical Psychiatry*, 48: 407–412.

Beatty, W.W., Zavadil, K.D. and Bailly, R.C. (1998) 'Preserved Musical Skills in a Severely Demented Patient', *International Journal of Clinical Neuropsychology*, 10, 158–164.

Bent, I. and Pople, A. (2001) 'Analysis', in S. Sadie (ed.), *The New Grove Dictionary of Music and Musicians 1*, London: Macmillan.

Berliner, P.F. (1994) *Thinking in Jazz: The Infinite Art of Improvisation*, University of Chicago Press.

Bernstein, L. (1976) *The Unanswered Question*, Harvard University Press.

Bion, W. (1962) *Learning from Experience*, London: Heinemann.

Blake, W. (ed. G. Keynes) (1966) *Notebook for the Year 1810*, Additions to Blake's Catalogue of Pictures, from the Complete Writings, Oxford University Press.

Bolton, R. (1998) 'Towards an Understanding of Structure and Process in Jazz Improvisation', Unpublished M.Mus. thesis, University of Sheffield.

Bonny, H.L. and Savary, L.M. (1973) *Music and your Mind*, New York: Station Hill.

Bowlby, J. (1969) *Attachment and Loss Vol. 1: Attachment*, 2nd edn, London: Pelican Books.

Boxill, E. (1985) *Music Therapy for the Developmentally Disabled*, Rockville, MD: Aspen Systems.

Boyce-Tillman, J. (2000) *Constructing Musical Healing: The Wounds that Sing*, London: Jessica Kingsley.

British Medical Association (11 June 1991) Personal Communication.

Brown D. and Pedder, J. (1991) *Introduction to Psychotherapy*, 2nd edn, London: Routledge.

Brown, S.M.K. (1994) 'Autism and Music Therapy: Is Change Possible, and Why Music?', *Journal of British Music Therapy*, 8, 1: 15–25.

Brown, S. (1997) 'Supervision in Context: A Balancing Act', *British Journal of Music Therapy*, 11, 1: 4–12.

Brown, S. (1999) 'Some Thoughts on Music, Therapy and Music Therapy', *British Journal of Music Therapy*, 13, 2: 63–72.

Bruscia, K. (1987) *Improvisational Models of Music Therapy*, Springfield, Illinois: Charles C. Thomas.

Bruscia, K. (1988) 'Standards for Clinical Assessment in the Arts Therapies', *The Arts in Psychotherapy*, 15: 5–10.

Bruscia, K. (ed.) (1991) *Case Studies in Music Therapy*, Phoenixville, Pennsylvania: Barcelona.

Bruscia, K. (1995a) 'Modes of Consciousness in Guided Imagery and Music (GIM): A Therapist's Experience of the Guiding Process', in C.B. Kenny (ed.), *Listening, Playing, Creating: Essays on the Power of Sound*, Albany: State University of New York Press.

Bruscia, K. (1995b) 'Differences between Quantitative and Qualitative Research Paradigms: Implications for Music Therapy', in B. Wheeler (ed.), *Music Therapy Research: Quantitative and Qualitative Perspectives*, Phoenixville, Philadelphia: Barcelona.

Bruscia, K. (1998) (ed.) *The Dynamics of Music Psychotherapy*, Gilsum, NH: Barcelona.

Bunt, L. (1994) *Music Therapy: An Art Beyond Words*, London: Routledge.

Bunt, L. (1997) 'Clinical and Therapeutic Uses of Music', in D. Hargreaves and A. North (eds), *The Social Psychology of Music*, Oxford University Press.

Bunt, L. (2001) 'Music Therapy', in S. Sadie (ed.), *The New Grove Dictionary of Music and Musicians 17*, London: Macmillan.

Bunt, L. (2002) *Entry on Music Therapy in A. Latham (ed.) Oxford Companion of Music*, Oxford University Press.

Bunt, L., Burns, S. and Turton, P. (2000) 'Variations of a Theme: The Evolution of a Music Therapy Research Programme at the Bristol Cancer Help Centre', *British Journal of Music Therapy*, 14, 2: 62–70.

Bunt, L. and Marston-Wyld, J. (1995) 'Where Words Fail, Music Takes Over: A Collaborative Study by a Music Therapist and a Counselor in the Context of Cancer Care', *Music Therapy Perspectives*, 13: 46–50.

Bunt, L. and Pavlicevic, M. (2001) 'Music and Emotion: Perspectives from Music Therapy', in P. Juslin and J. Sloboda (eds), *Music and Emotion*, Oxford University Press.

Burns, S.J.I., Harbuz, M.S., Hucklebridge, F. and Bunt, L. (2001) 'A Pilot Study into the Therapeutic Effects of Music Therapy at a Cancer Help Center', *Alternative Therapies in Health and Medicine*, 7, 1: 48–56.

Carpy, D.V. (1989) 'Tolerating the Countertransference: A Mutative Process', *International Journal of Psycho-analysis*, 70: 287–294.

Case, C. and Dalley, T. (1992) *The Handbook of Art Therapy*, London: Routledge.

Casement, P. (1985) *On Learning from the Patient*, London: Routledge.

Christophers, D. (2001) Personal Communication.

Clark, M. (1999) 'The Bonny Method of Guided Imagery and Music and Spiritual Development', *Journal of the Association for Music and Imagery*, 6: 55–62.

Clarke, E. (1988) 'Generative Principles in Musical Performance', in J. Sloboda (ed.), *Generative Processes in Music: The Cognitive Psychology of Music*, Oxford: Clarendon.

Clarkson, P. (1994) 'The Psychotherapeutic Relationship', in P. Clarkson and M. Pokorny (eds), *The Handbook of Psychotherapy*, London: Routledge.

Clarkson, P. and Pokorny, M. (eds) (1994) *The Handbook of Psychotherapy*, London: Routledge.

Clough, J. (1992) 'Music Therapy: A Description of Work with a Mentally Handicapped Young Man', *Journal of British Music Therapy*, 6, 2: 16–23.

Cobb, N. (1992) *Archetypal Imagination: Glimpses of the Gods in Life and Art*, Hudson, New York: Lindisfarne Press.

Cook, N. (1998) *Music: A Very Short Introduction*, Oxford University Press.

CPSM (1997) *The Council for Professions Supplementary to Medicine Annual Report*.

Cordess, C. and Cox, M. (eds) (1996) *Forensic Psychotherapy: Crime, Psychodynamics and the Offender Patient*, London: Jessica Kingsley.

Cowan, J. (1989) 'Role Limits in Music Therapy', *Journal of British Music Therapy*, 3, 1: 5–9.

Crystal, H. *et al.* (1989) 'Preservation of Musical Memory in Alzheimer's Disease', *Journal of Neurosurgical Psychiatry*, 52: 1415–1416.

Cummings, E.E. (1960) *Selected Poems 1923–1958*, London: Faber and Faber.

Darnley-Smith, D. (2001) 'Group Music Therapy for Older Adults with Memory Loss: Reflections upon Meaning and Purpose', Paper presented at the Fifth European Congress of Music Therapy, Naples, Italy.

Dass, R. and Gorman, P. (1985) *How Can I Help? Emotional Support and Spiritual Inspiration for Those who Care for Others*, London: Rider.

Davies, A. (1996) 'The Acknowledgement of Loss in Working Through Depression', *British Journal of Music Therapy*, 9, 1: 11–17.

Davies, A. and Richards, E. (1998) 'Music Therapy in Acute Psychiatry: Our Experience of Working as Co-therapists with Groups of Patients from Two Neighbouring Wards', *British Journal of Music Therapy*, 12, 2: 53–60.

Davies, A. and Richards, E. (forthcoming) *Music Therapy and Group Work*, London: Jessica Kingsley.

Davies, J.B. (1978) *The Psychology of Music*, London: Hutchinson.

Dawe, P. (1995) 'Autism and the Viola: A Proposed Model of Working', Unpublished student project, Department for Continuing Education, University of Bristol.

de Bernières, L. (1994) *Captain Corelli's Mandolin*, London: Minerva, Random House.

de Nora, T. (2001) *Music in Everyday Life*, Cambridge University Press.

Department of Health Social Services Inspectorate NHS Executive (2001) *London Learning Disability Strategic Framework*, DOH Website.

Dileo, C. (2000) *Ethical Thinking in Music Therapy*, Cherry Hill, New Jersey: Jeffrey Books.

Dokter, D. (ed.) (1995) *Arts Therapies and Clients with Eating Disorders: Fragile Board*, London: Jessica Kingsley.

Dunmore, H. (1997) *Talking to the Dead*, London: Penguin Books.

Durham, C. (1995) 'Music Therapy with Severely Head-injured Clients', in C. Lee (ed.), *Lonely Waters, Proceedings of the International Conference of Music Therapy in Palliative Care*, Oxford: Sobell Publications.

Dvorkin, J. (1999) 'Psychoanalytically Oriented Music Therapy Supervision', in T. Wigram and J. de Backer (eds), *Clinical Applications of Music Therapy in Psychiatry*, London: Jessica Kingsley.

Edwards, J. (1999) 'Considering the Paradigmatic Frame: Social Science Research Approaches Relevant to Research in Music Therapy', *The Arts in Psychotherapy*, 26, 2: 73–80.

Egan, G. (1994) *The Skilled Helper: A Problem-management Approach to Helping*, 5th edn, Pacific Grove, California: Brooks/Cole.

Eisler, J. (1990) 'Creative Music Therapy for the Mentally Handicapped or Emotionally Disturbed Child', in S.S. Segal (ed.), *Creative Arts and Mental Disability*, London: AB Academic Publishers.

Eisler, J. (1992) 'The Cinderella of Music Therapy in Great Britain: Music Therapy in Child Pyschiatry', in *Proceedings of First European Music Therapy Conference, Vol. 4*, London: BSMT.

Eisler, J. (1993) 'Music Therapy in the Context of the Multi-disciplinary Team', *Journal of British Music Therapy*, 7, 1: 23–24.

Eisler, J. (2001) 'The Lot of the Second Twin', Paper presented at the Fifth European Congress of Music Therapy, Naples, Italy.

Engler, J. (1986) 'Therapeutic Aims in Psychotherapy and Meditation: Developmental Stages in the Representation of Self', in K. Wilber, J. Engler and D.P. Brown (eds), *Transformations of Consciousness*, Boston: Shambhala.

Erdonmez, D. (1991) 'Rehabilitation of Piano Performance Skills Following a Left Cerebral Vascular Accident', in K. Bruscia (ed.), *Case Studies in Music Therapy*, Phoenixville, Pennsylvania: Barcelona.

Erdonmez, D. (1993) 'Music: A Mega-vitamin for the Brain', in M. Heal and A. Wigram (eds), *Music Therapy in Health and Education*, London: Jessica Kingsley.

Erdonmez Grocke, D. (1999) 'The Music which Underpins Pivotal Moments in Guided Imagery and Music', in T. Wigram and J. de Backer (eds), *Clinical Applications of Music Therapy in Psychiatry*, London: Jessica Kingsley.

Erikson, E.H. (1965) *Childhood and Society*, Harmondsworth: Penguin Books.

Ferrucci, P. (1990) *Inevitable Grace*, Wellingborough, Norhamptonshire: The Aquarian Press.

Fincher, S.F. (1991) *Creating Mandalas*, Boston: Shambhala.

Flower, C. (2001) 'The Spaces Between the Notes: Silence in Music Therapy', Paper presented at the BSMT/APMT Conference, *Children Need Music: Music Therapy and Children with Special Needs*, February.

Forinash, M. (2001) *Music Therapy Supervision*, Gilsum, NH: Barcelona.

Fox, M. (ed.) (1985) *Illuminations of Hildegard of Bingen*, Sante Fe: Bear and Company.

Fox, M. (1987) *Hildegard of Bingen's Book of Divine Works*, Sante Fe: Bear and Company.

Freud, S. (1905) *Case Histories: Dora and Little Hans*, A. Richards (ed.) (1977) The Pelican Freud Library, Vol. 8, London: Penguin.

Frohne-Hagemann, I. (2001) 'Music Therapy Aesthetic Dimensions', Paper presented at the Fifth European Music Therapy Conference, Naples, Italy.

Gaarder, J. (1991) *Sophie's World*, London: Phoenix.

Gabriel, P. (1996) *Eve: The Music and Art Adventure*, Real World MultiMedia Ltd.

Gaggero, G., Zanchi, B. and Bunt, L. (2001) 'Musical Interpretation and the Therapeutic Relationship', Paper presented at the Fifth European Music Therapy Conference, Naples, Italy.

Gale, C.P. (1989) 'The Question of Music Therapy with Mentally Handicapped Adults', *Journal of British Music Therapy*, 3, 2: 20–30.

Gantt, L. (2000) 'Assessments in the Creative Arts Therapies: Learning from Each Other', *Music Therapy Perspectives*, 18: 41–46.

Gardner, A. and Smyly, S.R. (1997) 'How Do We Stop "Doing" and Start Listening: Responding to the Emotional Needs of People with Learning Disabilities', *British Journal of Learning Disabilities*, 25: 26–29.

Gardner, H. (1985) *Frames of Mind: The Theory of Multiple Intelligences*, London: Heinemann.

Gfeller, K. (1995) 'The Status of Music Therapy Research', in B. Wheeler (ed.), *Music Therapy Research: Quantitative and Qualitative Perspectives*, Phoenixville, Philadelphia: Barcelona.

Gilroy, A. (1996) 'Our Own Kind of Evidence', *Inscape*, 1, 2: 52–60.

Gilroy, A. and Lee, C. (eds) (1995) *Art and Music: Therapy and Research*, London: Routledge.

Gordon, H.W. and Bogen, J.E. (1974) 'Hemispheric Lateralization of Singing After Interacarotoid Sodium Amylobarbitone', *Journal of Neurological and Neurosurgical Psychiatry*, 37: 727–738.

Gouk, P. (ed.) (2000) *Music Healing in Cultural Contexts*, Aldershot: Ashgate.

Gray, A. (1994) *An Introduction to the Therapeutic Frame*, London: Routledge.

Gregory, D. (2000) 'Test Instruments Used by *Journal of Music Therapy* Authors from 1984–1997', *Journal of Music Therapy*, 37, 2: 79–94.

Hansard 6 March 1997: 2026–2029.

Harvey, J. (1999) *Music and Inspiration*, London: Faber and Faber.

Hawkins, P. and Shohet, R. (1989) *Supervision in the Helping Professions*, Milton Keynes: Open University Press.

Heal, M. (1989) 'The Use of Pre-composed Songs with a Highly Defended Client', *Journal of British Music Therapy*, 3, 1: 10–16.

Heal Hughes, M. (1995) 'A Comparison of Mother–Infant Interactions and the Client–Therapist Relationship in Music Therapy Sessions', in T. Wigram, B. Sapertson and R. West (eds), *The Art and Science of Music Therapy: A Handbook*, London: Harwood Academic Press.

Heaney, S. (1996) 'The Rain Stick', in *The Spirit Level*, London: Faber and Faber.

Hibben, J. (ed.) (1999) *Inside Music Therapy: Client Experiences*, Gilsum, NH: Barcelona.

Higgins, R. (1993) *Approaches to Case study: A Handbook for those Entering the Therapeutic Field*, London: Jessica Kingsley.

Hillman, J. (1972) *The Myth of Analysis: Three Essays in Archetypal Psychology*, London: Harper and Row.

Hinde, R. (1979) *Towards Understanding Relationships*, London: Academic Press.

Hinde, R. (1997) *Relationships: A Dialectical Perspective*, Sussex: Psychology Press (Erlbaum) Taylor and Francis.

Holland, P. (1995) 'The Role of Music Therapy in the Effective Use of Stress', in T. Wigram, B. Sapertson, and R. West (eds), *The Art and Science of Music Therapy: A Handbook*, London: Harwood Academic Press.

Hooper, J. and Lindsay, B. (1990) 'Music and the Mentally Handicapped – the Effect of Music on Anxiety', *Journal of British Music Therapy*, 4, 2: 19–26.

Hopkins, G.M. (1953) 'Binsey Poplars', in W.H. Gardner (ed.), *Gerard Manley Hopkins: Poems and Prose*, London: Penguin.

Horden, P. (2000) (ed.) *Music as Medicine: The History of Music Therapy Since Antiquity*, Aldershot: Ashgate.

Hoskyns, S. (1995) 'Observing Offenders: The Use of Simple Rating Scales to Assess Changes in Activity During Group Music Therapy', in A. Gilroy and C. Lee (eds), *Art and Music: Therapy and Research*, London: Routledge.

Howat, R. (1995) 'Elizabeth: A Case Study of an Autistic Child in Individual Music Therapy', in T. Wigram, B. Sapertson and R. West (eds), *The Art and Science of Music Therapy: A Handbook*, London: Harwood Academic Press.

Hozeski, B. (translator) (1987) *Hildegard of Bingen's Scivias*, Santa Fe: Bear and Company.

Ibberson, C. (1996) 'A Natural End: One Story about Catherine', *British Journal of Music Therapy*, 10, 1: 24–32.

Isenberg-Grezda, C. (1988) 'Music Therapy Assessment: A Reflection of Professional Identity', *Journal of Music Therapy*, 25: 156–169.

John, D. (1995) 'The Therapeutic Relationship in Music Therapy as a Tool in the Treatment of Psychosis', in T. Wigram, B. Sapertson and R. West (eds), *The Art and Science of Music Therapy: A Handbook*, London: Harwood Academic Press.

Jolliffe, T., Lansdown, R. and Robinson, C. (1992) 'Autism: A Personal Account', *Communication*, 26, 3: 12–19.

Jung, C.G. (1968) *The Archetypes and the Collective Unconscious*, 2nd edn, trans. R.F.C. Hull, Bollingen Series XX, Princeton University Press.

Juslin, P. and Sloboda, J. (eds) (2001) *Music and Emotion*, Oxford University Press.

Kanner, L. (1943) 'Autistic Disturbances of Affective Contact', *Nervous Child*, 2: 217–250.

Kellogg, J. (1978) 'Mandala: Path of Beauty', Unpublished Master's thesis, Antioch University, Columbia.

Kenny, C.B. (1989) *The Field of Play: A Guide of the Theory and Practice of Music Therapy*, Atascadero, California: Ridgeview.

King's Fund (1980) *An Ordinary Life*, London: Kings Fund.

Klein, J. (1995) *Doubts and Certainties in the Practice of Psychotherapy*, London: Karnac Books.

Koger, S.M. and Brotons, M. (2000) 'Music Therapy for Dementia Symptoms (Cochrane Review)', *Cochrane Library*, 4, Oxford: Update Software.

Langenberg, M., Aigen, K. and Frommer, J. (1996) *Qualitative Music Therapy Research: Beginning Dialogues*, Gilsum, NH: Barcelona.

Lawrence, D.H. (1950) *Selected Poems*, London: Penguin.

Lee, C.A. (1989) 'Structural Analysis of Therapeutic Improvisatory Music', *Journal of British Music Therapy*, 3, 2: 11–20.

Lee, C.A. (1990) 'Structural Analysis of Post-tonal Therapeutic Improvisatory Music', *Journal of British Music Therapy*, 4, 1: 6–21.

Lee, C.A. (1995a) *Lonely Waters, Proceedings of the International Conference of Music Therapy in Palliative Care*, Oxford: Sobell Publications.

Lee, C.A. (1995b) 'The Analysis of Therapeutic Improvisory Music', in A. Gilroy and C. Lee (eds), *Art and Music: Therapy and Research*, London: Routledge.

Lee, C.A. (1996) *Music at the Edge: The Music Therapy Experiences of a Musician with AIDS*, London: Routledge.

Lee, C.A. (2000) 'A Method of Analyzing Improvisations in Music Therapy', *Journal of Music Therapy*, 37, 2: 147–167.

Lees, J. and Plant, S. (2000) *PASSPORT (Personal and Social Development in Schools Progression Organisation Rigour Training) – A Curriculum Framework for the Teaching of Personal and Social Development in Schools*, London: Calouste Gulbenkian Foundation.

Leuner, H. (1984) *Guided Affective Imagery*, New York: Thieme Stratton.

Levinge, A. (1993) 'Permission to Play. The Search for Self through Music Therapy: Research with Children Presenting with Communication Difficulties', in H. Payne (ed.), *Handbook of Inquiry in the Arts Therapies: One River Many Currents*, London: Jessica Kingsley.

Levinge, A. (1999) 'Music Therapy and the Theories of Donald Winnicott', Unpublished Ph.D. thesis, University of Birmingham.

Lewis, K. (1999) 'The Bonny Method of G.I.M.: Matrix for Transpersonal Experience', *Journal of the Association for Music and Imagery*, 6: 63–85.

Lincoln, Y.S. and Guba, E.G. (1985) *Naturalistic Inquiry*, Newbury Park, California: Sage.

Loewy, J. (2000) 'Music Therapy Assessment', *Music Therapy Perspectives*, 18: 47–58.

Loth, H. (1996) 'Music Therapy', in C. Cordess and M. Cox (eds), *Forensic Psychotherapy: Crime, Psychodynamics and the Offender Patient*, London: Jessica Kingsley.

MacKenzie, K., Matheson, E., McKaskie, K., Hamilton, L. and Murray, G. (2000) 'Impact of Group Training on Emotion Recognition in Individuals with a Learning Disability', *British Journal of Learning Disabilities*, 28, 4: 143–147.

MacLaverty, B. (1997) *Grace Notes*, London: Jonathan Cape.

MacMillan, J. (1999) Interview in *The Independent*, 26 March.

Magee, W. (1995) 'Case Studies in Huntingdon's Disease: Music Therapy Assessment and Treatment in the Early to Advanced Stages', *British Journal of Music Therapy*, 9, 2: 13–19.

Magee, W. (1998) 'Dialogues: In Response to "Lighting up the Mind" by Julia Usher', *British Journal of Music Therapy*, 12, 1: 29–31.

Magee, W. (1999) 'Singing My Life, Playing My Self,' in T. Wigram and J. de Backer (eds), *Clinical Applications of Music Therapy in Developmental Disability, Paediatrics and Neurology*, London: Jessica Kingsley.

Malloch, S.N. (1999) 'Mothers and Infants and Communicative Musicality', *Musicae Scientiae*, Special Issue, 1999–2000: 29–54.

Mansell, J. and Ericsson, K. (1996) *Deinsitutionalisation and Community Living*, London: Chapman and Hall.

Mark, P. (1986) 'Offending Behaviour or Better Adjusted Criminals?', *Probation Journal*, 33: 127–131.

McMaster, N. (1991) 'Reclaiming a Positive Identity: Music Therapy in the Aftermath of a Stroke', in K. Bruscia (ed.), *Case Studies in Music Therapy*, Phoenixville, Pennsylvania: Barcelona.

Michel, D. (2000) 'An Assessment of Music Therapy Over the Past Fifty Years and a Vision of its Future', *Music Therapy Perspectives*, 18: 72–77.

Miller, L., Rustin, M. and Shuttleworth, J. (1989) *Closely Observed Infants*, London: Duckworth.

Moog, H. (1976) *The Musical Experience of the Pre-school Child*, London: Schott.

Moore, G. (1962) *Am I too Loud: Memoirs of an Accompanist*, London: Hamish Hamilton.

Moore, T. (1990) *The Planets Within: The Astrological Psychology of Marsilio Ficino*, Great Barrington, MA: Lindisfarne Press.

Moore, T. (1992) *Care of the Soul*, London: Judy Piatkus.

Murphy, M. (1991) 'The Treatment of a Depressed Woman Following Neurological Trauma', in K. Bruscia (ed.), *Case Studies in Music Therapy*, Phoenixville, Pennsylvania: Barcelona Publishers.

Murray, G., McKenzie, K., Kidd, G., Lakhani, S. and Sinclair, B. (1998) 'The Five Accomplishments: A Framework for Obtaining Customer Feedback in a Health Service Community Learning Disability Team', *British Journal of Learning Disabilities*, 26, 3: 146.

Nachmanovitch, S. (1990) *Free Play: Improvisation in Life and Art*, New York: Penguin Putman.

Nettl, B. (2001) 'Improvisation', in S. Sadie (ed.), *The New Grove Dictionary of Music and Musicians 12*, London: Macmillan.

Nind, M. and Hewett, D. (1994) *Access to Communication*, London: David Fulton.

Nordoff, P. (1976) *Parents and Children*, BBC Television.

Nordoff, P. and Robbins, C. (1971) *Therapy in Music for Handicapped Children*, London: Gollancz.

Nordoff, P. and Robbins, C. (1977) *Creative Music Therapy*, New York: John Day.

Odell, H. (1979) 'Music Therapy in SSN Hospitals', Report of BSMT meeting in *British Journal of Music Therapy*, 10, 4: 12–15.

Odell-Miller, H. (1991) 'The Experience of a Man with Schizophrenia', in K. Bruscia (ed.), *Case Studies in Music Therapy*, Phoenixville, Pennsylvania: Barcelona Publishers.

Odell-Miller, H. (1995) 'Approaches to Music Therapy in Psychiatry with Specific Emphasis upon a Research Project with the Elderly Mentally Ill', in T. Wigram, B. Sapertson and R. West (eds), *The Art and Science of Music Therapy: A Handbook*, London: Harwood Academic Press.

Odell-Miller, H. (1997) 'Music Therapy and the Functions of Music with Older Mentally Ill People in a Continuing Care Setting', in M. Denham (ed.), *Continuing Care for Older People*, Cheltenham: Stanley Thornes.

Odell-Miller, H. (1999) 'Investigating the Value of Music Therapy in Psychiatry', in T. Wigram and J. de Backer (eds), *Clinical Applications of Music Therapy in Psychiatry*, London: Jessica Kingsley.

Okri, B. (1997) *A Way of Being Free*, London: Phoenix.

Oldfield, A. and Adams, M. (1990) 'The Effects of Music Therapy on a Group of Profoundly Mentally Handicapped Adults', *Journal of Mental Deficiency Research*, 34, 2: 107–125.

Oldfield, A., Bunce, L. and Adams, M. (2001) 'Mum Can Play Too: Short-term Music Therapy with Mothers and Young Children', *British Journal of Music Therapy*, 15, 2: 27–36.

Orton, R. (1992) 'From Improvisation to Composition', in J. Paynter, T. Howell, R. Orton and P. Seymour (eds), *The Companion to Contemporary Musical Thought*, London: Routledge.

Ovid, *Metamorphoses*, translation by Mary M. Innes (1955), London: Penguin Books.

Papoušek, M. (1996) 'Intuitive Parenting: A Hidden Source of Musical Stimulation in Infancy', in I. Deliège and J. Sloboda (eds), *Musical Beginnings*, Oxford University Press.

Pavlicevic, M. (1990) 'Dynamic Interplay in Clinical Improvisation', *British Journal of Music Therapy*, 4, 2: 5–9.

Pavlicevic, M. (1995a) 'Music and Emotion: Aspects of Music Therapy Research', in A. Gilroy and C. Lee (eds), *Art and Music: Therapy and Research*, London: Routledge.

Pavlicevic, M. (1995b) 'Interpersonal Processes in Clinical Improvisation: Towards a Subjectively Objective Systematic Definition,' in T. Wigram, B. Saperston and R. West (eds), *The Art and Science of Music Therapy: A Handbook*, London: Harwood Academic Press.

Pavlicevic, M. (1997) *Music Therapy in Context: Music, Meaning, and Relationship*, London: Jessica Kingsley.

Pavlicevic, M. (1999a) *Music Therapy: Intimate Notes*, London: Jessica Kingsley.

Pavlicevic, M. (1999b) 'Thoughts, Words and Deeds: Harmonies and Counterpoints in Music Therapy Theory', *British Journal of Music Therapy*, 13, 2: 59–63.

Pavlicevic, M. (2001) 'A Child in Time and Health: Guiding Images in Music Therapy', *British Journal of Music Therapy*, 15, 1: 14–21.

Pavlicevic, M. and Trevarthen, C. (1989) 'A Musical Assessment of Psychiatric States in Adults', *Psychopathology*, 22, 6: 325–334.

Payne, H. (ed.) (1993) *Handbook of Inquiry in the Arts Therapies: One River, Many Currents*, London: Jessica Kingsley.

Pedersen, I.N. (1999) 'Music Therapy as Holding and Re-organizing Work with Schizophrenic and Psychotic Patients', in T. Wigram and J. de Backer (eds), *Clinical Applications of Music Therapy in Psychiatry*, London: Jessica Kingsley.

Pelham, G. and Stacy, J. (1999) *Counselling Skills for Creative Arts Therapists*, London: Worth Publishing.

Phillips, A. (1998) *The Beast in the Nursery*, London: Faber and Faber.

Pines, M. (2000) 'Interpretation: Why, for Whom and When?', in D. Kennard, J. Roberts and D. Winter, *A Workbook of Group-analytic Interventions*, London: Jessica Kingsley.

Pribham, K. (1993) 'Brain, Music and Meaning', Keynote paper given at the Seventh World Congress of Music Therapy, Vitoria, Spain.

Priestley, M. (1975) *Music Therapy in Action*, London: Constable.

Priestley, M. (1994) *Essays on Analytical Music Therapy*, Phoenixville: Barcelona.

Purdie, H. and Baldwin, S. (1994) 'Music Therapy: Challenging Low Self-esteem in People with a Stroke', *Journal of British Music Therapy*, 8, 2: 19–24.

Racker, H. (1968) *Transference and Countertransference*, London: Hogarth.

Reason, P. and Rowan, J. (1981) *Human Inquiry: A Sourcebook of New Paradigm Research*, London: John Wiley.

Richer, J.M. (1983) 'The Development of Social Avoidance in Autistic Children', in A. Oliveiro and M. Zappella (eds), *The Behaviour of Human Infants*, New York: Plenum Press.

Richer, J.M. (2001) 'An Ethological Approach to Autism: From Evolutionary Perspectives to Treatment', in J. Richer and S. Coates (eds), *Autism: The Search for Coherence*, London: Jessica Kingsley.

Rinpoche, S. (1992) *The Tibetan Book of the Living and the Dead*, London: Rider Books.

Ritchie, F. (1991) 'Behind Closed Doors: A Case Study', *Journal of British Music Therapy*, 5, 2: 4–10.

Robarts, J. (1996) 'Music Therapy for Autistic Children', in C. Trevarthen, K. Aitken, D. Papoudi and J. Robarts (eds), *Children with Autism: Diagnosis and Interventions to Meet their Needs*, London: Jessica Kingsley.

Robarts, J. (ed.) (forthcoming) *Music Therapy Research: Growing Perspectives in Theory and Practice*, Vol. 2, London: BSMT Publications.

Robarts, J. and Sloboda, A. (1994) 'Perspectives on Music Therapy with People Suffering from Anorexia Nervosa', *Journal of British Music Therapy*, 8, 1: 7–15.

Robbins, C. (2000) Personal Communication.

Robbins, C. and Robbins, C. (1991) 'Creative Music Therapy in Bringing Order, Change and Communicativeness to the Life of a Brain-injured Adolescent', in K. Bruscia (ed.), *Case Studies in Music Therapy*, Phoenixville, Pennsylvania: Barcelona.

Rogers, C. (1980) *A Way of Being*, Boston: Houghton Mifflin.

Rogers, P. (1992) 'Issues in Working with Sexually Abused Clients in Music Therapy', *British Journal of Music Therapy*, 6, 2: 5–16.

Rogers, P. (1993) 'Research in Music Therapy with Sexually Abused Clients', in H. Payne (ed.), *Handbook of Inquiry in the Arts Therapies: One River, Many Currents*, London: Jessica Kingsley.

Rogers, P. (2000) 'Truth or Illusion: Evidence-based Practice in the Real World', in J.Z. Robarts (ed.), *Music Therapy Research: Growing Perspectives in Theory and Practice*, Vol. 1, London: British Society for Music Therapy.

Rooley, A. (1990) *Performance: Revealing the Orpheus Within*, Shaftesbury, Dorset: Element.

Rowan, J. (1993) *The Transpersonal: Psychotherapy and Counselling*, London: Routledge.

Ruud, E. (1995) 'Improvisation as a Liminal Experience: Jazz and Music Therapy as Modern "Rites de Passage"', in C.B. Kenny (ed.), *Listening, Playing, Creating: Essays on the Power of Sound*, Albany: State University of New York.

Ruud, E. (1998) *Music Therapy: Improvisation, Communication and Culture*, Gilsum, NH: Barcelona.

Ryan, J. and Thomas, F. (1987) *The Politics of Mental Handicap*, London: Free Association Books.

Sackett, D.L., Rosenberg, W.M.C., Gray, J.A.M. *et al.* (1996) 'Evidence-based Medicine: What it Is and What it Isn't', *British Medical Journal*, 312: 71–72.

Sacks, O. (1985) *The Man who Mistook his Wife for a Hat*, London: Picador.

Sacks, O. (1991) *Awakenings*, revised edn, London: Pan.

Samson, S. and Zatorre, R.J. (1993) 'Contribution of the Right Temporal Lobe to Musical Timbre Discrimination', *Neuropsychologia*, 32, 2: 231–240.

Santos, K. and Loth, H. (1993) 'Music Therapy in Forensic Psychiatry', Paper presented at the Seventh World Congress of Music Therapy, Vitoria, Spain, July.

Shah, I. (1964) *The Sufis*, London: Octagon Press.

Sidoli, M. (1998) 'Hearing the Roar', *Journal of Analytical Psychology*, 43, 1: 23–33.

Siegel, S. (1956) *Nonparametric Statistics for the Behavioral Sciences*, New York: McGraw-Hill.

Simpson, F. (2000) 'Creative Music Therapy: A Last Resort?', in D. Aldridge (ed.), *Music Therapy in Dementia Care*, London: Jessica Kingsley.

Sinason, V. (1992) *Mental Handicap and the Human Condition*, London: Free Association Books.

Sines, D. (1988) 'Maintaining an Ordinary Life', in D. Sines (ed.), *Towards Integration: Comprehensive Services for People with Mental Handicaps*, London: Chapman and Hall.

Skille, O. and Wigram, T. (1995) 'The Effects of Music, Vocalisation and Vibration on Brain and Muscle Tissue: Studies in Vibroacoustic Therapy', in T. Wigram, B. Saperston and R. West (eds), *The Art and Science of Music Therapy: A Handbook*, London: Harwood Academic Press.

Sloboda, A. (1996) 'Music Therapy and Psychotic Violence', in E. Welldon and C. van Velsen (eds), *A Practical Guide to Forensic Psychotherapy*, London: Jessica Kingsley.

Sloboda, J.A. (1985) *The Musical Mind: The Cognitive Psychology of Music*, Oxford University Press.

Small, C. (1998) *Musicking*, Hanover, NH: Wesleyan University Press.

Smeijsters, H. (1997) *Multiple Perspectives: A Guide to Qualitative Research in Music Therapy*, Gilsum, NH: Barcelona.

Snedecor, G.W. and Cochrane, W.G. (1980) *Statistical Methods*, 7th edn, Aimes, Iowa: Iowa State University Press.

Sobey, K. (1992) 'Relatedness in Music Therapy and Psychotherapy', *Journal of British Music Therapy*, 6, 1: 19–21.

Sobey, K. (1993) 'Out of Sight – Out of Mind? Reflections on a Blind Young Woman's Use of Music Therapy', *Journal of British Music Therapy*, 7, 2: 5–12.

Sobey, K. and Woodcock, J. (1999) 'Psychodynamic Music Therapy: Considerations in Training', in A. Cattanach (ed.), *Process in the Arts Therapies*, London: Jessica Kinsgley.

Solomon, A.L. (1995) 'Historical Research', in B. Wheeler (ed.), *Music Therapy Research: Quantitative and Qualitative Perspectives*, Phoenixville, Philadelphia: Barcelona.

Spingte, R. (1998a) 'Introductory Comments', in R.R. Pratt and D.E. Grocke (eds), *MusicMedicine 3 MusicMedicine and Music Therapy: Expanding Horizons*, Melbourne, Australia: Faculty of Music, University of Melbourne.

Spingte, R. (1998b) 'MusicMedicine: Applications, Standards and Definitions', in R.R. Pratt and D.E. Grocke (eds), *MusicMedicine 3 MusicMedicine and Music Therapy: Expanding Horizons*, Melbourne, Australia: Faculty of Music, University of Melbourne.

Steele, P. (1988) 'Children's Use of Music Therapy', Paper presented at the British Society for Music Therapy Conference, London: BSMT.

Steele, P. (1991) 'Aspects of Psychodynamic Music Therapy', Unpublished paper presented at the Scottish Music Therapy Conference.

Steele, P. and Leese, K. (1987) 'The Music Therapy Interactions of One Session with a Physically Disabled Boy', *British Journal of Music Therapy*, 1, 1: 7–12.

Stern, D. (1985) *The Interpersonal World of the Infant: A View from Psychoanalysis and Developmental Psychology*, London: Academic Press.

Stevens, J. (1985) *Search and Reflect: A Music Workshop Handbook*, London: Community Music Ltd.

Stewart, D. (1996) 'Chaos, Noise and a Wall of Silence: Working with Primitive Affects in Psychodynamic Group Music Therapy', *British Journal of Music Therapy*, 10, 2: 21–34.

Stewart, D. (2000) 'The State of the UK Music Therapy Profession: Personal Qualities, Working Models, Support Networks and Job Satisfaction', *British Journal of Music Therapy*, 14, 1: 13–32.

Stige, B. (1998) 'Perspectives on Meaning in Music Therapy', *British Journal of Music Therapy*, 12, 1: 20–29.

Stige, B. (2001) 'Writing Music Therapy: Clinical Research as Ethnography', in D. Aldridge, G. di Franco and T. Wigram (eds), *Music Therapy in Europe*, Rome: ISMEZ/Onlus.

Sting (1998) 'Music and Silence', *Resurgence*, November/December, 191, 32–33.

Stokes, J. (1987) 'Insights from Psychotherapy', *International Symposium on Mental Handicap*, Royal Society of Medicine.

Storr, A. (1997) *Music and the Mind*, London: HarperCollins.

Streeter, E. (1978) 'The Role of Music Therapy in the Assessment and Treatment of a Pre-school Language Delayed Child', *British Journal of Music Therapy*, 9, 1: 2–6.

Streeter, E. (1979) 'A Theoretical Background to the Interpretation of Rhythmic Skills with Particular Reference to the Use of Music Therapy as an Aid to the Clinical Assessment of Pre-school Handicapped Children', Unpublished MA thesis, University of York.

Streeter, E. (1999a) 'Finding a Balance between Psychological Thinking and Musical Awareness in Music Therapy Theory', *British Journal of Music Therapy*, 13, 1: 5–21.

Streeter, E. (1999b) 'Definition and Use of the Musical Transference Relationship', in T. Wigram and J. de Backer (eds), *Clinical Applications of Music Therapy in Psychiatry*, London: Jessica Kingsley.

Streeter, E. (2001) *Making Music with the Young Child with Special Needs: A Guide for Parents*, London: Jessica Kingsley.

Swartz, K., Hantz, E., Crummer, G., Walton, J. and Frishna, R. (1989) 'Does the Melody Linger On? Music Cognition in Alzheimer's Disease', *Seminars in Neurology*, 9: 152–158.

Tarnas, R. (1991) *The Passion of the Western Mind*, London: Pimlico.

Tate, D. (1958) 'On Ego Development', *Journal of Analytical Psychology*, 3, 2: 149–155.

Tavistock and Portman NHS Trust (2001) *Learning Disability Service New Update*, London: Tavistock and Portman NHS Trust.

Tessimond, A.S.J. (1985) 'This is not Love Perhaps', in H. Nicholson (ed.), *Collected Poems*, University of Reading: Whiteknights Press.

Tinbergen N. and Tinbergen, E.A. (eds) (1983) *Autistic Children: New Hope for Cure*, London: Allen & Unwin.

Tingle, E. (2000) 'Searching for the Meeting Place: A Study of Moments of Contact between Client and Therapist in a Music Therapy Session', Unpublished M.Phil. thesis, University of Bristol.

Toolan P. and Coleman, S. (1995) 'Music Therapy: A Description of Process: Engagement and Avoidance in Five People with Learning Difficulties', *British Journal of Music Therapy*, 9, 1: 17–25.

Torbert, W.R. (1981) 'Why Educational Research has been so Uneducational: The Case for a New Model of Social Science Based on Collaborative Inquiry', in P. Reason and J. Rowan (eds), *Human Inquiry: A Sourcebook of New Paradigm Research*, Chichester: John Wiley.

Towse, E. (1995) 'Listening and Accepting', in T. Wigram, B. Saperston and R. West (eds), *The Art and Science of Music Therapy: A Handbook*, London: Harwood Academic Press.

Towse, E. (1997) 'Group Analysis and Improvisation: A Musical Perspective', *British Journal of Music Therapy*, 11, 2: 51–56.

Towse, E. and Flower, C. (1993) 'Levels of Interaction in Group Improvisation', in M. Heal and T. Wigram (eds), *Music Therapy in Health and Education*, London: Jessica Kingsley.

Trehub, S., Schellenberg, G. and Hill, D. (1997) 'The Origins of Music Perception and Cognition: A Developmental Perspective', in C. Deliège and J. Sloboda (eds), *Perception, Cognition and Music*, Hillsdale, NJ: Erlbaum.

Trevarthen, C. (1993) 'The Function of Emotions in Early Infant Communication and Development', in J. Nadel and L. Camaioni (eds), *New Perspectives in Early Communicative Development*, London: Routledge.

Trevarthen, C. (1999) 'Musicality and the Intrinsic Motive Pulse: Evidence from Human Psychobiology and Infant Communication', *Musicae Scientiae*, Special Issue, 1999–2000: 155–211.

Trevarthen, C. and Malloch, S.N. (2000) 'The Dance of Wellbeing: Defining the Musical Therapeutic Effect', *Nordic Journal of Music Therapy*, 9, 2: 3–17.

Tustin, F. (1992) *Autistic States in Children*, London: Routledge.

Tyler, H. (1999) Personal Communication.

Tyler, H. (2000) 'The Music Therapy Profession in Modern Britain', in P. Horden (ed.), *Music as Medicine: The History of Music Therapy since Antiquity*, Aldershot: Ashgate.

Usher, J. (1998) 'Lighting up the Mind: Evolving a Model of Consciousness and its Application to Improvisation in Music Therapy', *British Journal of Music Therapy*, 12, 1: 4–19.

Verney, R. (2001) 'Fine Tuning: Musical Listening During and After Music Therapy Sessions', Paper Presented at the BSMT/APMT Conference *Children Need Music: Music Therapy and Children with Special Needs*, February.

Voss, A. (2000) 'Marsilio Ficino, the Second Orpheus', in P. Horden (ed.), *Music as Medicine: The History of Music Therapy since Antiquity*, Aldershot: Ashgate.

Warwick, A. (1995) 'Music Therapy in the Education Service: Research with Autistic Children and their Mothers', in T. Wigram, B. Saperston and R. West (eds), *The Art and Science of Music Therapy: A Handbook*, London: Harwood Academic Press.

Welldon, E. and van Velsen, C. (1996) *A Practical Guide to Forensic Psychotherapy*, London: Jessica Kingsley.

Wheeler, B. (ed.) (1995) *Music Therapy Research: Quantitative and Qualitative Perspectives*, Phoenixville, Philadelphia: Barcelona.

Whittaker, A. and McIntosh, B. (2000) 'Changing Days', *British Journal of Learning Disabilities*, 28, 1: 3–8.

Wigram, T. (1995) 'A Model of Assessment and Differential Diagnosis of Handicap in Children through the Medium of Music Therapy', in T. Wigram, B. Saperston and R. West (eds), *The Art and Science of Music Therapy: A Handbook*, London: Harwood Academic Press.

Wigram, T. (2000) 'A Method of Music Therapy Assessment for the Diagnosis of Autism and Communication Disorders in Children', *Music Therapy Perspectives*, 18: 13–22.

Wigram, T. and Dileo, C. (1997) *Music Vibration*, Cherry Hill, New Jersey: Jeffrey Books.

Wigram, T. and de Backer, J. (1999a) *Clinical Applications of Music Therapy in Developmental Disability, Paediatrics and Neurology*, London: Jessica Kingsley.

Wigram, T. and de Backer, J. (1999b) *Clinical Applications of Music Therapy in Psychiatry*, London: Jessica Kingsley.

Wigram, T., Saperston, B. and West, R. (1995) *The Art and Science of Music Therapy: A Handbook*, London: Harwood Academic Press.

Wilber, K. (1983) *Eye to Eye: The Quest for the New Paradigm*, Boston: Shambhala.

Wilber, K. (1993) *No Boundary: Eastern and Western Approaches to Personal Growth*, Boston: Shambhala.

Wilber, K. (1998) *The Marriage of Sense and Soul: Integrating Science and Religion*, Dublin: Newleaf.

Wilber, K. (2000) *Integral Psychology: Consciousness, Spirit, Psychology, Therapy*, Boston: Shambhala.

Wilber, K., Engler, J. and Brown, D.P. (1986) *Transformations of Consciousness*, Boston: Shambhala.

Williams, D. (1996) *Autism – an Inside-out Approach*, London: Jessica Kingsley.

Williams, W.E. (1950) *Introduction to DH Lawrence: Selected Poems*, London: Penguin.

Wilson, B.L. and Smith, D.S. (2000) 'Music Therapy Assessment in School Settings: A Preliminary Investigation', *Journal of Music Therapy*, 37, 2: 95–117.

Wing, C. (1968) 'Music Therapy in a Hospital for Subnormal Adults', *British Journal of Music Therapy*, Autumn: 4–10.

Wing, L. (1993) *Autistic Continuum Disorders: An Aid to Diagnosis*, London: National Autistic Society.

Winnicott, D.W. (1965) *The Family and Individual Development*, London: Tavistock.

Winnicott, D.W. (1974) *Playing and Reality*, London: Penguin Books.

Winnicott, D.W. (1986) *Home is Where We Start From*, London: Pelican Books.

Winnicott, D.W. (1990) *Maturational Processes and the Facilitating Environment*, London: Karnac Books and the Institute of Psychoanalysis.

Woodcock, J. (1987) 'Towards Group Analytic Music Therapy', *Journal of British Music Therapy*, 1, 1: 16–22.

Woodcock, J. and Lawes, C. (1995) 'Music Therapy and People with Severe Learning Difficulties who Exhibit Self-injurious Behaviour', in T. Wigram, B. Saperston and R. West (eds), *The Art and Science of Music Therapy: A Handbook*, London: Harwood Academic Publishers.

World Health Organisation (1992) *International Classification of Diseases*, World Health Organisation.

Zackey, G. (1999) Personal Communication.

Zanchi, B. (2001) Personal Communication.

Zeldin, T. (1995) *An Intimate History of Humanity*, London: Minerva.

Zulueta, F. de (1993) *From Pain to Violence: The Traumatic Roots of Destructiveness*, London: Whurr.

Name index

Subject index